# PRESUMPTION OF INNOCENCE UNDER CHINA'S 'NATIONAL CONDITIONS'

Drawing on broader legal-political discourses within the party-state and institutionalised academia, this book shines a light on one of the most controversial legal principles in Chinese criminal justice: the presumption of innocence.

It argues the reasons why there is no presumption of innocence in China, tracing the curve, or evolution, of academic discourse about presumption of innocence against the backdrop of changing politics, or varying emphases on national conditions, from Mao Zedong to Xi Jinping. The book deepens our understanding of the trajectory of criminal justice reforms in the party-state and shows how the more open and liberal phases of the reform era opened up some space for pluralist views and constructive criticism. In comparison, the second wave of autocratisation of the system influenced the conception of the criminal and paved the way for an illiberal turn.

# Presumption of Innocence Under China's 'National Conditions'

Alexandra Kaiser

•HART•
OXFORD • LONDON • NEW YORK • NEW DELHI • SYDNEY

HART PUBLISHING

Bloomsbury Publishing Plc

Kemp House, Chawley Park, Cumnor Hill, Oxford, OX2 9PH, UK

1385 Broadway, New York, NY 10018, USA

Bloomsbury Publishing Ireland Limited, 29 Earlsfort Terrace, Dublin 2, D02 AY28, Ireland

HART PUBLISHING, the Hart/Stag logo, BLOOMSBURY and the Diana logo are trademarks of Bloomsbury Publishing Plc

First published in Great Britain 2025



A catalogue record for this book is available from the British Library.

A catalogue record for this book is available from the Library of Congress.

Library of Congress Control Number: 2025945743

ISBN: HB: 978-1-50997-310-1
ePDF: 978-1-50997-312-5
ePub: 978-1-50997-311-8

Typeset by Compuscript Ltd, Shannon

For product safety related questions contact productsafety@bloomsbury.com

To find out more about our authors and books visit www.hartpublishing.co.uk. Here you will find extracts, author information, details of forthcoming events and the option to sign up for our newsletters.

# ACKNOWLEDGEMENTS

This book is based on my doctoral research. There are many people to whom I owe a great debt of gratitude and who discussed this research with me, helped me develop my thoughts, and articulate my ideas, but not all of them can be mentioned by name here, as I promised some of them that their identities would remain anonymous.

My special thanks go to Professor Eva Pils. Without her constant encouragement, support and trust, this work would not have been the same. She taught me a lot about academic writing and always inspired me with her creativity. I am very happy to be back at Friedrich-Alexander-University Erlangen-Nürnberg (FAU) and to be working with her again.

I would like to thank Professor Björn Ahl for giving me the opportunity to work at the Chair of Chinese Legal Culture at the University of Cologne during my doctoral studies. I am very grateful to Dr Daniel Sprick, who had the misfortune of sharing an office with me and who was always willing to discuss my research with me. His excellent comments and ideas on this research have been a great support over the years and have always pushed me forward.

I would also like to thank Professor Katrin Kinzelbach and other colleagues and friends at FAU who have made me feel very welcome. I had my first postdoc position with her, and I learned a lot and greatly appreciate her support and trust during these years.

Furthermore, a big thank you to the Institutum Iurisprudentiae at Academia Sinica, in particular Dr Chen Yu-Jie, for the hospitality and support I received during my work there. This has certainly been an inspiring time, and I feel very privileged to call Taiwan my second home.

Finally, I am very grateful to my mother for raising us children – writing a book seems like a piece of cake by comparison.

# CONTENTS

# 1

# Introduction

'There is no presumption of innocence in China.'[1] This brief remark by a Chinese law professor on the campus of a Chinese university in late 2018, mentioned only in passing when I spoke about my research on the presumption of innocence in the People's Republic of China (PRC or China), surprised me. It appeared to be a rather disillusioning view on one of the most controversial legal issues that has been debated amongst scholars and practitioners in China for the last decades. It turned out to be true. However, going a step back. Having talked to several Chinese legal scholars between 2017 and 2019, my overall impression was that they tend to highlight the progress of China's criminal justice system whilst defending deficiencies by pointing to the continuing transformative phase. In other words, in the process of perfecting the system, some systemic flaws, such as the appearance of wrongful convictions, were inevitable. Nonetheless, China would have achieved great progress with respect to criminal justice.[2] To some extent, this view reflects the official position of the party-state that stresses China's transformative phase, justifying the need for a gradual development of the legal system that ought to improve gradually through practice, suggesting a developmentalist approach to criminal justice. However, as we will see, legal reforms should not necessarily be associated with progress in terms of rights protection.

Admittedly, when comparing the 'lawless' Mao era with the reformist Deng era, any legislative reforms to establish a relatively stable legal order appeared to have marked some progress. The criminal justice system was part of these efforts, and despite all shortcomings, post-Mao criminal justice was rightly considered a great improvement,[3] even though the idea of fairness – as well as the empirical reality of criminal justice – was in stark contrast to international standards of fairness. In 1979, China's first Criminal Procedure Law (CPL 1979) was enacted, and since then the law has been amended three times. In comparison to the thin CPL of 1979 the 1996 and 2012 reforms had incorporated some minimum fair trial standards,

[1] Conversation with a Chinese law professor#1 (Site A).

[2] As a defensive argument, it has sometimes been pointed out to me that China would not differ so much from other countries, which they considered to already have gone through this 'process of transformation', thereby relativising any divergences. However, the latent threat that is inherent in such comments is relativising systemic flaws that are, one might suspect, rooted in deeper ideological and political values and ideas rather than in the stage of development.

[3] Shao-Chuan Leng and Hungdah Chiu, *Criminal Justice in Post-Mao China* (Albany, State University of New York Press 1985) 86–87, 168–172.

but a trend of legal regression in the sense of a return to crime control was already tangible in 2012 and further cemented during the 2018 overhaul of the law.

Undoubtedly, the right to a fair trial, with the presumption of innocence constituting a central fair trial safeguard, is universally recognised and should be part of any decent criminal justice system. The right to a fair trial consists of a conglomerate of rules and principles. A fair trial in accordance with Article 14 ICCPR requires equality before the courts and tribunals and the right to a fair and public hearing by an independent and impartial tribunal, which is an 'institutional guarantee' (see paragraph 1). The latter has been described as manifesting the essence of 'due process of law', while the provisions in Article 14(2) to (7) (and Article 15) are specifications of what constitutes a fair trial.[4] The presumption of innocence is protected in paragraph 2 of this provision, and a fair trial encompasses a catalogue of *minimum* guarantees (paragraph 3(a) to (g)) that a criminal accused should be entitled to and which are partly deeply interwoven with it.

In the drafting of international human rights instruments after WWII, the need for introducing individual fair trial safeguards and limiting the state's power to impose sanctions was beyond dispute. The conception of human dignity played an important role in the construction of fair trial at the international level from which a plethora of fair trial guarantees can be deduced, and, even though not explicitly saying this, the realisation of a fair trial is dependent upon normative considerations and institutional arrangements that underpin liberal democratic systems. As a fair trial safeguard, the presumption of innocence aims to protect the integrity and dignity of the accused and shield innocent persons from conviction. If we recognise this raison d'être of the presumption of innocence and the moral authority of it in the criminal process, we must accept that a guilty person might escape punishment because we embrace the idea that an innocent person ought not to be punished. Where guilt cannot be proved according to the law the accused must thus be acquitted. Therefore, looking at domestic conceptions of fair trial can reveal much about the relationship between the ruler and the ruled. What might the concept of fair trial, as enshrined under international law, imply for fair trials in non-democratic systems where, for instance, a genuine separation of powers or judicial oversight is lacking?

In terms of Chinese criminal justice that operates in an autocratic environment, as already mentioned, empirically speaking, we could observe some improvements in the post-Mao era. However, despite initial progress made with respect to written law, the actual impact of more than 20 years of criminal justice reforms on the practice of criminal justice – on the reality of what happens in the criminal process from investigation to trial and conviction, in detention centres, or in courtrooms – appears to have been limited. Indeed, with increasing law-making efforts, the gap between how the criminal process ought to operate and how it is operating in practice has become wider.

[4] Manfred Nowak, *U.N. Covenant on Civil and Political Rights, CCPR Commentary*, 2nd edn (Kehl, N P Engel 2005) 314.

In the light of China's participation in the international human rights regime, the protection of human rights in the criminal justice process has been critically examined, domestically as well as internationally. Observers have analysed the national legal framework, as well as other relevant normative and political documents, and critically observed their implementation. Over the last decades a solid corpus of academic writing and reports has emerged, and persistent shortcomings may be summarised as follows: coerced confessions[5] and confession reliance;[6] inadequate defence rights;[7] ineffective exclusionary rules;[8] excessive and prolonged use of custodial compulsory measures and ineffective mechanisms to challenge deprivations of personal liberty;[9] or the lack of an effective right against self-incrimination and right to silence.[10] Although all the shortcomings are related

[5] Wei Wu and Tom Vander Beken, 'Police Torture in China and Its Causes: A Review of Literature' (2010) 43 *The Australian and New Zealand Journal of Criminology* 557; Ira Belkin, 'China's Tortuous Path toward Ending Torture in Criminal Investigations', *Comparative Perspectives on Criminal Justice in China* (Cheltenham, Edward Elgar, 2013); Elisa Nesossi, 'The Politics of Torture and Miscarriages of Justice in Contemporary China' (2017) 11 *Journal of Comparative Law* 166; Na Jiang, 'Excluding Tortured Confessions in the People's Republic of China: A Long March towards the Eventual Abolition of Torture?' (2018) 54 *International Journal of Law, Crime and Justice* 1; Amnesty International, 'No End in Sight – Torture and Forced Confessions in China' (2015) www.amnesty.org/en/documents/asa17/2730/2015/en/ accessed 30 March 2020; Human Rights Watch, 'World Report 2019 (China, Events of 2018)' (2019) www.hrw.org/world-report/2019/country-chapters/china-and-tibet accessed 5 May 2020.

[6] Mike McConville and (with Satnam Choongh, Pinky Choy, Dick Wan, Eric Chui, Wing Hong, Ian Dobinson and Carol Jones), *Criminal Justice in China: An Empirical Inquiry* (Cheltenham, Edward Elgar, 2011); Yu Mou, *The Construction of Guilt in China, An Empirical Account of Routine Chinese Injustice* (Oxford, Hart Publishing, 2020); Yu Mou, 'Overseeing Criminal Justice: The Supervisory Role of the Public Prosecution Service in China' (2017) 44 *Journal of Law and Society* 620; Yu Mou, 'The Constructed Truth: The Making of Police Dossiers in China' (2017) 26 *Social & Legal Studies* 69.

[7] Eva Pils, 'Disappearing China's Human Rights Lawyers' in Mike McConville and Eva Pils (eds), *Comparative Perspectives on Criminal Justice in China* (Cheltenham, Edward Elgar, 2013); Eva Pils, *China's Human Rights Lawyers: Advocacy and Resistance* (Abingdon, Routledge, 2014); Hualing Fu, 'When Lawyers Are Prosecuted … The Struggle of a Profession in Transition' (2007) 2 *Journal of Comparative Law* 95; Hualing Fu, 'Criminal Defence in China: The Possible Impact of the 1996 Criminal Procedure Law Reform' [1998] *The China Quarterly* 31; Sida Liu and Terence Halliday, *Criminal Defense in China, The Politics of Lawyers at Work* (Cambridge, Cambridge University Press, 2016).

[8] Zhiyuan Guo, 'Exclusion of Illegally Obtained Confessions in China: An Empirical Perspective' (2017) 21 *The International Journal of Evidence & Proof* 30; Zhiyuan Guo, 'Torture and the Exclusion of Evidence in China' [2019] *China Perspectives* 45; Jiang (n 5).

[9] McConville and (with Satnam Choongh, Pinky Choy, Dick Wan, Eric Chui, Wing Hong, Ian Dobinson and Carol Jones) (n 6); Elisa Nesossi and others (eds), *Legal Reforms and Deprivation of Liberty in Contemporary China* (Abingdon, Routledge, 2016); Alexandra Kaiser, 'A New Model of Habeas Corpus in China? Procuratorial Necessity Examination of Pretrial Custody' in Björn Ahl (ed), *Post-2013 Reforms of Chinese Courts and Criminal Procedure* (Cambridge, Cambridge University Press, 2021).

[10] Xifen Lin and Casey Watters, 'Understanding the Presumption of Innocence in China: Institution and Practice' in Yun Zhao and Michael Ng (eds), *Chinese Legal Reform and the Global Legal Order: Adoption and Adaptation* (Cambridge, Cambridge University Press, 2018); Chen Weidong and Chen Fei, 'Lun chenmoquan yu tanbai congkuan (On the Right to Silence and Leniency for Those Who Confess)' [2005] *Journal of Henan Administrative Institute of Politics and Law* 50; Sun Changyong, 'Chenmoquan yu zhongguo xingshi susong (The Right to Silence and the Chinese Criminal Process)' (2000) 22 *Modern Law Science* 18; Bai Dong, 'Rushi huida yu chenmoquan de gongneng zhuyi fenxi

to presumption of innocence, so far less research has been devoted to the fate of presumption of innocence in China; or perhaps to the question of why there is no presumption of innocence.

Since we already know that the Chinese party-state clearly falls short of international fair trial standards, this book could not add much to these rich studies on the reality of Chinese criminal justice; it thus looks at criminal justice reforms from a different perspective. For those readers who are familiar with the study of the Chinese legal system, it will be clear that a purely doctrinal examination of legal provisions is also not helpful in understanding criminal justice in China. My analysis will be largely theoretical in the sense that it looks at criminal justice reforms and the interplay between law and politics from a discursive angle. This obviously requires some explanation.

Going back to the quote of the Chinese law professor, I wonder why there is no place for presumption of innocence in the Chinese criminal justice system. The Chinese government signed the ICCPR in October 1998 but has not ratified it, though it has reiterated its efforts to meet ICCPR standards.[11] This raises the question of how far this commitment goes, but a purely doctrinal approach, or a compliance assessment, would not be helpful in the Chinese context, as law is political. Rather, it is necessary to look at the party-state's official human rights position. While it officially recognises the *universal aspiration* of human rights, it claims that their realisation, or implementation, must differ according to 'national conditions' (*guoqing*).[12] I will refer to this as the official doctrine of national conditions, which reflects the idea of human rights 'with Chinese characteristics'. Indeed, prima facie, it appears not to be hostile towards the idea, or category, of civil rights and liberties, nor has it *explicitly* rejected this category of rights. As we will see, the Constitution of 1982 contains a catalogue of fundamental rights, including civil rights and liberties, which suggest the recognition of at least some rights, and legislation has adopted some fair trial safeguards. Moreover, the human rights white papers or action plans make references to the legal protection of civil rights.[13] It predominately posits the maxim of proceeding from China's actual conditions that has also permeated the legal sphere.

It may be fair to say that the criminal justice system belonged to those areas in which more legal reforms have taken place to ensure a *fairer* trial, even if Party

yu wenhua jieshi (Functional Analysis and Cultural Interpretation to Truthful Answer and Right to Silence)' [2012] *Law Science Magazine* 113.

[11] Katie Lee, 'China and the International Covenant on Civil and Political Rights: Prospects and Challenges' (2007) 6 *Chinese Journal of International Law* 445, 457; UNHRC, 'National Report Submitted in Accordance with Paragraph 5 of the Annex to Human Rights Council Resolution 16/21 – China' (2018) UN Doc A/HRC/WG.6/31/CHN/1, para 14.

[12] State Council Information Office, 'Zhongguo de renquan zhuangkuang (On the Human Rights Situation in China)' (1991) www.scio.gov.cn/zfbps/index.htm accessed 15 May 2019. Later white papers on human rights have maintained this basic position.

[13] See, eg, State Council Information Office, 'Guojia renquan xingdong jihua (2012-2015 nian) (National Human Rights Action Plan of China (2012-2015))' (2012) www.scio.gov.cn/zfbps/index.htm accessed 7 August 2019.

leaders never explained a systematic approach to a gradual broadening of fair trial safeguards. To examine in what sense and in what aspects the official doctrine of national conditions has indeed impacted the trajectory of criminal justice is crucial. Implications of how the realisation of human rights does depart from international recognised human rights standards and the consequences following from such deviations can only be drawn from empirical evidence. Therefore, I take the presumption of innocence in Chinese criminal justice as a study to examine the impact of the official doctrine of national conditions specifically with respect to this human right and look behind the scenes of law-making, as well as negotiations between scholars and party-state agencies.

The earlier mentioned shortcomings indicate that many rights violations take place in the pre-trial phases of the criminal justice process, crucially, due to a lack of equality of arms between prosecution and defence. Consequently, the trial itself is marginalised, as the question of guilt or innocence has already been established in the pre-trial phases. This is reflected in the rate of conviction of over 99 per cent.[14] As already mentioned, recurring themes and areas of concern in Chinese academic discourses include the criminal defence system, protection of personal liberty and checks and balances among state agencies in the criminal process. As will be shown in chapter two, these themes are relevant to presumption of innocence. My book will thus pay particular attention to criminal pre-trial proceedings in China. It traces the different periods of discourses about presumption of innocence in the context of criminal justice reforms from Mao in the 1950s over the reform era to the present day to show how the official human rights conception of national conditions and changing political agendas thereof have impacted its fate. This introductory chapter will explain the backdrop of the official view on law and human rights and in what sense the idea of national conditions is relevant in the context of criminal justice to provide some guidance for the chapters to follow.

## I. Maoism, Socialist Attitudes Towards Law and Human Rights

The Chinese party-state follows a type of socialist law but claims it has 'Chinese characteristics.' Before we delve into the depths of the conception of human rights 'with Chinese characteristics', a few words about socialist law will be helpful. In accordance with the classical understanding of the base-superstructure theorem, law is neither autonomous nor a self-contained objective system in a socialist country. The totality of productive forces forms the economic structure of society – the economic base – on which a political and legal superstructure rests.[15] It is the purpose of law to serve the interests of the ruling class. Therefore, law and

[14] See, eg, China Law Yearbooks (*Zhongguo Falü Nianjian*).
[15] Karl Marx, *Zur Kritik Der Politischen Ökonomie* (Karl-Maria Guth ed, Contumax, 2017) 5.

legal institutions belong to the superstructure of the economic base, as famously captured in the phrase, '[r]ight can never be higher than the economic structure of society and its cultural development conditioned thereby'.[16]

Consequently, law as well as politics both belong to the superstructure and are servants of the economic base. This theorem not only emphasises the political function of law as an instrument of the ruling class but also elevates the status of politics and policies over formal laws. Yet, apart from this base-superstructure theorem, Marx and Engels did not explain in any detail how to establish a formal socialist legal doctrine.[17] Indeed, classical Marxism-Leninism had little respect for positive law. Lenin had put forward the idea that positive law in a socialist country would gradually die out. In his view, law imposes external and coercive constraints; it is always oppressive, and society will be truly free only in the absence of positive law. The state apparatus is not abandoned but rather becomes superfluous with the dissolution of all class relations and antagonisms.[18]

Indeed, there are some caveats with respect to socialist law or socialist legality that should be observed. The claim of socialist legality is insofar self-contradictory as socialism is traditionally anti-legalist, and the view of legal nihilism initially dominated.[19] There have been many questions about the actual particularities of socialist law. As mentioned, Lenin had advanced the idea that under socialism law would die out, and the Russian revolutionaries did thus not envisage the establishment of a new type of law. Since prior to 1917, Russian codes had accommodated many features of western civil law systems, observers had long contended that Soviet law was essentially 'bourgeois' law, which served the proletarian dictatorship in the period of transition to socialism. It was only in the mid-1930s when the idea of 'socialist law' as a 'new type' of law emerged under Stalin, distinguishing it from common law or civil law systems.[20] In 1937, Vyshinski attacked the 'nihilists', saying that such 'anti-Party theories of the withering away of law and the State' would lead to counterrevolution. He rejected the claim of socialist law being self-contradictory, claiming that socialist law was a political expression of the dictatorship of the proletariat and a withering away could only be achieved through a strengthening of the law. Therefore, the proletarian dictatorship was the source of legitimacy for the socialist law, and the law was declared a tool to protect the interests of the development of the socialist society. The existence of law was associated with stability, and the passage of the 1936 Stalinist Constitution marked the final turn. The new era of socialist legality was born.[21] Since the authority of the state had been strengthened, its role in the protection of human rights became a decisive

[16] Karl Marx, *Critique of the Gotha Program* (Maryland, Wildside Press, 2008) 26.

[17] Yin Bo and Peter Duff, 'Criminal Procedure in Contemporary China: Socialist, Civilian, or Traditional?' (2010) 59 *International & Comparative Law Quarterly* 1099, 1102–1103.

[18] George L Kline, '"Socialist Legality" and Communist Ethics' (1963) 8 *Natural Law Forum* 21, 22; Harold J Berman, 'What Makes "Socialist Law" Socialist?' (1971) 20 *Problems of Communism* 24, 25.

[19] Kline (n 18) 25.

[20] Berman (n 18) 25.

[21] Kline (n 18) 24.

element of the socialist human rights conception, which – just like the view on law – was greatly shaped by the Communist worldview.[22]

The socialist human rights conception rejects any natural origin of human rights. It connects them to the political objectives of the state. Human rights must thus be seen in the light of the objectives pursued by socialist states. As indicated above, classical Marxism presumes that, in an ideal Communist society, the individual will observe the rules of community living internally, without external coercion (meaning without law). To this end, everything, including the rights and interests of individuals, is subordinated to achieving this ultimate objective and ideal society.[23]

Following the Marxist understanding, human rights are the result of a historical evolution on social and economic levels, meaning the development of human rights is a dynamic process.[24] In this sense, human rights are not seen as a precondition for development – human rights develop out of practice. The historical condition is thus a continuously underlying condition to justify a gradual human rights development. However, the flipside of it is that the state is considered responsible for laying the social, economic, and political conditions, as well as the legal guarantees, to ensure genuine implementation of human rights against the backdrop of national conditions.[25]

A caveat to this is, however, that the state can decide which (human) rights should be granted at a certain point in time. Here, it may be worth noting that, according to socialist doctrine regarding the relationship between the state and the individual, the unity of state and society ought to prevent any abuse of the law. The logic of this is as follows: By entering society, the individual gives all his rights to the state. Since all rights of the individual derive from the society/state, it is therefore not surprising that collective rights prevail over individual rights. This moreover underlines the role of the state in the realisation of human rights. Genuine individual freedom can be realised only in the Communist society, though it will never be absolute in the sense that collective interests, the interests of whole society, justify the limitations of individual liberties. And because the state defines individual behaviour in accordance with the interests of society, the individual has the duty to observe the laws and show absolute obedience to the state. It is through this internal conviction to obey that he finds his true freedom. Clearly, the vagueness of the notion of 'the interests of the state' calls for an explanation. It is presumed that what comes from the state is good, when it is – in fact – a convenient excuse for violating human rights.[26]

[22] Franciszek Przetacznik, 'The Socialist Concept of Human Rights: Its Philosophical Background and Political Justification' (1977) 13 *Revue Belge De Droit International* 238, 245–246.

[23] ibid 240–242.

[24] LJ Macfarlane, 'Marxist Theory and Human Rights' (1982) 17 *Government and Opposition* 414, 414–416.

[25] Przetacznik (n 22) 270.

[26] ibid 246–248.

In this context, it is helpful to recall some fundamental purposes of socialist law, especially the element of 'mobilization for total social involvement'. Hazard uses the example of the duty to work to illustrate how social duties are a part of this mobilisation. This is closely connected to another centrally important tenet, the creation of a new type of 'socialist man' through criminal law, who is aware of such rules as 'he who does not work shall not eat', which emphasises the educational function of law.[27] I owe everything to the state, and thus I must sacrifice everything to it, including my life and freedom, seems to be the more accurate interpretation. In other words, the right to life belongs to the party-state – not to the individual.

Mao himself developed a line of thinking that was consistent with the classical Marxist theory of base and superstructure and the socialist attitude towards law. In 1938, Mao Zedong put forward the idea of 'sinicisation of Marxism' or 'Sino-Marxism' (*Makesi zhuyi zhongguo hua*), stressing that China should adhere to Marxism as a guiding ideology while accommodating domestic realities.[28] In 1957, China began to repudiate Soviet law entirely due to its 'bourgeois' nature.[29] By emphasising 'Chinese characteristics', the Party could signal a break with such law. Even if Mao had increasingly departed from Soviet ideology, his mantra of integrating theory and practice had influenced the attitude towards law, including criminal justice, in China.[30]

However, the Mao era was characterised by waves of internal consolidation and reorganisation, as well as political campaigns. Mao himself was a declared anti-legalist, even if the party-state made some modest efforts to establish formal laws, procedures, and institutions in the mid-1950s. Legal protections for the Chinese 'people' were enshrined in the Common Program of 1949 or the Constitution of 1954, which adopted notions of equality,[31] but the class struggle, with its overwhelming emphasis on the suppression of class contradictions, meant that alleged class enemies were deprived of legal safeguards.[32] It is therefore commonly held that the Mao era was characterised by 'human rights nihilism', as legal provisions provided little or even no protection at all in practice.[33] Moreover, scholarly discourses on human rights that emerged in the 1950s and continued throughout the 1970s were largely politicised,[34] and the denialist view on positive law as well

[27] John N Hazard, *Communists and Their Law* (Chicago, University of Chicago Press, 1969) 523–524.

[28] Cao Peiqiang and Liu Junhan, *Mao Zedong sixiang he zhongguo tese shehui zhuyi lilun tixxi gainian (Mao Zedong Thought and the Theoretical System of Socialism with Chinese Characteristics)*, 2nd edn (Beijing, Beijing Institute of Technology Press, 2011) 2.

[29] Berman (n 18) 25.

[30] Shao-Chuan Leng, *Justice in Communist China: A Survey of the Judicial System of the Chinese People's Republic* (New York, Oceana Publications, 1967) xi–xv.

[31] Marina Svensson, *Debating Human Rights in China: A Conceptual and Political History* (Lanham, Rowman & Littlefield, 2002) 221.

[32] Albert Chen, *An Introduction to the Legal System of the People's Republic of China*, 4th edn (London, LexisNexis, 2011) 71.

[33] Michael C Davis, 'Chinese Perspectives on Human Rights' in *Human Rights and Chinese Values* (Oxford, Oxford University Press, 1995) 9.

[34] See, eg, Ye Xiaoxin, '1789 nian faguo "renquan xuanyan" de pipan – cong lao gen shang qingsuan youpai fenzi guanyu minzhu, ziyou, fazhi deng de huangyan (Critique of the 1789 French "Declaration

as the denial of individualism had dominated the official and academic discourse in the Mao era. Echoing the official view, human rights were condemned as 'a bourgeois slogan' and thus seen as incompatible with socialism. Although there was no place to lay the foundation for a human rights theory, the notion of 'human rights' (*renquan*) was in usage. It appeared in provisions even prior to the founding of the PRC in 1949,[35] and the press denounced human rights violations by cadres from the early 1950s. The number of accounts that can be found in the *People's Daily* indicates that there had been some kind of human rights propaganda among the population.[36] For this introductory discussion, it is sufficient to bear in mind that the Mao era culminated in the Cultural Revolution (1966–76), during which formal laws and institutions were largely set aside. While the absence of state coercion and constraints has never been practiced in China – the withering away of law and the state was soon out of the question – it is perhaps these attitudes towards law that have shaped the underlying principles of socialist law and thus the human rights view in the Chinese party-state the most. Indeed, the autocratic elements of the classical socialist human rights conception have been maintained and modified.

## II. The Evolution of Human Rights 'with Chinese Characteristics' in the Reform Era

The chapter now turns to the beginning of the reform in the late 1970s. The Third Plenary Session of the 11th Central Committee of the CCP in 1978 ('Third Plenum 1978') marked a crucial turning point in the Party's official stance towards law. The state and its citizens were now to abide by law and order after the horrors of the Mao era; 'rule by man' (*renzhi*) had been abolished. At the time, it was clear that a functioning legal system was needed to facilitate the economic reform,

of the Rights of Man" – Exposing the Lies of Rightists About Democracy, Freedom or Legal Systems from the Roots)' [1958] *Law Science* 35.

[35] See, eg, Regulations on the Protection of Human Rights and Property Rights in the Shanxi-Gansu-Ningxia Border Region, Adopted by the First General Meeting of the Second Senate of the Shanxi-Gansu-Ningxia Border Region on 6 November 1941; Notice of the Harbin Special Municipal Government – Prohibition of Unlawful Confinement, Interrogation and Violation of the Human Rights of Others, Adopted on 13 April 1948; Order of the Yu-Wan-Su Border Region Administrative Office to Governments at all Levels on Earnestly Protecting Human Rights, Strictly Prohibiting Arbitrary Confinement, and Extortion of Confessions by Torture, Adopted on 13 April 1948.

[36] See, eg, 'Fandui Qiangpo Mingling – Guanche Baozhang Renquan: Tianjin Zhuanqu Jiuzheng Ganbu Buliang Zuofeng (Oppose Forced Orders and Thoroughly Safeguard Human Rights. Tianjin Prefecture Rectifies the Undesirable Work Styles of Cadres)' *People's Daily* (31 May 1950); 'Guanyu ganbu qinfan renquan shijian Rongcheng xianfu xianwei ziwo jiantao (Self-Criticism by Rongcheng County Committee Regarding Cadres Who Violated Human Rights)' *People's Daily* (11 August 1950); 'Sanhe xian renmin fayuan: qinfan renquan wugu juya cunmin: Han Guang tongzhi laixin piping (Sanhe County People's Court: Human Rights Violation and Groundless Detention of Villagers: Comrade Han Guang writes Criticism)' *People's Daily* (24 August 1950).

or, in official parlance, the socialist modernisation.[37] However, the ideological reservation that the law can never take primacy over politics – meaning the Party – remained intact. While ideologically the leadership under Deng Xiaoping officially remained loyal to Marxism-Leninism, Maoism, and thus socialism 'with Chinese characteristics' (*zhongguo tese shehui zhuyi*), the attitude towards law became more pragmatic, and pragmatism henceforth competed with ideology.[38] In other words, concerns of economic development could initially suppress political concerns. The entry of pragmatism also meant that the classical socialist attitude towards law had to be revisited, and scholars had more room to interpret it in a way to accommodate the turn towards formal law. Indeed, this turn also meant that the superstructure shaped the economic base and increasingly regulated the behaviour of individuals, even if the Party maintained that the conditions of the base restrain the contents of such law.

The decision to construct a legal system, albeit it was to be socialist in nature, was arguably favourable to at least minimal (formal) legal rights protections, an increased recognition of the individual, and the extension of rights protections to a larger group of society.[39] In 1979, the Chinese legislator enacted criminal laws and thus, for the first time in the PRC's history, established formal proceedings, complemented by the passage of the Constitution in 1982.[40]

In the view of scholars like Chen Yaobin or Wan Qianhui, the Third Plenum of 1978 marked the beginning for the development of an especially Chinese human rights view, as it was the official green light to deepen the research on Sino-Marxism, including the question of a Marxist human rights theory.[41] At the time, the leadership had remained rather imprecise and did not predefine the notion of human rights; there was some room for pluralistic views, and scholars could advance more specific ideas.

[37] 'Communiqué of the Third Plenary Session of the 11th Central Committee of the CCP' www.bjreview.com/Special_Reports/2018/40th_Anniversary_of_Reform_and_Opening_up/Timeline/201806/t20180626_800133641.html accessed 20 March 2018.

[38] Carlos Wing-hung Lo, *China's Legal Awakening: Legal Theory and Criminal Justice in Deng's Era* (Hong Kong, Hong Kong University Press, 1995) 21–24.

[39] Ann Kent, *Between Freedom and Subsistence, China and Human Rights* (Oxford, Oxford University Press, 1993) 84; Feng Zhu, 'Human Rights and the Political Development of Contemporary China, 1979-1994' in Michael C Davis (ed), *Human Rights and Chinese Values* (Oxford, Oxford University Press, 1995) 126–133; Qianfan Zhang, *The Constitution of China: A Contextual Analysis* (Oxford, Hart Publishing, 2012) 57, 65–79.

[40] Constitution of the People's Republic of China of 4 December 1982. While it should be observed that, until today, China's Constitution is unenforceable – the party-state does not tolerate its interpretation and application by the judicial system or a constitutional court – this will not be at the centre of attention.

[41] Wan Qianhui, 'Zhongguo tese renquanguan de lishi fazhan yu neizai luoji (Historical Development and Internal Logic of the View of Human Rights with Chinese Characteristics)' [2017] *Human Rights* 33, 37; Chen Yaobin, 'Lun zhongguo tese de renquan guan (On the View of Human Rights with Chinese Characteristics)' [1995] *Hebei Tribune of Social Science* 33, 34.

Revising the denialist view, scholars now recognised the significance of human rights in a socialist society,[42] even if echoing the official view that human rights in the West and in China were two different things,[43] as famously declared by Deng Xiaoping in 1985.[44] In the view of Dong Yunhu, Deng thereby raised the question of what kind of human rights socialism is concerned with.[45] And Chen Yaobin believed that, by deepening the practice of socialism 'with Chinese characteristics', China's understanding of human rights 'with Chinese characteristics' would also flourish:

> We are building socialist human rights with Chinese characteristics. [Our] understanding of human rights is immediately linked to [our] understanding of socialism. Because the essence of socialism also determines the nature and development trend of socialist human rights, a clear understanding of socialism will inevitably advance the building of human rights with Chinese characteristics. It is the right to subsistence, in particular, that has an immanent relationship with the essence of socialism.[46]

Chen emphasises the linkages between the development of socialism and human rights. Of particular interest is his reference to the right to subsistence. The interdependence of the development of productive forces and human rights had become a core element of the theory of human rights 'with Chinese characteristics'.[47] As mentioned in the previous section, because the economic base conditions the superstructure, the economic structure of society (ie, economic conditions) predefines the scope of human rights. By prioritising the right to subsistence, human rights 'with Chinese characteristics' was understood to be essentially Marxist by drawing on historical materialism. Accordingly, Dong Yunhu believed that the Party's determination that China will remain in the primary stage of socialism for a long time, combined with the goal of building socialism 'with Chinese characteristics', decisively influenced the human rights view.[48] Indeed, the thesis that China has not yet overcome the primary stage of socialism was first formally set forth

[42] Shi Daxin, 'Lun renquan he renquan de guoji baohu (On Human Rights and the International Protection of Human Rights' [1982] *Journal of Anhui University* (Philosophy and Social Sciences Edition) 52, 52–57; Xu Bing, 'Renquan lilun de chansheng he lishi fazhan (The Emergence and Historical Development of the Human Rights Theory)' [1989] *Chinese Journal of Law* 1, 1–10.

[43] Hefu Chen, 'Renquan wenti qian yi (A brief discussion on Human Rights)' [1985] *CASS Journal of Political Science* 12, 14.

[44] Xiaoping Deng, 'Bourgeois Liberalization Means Taking the Capitalist Road, May and June 1985', *Deng Xiaoping wenxuan (Selected Works of Deng Xiaoping)*, vol III (Beijing, People's Publishing House, 1993) 125.

[45] Dong Yunhu, 'Zhongguo renquan fazhan lishi shang de yige zhongyao lichengbei – "zhongguo de renquan zhuangkuang" baipishu fabiao 10 zhounian huigu (An Important Milestone in the Development of Human Rights in China – a Review of the 10th Anniversary of the Publication of the White Paper "the Human Rights Situation in China")' [2002] *Human Rights* 24, 26.

[46] Chen Yaobin (n 41) 34.

[47] ibid 35.

[48] Dong Yunhu (n 45) 26.

by the CCP in the early 1980s and then written into the Constitution of 1982,[49] though the idea of an 'initial stage of socialism' had already been vaguely put forward by Mao Zedong in 1958.[50]

In 1984, Deng Xiaoping thus stressed the need to develop the productive forces in this stage of socialism and formulated the 'Four Cardinal Principles' (*sixiang jiben yuanze*) through which China's modernisation could succeed, namely, socialism, the people's democratic dictatorship, CCP leadership, and Marxism-Leninism-Maoism, as enshrined in the 1982 Constitution.[51] There would be obvious constraints following from these principles for a liberal rule of law conception.[52]

In 1987, Zhao Ziyang reaffirmed the basic strategy of pursuing modernisation under the conditions of socialism and elaborated on the implications of 'building socialism with Chinese characteristics'. He emphasised the correctness of the primary stage theory, which would entail two aspects. First, that the Chinese society is a socialist society and, second, that the Chinese society is still in the primary stage. Because China could not skip this stage, the Party leaders would have to proceed from this reality and formulate policies upon this axiomatic determination.[53] Even though it reads somewhat tautological, this reasoning has been largely maintained, and 'the primary stage of socialism' as well as 'socialism with Chinese characteristics' had been written down as state doctrine in the Chinese Constitution in 1993.[54] In the view of Dong Yunhu, Jiang Zemin had cemented the official stance that the human rights question could be resolved ideologically only through the lens of Marxism, emphasising that more research was needed to respond to 'Western hostile forces', to show that 'Chinese socialism respects human rights' and that 'the Chinese system of democracy suits the actual conditions of China'.[55] The Party's defensive attitude was due to the isolation and sanctions it had faced following the Tiananmen Massacre in 1989.[56]

[49] 'Resolution of the Central Committee of the CCP on Certain Questions in the History of Our Party since the Founding of the PRC, Issued on 27 June 1981' www.gov.cn/test/2008-06/23/content_1024934.htm accessed 20 July 2017; Yannian Dai, 'An Important Thesis on Building Socialism' *Beijing Review* (9 November 1987).

[50] Guocheng Li, *A Glossary of Political Terms of the People's Republic of China* (Hong Kong, Chinese University Press, 1995) 399–400.

[51] See seventh preambular paragraph of the 1982 Constitution; Xiaoping Deng, *Building Socialism with Chinese Characteristics* (Peking, Foreign Language Press, 1985) 38.

[52] Qianfan Zhang, *The Constitution of China: A Contextual Analysis* (Oxford, Hart Publishing, 2012) 50–51.

[53] Zhao Ziyang, 'Yanzhe you zhongguo tese shehuizhuyi daolu qianjin (Follow the Road of Socialism with Chinese Characteristics), Report to the 13th National Congress of the CCP on 25 October 1987' s 2 cpc.people.com.cn/BIG5/64162/64168/64566/65447/4526368.html accessed 15 August 2017.

[54] Constitution of 1982 (1993 Amendment). seventh preambular paragraph.

[55] Dong Yunhu (n 45) 24–25.

[56] Katrin Kinzelbach, 'Human Rights in Chinese Foreign Policy: A Battle for Global Public Opinion' in Sarah Biddulph and Joshua Rosenzweig (eds), *Handbook on Human Rights in China* (Cheltenham, Edward Elgar, 2019) 85–87.

In response, the party-state first officially outlined its basic human rights standpoint in a White Paper in 1991, which reportedly had been based on several instructions compiled under the leadership of Jiang Zemin and Li Peng between 1989 and 1990, as well as reportedly been based on the views of experts and scholars. This position has largely remained unchanged until today, albeit with some modifications, which will be discussed throughout this chapter. Even if it was being primarily addressed to the outside world, the party-state officially recognised the existence of human rights in China as well as shortcomings in terms of human rights protection. Many Chinese scholars believe the 1991 White Paper had laid the foundation for the question of Marxism and human rights and that, for the first time, a socialist country had officially acknowledged the need for human rights protection. The issuance of the 1991 White Paper was therefore a momentum for the domestic research on human rights.[57] Echoing the official stance, Chinese scholars have henceforth called for the development of a socialist human rights 'with Chinese characteristics'.[58]

This move was considered a dramatic shift in politics because the party-state had officially recognised that human rights were higher than class boundaries.[59] Apart from this, the 1991 White Paper largely reaffirmed the basic position by recognising the importance of the Universal Declaration while emphasising the different historical and cultural conditions of countries, manifesting the idea of national conditions. Following the official discourse, and as a matter of axiomatic constitutional assumption, China is a socialist developing country in the primary stage of socialism, and crucially, on this basis, the Party ascribes priority to the 'right to subsistence' (*shengcun quan*) and the 'right to development' (*fazhan quan*) as the 'foremost human rights'. Realising the right to subsistence requires guaranteeing basic means of livelihood, ie, 'having enough to wear and to eat' (*wenbao*). Therefore, as of 1979, the government's efforts have concentrated on furthering economic reforms. Although, according to the 1991 White Paper, the *wenbao* problem has largely been resolved, economic development remains on top of the government agenda.[60]

Consequently, human rights become historically relative and contingent. As the argument goes, human rights in China possess three distinctive characteristics: 'extensiveness'; 'equality'; and 'authenticity'. This means all Chinese citizens will at some point equally be granted the entire UN scope of human rights, but only those human rights as codified in Chinese legislation. As an explanation for the preference of the right to subsistence, it states that without this human right, other rights cannot be realised. Therefore, for historical reasons, it would be the

[57] Dong Yunhu (n 45) 24–26.

[58] Chen Yaobin (n 41) 33; WanQianhui (n 41) 37; 'Renquan zhuanjia tichu zhongguo tese de shehuizhuyi renquan guan (Human Experts Put Forward the Socialist Outlook on Human Rights with Chinese Characteristics)' (*China News*, 13 April 2001) www.chinanews.com/2001-04-13/26/85361.html accessed 24 May 2020.

[59] Zhu (n 39) 138.

[60] State Council Information Office, 'Human Rights White Paper (1991)' (n 12).

most important task for the party-state to first secure the right to subsistence.[61] The key takeaway is that, by relying on objective laws of development, the Party can remedy a lack of legitimacy. The leadership alone determines those objective laws of development, and political decisions are justified based on those supposed objective conditions.[62]

Following this official view, the right to development and the right to subsistence may be understood to form the core, or even root, of human rights in China from which all the other human rights (in principle, the UN scope) are understood to be deduced in the sense that their realisation depends on the realisation of those primary human rights. Even though at the time the Chinese official position was not yet fully construed, the idea of a Chinese-style human rights doctrine was basically born. While Marxism remained the guiding ideology,[63] the UN human rights framework, especially the International Bill of Rights (consisting of the principles of universality, egalitarianism, individualism, indivisibility, and interdependence),[64] served as a reference benchmark to justify and explain the official human rights standpoint.[65]

While the Party uses allegedly objective conditions, it must explain how this approach reflects the interests of society. To this end, the history of human rights is written from the perspective of Chinese society. This 1991 White Paper stated that '[t]he Chinese people have taken their historical and national conditions as starting point and, by being based on their long practical experience, the Chinese people have developed their own view on the human rights question.'[66] The party-state used the idea of 'democratic centralism (*minzhu jizhongzhi*)', which means that – theoretically – all state power belongs to the people and state organs should represent the interests of Chinese citizens,[67] to create the narrative that the prioritisation of human rights reflects the will of society; this element was indeed later more explicitly accommodated. As shown in the preceding section, this is a classical socialist human rights position. It is about this line of reasoning that the duty of obedience is required from the individual, as being a member of society, whose interests are realised through the state.

This connects to the party-state's principle of 'law-based governance' (*yifa zhiguo*), as endorsed as a basic strategy of governance at the 15th CCP National Congress in 1997. Since then, the discursive focus has shifted from the narrower

[61] ibid.

[62] Valentin Petev, *Kritik Der Marxistisch-Sozialistischen Rechts- Und Staatsphilosophie* (Berlin, Duncker & Humbolt, 1989) 137–139.

[63] Wan Qianhui (n 41) 36.

[64] Ie, the Universal Declaration of 1948 and the two Covenants of 1966.

[65] Harro von Senger, 'Die UNO-Konzeption Der Menschenrechte Und Die Offizielle Menschenrechts-Position Der Volksrepublik China' in Gregor Paul (ed), *Die Menschenrechtsfrage: Diskussion über China – Dialog mit China* (ein wissenschaftliches Symposium (Schriften der Deutschen China-Gesellschaft) 1998) 66.

[66] State Council Information Office, 'Human Rights White Paper (1991)' (n 12).

[67] See fifth preambular paragraph, arts 2 and 3 of the 1982 Constitution.

*fazhi* ('legal system' or 'rule by law') to the broader *fazhi* ('rule of law' or 'legal governance'; often translated as the rule *of* law, although it also entails rule *by* law in the Chinese context) that touches upon the issue of power relations in the political-legal system and encompasses more ideological implications.[68] In this context, Jiang also elaborated on the relationship between reform, development, and stability in the primary stage of socialism. It should be observed that stressing the stability of the legal system is a very un-Marxian claim.[69] We may first wonder what precisely is meant by stability. Maintaining stability in society was the overriding aim, but the law was not stable in the sense of being inflexible; stability has been closely linked to the existence of the Party. Deng focused on economic reform, but stability was unambiguously understood to depend on the survival of the Party, and this narrative had not been challenged by his successors[70] – not until today. He emphasised that stability could only be maintained by adhering to the leadership of the Party and the people's democratic dictatorship, meaning people being the 'masters of the nation', while 'destabilising' factors, including 'bourgeois liberalisation', and 'hostile forces' should be suppressed. Jiang applied the same paradigm to the development of law-based governance.[71]

Jiang thus emphasised that the principles of Party leadership and people-centredness are inseparable and equally ranked. As regards the official doctrine of national conditions, the Party has framed this relationship in a way to use democratic centralism as a legitimisation strategy for the ranking of human rights. In official parlance and in accordance with the classical Socialist doctrine, there is no conflict between the interests of the state and society because all state organs practice democratic centralism.[72] From this perspective, it is only logical that the 'foremost human right' (*shouyao renquan*) is to be determined in accordance with the different needs in different times and different countries. In other words, those human rights that are considered to facilitate the development of society should be prioritised.[73]

Principles underlying the official human rights conception thus correspond to basic principles of governance. Democratic centralism ('for the people') is both

[68] Chongyi Feng, 'China's Socialist Rule of Law: A Critical Appraisal of the Relationship Between the Communist Party and Comprehensive Law Reform' in John Garrick, and Yan Chang Bennett (eds), *China's Socialist Rule of Law Reforms Under Xi Jinping* (Abingdon, Routledge, 2016) 45–46.

[69] Alice Erh-Soon Tay and Eugene Kamenka, 'Marxism and the Problem of Legal Continuity – Recent Trens in Communist Legal Theory' [1980] *Bulletin of the Australian Society of Legal Philosophy* 31, 36–38.

[70] Stanley B Lubman, *Bird in a Cage* (Redwood, Stanford University Press, 1999) 123–126.

[71] Jiang Zemin, 'Gaoju Deng Xiaoping lilun weida qizhi, ba jianshe you zhongguo tese shehuizhuyi sheye quanmian tui xiang ershiyi shiji (Hold High the Great Banner of Deng Xiaoping Theory for an All-round Advancement of the Cause of Building Socialism with Chinese Characteristics into the 21st Century), Report to the 15th National Congress of the CCP' (1997) www.gov.cn/test/2007-08/29/content_730614.htm accessed 29 December 2018.

[72] Constitution of 1982, art 2.

[73] Chen Youwu and Li Buyun, 'Zhongguo tese shehui zhuyi renquan lilun tixi lun gang (Outline of the Theoretical System of Socialist Human Rights with Chinese Characteristics)' [2012] *Political Science and Law* 54, 57.

an ideological and organisational principle of the Party and state. As an ideological basis of governance, it presumes that the Party is responsive to the needs and interests of the people, as reflected in the 'mass line' (*qunzhong lüxian*), meaning it secures democracy through centralised control. It is, however, also designed as a mechanism by which the people should unconditionally embrace the policies and decisions and to mobilise them to action. Democratic centralism thus emphasises the unity of the party-state and society. It logically entails the subordination of individual interests to collective ones. In the Mao era, the pendulum had swung between democracy and centralism, with a clear tendency towards the latter. The mass line had become a tool of mass mobilisation, often to consolidate central control at the expense of peoples' interests. In the reform era after 1978, Deng acknowledged the lack of democracy, and through the introduction of the principle of law-based governance, there now was a triangular relationship. Democratic centralism realises the integration between Party leadership, the position of the people as of the nation, and legal governance.[74]

Indeed, in his work report in 2010, Wen Jiabao emphasised that the Party's efforts would concentrate on 'making people's lives happier and more dignified' – a similar formulation found its way into the foreword of a human rights White Paper.[75] In the view of Liu Huawen, taking a people-centred approach, the Party leadership had crucially embraced the idea of dignity as a governance objective and would now proceed from the notion of dignity to strengthen human rights, which he considers to be reflected in the increasing legal protection of dignity.[76] Liu later called this the Party's turn towards a 'theory of dignity'.[77] Wen frames human dignity in a purely materialistic sense, being connected to well-being. It is simply framed as an end to the means to achieve a more harmonious society. The official narrative has accommodated liberal notions such as dignity to enhance the image of a 'benevolent' leadership. The official discourse that equates economic development with human rights progress assumes that everything that comes from the state is good.

[74] Sarah Biddulph, 'Democratic Centralism and Administration in China' in Hualing Fu and others (eds), *Socialist Law in Socialist East Asia* (Cambridge, Cambridge University Press, 2018) 200.

[75] State Council Information Office, '2009 nian zhongguo renquan shiye de jinzhan (Progress of Human Rights in China in 2009)' (2010) www.scio.gov.cn/zfbps/index.htm accessed 23 October 2020; '2011 nian guowuyuan zhengfu gongzuo baogao (Report of the State Council on the Work of the Government, presented by Wen Jiabao at the 4th Session of the 11th National People's Congress' (2010) www.gov.cn/test/2012-03/15/content_2067314.htm accessed 17 April 2018.

[76] Liu Huawen, 'Jiyu "zunyan lun" queli renquan lilun (Establishment of the concept of human rights based on the "Doctrine of Dignity")' (22 September 2011) 9 www.iolaw.org.cn/showArticle.aspx?id=3019 accessed 20 February 2020.

[77] Liu Huawen, 'Zhongguo tese shehuizhuyi requan guan – jiehe Xi Jinping Zhi "2015" – Beijing Renquan Luntan 'de Hexin (The Socialist Outlook on Human with Chinese Characteristics: Interpretation of Xi Jinping's Congratulatory Letter at the 2015 Beijing Human Rights Forum)' [2016] *Chinese Review of International Law* 3, 9.

The mantra of people-centredness has become clearly articulated to legitimise the narrative of foremost human rights in accordance with China's (objective) national conditions; it has another dimension. Society, here, is construed as a homogenous and collective unity, which has been used to suppress the notion of individualism. Individual and collective rights unambiguously form an organic unity, which connects to the classical unity of rights and duties.[78] While the idea of individual empowerment cannot be found, society is seen as an important pillar through which human rights ought to be realised, which reflects the idea of social involvement. Against the backdrop of this ideological choice, it is not surprising that the party-state has formulated human rights as collective goals; rights take the form of privileges or space rather than empowerment. Social engagement in economic development to enhance human rights protection has remained the dominant position. In 2012, Hu Jintao formulated the goal of completing the building of a moderately prosperous society in all respects by 2020.[79]

When Xi Jinping assumed power in 2012–13, the official human rights position substantially remained unchanged. Xi, who has put his personal stamp on the Chinese human rights view, continues to follow a developmentalist approach that links human rights to economic development. The leadership under Xi has reiterated this policy goal and, moreover, set the goal of building a great modern socialist country by 2050 under the label of the 'Two Centenary Goals'.[80] Xi has proclaimed a 'New Era' of socialism 'with Chinese characteristics' under his guidance, which has been cemented under the label of 'Xi Thought on Socialism with Chinese Characteristics for a New Era' and enshrined as the guiding ideology in the CCP Charter in 2017.[81] In the words of Xi, 'The Chinese people are currently striving for realizing the Chinese dream of national rejuvenation, this will raise the

[78] 'Weishenme shuo "renquan shi ren de quanli he yiwu de tongyi"? (Why do we say that human rights are the unity of rights and duties?)' (*China Human Rights*, 12 June 2014) www.humanrights.cn/html/2014/rqzs_0612/532.html accessed 27 August 2018.

[79] Hu Jintao, 'Jianding bugou yanzhe zhongguo tese shehuizhuyi daolu qianjin wei quanmian jiancheng xiaokangshehui er fendou (Firmly March on the Path of Socialism with Chinese characteristics and Strive to Complete the Building of a Moderately Prosperous Society in all Respects), Report to the 18th National Congress of the CCP on 8 November 2012' www.npc.gov.cn/zgrdw/npc/zggcddsbc-qgdbdh/2012-11/09/content_1742519.htm accessed 8 May 2018; Jiabao Wen, 'Our Historical Tasks at the Primary Stage of Socialism and Several Issues Concerning China's Foreign Policy' www.fmprc.gov.cn/ce/ceno/eng/dtxw/t301338.htm accessed 26 May 2020.

[80] Xi Jinping, 'Juesheng quanmian jiancheng xiaokangshehui duoqu xinshidai zhongguo tese shehuizhuyiweida shengli (Secure a Decisive Victory in Building a Moderately Prosperous Society in All Respects and Strive for the Great Success of Socialism with Chinese Characteristics for a New Era), Report to the 19th National Congress of the CCP on 18 October 2017' www.gov.cn/zhuanti/2017-10/27/content_5234876.htm accessed 13 July 2018.

[81] State Council Information Centre, '"Wei renmin mou xingfu: xin zhongguo renquan shiye fazhan 70 nian" baipishu (Seeking Happiness for People: 70 Years of Progress on Human Rights in China)' (2019) www.scio.gov.cn/zfbps/index.htm accessed 24 August 2020; Charter of the Communist Party of China, Adopted at the 12th CCP National Congress on 6 August 1982, Amendments adopted at the 19th National Congress of the CCP on 24 October 2017; Xi Jinping (n 80).

level of human rights protection in China and promote an overall human rights development.'[82]

Human rights protection remains unambiguously dependent on development,[83] and it is crucially linked to 'Socialism with Chinese characteristics for a New Era' to build a moderately prosperous society. And because, as a matter of axiomatic constitutional assumption, China is in the primary stage of socialism, and since the goal is to achieve a moderately prosperous society for the Chinese people, the current leadership under Xi has maintained the developmentalist view on human rights.[84] Poverty alleviation thus remains on top of the agenda of the party-state to guarantee, in the words of the Party, a 'happy life', which is deemed the 'greatest human right'.[85] The inclusion of 'happiness' is a newer, modified feature of the official human rights view and is to be achieved only through material well-being. Since the goal is to build a moderately prosperous society, which can only be achieved by upholding the leadership of the Party, the narrative of a 'happy life' is to be complemented by other aspects, such as environmental protection, health, security and so on.

Since the 1990s, scholars began to more critically discuss the prioritisation of human rights, challenging the official discourse on the rights to subsistence and development as the 'foremost human rights'. For example, Guo Daohui interpreted the classical Marxist view on human rights differently. Guo was sceptical that the right to existence was *the* foremost human right; the quality of life would not be determined by this right as such but by the environment in which it exists. Indeed, the claim, 'without the right to subsistence, all the other human rights are out of the question' could be easily applied to other human rights. In the view of Guo, political human rights – the right to revolution and the right to democracy and freedom – were the most foremost human rights in the Chinese context in order to create an environment that was beneficial for the development of human rights such as economic human rights.[86] Indeed, the classical Socialist human rights conception rejects a categorisation of human rights because they constitute an organic whole and thus recognises the interdependence of human rights to ensure full realisation,

[82] Xi Jinping, 'Xi Jinping zhi "2015" – Beijing renquan luntan" de hexin (Xi Jinping's Congratulatory Letter at the 2015 Beijing Human Rights Forum)' (16 September 2015) www.mfa.gov.cn/web/ziliao_674904/zyjh_674906/201509/t20150916_7945447.shtml accessed 16 October 2018.

[83] State Council Information Office, 'Guojia renquan xingdong jihua (2012-2015 nian) (National Human Rights Action Plan of China (2012-2015))' (n 13).

[84] Xi Jinping, 'Gaoju zhongguo tese shehuizhuyi weida qizhi wei quanmian jianshe shehuizhuyi xiandaihua guojia er tuanjie fendou (Hold High the Great Banner of Socialism with Chinese Characteristics and Strive in Unity to Build a Modern Socialist Country in All Respects), Report to the 19th CCP National Congress on 16 October 2022)' (2022) www.gov.cn/xinwen/2022-10/25/content_5721685.htm accessed 29 November 2023.

[85] State Council Information Centre (n 81).

[86] Guo Daohui, 'Renquan de benxing yu jiazhi wei jie (The Nature and Value Hierarchy of Human Rights)' (2004) 22 *Tribune of Political Science and Law (Journal of China University of Political Science and Law)* 3, 8.

even if it ranks human rights in the sense that it considers certain rights, such as the right to life, as prerequisites for the realisation of all other human rights.[87]

The underlying relativism of the official doctrine of national conditions had not been unnoticed by Chinese scholars.[88] Liu Junning, a liberal scholar and outspoken critic of the 'Asian Values' discourse, which came into being in April 1993 through the Bangkok Declaration and had culminated in various counterarguments to human rights universalism,[89] has advocated human rights as universal moral rights that belong to all human beings beyond state-level. While Liu concedes that the level of economic and social development may indeed influence the level of human rights protection domestically, in his view, there was no contradiction between the right to existence and human rights universalism. Liu voiced concerns as to the developmentalist argument, because the protection of human rights was the precondition for development and not the other way around. Furthermore, the state-centric view of the right to development and existence could not explain why other fundamental human rights and freedoms must be denied. However, Liu emphasises that the 'theory of national particularism' was distinct from human rights relativism and a rather realistic approach. Liu does not directly criticise the Party or the Chinese government, but he criticises the line of reasoning often brought forward by autocratic rulers.[90] Liu presumably means that human rights universalism does not deny cultural diversity but that culture is no excuse for non-compliance with fundamental human rights.[91]

In academic circles, the official prioritisation of human rights continues to remain a point of controversy among academics, even if the tolerance for constructive criticism has shrunk to a minimum under Xi Jinping.[92] In late 2019, a group of scholars criticised the Chinese government's advocacy, as they saw it, of a relativistic human rights concept. Moreover, according to these critics, even within this 'relativist' conception, the rights to subsistence and development are understood

[87] Przetacznik (n 22) 167–169.

[88] Human rights relativists claim that human rights conceptions are relative to the idea of man in a specific culture and cannot be based on the standards of any single culture or determined by any single people. Therefore, it is usually referred to as *cultural* or *moral* relativism. *Cultural* relativism is essentially 'a theory about the nature of morality'. Cultural relativists thus deny the existence of a universal truth in ethics, since morality is culture-bond, see James Rachels, *The Elements of Moral Philosophy*, 4th edn (New York, McGraw-Hill, 2003) 15–29. The related *moral* relativism encompasses different claims, which are more or less but not necessarily incompatible with the notion of universality. More moderate advocates of moral relativism thus in principle support a minimum universalism, see James W Nickel, *Making Sense of Human Rights* (Oakland, University of California Press, 1987) 68–81.

[89] Bangkok NGO Declaration on Human Rights (Geneva, 19 April 1993).

[90] Liu Junning, 'Renquan de pubianxing ji qi fandiao (The Universality of Human Rights and their Antitheses)' [1998] *Open Times* 5, 6–10.

[91] It should be observed that advocates of human rights universalism are not necessarily hostile towards cultural diversity but rather try to reconcile cultural diversity with universal human rights. The international human rights framework recognises the *fact* of cultural diversity, see Vienna Declaration (1993), Preamble, I (5).

[92] See, eg, Alexandra Kaiser, 'The Shaping of Authoritarian Law under the "Socialist Rule of Law": Academics and Obedience in the Chinese Party-State' [2024] *Taiwan Human Rights Journal* 15.

to be granted in only very narrow terms, largely focusing on material well-being.[93] However, it should be noted that certain scholars – at least based on their writing – are supportive of the official human rights stance. For example, Luo Haocai, then president of the China Society for Human Rights Studies,[94] has defended the Party's developmentalist human rights view.[95]

The point is the official doctrine of national conditions is not a rights-based discourse. Rather, it is a manifestation of the amalgam of law and politics. In accordance with classical Marxism, it elevates politics over law. The party-state has not explained how precisely human rights, including civil rights, will develop gradually, nor has it formulated a coherent system of established norms and principles. It makes sense to distinguish economic and social goals from rights. Many of the arguments developed by the party-state are expressed in political documents that outline general socio-economic goals, which cannot explain the absence of certain fundamental human rights. For the Party, the official doctrine of national conditions is used to frame political imperatives and remains a very convenient and flexible rhetoric to defend its human rights position in a particular situation. Overall, it remains ambiguous and is often used in absolute terms. This leads to the question of the implications for the human rights protection in certain areas such as criminal justice.

## III. The Notion of 'National Conditions' in the Context of Criminal Justice

In the light of the previous discussions, one may wonder in what sense the official doctrine of national conditions in the context of human rights is relevant for criminal justice. As the discussions to follow will show, while debates on criminal justice in the late 1970s developed in parallel and independently from human rights discourses, the idea of national conditions had already been a central aspect of criminal justice discourses, as it is reflected in the official stance of not blindly copying other systems but rather combining national conditions with foreign experience. Even though these two discourses initially developed independently and only began to merge in the early 1990s, they both rest on the Marxist theory of historical and dialectical materialism. This is an important rhetorical caveat, as it sets limits to scholarly claims to improve rights protection in the criminal justice system. As explained in the previous sections, the doctrine of national

[93] Conversation with Chinese scholars#2 (Site B).

[94] The China Society for Human Rights Studies, founded in 2003, is under the State Council and committed to the CCP leadership; it publishes the Human Rights Journal, see 'China Society for Human Rights Studies' www.humanrights.cn/2023/11/23/4fe07426ddf54a2cb3badfac87565a0c.html accessed 6 December 2024.

[95] Luo Haocai, 'Zhongguo renquan shiye qianjing guangkuo (The Cause of Human Rights in China has a Bright Future)' (2014) 73 *Human Rights* 2, 2.

conditions is rooted in the base-superstructure theorem. Since the conception of human rights is said to be an intrinsic element of socialism 'with Chinese characteristics' and because it was shaped or conditioned thereby, the harmonisation of the two discourses was imperative. The legal system is a subconstruct of socialism 'with Chinese characteristics', to which human rights belong, and this links human rights and criminal justice.[96] And because the idea of national conditions is the basis for 'building of socialism with Chinese characteristics', it sets the framework for the legal system and thus criminal justice. With the growing interest in human rights, these two discourses had begun to gradually merge from the early 1990s onwards, crucially through the issuance of the 1991 White Paper that had officially recognised human rights shortcomings in the criminal justice system, leading to greater demands for human rights protection in the criminal process and thus to greater tensions. However, such calls were constrained by the idea of human rights 'with Chinese characteristics'. In other words, and following the official stance, as human rights must be implemented according to national conditions, so must human rights in the field of criminal justice.

A brief theoretical detour may illustrate this better. As already suggested, the Party's developmentalist view presumes a top-down approach to human rights implementation. As outlined in the previous section, the party-state has remained loyal to the position that human rights at the domestic and international level were two different things. Maintaining a classical socialist stance, the party-state does not recognise human rights to exist on a meta-level, meaning above the state level; it does not distinguish between human rights and the rights of citizens because all positive rights derive from the state. Since – in the view of the Party – human rights remain socially bound and only acquire their legal significance through the state by being defined in legislation, the party-state considers itself to play a crucial role in the legal protection of human rights. This legalist top-down approach to human rights implementation has been asserted in several Party-government documents, especially in the context of developing a socialist legal system 'with Chinese characteristics' by 2010. Viewing human rights 'with Chinese characteristics' as a branch of socialism 'with Chinese characteristics', the legal substantiation of the former can only be achieved through the legal system.[97] At first glance, this appears to reflect the principle of legality, but it makes a broader claim because it relates to political imperatives, as well as the Party's role and power in law-making, which manifests the idea of national conditions.

Following the official discourse, the legal system places the Constitution at the 'core', which thus guides the development of the 'branches', namely, the Criminal

[96] Hu Jintao (n 79).

[97] State Council Information Office, 'Zhongguo tese shehuizhuyi falü tixi (The Socialist Legal System with Chinese Characteristics)' (2011) www.scio.gov.cn/zfbps/index.htm accessed 19 May 2020; State Council Information Office, 'Zhongguo renquan fazhihua baozhang de xin jinzhan (New Progress in the Legal Protection of Human Rights in China) (White Paper on the Legal Protection of Human Rights in China)' (2017) www.scio.gov.cn/zfbps/index.htm accessed 12 January 2018.

Procedure Law and human rights. Political documents have asserted the assumption that criminal justice reforms are conditioned by the socialist legal system 'with Chinese characteristics'. Demands of national conditions (for example, an imbalanced national development due to regional differences) and requirements resulting from different historical and legal traditions and social conditions are mentioned as two features of the socialist legal system 'with Chinese characteristics', whose development is a 'dynamic' process. According to the White Paper on the Socialist Legal System of 2011, the Constitution and the laws have established a unified and multi-layered legislative structure 'with Chinese characteristics' to accommodate these two features.[98]

The party-state thereby cemented the subordination of law under politics, as well as the contingency of rights – an inherent claim of the 'socialist legal system with Chinese characteristics'. Therefore, the idea of a gradual development (historical materialism) is a claim of the official doctrine of national conditions, which has also shaped the understanding of rights protection in criminal process. The economic base, which, of course, is always in flux, is understood to be the most fundamental national condition – an objective condition – which legitimises the contingency of human rights. Consequently, both the official conceptions of human rights and criminal justice reflect a relativistic – if invoked against universal human rights – and positivistic top-down approach, which is in stark contrast to the idea of the right to a fair trial under international law.

At the more practical level, this raises the question of what precisely national conditions are in the context of criminal justice and how they ought to guide the implementation of human rights. The party-state, as the sole determinator of what ought to constitute any national condition(s), has not explained this – at least not beyond the primary stage of socialism. And even if official and academic discourses have divided national conditions vaguely into the historical, social, economic, and cultural conditions,[99] the concrete conditions often remain unnamed. Indeed, we will see that their interpretation depends on who invokes the claim of national conditions to argue either in one or the other direction, meaning for or against more human rights. There was no sophisticated blueprint for the development of human rights in China. Indeed, both official and academic discourses have elaborated on the interdependence of the economic base and legal superstructure, and the fact that national conditions can also be invoked in favour of human rights has led to greater tensions between the different stakeholders.

In the party-state, criminal justice reforms can be described as a process of negotiations between different stakeholders. Especially in the reform era, many leading scholars that are discussed in this book assumed a more moderate or

[98] State Council Information Office, 'Zhongguo tese shehuizhuyi falü tixi (The Socialist Legal System with Chinese Characteristics)' (n 97) 16.

[99] State Council Information Office, 'Human Rights White Paper (1991)' (n 12); Chen Yaobin (n 41) 34; Dong Yunhu (n 45) 26; Dingding Chen, 'Explaining China's Changing Discourse on Human Rights, 1978–2004' (2005) 29 *Asian Perspective* 155, 159.

pragmatic approach and tried to reconcile national conditions with international fair trial standards, even if promoting rights and freedoms that are associated with liberalism such as presumption of innocence; such an approach may be due to strategic considerations. In the process of law-making, the notion of national conditions has been used, especially by state agencies and/or those who hold political power, as a codeword to frame political imperatives. It has provided the 'iron triangle',[100] notably the public security organs (the police), with useful rhetoric to reject international fair trial standards. In this context, especially the supremacy of collectivism, the emphasis on crime control as a guarantor for social stability and thus collective interests or the educational function of law have competed with liberal notions and procedural justice, as enshrined under international law. All these ostensible 'conditions' connect to the underlying values of criminal justice.

For example, rhetorically, various justifications can be derived from the unity of individual and collective rights to allow for restricted individualism. Such claims have been crucially supported by the Chinese legal system. While notions of equality and individualism had become more tangible in the reform era, the legal system retained notions of collectivism and individual duties, also in the context of criminal justice.[101] And even if the idea of duties is not alien to international human rights law,[102] this overemphasis on collectivism and social duties has competed with the idea of empowerment and individualism underlying the international human rights concept.[103]

Considering the earlier outlined classical socialist attitudes towards law, human rights are about social involvement. In the context of Chinese criminal justice, the mobilisation for social involvement is reflected in crime control elements, such as anti-crime campaigns or the social duty to denounce fellows and cooperate with state agencies. Therefore, social control has always been an important aspect of criminal justice. The underlying assumption of social involvement or mobilisation means that disobedience of law is an immediate threat to socialism, to society, and to collective interests – and ultimately to the leadership of the Party. The objective of crime control is moreover manifested in the search for factual guilt and swift resolution of cases. With growing concern for human rights, we will see that the dual objectives of human rights protection and crime control have been touted to run in parallel, especially in official discourses, although they indeed reflect

[100] The so-called 'iron triangle' consists of the three agencies (the police, the procuratorates, and the courts) that dominate the criminal justice process.

[101] Constitution of 1982, arts 33(4), 51, and 53. Tang Congyao, *Xingshi beigaoren de susong quanli he yiwu (The Procedural Rights and Duties of the Criminal Defendant)* (Fuzhou, Fujian Renmin University Press, 1982) 64–87.

[102] Kathryn Sikkink, *Evidence for Hope: Making Human Rights Work in the 21st Century* (Princeton, Princeton University Press, 2017) 74–77.

[103] Expect for the right to self-determination (ICCPR, art 1), the rights of the Covenant are all human rights of individuals, see Nowak (n 4) xxv; Jack Donnelly, *Universal Human Rights in Theory and Practice*, 3rd edn (Ithaca, Cornell University Press, 2013) 29.

competing values, as the latter has been understood to emphasise national conditions to justify rights restrictions.

As already indicated, reform-minded legal scholars have interpreted the fluid national conditions differently. In the context of criminal justice, the party-state's narrative of an interdependence of the economic base and legal superstructure had faced a dilemma. In the face of China's rapid economic development, certain scholars have interpreted national conditions in favour of human rights, and claims for greater protection of human rights grew. Scholars used the theory of a (increasingly prosperous) base and (by comparison a still inferior) superstructure to advocate the strengthening of fair trial guarantees, amongst which the presumption of innocence became one of the most prominent yet contested guarantees. As an additional factor, the international human rights regime has led to a greater convergence of legal systems and, as we will see in the chapters to follow, has greatly influenced academic discourses in China as well, especially from the 1990s onwards. Calls for better rights protection were crucially supported by the Chinese government's official commitment to international human rights from the late 1980s onwards, as well as the Party's agenda of legal governance. A critical moment was the signature of the ICCPR in October 1998. This official green light and the overall more open atmosphere had created new spaces for more pluralistic discourses, which was tolerated by the party-state, at least to some degree.

However, national conditions remained a powerful rhetoric against human rights, crucially supported by changing politics and greater central control over values discourses that impacted the trajectory of criminal justice. The tensions between human rights and national conditions were growing, especially from the mid-1990s onwards, and became particularly tangible early in the tenure of Xi Jinping. In the era of Xi, advocacy for universal values and human rights has become dangerous. More insistent on specifically Chinese values, while openly even considering their advocacy as a threat to its leadership role, the party-state has largely closed this discursive vacuum. It is observable that these developments have also impacted the underlying values of criminal justice, with a renewed emphasis on crime control mechanisms, which are now codified in Chinese legislation. And while the continuing process of legalisation is framed as progress, it should not be confused with liberalism. It should be observed that the autocratic elements of the socialist attitudes towards law and human rights, both crucially impacted by the Communist worldview and resting on the doctrine of national conditions that had never been abandoned, facilitated such an illiberal turn of the legal system.

Therefore, the pros and cons of national conditions ultimately reflect different value choices and ideologies underlying both human rights and criminal justice. Whereas the official discourse and state agencies tended to use alleged conditions in rather absolute and vague terms, scholars had been more nuanced in their engagement with this official discourse. Conflicting interpretations of the paradigm of national conditions can thus serve both sides: illiberalism and liberalism. However, success or failure of human rights claims was dependent upon political preferences. While the pendulum swung between these two choices in the reform era, with attempts to find a compromise, it appears to have settled with the choice of illiberalism in the era of Xi, as orchestrated from the Party Central. This meant the end of presumption of innocence discourses in China.

## IV. Organisation of the Book

Chapter two introduces the subject of this book and lays the foundation for an engagement with presumption of innocence in the Chinese context. It begins by illuminating the bottom-conception of the right to a fair trial under international law and demonstrates the non-derogable nature of the presumption of innocence as a central aspect of fairness. In a further step, this chapter illustrates the three dimensions of the presumption of innocence as a right, a rule, and a principle and thus argues that a broad approach to presumption of innocence is not only defensible but also necessary to give full moral force to this fair trial guarantee.

The chapters to follow, chapters three to six, follow a period approach and explain the curve, or evolution, of academic discourse about presumption of innocence against the backdrop of changing politics, or varying emphases on national conditions, which demonstrates the amalgam of law and politics in the context of criminal justice. Scholars have divided the academic discourses in China into four phases. The first phase began in the mid- to late-1950s, unleashed by the Eighth National Congress of the CPC in 1956, and it was a rather short-lived discourse. The Third Plenum in 1978 and the passage of the first Criminal Procedure Law in 1979 (CPL 1979) commenced the second phase of presumption of innocence discourses. In the late 1980s, when an overhaul of the CPL 1979 was already under consideration, another round of debates began, marking the third phase of the discourse on the presumption of innocence. The Criminal Procedure Law 1996 (CPL 1996) facilitated the fourth phase of the discourse on the presumption of innocence, with many scholars advocating the explicit adoption of the presumption of innocence.[104] The fourth phase was the final phase, which ended with the Criminal Procedure Law 2012 (CPL 2012). No new round of presumption of innocence discourses emerged when a refined version of the Criminal Procedure Law was adopted in 2018 (CPL 2018).

Chapter three sheds light on the first two phases of presumption of innocence in China. It sets out in the early years of the PRC under Mao Zedong. The official discourse rejected the 'bourgeois' presumption of innocence as 'reactionary' and incompatible with the socialist legal system. However, in the mid-1950s, when

[104] Yue Liling, *Gongmin quanli he zhengzhi quanli guoji gongyue yu zhongguo xingshi sifa (International Covenant on Civil and Political Rights and Criminal Justice in China)* (Beijing, Law Press China, 2007) 131; Chen Guangzhong, Jiang Jiahua and Xiao Peiquan, 'Lun wuzui tuiding jiqi zai zhongguo de shiyong (On the Presumption of Innocence and its Application in China)' [2013] *Law Science Magazine* 1, 5–6.

the Party had consolidated its power and decided to shift its focus to economic developments for which some regulation was considered indispensable, some few scholars openly advocated this procedural safeguard. Yet, such views were suppressed by the Anti-Rightist Campaign (1957–58), and the various following political campaigns in the Mao era largely suppressed any further engagement with presumption of innocence. In the early reform era, stability was emphasised to support economic development, and with the official end of the class struggle and the elevation of law over politics, at least nominally, the presumption of innocence gained a new momentum, even if scepticism and misconceptions of this guarantee remained prevalent during this time. Many scholars read the presumption of innocence as a rule of evidence, while its broader dimension of principle had not yet been widely recognised, and some even claimed that the first Criminal Procedure Law, 1979, showed signs of presumption of innocence. The chapter argues that there was no place for presumption of innocence in the law.

Chapter four discusses the third phase of the discourse on the presumption of innocence and the first overhaul of the Criminal Procedure Law, which was underway from the early 1990s onwards. In addition to the many shortcomings of the law, theorists and practitioners agreed that the dramatic socio-economic changes required legal reforms. Crucially, as this chapter demonstrates, the discourses on human rights and criminal justice merged, and calls for better human rights protection in the criminal process grew. Some scholars have viewed the CPL 1996 as the beginning of a presumption of innocence 'with Chinese characteristics' increasingly found new grounds among Chinese scholars. The legislator assigned a group of scholars the production of a Criminal Procedure Law draft proposal. Even if some of the scholarly proposals were adopted and even though the law showed signs of improvements in terms of fair trial safeguards, there was no genuine endorsement of presumption of innocence, and the law maintained many controversial provisions or counter-norms. This chapter concludes that the official doctrine of national conditions has triumphed over international presumption of innocence standards and the claim of a partial acceptance of the presumption of innocence stood on very fragile grounds.

Chapter five looks at the fourth and final phase of the discourse on the presumption of innocence and the lengthy law-making of the CPL 2012 that took almost ten years. In the 2000s, international law arguably became the most important benchmark for reform-minded scholars, which also meant that the broader principle of presumption of innocence was increasingly recognised among scholars. Even if not being formally entrusted, some leading scholars prepared comprehensive Criminal Procedure Law draft proposals. A competing, largely academic discourse on the human right of presumption of innocence emerged, but the continued insistence on national conditions had forced the destruction of the human right to presumption of innocence into various elements, leading to a fragile presumption of innocence in the CPL 2012, at best. This chapter argues that the 2012 CPL showed initial signs of an illiberal turn and marked a crucial turning point in the genesis of criminal justice in China. Advocacy for universal human rights has been increasingly seen as a threat to the leadership role of the Party.

Chapter six illuminates the domestic developments after 2012 and shows the marginalisation of such liberal values as presumption of innocence due to re-ideologisation and autocratic closure on the ground. The Party has become the highest moral authority and lawmaker. There is a strong reemphasis on 'Chinese characteristics', ie, national conditions, and the political agenda had shifted towards crime control. In the aftermath of the CPL 2012, the presumption of innocence has been in decline, and there was no new round of discourse. This trend became particularly tangible in the wake of the Criminal Procedure Law 2018 (CPL 2018). A new political wind has impacted the path of criminal justice, even if the official discourse frames the latest reform as progress due to further legalisation or standardisation of proceedings. This chapter discusses the new supervisory mechanism and the legalisation of the policy of combining leniency with severity to suggest that the law had made a further return to crime control and illiberalism.

Chapter seven is the concluding chapter, summarising the findings of this book.

# 2

# Defending a Broad Presumption of Innocence

Chapter two lays the foundation for the remainder of this book and will be helpful for our understanding of the challenges the presumption of innocence has been facing in the Chinese context. Drawing on international law and discourses, it illuminates the bottom-up conception of fairness, as enshrined in international law.[1] The chapter shows that, as a concrete manifestation of the right to a fair trial, the presumption of innocence is based on the concept of human dignity, which justifies its raison d'être. In other words, minimum fair trial guarantees, which are associated with the presumption of innocence, can be deduced from human dignity. I understand this as the bottom-up conception of the right to a fair trial under international law. In a further step, I elaborate on the three different dimensions of presumption of innocence as a right, a rule, and a principle – conceptualising it in this sense helps to further explain its raison d'être. Based on these three dimensions, I will defend a broader approach to presumption of innocence. I do not intend to create a 'super presumption of innocence',[2] absorbing such a plethora of fair trial safeguards under it that every procedural defect immediately also violates presumption of innocence. Rather, I demonstrate that the right to a fair trial belongs to a core of human rights and that the essence of this right, which is based on centrally important human rights, is non-negotiable. The chapter then discusses in what sense and in what aspects the ICCPR nevertheless allows states a flexible implementation of presumption of innocence standards to demonstrate further that the presumption of innocence, as part of a fair trial, allows for some variation but that the essence of fairness can never be compromised.

## I. The Bottom-up Conception of Fairness

From a moral point of view, the modern human rights concept assumes that every human being should equally enjoy all human rights due to their inherent dignity.

[1] When speaking of the 'right to a fair trial' or 'a fair trial', I mean Article 14 ICCPR in its entirety.

[2] Carl-Friedrich Stuckenberg, 'Who Is Presumed Innocent of What by Whom?' (2014) 8 *Criminal Law and Philosophy* 301.

Legally speaking, this conception centres on individual autonomy, fairness and equality, all of which should be guaranteed through positive law. In this section I explain what I will call the bottom-up conception of fairness in international law. Some contextualisation might be useful to understand what the drafters had in mind when formulating international fair trial standards, which will be outlined in detail in the next section. In the aftermath of World War II, the establishment of fair trial guarantees was based on both epistemic and non-epistemic considerations. Undoubtedly, the atrocities of Nazi Germany had raised awareness of individual safeguards. Regardless of the disagreements that arose in the process of drafting the right to a fair trial, no one questioned the need for such individual safeguards in the abstract.[3] Articles 10 and 11 of the Universal Declaration of 1948 established minimum standards of fair trial that suggest limits on a government's power to impose and enforce criminal punishment to ensure the protection of human rights. Indeed, the right to a fair trial under international law is associated with liberal-democratic values. Moral considerations had crucially shaped the contemporary understanding of minimum standards of fairness. Recall that a government is a 'moral agent' and at the same time holds the monopoly on the power to impose sanctions. To legitimise this monopoly, a government should observe legal constraints on its power, even if it might result in sacrificing the efficient prosecution of crimes. In the words of Lee:

> Fundamental legal protections that are promised to individuals [...] are not merely requirements that flow directly from laws of morality that dictate how individuals ought to treat one another. They also spell out the proper relationship between the government and the governed, and they are among the many conditions that attach to the government's exclusive possession and use of the power to criminalize and punish. These conditions, in turn, take the form of constraints that are resistant to trade-offs in order to protect their viability as restrictions on the government's power to blame.[4]

As part of a fair trial, the presumption of innocence is not only a fundamental human right; it is a procedural means to realise the rule of law.[5] Ashworth has held that the presumption of innocence represents 'a moral and political principle, based on a widely shared conception of how a free society (as distinct from an authoritarian society) should exercise the power to punish'.[6]

As regards the theoretical foundation of universal human rights, the incorporation of human dignity facilitated an overlapping consensus, despite different prevalent philosophical and political convictions.[7] Owing to the absence of any

[3] Johannes Morsink, *The Universal Declaration of Human Rights: Origins, Drafting, and Intent* (Philadelphia, University of Pennsylvania Press, 1999) 50–52.

[4] Youngjae Lee, 'Deontology, Political Morality, and the State: Political Theory and Criminal Punishment' (2011) 8 *Ohio State Journal of Criminal Law* 385, 399.

[5] General Comment No. 32, Article 14: 'Right to equality before courts and tribunals and to a fair trial' (GC NO. 32) 2007 (UN Doc CCPR/C/GC/32) para 2.

[6] Andrew Ashworth, 'Four Threats to the Presumption of Innocence' (2006) 10 *The International Journal of Evidence & Proof* 241, 249–250.

[7] Jürgen Habermas, 'The Concept of Human Dignity and the Realistic Utopia of Human Rights' (2010) 41 *Metaphilosophy* 464, 467.

other basis for facilitating consensus among the drafters and to avoid the impression of a particular ideological foundation, the notion of human dignity could create a transcultural theory of human rights, allowing for cross-cultural acceptance. From a utilitarian perspective, the lack of definition of dignity meant it could accommodate different meanings, depending on the reader.[8] While the notion of dignity in international law is understood to have its roots in the Kantian conception of dignity,[9] it remained undefined. Schachter believes that this explains why the notion of human dignity has become such a widely applied concept:

> [The] intrinsic meaning [of human dignity] has been left to intuitive understanding, conditioned in large measure by cultural factors. When it has been invoked in concrete situations it has been generally assumed that a violation of human dignity can be recognized even if the abstract term cannot be defined. "I know it when I see it even if I cannot tell you what it is."[10]

The notion of human dignity can be found in both the Universal Declaration and Covenant. The first preambular paragraph of the Universal Declaration reads:

> [The] recognition of the *inherent* dignity and of the equal and inalienable rights of all members of the human family is the foundation of freedom, justice and peace in the world.[11] [Emphasis added]

Moreover, Article 1 UDHR equates dignity with rights, stating that '[a]ll human beings are born free and equal in dignity and rights.'[12] The first paragraph of the preamble to the Universal Declaration was later incorporated in identical wording in the first paragraph of the preamble of the International Covenant on Civil and Political Rights (ICCPR or Covenant), which moreover recognised 'that these rights derive from the inherent dignity of the human person'.[13] Even if it cannot establish an immediate link between dignity and law as such, it recognises a substantive link between dignity and human rights law,[14] and thus detaches human rights from state authority. Although both the Universal Declaration and the Covenant are silent on the precise meaning of 'human dignity', or they

[8] Christopher McCrudden, 'Human Dignity and Judicial Interpretation of Human Rights' (2008) 19 *The European Journal of International Law* 655, 675–678.

[9] James Rachels, *The Elements of Moral Philosophy*, 4th edn (New York, McGraw-Hill, 2003) 130. Considering the relationship between law and morality, it is not surprising that justifications for the presumption of innocence have been sought in natural law as well, see, eg, Joseph C Cascarelli, 'Presumption of Innocence and Natural Law: Machiavelli and Aquinas' (1996) 41 *The American Journal of Jurisprudence*.

[10] Oscar Schachter, 'Human Dignity as a Normative Concept' (1983) 77 *The American Journal of International Law* 848, 849.

[11] See also fifth preamble paragraph, Arts 1, 22, and 23 of the Universal Declaration of Human Rights (Paris, 10 December 1948).

[12] Georg Lohmann, 'Echo Des Naturrechts? Menschenwürde, Menschenrechte und Demokratie' in Pirmin Stekeler-Weithofer and Benno Zabel (eds) *Philosophie der Republik* (Mohr Siebeck GmbH and Co KG 2018) 450.

[13] See fifth preambular paragraph of the International Convention on Civil and Political Rights (Covenant or ICCPR) (New York, 16 December 1966).

[14] Jeremy Waldron, 'How Law Protects Dignity' (2012) 71 *Cambridge Law Journal* 200, 201.

are silent on how precisely it serves as the foundation of human rights,[15] the key takeaway is that human dignity is an inherent value claim of international human rights.

The idea that human rights derive from human dignity had facilitated scholarly discourses about the implications of such a conception and the legal concept of dignity. While Lohmann believes that the normative concept of dignity manifests the equal value and legal equality of all human beings.[16] Habermas views human rights as 'specifications of human dignity', believing that there has always existed an intrinsic and conceptual relationship between these two from the very beginning, precisely because the concept of human rights emerged in response to tyranny, oppression, and humiliation. A case in point and perhaps the most obvious example may be the prohibition against torture in Article 5 UDHR, spelling out what amounts to humiliation. Therefore, Habermas believes that human dignity is the moral source of fundamental human rights.[17]

However, one may wonder how law protects dignity. Waldron has argued that law protects dignity by acknowledging individual autonomy and self-control, and the most obvious way in which it does so is by prohibiting violations of human dignity, including Article 7 ICCPR or Article 5 UDHR or Article 3 of the Geneva Conventions, which prohibits 'outrages upon personal dignity, in particular humiliating and degrading treatment'.[18] In the context of criminal proceedings, the dignity of the accused would be protected by a robust set of rules to ensure compliance with the principles of equality and fairness.[19] Again, the link between dignity and torture may be one of the most evident examples.[20]

Consequently, Lippke has held that human dignity is a fundamental value underlying criminal proceedings, which would impose normative restrictions on the way in which proceedings may be conducted. For example, rights violations, such as unlawful obtainment of evidence, would not only be a violation of dignity but also of other human rights. Again, the most obvious example would be the prohibition against torture. In other words, interferences with human dignity can never be justified or balanced against other human or fundamental rights. Although interferences with fundamental rights were possible, the requirements

[15] Jack Donnelly, *Universal Human Rights in Theory and Practice*, 3rd edn (Ithaca, Cornell University Press 2013) 28.

[16] Lohmann (n 12) 454.

[17] Habermas (n 7) 466–468.

[18] The Four Geneva Conventions of 12 August 1949 (Geneva Convention I for the Amelioration of the Condition of Wounded and Sick in Armed Forces in the Field, Geneva Convention II for the Amelioration of the Condition of Wounded and Sick and Shipwrecked Members of Armed Forces at Sea, Geneva Convention III Relating to the Treatment of Prisoners of War, Geneva Convention IV Relating to the Protection of Civilian Persons in Times of War).

[19] Waldron (n 14) 200–210.

[20] McCrudden (n 8) 670; Vienna Declaration and Programme of Action (Vienna, 25 June 1993) para 5. It can also be found in the Vienna Declaration, which reaffirms the conception of human dignity as the basis of human rights and states, 'one of the most atrocious violations against human dignity is the act of torture, the result of which destroys the dignity [...]'.

for justifying such interferences would be high, for example, in the context of deprivations of personal liberty. The use of coercive measures against an accused person could nonetheless never justify undignified treatment.[21] Indeed, Article 10 ICCPR refers to dignity in the context of deprivation of personal liberty and emphasises the requirements of dignified treatment in the second paragraph of this provision.

Against this backdrop, it may become clearer that international law only outlines minimum requirements of fair trial – the bottom line of fairness – which are needed to protect human dignity and which will become clearer in the sections to follow, the right to a fair trial with the presumption of innocence rests on human dignity and brings it to life by giving it substance. The presumption of innocence, as a specification of human dignity, tells us where the bottom line of decency lies. The interdependence of dignity and fair trial reinforces the assumption that it can never be justified to compromise what lies at the core of presumption of innocence – the idea of fairness. Therefore, it makes more sense to consider the bottom-up conception of fairness, or the right to a fair trial. While it would be misleading to view the right to a fair trial as a core value on which the construct as such and all safeguards rest.

## II. The Universality of Fair Trial

The right to a fair trial is enshrined in Articles 10 and 11 UDHR. These provisions protect a general right to an equal, fair and public hearing before an independent, impartial tribunal; the principle of presumption of innocence as well as the legal principle of *nulla poena sine lege* ('no penalty without a law').[22] Paragraph 1 of Article 11 UDHR closely links the presumption of innocence to the general fair trial guarantee:

> Everyone charged with a penal offence has the right to be presumed innocent until proved guilty according to law in a public trial at which he has had all the guarantees necessary for his defence.[23]

Even if one rejects the view that the Universal Declaration in its entirety constitutes customary law, and even though so-called 'soft law' in the form of resolutions and declarations is not legally binding, it is morally binding upon UN members – ethically and politically. It moreover indicates that states have reached a consensus as regards the aspiration of human rights, meaning how such human rights ought to ideally operate in reality. Moreover, UN 'soft law' has evolved, and often does evolve, into binding law, as has been the case with respect to the Universal

[21] Richard L Lippke, 'Fundamental Values of Criminal Procedure' in Darryl K Brown, Jenia I Turner and Bettina Weisser (eds), *The Oxford Handbook of Criminal Process* (Oxford, Oxford University Press, 2019) 27–30.

[22] UDHR, arts 10, 11.

[23] Stefan Trechsel, *Human Rights in Criminal Proceedings* (Oxford, Oxford University Press, 2005) 154.

Declaration.[24] While the status of declarations corresponds to recommendations, they remain significant instruments on their own, especially vis-à-vis non-state parties.[25]

In terms of legally binding treaties, the right to a fair trial is codified in Article 14 ICCPR. It is of a complex nature; it combines various institutional and procedural guarantees.[26] A fair trial requires equality before the courts and tribunals and the right to a fair and public hearing by an independent and impartial tribunal, which is an 'institutional guarantee' (Article 14(1)). The latter has been described as manifesting the essence of 'due process of law', while the provisions in Article 14(2) to (7) (and Article 15) are specifications of what constitutes a fair trial.[27] The presumption of innocence is protected in paragraph 2 of this provision:

> Everyone charged with a criminal offence shall have the right to be presumed innocent until proved guilty according to law.

Furthermore, a fair trial encompasses a catalogue of *minimum* guarantees a criminal accused should be guaranteed, including the right to be promptly and in detail informed of the charge against him (paragraph 3(a)), to have adequate time and facilities to prepare for defence and access to legal counsel (paragraph 3(b)). It requires the right to be tried without undue delay (paragraph 3(c)), the right to defence (paragraph 3(d)), the right to call and examine witnesses (paragraph 3(e)), free assistance of an interpreter (paragraph 3(f)), and the privilege against self-incrimination (paragraph 3(g)). Moreover, paragraphs 1 and 4 of Article 14 (as well as Articles 6(5) and 10(2) ICCPR) make references to juvenile criminal trials.[28] A fair trial further requires ensuring the right to have a criminal conviction reviewed by a higher tribunal (paragraph 5). Paragraph 6 protects the right to compensation in cases of miscarriages of justice. This right applies to persons who have been convicted of a criminal offence by a final decision and have 'suffered punishment' based on such miscarriage of justice. Their conviction must be later reversed, or the person convicted must be pardoned on the grounds of 'a new or newly discovered fact shows conclusively that there has been a miscarriage of justice'.[29] Finally, double jeopardy is prohibited (paragraph 7). Article 14 ICCPR establishes only minimum requirements for ensuring fair and reasonable outcomes of criminal trials. It should be observed that the right to a fair trial, moreover, aims to protect

[24] Walter Kälin and Jörg Künzli, *The Law of International Human Rights Protection*, 2nd edn (Oxford, Oxford University Press 2019) 65–67.

[25] See, eg, Body Principles for the Protection of All Persons under Any Form of Detention or Imprisonment 1988 [UNGA res. 43/173]; Declaration on the Protection of All Persons from Being Subjected to Torture and Other Cruel, Inhuman or Degrading Treatment or Punishment 1975 [UNGA res. 3452 (XXX)]; Declaration on the Protection of All Persons from Enforced Disappearance 1992 [UNGA res. 47/133]; Kälin and Künzli (n 24) 65–67.

[26] GC No. 32 para 3.

[27] Manfred Nowak, *U.N. Covenant on Civil and Political Rights, CCPR Commentary*, 2nd edn (Kehl, N P Engel, 2005) 314.

[28] These provisions were incorporated and further specified in art 40 CRC, see ibid 346–347.

[29] GC No. 32 para 52; Nowak (n 27) 353.

negative freedoms by minimising the risk of interferences. In this sense, the full realisation of the right to a fair trial is not a *purely* positive right in the sense that it entails affirmative duties on the state. Considering the 'trias of state obligations' (respect, protect, and fulfil), there must be some interplay between negative freedoms and positive guarantees.[30]

Thus far, 173 countries are state parties to the ICCPR.[31] The presumption of innocence is thus a *universally* recognised procedural safeguard and human right.[32] However, the idea of human rights *universalism* remains controversial. Advocates of universality of human rights have developed different but partly overlapping justifications to defend universal human rights based on various moral, legal and political considerations. For the purpose of this chapter, it is sufficient to bear in mind that human rights are commonly seen as inherent and inalienable, as being derived from human dignity and possessed by all persons equally solely in virtue of being human.[33] The critical issue here is the meaning of universality. Human rights are universal because they are enjoyed universally by all human beings and thus should possess universal applicability and validity.[34] Such views are in line with the UN human rights doctrine, according to which human rights are universal, egalitarian, individualistic,[35] indivisible, and interdependent.[36] Interdependence means that there is a functional link between rights. Indivisibility indicates that human rights cannot be ranked; they can only ensure full realisation if they are considered equally important.[37] Universality, therefore, means that *all* people (ought to) have *all* human rights. Legally speaking, human rights create entitlements, whose *beneficiaries* are individuals.[38] However, this is where the problems begin. Even if, in principle, we advocate human rights universalism, *which* rights are human rights? And in what sense are they universal?

From a moral perspective, few would protest human rights universalism, or at least the idea of it. From a normative point of view, however, the scope of enjoyment of '*all* human rights' remains highly controversial, as there is no agreement on how broad it should be. Apart from a few human rights, which are internationally

[30] Nowak (n 27) xx–xi.

[31] Status of Ratification, see treaties.un.org/Pages/ViewDetails.aspx?src=TREATY&mtdsg_no=IV-4&chapter=4&clang=_en accessed 14 February 2025.

[32] See also art 7(1) of the African Charter on Human and Peoples' Rights (Nairobi, 27 June 1981); Art 6 of the Convention for the Protection of Human Rights and Fundamental Freedoms (ECHR) (Rome, 4 November 1950); art 40(2)(b)(i) Convention on the Rights of the Child (CRC) (New York, 20 November 1989); art 8(2) of the American Convention on Rights (San José, 22 November 1969).

[33] Donnelly (n 15) 7.

[34] Michael Freeman, *Human Rights: An Interdisciplinary Approach*, 2nd edn (Cambridge, Polity Press, 2011) 61–74; Jack Donnelly, 'The Relative Universality of Human Rights' (2007) 29 *Human Rights Quarterly* 281, 282–283; Charles Beitz, *The Idea of Human Rights* (Oxford, Oxford University Press, 2009) 5.

[35] Except for the right to self-determination, eg, in art 1(1) of the ICCPR.

[36] The wording of the Universal Declaration indirectly recognises human rights universalism, see Freeman (n 34) 119.

[37] Donnelly (n 15) 31–32.

[38] Kälin and Künzli (n 24) 28.

recognised as belonging to the core of human rights (ie, *jus cogens* norms),[39] beyond this there is no consensus.[40]

In the present context, it is important to mention that, in order to facilitate consensus amongst states as to a core set of universal values or rights, international human rights treaties allow for a considerable degree of discretion in terms of interpreting concrete human rights standards and norms – with the ICCPR being no exception. After all, the implementation of human rights into domestic legislation predominately depends on the willingness of a state – regardless of whether it is being legally obliged or not. In other words, it is ultimately upon a state to respect, protect and fulfil human rights.

Therefore, even if agreeing on a core set of international human rights (beyond human rights treaties and the few human rights norms that have the status of *jus cogens*), the lacking enforcement of such norms considerably weakens their effectiveness. Indeed, Kälin and Künzli believe that

> positivist arguments are insufficient in cases where there is no consensus on the precise content of particular rights, on the scope of the restrictions to which they may be subjected or on their relative status. It is equally insufficient in cases where the validity of a right is disputed because of the need to protect cultural traditions or even by reference to a divine law.[41]

In such cases, they conclude, universality of human rights cannot be justified by factual cross-cultural adherence to international human rights treaties.[42] In other words, consensus in the form of signatures or ratifications may be driven by mere unawareness, hypocrisy, or even arrogance, rather than by a genuine intention to comply with such treaties.[43] Although there appears to be some consensus on the universality of human rights as a *universal aspiration*, and even if we agree on a core of human rights, we would thereby not automatically clarify the *meaning* of universality in terms of the concrete *scope* and *content* of particular human rights norms. Take the presumption of innocence, for example. In 1984, the UN Human Rights Committee

> has noted a lack of information regarding article 14(2) and, in some cases, has even observed that the presumption of innocence, which is fundamental to the protection of human rights, is expressed in very ambiguous terms or entails conditions which render it ineffective.[44]

[39] Kälin and Künzli, for example, argue that only those human rights that 'form part of *jus cogens*, that is, peremptory norms of international law, constitute the hard core of human rights', see ibid 61.

[40] James Rawls, *The Law of Peoples* (Massachusetts, Harvard University Press, 1999); Amy Gutmann, *Human Rights as Politics and Idolatry* (Princeton, Princeton University Press, 2001).

[41] Kälin and Künzli (n 24) 19–20.

[42] ibid.

[43] Rein Müllerson, 'Universal Human Rights in Multicultural World' in ER May and AE Laiou (eds), *The Dumbarton Oaks Conventions and the United Nations 1944–1994* (Dumbarton Oaks Research Library and Collection, 1998) 112–113.

[44] CCPR General Comment No. 13: Article 14 (Administration of Justice), Equality before the Courts and the Right to a Fair and Public Hearing by an Independent Court Established by Law (GC No. 13) 1984 para 7.

Therefore, the issue of universality becomes even more complex when we consider the *content* of individual human rights norms like the presumption of innocence in Article 14(2) ICCPR, even if a state has agreed to be bound by it. Moreover, a too narrow positivist approach to international human rights law may neglect non-binding standards such as UN soft law. It should furthermore be observed that disagreements may not merely be grounded in relativistic claims, but the content of a specific human right may be called into question by states that do not necessarily embrace any form of relativism as such.[45] Therefore, even if we can agree that the presumption of innocence is a universally recognised human right, we have not yet established the precise content of it. To determine what precisely is required to protect the presumption of innocence, it is necessary to first consider if and to what extent states are permitted to depart from the right to a fair trial with the presumption of innocence.

## III. Non-Derogability of the Presumption of Innocence

The question of non-derogability of the presumption of innocence in Article 14(2) ICCPR must be addressed to facilitate the argument that the presumption of innocence must be part of any decent criminal justice system. To answer this question, it is necessary to consider the place of the presumption of innocence in the context of the right to a fair trial. In this context, the Human Rights Committee has held that

> a general reservation to the right to a fair trial [with the intent of excluding or to modifying the legal effect of that provision] would be incompatible with the object and purpose of the Covenant.[46]

A general reservation to the right to a fair trial would thus violate the fundamental principles and values underlying the Convention. This raises the question of whether there can be *any* derogations from specific fair trial guarantees like the presumption of innocence. Here it is helpful to go back to the drafting history of the Covenant. In fact, proposals were made to include the right to a fair trial in Article 14 on the list of non-derogable rights.[47] Yet, such proposals were defeated due to unease about imposing too far-reaching obligations on state parties to accept such a characterisation of certain aspects of fair trial guarantees like the right to a public hearing.[48] As shown in the previous section, this provision does

[45] Jeremy Waldron, 'How to Argue for a Universal Claim' (1999) 30 *Columbia Human Rights Law Review* 306, 306–314.

[46] GC No. 32 para 5.

[47] Note that not every non-derogable human right norm necessarily constitutes a norm of *jus cogens*, see General Comment No. 29, States of Emergency (article 4) (GC No. 29) 2001 (UN Doc CCPR/C/21/Rev1/Add11) para 11.

[48] Stephanos Stavros, 'The Right to a Fair Trial in Emergency Situations' (1992) 41 *Comparative Law Quarterly* 343, 347–348.

consist of a complex plethora of safeguards, which may explain reluctance to make it non-derogable in its entirety. Since Article 14 is not included on the list of non-derogable rights, as provided by Article 4(2) of the Covenant, derogations from this right may be permitted, but only 'in time of public emergency'.[49]

This is an important caveat. While practice demonstrates that states have departed from the right in cases of public emergency,[50] there seems to be an agreement that Article 14 – including the presumption of innocence in paragraph 2 of this provision – is non-derogable in the absence of public emergency.[51] In fact, derogations are made even more difficult due to the absolute nature of some of the safeguards on which the right to a fair trial basically rests. In the words of the Human Rights Committee:

> The enumeration of non-derivable provisions in article 4 is related to, but not identical with, the question whether certain human rights obligations bear the nature of peremptory norms of international law. [...] Furthermore, the category of peremptory norms extends beyond the list of non-derogable provisions as given in article 4, paragraph 2. States parties may in no circumstances invoke article 4 as justification for acting in violation of humanitarian law or peremptory norms of international law [...] by deviating from fundamental principles of fair trial, including the presumption of innocence.[52]

It is thus under no circumstances justified to depart from fundamental fair trial principles such as the presumption of innocence. Since certain elements of the right to a fair trial are guaranteed under international humanitarian law in armed conflicts, the Human Rights Committee has stated that 'the principles of legality and the rule of law require that fundamental requirements of fair trial must be respected during a state of emergency'. In other words, the presumption of innocence and the habeas corpus guarantee, as well as impartial and independent tribunals, must be guaranteed even in time of public emergency.[53] Therefore, even in times of emergency, under humanitarian law, some fair trial minimum requirements must be protected, including the presumption of innocence, which suggests a high threshold to justify any erosion of the right to a fair trial.[54]

Therefore, even if derogations from internationally recognised fair trial standards may be permitted in a state of emergency, the notion of *fairness* of proceedings must be preserved at all times; non-derogable elements of *fairness* are set out in Article 14 ICCPR, which has been outlined in the previous section.

[49] A time of public emergency refers to a condition that 'threatens the life of the nation and the existence of which is officially proclaimed', see art 4(1) ICCPR.

[50] See, eg, Andreas Zimmermann, 'The Right to a Fair Trial in Situations of Emergency and the Question of Emergency Courts' in David Weissbrodt and Rüdiger Wolfrum (eds), *The Right to a Fair Trial* (Princeton, Springer, 1998).

[51] Judge Patrick Robinson, 'The Right to a Fair Trial in International Law, with Specific Reference to the Work of the ICTY' (2009) 3 *Berkeley Journal of International Law* 1, 6–7.

[52] GC No. 29 para 11.

[53] ibid para 16.

[54] Stavros (n 48) 351–358.

From this it follows that the essence of the right to a fair trial is grounded on such centrally important rights that the *procedure* of a fair trial might allow for minor variables, but the *essence* of the fair trial (the principle of fairness) cannot be undermined. The notion of *fairness* must be guaranteed at all times. What this means precisely will be explained in the next section. The presumption of innocence is non-derogable even in emergency situations, which demonstrates that it is a centrally important safeguard of fairness. It might be worth noting that even when states do derogate from the right to a fair trial in emergency situations, they would not openly admit to an *unfair* trial.[55] Such an open denial of the right to a fair trial would arguably backfire; this once again emphasises the importance this human right has acquired.

Furthermore, considering the interdependence of fair trial safeguards, derogations are made almost impossible in practice. The Human Rights Committee has pointed this out by saying that 'guarantees of fair trial may never be made subject to measures of derogation that would circumvent the protection of non-derogable rights'.[56] For example, the prohibition against torture in Article 7 ICCPR is non-derogable in its entirety. This means that it is prohibited to invoke statements, confessions or other evidence that has been obtained in violation of this provision as evidence in any proceedings covered by Article 14 ICCPR, including in emergency situations. In accordance with the Convention against Torture, such evidence may only be invoked as evidence to prove that torture or other forms of treatment in violation of this provision occurred.[57] For example, the use of torture to obtain evidence in violation of Articles 7, 14(2), 14(3)(g) ICCPR would render a trial unfair. Furthermore, the prohibition of all forms of arbitrary deprivation of liberty is non-derogable under both treaty law and customary international law and constitutes a *jus cogens* norm.[58]

These considerations appear to further render the right to a fair trial with the presumption of innocence non-negotiable, as the *jus cogens* elements of it forbid any state from departing from the principle of a *fair* trial. Martin describes such norms that are necessary to guarantee the protection of other *jus cogens* norms as 'derivative *jus cogens*'.[59] Even if recognising the non-derogable nature of the presumption of innocence and viewing it as a derivative *jus cogens* norm, the question of what exactly is required under the presumption of innocence has not yet been answered.

[55] Robinson (n 51) 6–7.

[56] GC No. 32 para 6.

[57] Article 15 of the Convention against Torture and Other Cruel, Inhuman or Degrading Treatment or Punishment (Convention against Torture or CAT) (New York, 10 December 1984); GC No. 32 para 6.

[58] Human Rights Council, 'Report of the Working Group on Arbitrary Detention' (2012) UN Doc A/HRC/22/44 paras 47 and 49.

[59] Here, 'derivative' means how we should perceive such norms from an international law perspective when international instruments have not described them as non-derogable or peremptory, see Francisco Forrest Martin and et al., *International Human Rights and Humanitarian Law: Treaties, Cases, and Analysis* (Cambridge, Cambridge University Press, 2011) 37–39.

## IV. Flexible Universalism of the Presumption of Innocence

In this section, I use the idea of 'flexible or variable universalism' of the presumption of innocence to support my argument that the *procedure* of a fair trial allows for minor variations, while the *essence* of what constitutes *fairness* must be protected. As the previous discussions have shown, some elements of the right to a fair trial are absolute, or are centrally important, in the sense that they either do not allow derogations (eg, the presumption of innocence), provide no justification for interferences, or leave few rooms for discretionary implementation. Therefore, some elements of the right to a fair trial are more rigid than other elements. This would mean that the implementation of such universal human rights also leaves less room for flexibility. The question is how this relates to debates about domestic particularities. Donnelly, for example, has advocated a form of 'relative universality of human rights', as human rights universalism leaves room, at least to a certain extent, for claims of relativism. Therefore, legitimate claims might be invoked at both ends of the spectrum – universality and relativity. In a way, such defensible claims thus display the limits of universality. Donnelly distinguishes between 'conceptual' and 'substantive universality'. From a conceptual point of view, human rights are universal because they are equal and inalienable and thus held by all humans; but they are only 'relatively universal' in the sense that they leave room for diversity and relativity.[60] However, this does not really answer the question of how much room for manoeuvre states have with respect to relatively rigid human rights.

Lohmann has developed a similar approach to determine the scope of core human rights and adopts a more nuanced approach to establish grounds for minimum universalism, which also takes into consideration questions of implementation of human rights. For Lohmann, universalism is less flexible with respect to rights that encompass negative duties (eg, the prohibition on torture, personal liberty), while it can be implemented in a more flexible way with regard to rights that encompass positive rights – he calls this 'variable universalism'.[61] His approach connects to the discussion in the previous section. Therefore, many human rights norms, at least to a certain extent, leave room for interpretation and flexible universalism, while only a few international human rights fall within the scope of absolute rights, and many human rights are relative in the sense that they allow for limitations, including negative freedoms, provided they are justified. In addition to reservations, state parties can also submit declarations with the

[60] Donnelly (n 15) 93–102; Donnelly (n 34) 282–283.

[61] Georg Lohmann, 'Zu Einer Relationalen Begründung Der Universalisierung Der Menschenrechte' in Günter Nooke, Georg Lohmann and Gerhard Wahlers (eds), *Gelten Menschenrechte universal?: Begründungen und Infragestellungen* (Freiburg im Breisgau, Herder Press, 2008) 225–227.

intention to reinterpret (ie, modify) the content of a specific provision.[62] However, there must be limits to flexible universalism.

The Siracusa Principles on the Limitation and Derogation of Provisions in the International Covenant on Civil and Political Rights ('Siracusa Principles') provide guidance on the conditions under which limitations may be generally permissible.[63] The Siracusa Principles specify general principles to be observed when restricting rights guaranteed by the Covenant. In any case, permissible limitations, or grounds, are only those immediately provided for by the ICCPR itself, and the scope of limitation, as provided by the Covenant, must be interpreted in a way that the essence of a specific right is not compromised. In other words, extensive limitations on a right are prohibited; ie, 'all limitation clauses shall be interpreted strictly and in favour of the rights at issue'.[64] Obviously, any interference with a right must be grounded on a legal basis and be compatible with the objects and purposes of the Covenant,[65] thus setting limits to the principle of legality; limitations should not be applied in an 'arbitrary' manner.[66] Moreover, rights limitations must be proportionate, meaning 'necessary' in the sense of pursuing a legitimate aim and appropriate for the purposes of fulfilling a specific aim.[67] Therefore, to balance the interests involved, there must be an element of proportionality. De Schutter has summarised those three principles as the 'condition of legality', the 'condition of legitimacy', and the 'condition of proportionality'.[68]

The burden to justify limitations on rights protected under the Covenant is on the state.[69] The Siracusa Principles also require that '[e]very limitation imposed shall be subject to the possibility of challenge to and remedy against its abusive application',[70] ensuring checks and balances by enabling the individual to challenge rights limitations imposed by the state. There are further limitations to rights restrictions. As a general rule, limitations on a right guaranteed under the Covenant may never contravene Article 2(1), which prohibits discrimination on such various grounds as religion, sex, race, etc.[71] Moreover, the requirement expressed in Article 12 ICCPR, which enshrines the right to liberty of movement and freedom

[62] ICCPR, art 41; CCPR General Comment No. 24: Issues Relating to Reservations Made upon Ratification or Accession to the Covenant or the Optional Protocols thereto, or in Relation to Declarations under Article 41 of the Covenant (GC No. 24) 1994 (UN Doc CCPR/C/21/Rev1/Add6) paras 3, 19.

[63] UNCHR, 'Siracusa Principles on the Limitation and Derogation of Provisions in the International Covenant on Civil and Political Rights' (The Siracusa Principles) (28 September 1984) UN Doc E/CN.4/1984/4.

[64] ibid I A 3.

[65] ibid I A 5.

[66] ibid I A 7.

[67] ibid I A 10 (a) to (d).

[68] Olivier de Schutter, *International Human Rights Law: Cases, Materials, Commentary*, 2nd edn (Cambridge, Cambridge University Press, 2014) 339–344.

[69] UNCHR The Siracusa Principles (n 63) I A 12.

[70] ibid I A 8.

[71] ibid I A 9.

to choose one's residence, entails that any limitations on a right must be consistent with other rights guaranteed under the Covenant; this implies additional obstacles to justify rights restrictions. As another example, and as will be discussed in the sections to follow, in accordance with the privilege against self-incrimination in Article 14(3)(g) ICCPR, it is prohibited to use any information obtained in violation of the prohibition on torture or other forms of ill-treatment, which would also amount to a violation of Article 7 ICCPR and possibly Article 10 ICCPR. This rule is absolute in the sense that it does not permit any limitations. Restrictions on the right to legal counsel are only permitted on a small scale and subject to strict requirements, for example, on grounds of terrorism charges.[72] Derogation, as embodied in Article 4 ICCPR, is subject to safeguards based on the principles of legality and the rule of law underlying the Covenant.

Therefore, the Siracusa Principles provide a relatively comprehensive guide on general rules as to rights limitations, which has been supplemented by authoritative interpretations of the right to a fair trial, as guaranteed under the Covenant. This flexible universalism is further supported by the three dimensions of presumption of innocence that demonstrate what is needed to fully realise this fair trial safeguard.

## V. Three Different Dimensions of the Presumption of Innocence

This section engages with international law and international discourses. I explain why I defend a broad approach to presumption of innocence by outlining its three different dimensions of a right, a rule and a principle. Based on this conception, the requirements flowing from these three dimensions can be fleshed out. The previous discussions have shown that the presumption of innocence is understood to protect human rights in criminal proceedings. This is relatively uncontested. For example, its international acceptance was highlighted in the prominent case of *Coffin v United States*:

> The principle that there is a presumption of innocence in favour of the accused is the undoubted law, axiomatic and elementary, and its enforcement lies at the foundation of the administration of our criminal law.[73]

However, the presumption of innocence is silent on its precise scope of application, ie, whether it is limited to the trial stage or extends to the pre-trial stage,[74] as

[72] UN General Assembly, 'Protection of Human Rights and Fundamental Freedoms While Countering Terrorism' (2008) UN Doc A/63/223 paras 37 to 41; UN Working Group 'Protecting human rights while countering terrorism', 'Basic Human Rights Reference Guide: Right to a Fair Trial and Due Process in the Context of Countering Terrorism' (2014) paras 63 to 73.

[73] *Coffin v United States* US 156 U.S. 432 (4 March 1895).

[74] Stuckenberg (n 2) 308–309.

well as its precise meaning and content.[75] Some jurisdictions limit the scope of the presumption of innocence to the trial stage. For example, the US Supreme Court has rejected the application of the principle in the pre-trial context,[76] while the European Court of Human Rights (ECtHR) has supported a broader approach.[77] The Human Rights Committee has also embraced such a broader approach, saying that 'the presumption of innocence implies a right to be treated in accordance with this principle'.[78] In international discourses, it is especially this broader approach towards presumption of innocence that remains controversially discussed, while its narrow evidential conception is relatively uncontested.[79]

A reason for these controversies is the notion of 'presumption' in presumption of innocence in Article 14(2) ICCPR. The usage of 'presumption' may appear contradictory, as a person has the right to be presumed innocent while being a crime suspect. However, the provision refers to a scenario in which a person is suspected of having committed an offence without saying that he or she is actually guilty. This becomes even clearer when one considers the interplay between the notions of 'suspicion' (paragraph 2 speaks of 'charges') and 'presumption'. Even if an accused person should be treated as if he or she were innocent, the proceedings continue on the basis of the possibility or hypothesis that he or she may be guilty.[80] This may require some explanation.

There are different legal presumptions. They appear in the form of 'rebuttal' or 'irrebuttable' presumptions; the latter essentially operates as a rule. There are 'derivate' presumptions, meaning where proof of a certain fact compels the court to draw a particular conclusion, and 'foundational' presumptions, meaning where a court accepts a proposition without requiring proof for it. The presumption of innocence is a foundational and rebuttable presumption.[81] Even if it were possible to construe the presumption of innocence as a presumption of 'real' innocence, such a presumption would have a place only in the trial itself, for example, by treating insufficient proof of guilt as a presumption of 'real' innocence. This is because a presumption of real innocence would be irrebuttable and exclude the possibility of initiating criminal proceedings against a person based on his or her suspected guilt a priori.[82] The presumption of innocence, on the other hand, is neither factually nor empirically based. Indeed, reality would tell us that most persons accused

[75] ibid 302–303; Ashworth (n 6) 243; PJ Schwikkard, 'The Presumption of Innocence: What Is It?' (1998) 11 *South African Journal of Criminal Justice* 396, 396.

[76] Richard L Lippke, *Taming the Presumption of Innocence* (Oxford, Oxford University Press, 2016) 16–17.

[77] Ashworth (n 6) 243. Stuckenberg (n 2) 302.

[78] GC No. 13 para 7.

[79] See, eg, Schwikkard (n 75) 406; Ashworth (n 6) 252.

[80] Trechsel (n 23) 154–147; Carl-Friedrich Stuckenberg, *Untersuchungen Zur Unschuldsvermutung* (Berlin, De Gruyter, 1998) 438–447.

[81] Pamela R Ferguson, 'The Presumption of Innocence and Its Role in the Criminal Process' (2016) 27 *Criminal Law Forum* 131, 135–137.

[82] Stuckenberg (n 2) 307–308.

of a criminal offence are 'factually' guilty.[83] The presumption of innocence is thus a foundational but rebuttable presumption – foundational in the sense that a court must initially accept a certain proposition (proposition X) without requiring proof for that proposition.[84] Stuckenberg has called this an 'unconditional' presumption or assumption.[85]

The presumption of innocence itself formulates the condition for its rebuttal: 'until proved guilty according to law'.[86] A presumption of 'formal' innocence means that a person should be treated as someone whose guilt has not (yet) been established in accordance with the prescribed procedure. It thus determines the legal status of a person who has not (yet) been convicted, which entails further normative considerations that often include broader human rights considerations.[87] Yet, it only follows immediately from the presumption of innocence that deprivation of the accused's personal liberty in criminal proceedings cannot be based on that person's guilt as long as guilt has not (yet) been proven.[88] Therefore, the presumption of innocence is an assumption or a legal fiction rather than a legal presumption.[89] However, the presumption of innocence itself does not even spell out the standard of proof required to rebut it, ie, for proving guilt and for conviction, nor does it clarify the distribution of the burden of proof.[90]

In light of all these ambiguities, legal scholars have described the presumption of innocence as resembling

> [...] a wonderful carved and polished gem which reflects the light in various sparkling tones – but at closer inspection it is nothing but a piece of glass.[91]

In my view, the presumption of innocence is not of such an illusionary nature. However, the function, rationale and raison d'être of presumption of innocence can be fully grasped only by recognising all three dimensions of it. I argue that the presumption of innocence has three dimensions, namely, that of a right, a principle, and a rule. The right to presumption of innocence – the right dimension – is codified in international law, but neither the Universal Declaration nor the Covenant explains whether it functions as a principle or a rule. I will show that it operates as a legal moral principle underlying the entire criminal process, including pre-trial

[83] Ferguson (n 81) 135–137. Packer (1964) refers to 'factual' and 'legal' innocence or guilt, while Stuckenberg calls uses 'real' and 'material' innocence or guilt, see ibid 303–304; Herbert L Packer, 'Two Models of the Criminal Process' (1964) 113 *University of Pennsylvania Law Review* 1, 13–22.

[84] Ferguson (n 81) 135–137.

[85] Stuckenberg (n 2) 305–307.

[86] ibid; Trechsel (n 23) 154–157.

[87] Stuckenberg believes that it would be possible to create a 'super-presumption of innocence' domestically by filling it with a broad array of substantive and procedural guarantees for its rebuttal, whose violation would also mean a violation of the presumption of innocence, see Stuckenberg (n 2) 308–309.

[88] ibid.

[89] ibid 305–307; Stuckenberg (n 80) 438–494.

[90] Stuckenberg (n 2) 305–307.

[91] Thomas Weigend, 'Assuming the Defendant Is Not Guilty: The Presumption of Innocence in the German System of Criminal Justice' (2014) 8 *Criminal Law and Philosophy* 285, 285–286.

proceedings and moreover, connects to rules, in particular evidence rules, illuminating its dimension as a rule. Viewed from these three dimensions, a concrete set of requirements flows from the presumption of innocence.

Before we begin, it is important to bear in mind three fundamental caveats. First, neither Article 14 ICCPR itself nor any other provision prescribes a specific criminal trial model, meaning an inquisitorial or adversarial criminal trial model or hybrid model. It should be observed that the creation of the right to a fair trial under international law, which was greatly influenced by the Anglo-Saxon common law tradition of 'due process of law', has brought new dynamics into the existing models and increasingly merged the traditional inquisitorial model with adversarial features to the extent that the traditional two trial models have evolved into 'mixed' or 'hybrid legal systems'.[92]

Second, as concerns the scope of application of Article 14 ICCPR, the first half sentence of paragraph 1 states, 'Everyone charged with a criminal offence [...]', and thereby narrows the scope of this norm to criminal trials, even if it does not provide an authoritative definition of 'criminal offence' but to a certain degree allows for autonomous interpretation by states' parties. This is important insofar as those two aspects determine the scope of application of the presumption of innocence and lay the ground rules for the framework of a criminal trial.

Third, regarding the method of implementation of the presumption of innocence in Article 14(2) ICCPR, states are not required to codify the right to presumption of innocence (ie, the label itself) into domestic legislation in expressive terms, because it can nonetheless be realised in practice.[93] A more complex question concerns the permitted degree of flexible implementation, which will be addressed in the following sections.

## A. The (Subjective) Right Dimension

Both the Universal Declaration and the Covenant have codified the presumption of innocence as a *right* on its own.[94] This dimension of a right has different legal implications than the dimensions of rule and principle. According to the right to presumption of innocence, every person charged with a criminal offence enjoys the right to be presumed innocent until proven guilty according to law. It can thus be invoked by persons who have been accused of a criminal offence. The right to presumption of innocence hence can be interpreted as a procedural right that entitles the accused to various safeguards, ensuring that he or she is treated in accordance with their status as an innocent individual and that they receive a fair trial. Furthermore, the right to presumption of innocence can be

[92] Thomas Weigend, 'Should We Search for the Truth, and Who Should Do It?' (2011) 36 *North Carolina Journal of International Law and Commercial Regulation* 388, 401–406; Nowak (n 27) 305–307.

[93] Stuckenberg (n 2) 302.

[94] ECHR, art 6(2); ICCPR, art 14 (2).

invoked to prevent unjustified interferences with his basic liberties and welfare, more widely,[95] even though it is debatable whether the additional guarantee of a right is somewhat redundant. For example, Article 6(2) ECHR does not provide such an additional guarantee, at least not explicitly, even though the jurisdiction has recognised the 'right' to presumption of innocence.[96]

Notwithstanding this unambiguous formulation of a right to presumption of innocence, there remain some uncertainties as regards its implications. In my view, the right to presumption of innocence is of particular importance where other fair trial safeguards are lacking, as it seems to confer obligations on the state. It empowers the individual to invoke this right vis-à-vis the state and hold it accountable in the event of absence or violation of other centrally important fair trial guarantees. In this sense, the focus is on protecting the integrity and dignity, as well as the status, of an accused as an innocent. In such a constellation, the right to presumption of innocence can be invoked to claim some minimum protection.

The dimension of the right to the presumption of innocence raises the question of whether it can be waived, especially in the event of a confession of guilt. In the case of *Lutz v Germany*, the European Commission of Human Rights addressed precisely this question. In this context, Mr Trechsel has held that:

> Art 6 (2) of the Convention protecting the right of an accused to be presumed innocent is a guarantee designed to protect the accused's personal interest. I can see no reason why this interest should not be at the free disposal of the accused in the sense that he can waive the right to be presumed by pleading guilty.[97]

Although such a waiver would affect the presumption of innocence, unfortunately he did not explain in what sense it would do so.[98] If the accused voluntarily decides not to remain silent and incriminate themselves by making an admission of guilt, they arguably waive the right to the presumption of innocence. However, in my view, such a waiver would not affect the other two dimensions. Even if making an admission of guilt, guilt must nevertheless be established in accordance with the prescribed procedure, and the accused still has the right to be treated in accordance with the principle of presumption of innocence.[99] In other words, the other two dimensions – rule and principle – remain intact.

## B. The Rule Dimension

The presumption of innocence operates as a principle, but it connects to rules of the criminal process. Especially in the trial context, the presumption of innocence

[95] Lippke (n 76) 33–35.
[96] Trechsel (n 23) 153.
[97] 'Lutz v. Germany, Report of the Commission, Application No 9912/82 (Report of the European Commission of Human Rights, 18 October 1985)' 15.
[98] ibid 16.
[99] Lippke (n 76) 55.

exposes its evidential dimension (ie, the trial-centred evidential dimension) and is applied as a rule.[100] In a Dworkinian sense, a rule is applicable in an 'all-or-nothing fashion' (if A, then B), meaning it is either met or not. If it is met, then the rule is valid, and the legal consequences attached to it must be accepted. Rules cannot be balanced against each other; in case of conflict, only one can be valid. Since such conflicts will be anticipated, a legal system installs mechanisms to overcome them. Yet, the application of a rule may depend on principles lying beyond that rule, and, indeed, sometimes what is labelled a rule may rather function as a principle in practice.[101] The trial-centred aspect of the presumption of innocence is relatively uncontested and widely recognised by different systems,[102] even if controversies may arise in this context as well.[103] According to the narrow conception of the presumption of innocence, the burden of proof is principally on the prosecution, and proof must be 'beyond reasonable doubt', and the accused has the benefit of doubt, which refers to the maxim of *in dubio pro reo* ('[when] in doubt, for the accused').[104]

To realise the presumption of innocence in Article 14(2) ICCPR, state parties must apply the requirements of beyond reasonable doubt and *in dubio pro reo* and establish exclusionary rules in domestic legislation. Yet, the method of proof, the standard of proof that is required for criminal conviction, is not regulated by international law but remains a matter of domestic legislation, even if it must meet certain conditions, as confirmed by the Human Rights Committee

> [...] in general, the facts and evidence submitted on a case are for the domestic courts to evaluate unless it can be shown that their evaluation has been manifestly partial, arbitrary or tantamount to a denial of justice.[105]

Therefore, the presumption of innocence itself does not regulate the standard of proof needed for conviction, nor does it explain when *in dubio pro reo* is to be applied, but it is a reminder that a fair criminal trial should adhere to these evidential rules. The maxim of *in dubio pro reo* manifests the moral authority of the presumption of innocence, the idea that no innocent person should be convicted of a crime they have not committed. The rationale of the evidential rule is hence to protect the innocent individuals from conviction.[106] The standard of proof needed for conviction is met or it is not; if not, then the defendant must be acquitted. This is a 'dogmatic rule' in the sense that the law requires the addressee to comply with

[100] GC No. 32 para 30.
[101] Ronald M Dworkin, 'The Model of Rules' (1967) 35 *The University of Chicago Law Review* 14, 27.
[102] Richard L Lippke, 'The Presumption of Innocence in the Trial Setting' (2015) 28 *Ratio Juris* 159, 159.
[103] Lippke (n 76) 17; Trechsel (n 23) 167–171.
[104] GC No. 32 para 30.
[105] *Fernández v Spain*, Human Rights Committee, Communication No 1007/2001, CCPR/C/78/D/1007/2001 (7 August 2003) para 6.5.
[106] John D Jackson and Sarah J Summers, *The Internationalisation of Criminal Evidence* (Cambridge, Cambridge University Press, 2012) 205.

that rule.[107] This narrow understanding thus treats the presumption of innocence synonymously with a rule of evidence.[108]

Since the burden of proof is on the prosecution and proof must be beyond reasonable doubt, Article 14(3) ICCPR guarantees the privilege against self-incrimination, meaning the right of the accused not to be compelled to make detrimental statements or to confess guilt in the determination of any criminal charge against them. In this context, self-incrimination can be understood to refer to information provided by the accused that could increase the probability of prosecution of that person.[109]

Regarding the relationship of this guarantee with the right to silence, it is important to stress that the two are distinct and yet interrelated and partly overlapping guarantees. The right to silence is narrower, as it only applies to oral communications, while the privilege against self-incrimination also protects against pressure to hand over documents. The right to silence is a direct effect and logical consequence of the privilege against self-incrimination; or it may be said that it encompasses silence, otherwise the guarantee would indeed make little sense. Yet, the scope of the right to silence is broader than that of the privilege, because it does not only protect the accused from making any possible incriminating (or unfavourable) statements but from making any statements at all. Trechsel believes that formulations such as the one in the Covenant, which appears to be limited to detrimental statements, should be interpreted by going beyond the rigid adherence to the text. However, the privilege against self-incrimination is arguably one of the most complex guarantees among all fair trial guarantees; many issues have arisen in specific cases, especially as regards the relativity or absoluteness of the guarantee.[110]

The privilege against self-incrimination in Article 14(3)(g) ICCPR does not spell out whether exceptions are permissible, nor does any other provision in the Covenant. Interestingly, the European Human Rights Convention does not contain such a provision at all, but the ECtHR has recognised the privilege against self-incrimination and the right to silence as core guarantees of the right to a fair trial, as protected under Article 6 ECHR, and a violation may render the proceedings unfair.[111] Clearly, a legally guaranteed right to silence should be part of any *decent* criminal justice system,[112] but a number of questions have arisen as regards the absoluteness of the guarantee and the consequences of silence.

[107] Magnus Ulväng, 'Presumption of Innocence Versus a Principle of Fairness, A Response to Duff' (2013) 42 *Netherlands Journal of Legal Philosophy* 205, 208–209.

[108] Andrew Stumer, *The Presumption of Innocence: Evidential and Human Rights Perspectives* (Oxford, Hart Publishing, 2010) 52.

[109] Andrew LT Choo, *The Privilege Against Self-Incrimination and Criminal Justice* (Oxford, Hart Publishing, 2013) 1.

[110] Trechsel (n 23) 342–350.

[111] Choo (n 109) 20; Directive (EU) 2016/343 of the European Parliament and of the Council of 9 March 2016 on the strengthening of certain aspects of the presumption of innocence para 45.

[112] Thomas Weigend, 'The Suspect as a Source of Information' in Michael Lindemann and Andreas Ransiek (eds), *Interrogation, Confession, and Truth* (Baden-Baden, Nomos, 2020) 23.

Regarding the question of the absoluteness of the privilege against self-incrimination, the ECtHR did not give a clear answer in *Saunders*, even though it did affirm the absoluteness of the right not to incriminate oneself in the sense that it must be applied equally to all accused persons, regardless of the category or nature of the accusations – regardless of whether a person is accused of fraud or of murder; nor may public interest be used as an excuse to compromise the guarantee. It moreover found the privilege to be absolute in the sense that information obtained under compulsion in a non-judicial investigation cannot be used to incriminate the accused during the trial proceedings.[113]

In *Murray*, however, the ECtHR had to first deal with the question as to whether the guarantee is relative in the sense that inferences may be drawn from silence under certain circumstances, as permitted by the UK anti-terrorism legislation, and whether such adverse inferences from the suspect's silence were compatible with Article 6. In other words, whether silence can be used against the accused or whether it is 'improper compulsion' if the accused is informed in advance that, under certain conditions, silence will be used against them and thus have adverse conclusions. In this case, Mr Murray was coming down the stairs of a house when the police entered to free a hostage who had been kidnapped by the IRA and was being held in the house in question. The ECtHR held that this may be the case 'in situations which clearly call for an explanation from him' when assessing the persuasiveness of the evidence presented by the prosecution,[114] provided the suspect was informed about the consequences of remaining silent and understood the warning, had access to legal advice, and the court drew fair and reasonable inferences. Inferences from silence are thus only permissible where sufficient evidence already and independently exists to support a case. The purpose is that inferences should not help the prosecution in an otherwise weak case.[115] Yet, issues have arisen as regards the evidential purposes for which inferences are drawn from silence that can be used (except for weakening the defence's case) or the varying threshold requirements for the drawing of inferences; this is partly due to the absence of a precise scope of the procedural safeguards that need to be met.[116] The making of the EU Directive on the Presumption of Innocence revealed the debates surrounding adverse inferences from silence. Although the ECtHR reaffirmed the somewhat absoluteness of the guarantee, it said that while the exercise of silence cannot be used against a suspect or accused person or in itself be considered incriminating evidence, it recognised that the assessment of evidence by courts or

[113] *Saunders v UK* App No 19187/91 (ECtHR, 17 December 1996) paras 70 and 71.
[114] Trechsel (n 23) 344–345.
[115] Yvonne Daly and others, 'Human Rights Protections in Drawing Inferences from Criminal Suspects' Silence' (2021) 21 *Human Rights Law Review* 696, 699.
[116] Daly and others (n 115) 708–709.

judges remains a matter of national law as long as the rights of the defence are protected.[117]

Trechsel has therefore suggested that the right to silence is 'relative' in the sense that it is impossible to set sharp boundaries and say how much pressure is acceptable in absolute terms. Considering the inherently coercive nature of the criminal process, it is indeed difficult to claim that the accused is not put under any pressure at all. There is no denying that silence (as opposed to 'cooperative behaviour') may have an impact on the procedure and outcome of a case in terms of costs and sentencing in the event of conviction.[118] It should be observed that the rationale of the privilege against self-incrimination, inter alia, lies in the prevention of miscarriages of justice and in the realisation of the right to a fair trial. Therefore, the guarantee is deeply interwoven with the presumption of innocence.[119]

However, the question is under what circumstances the prohibition against self-incrimination will be violated. Both the Human Rights Committee and the ECtHR have undertaken a balancing act when assessing a possible violation of the privilege against self-incrimination in a specific case. As already discussed, the right to remain silent is a direct effect of the privilege and the will of the accused to choose silence and thus must be respected. The privilege essentially aims to ensure the integrity and dignity of an accused person, and there is thus an evident link between the privilege and the absolute prohibition against torture. There is no method that could be employed to compel the accused to make a statement without thereby violating some of the most fundamental human rights standards.[120] The Human Rights Committee has illustrated this link by emphasising 'the absence of any direct or indirect physical or undue psychological pressure from the investigation authorities on the accused'.[121]

To amount to a violation of the privilege, there must be some threat involved, while, for example, merely urging an accused person to speak the truth does not violate the right to silence. The ECtHR has clarified that a distinction must be drawn between compelling the accused 'to provide the evidence of offences he had allegedly committed'[122] and the obtainment of evidential materials by coercive investigation powers (also presumably against the will of the accused) but which exist 'independent of the will of the suspect', eg, materials obtained through

[117] ibid 697; Directive (EU) 2016/343 of the European Parliament and of the Council of 9 March 2016 on the strengthening of certain aspects of the presumption of innocence (n 111) art 7(5).
[118] Trechsel (n 23) 344–346; Directive (EU) 2016/343 of the European Parliament and of the Council of 9 March 2016 on the strengthening of certain aspects of the presumption of innocence (n 111) art 7.
[119] Trechsel (n 23) 166; *Saunders v UK* (n 113) para 68.
[120] Trechsel (n 23) 348–350.
[121] GC No. 32 para 41.
[122] *Funke v France* App No 10828/84 (ECtHR, 25 February 1993) para 44.

a warrant. In the latter case, the privilege cannot be applied.[123] It may be worth noting that, in the *Allan* case, in which the applicant had been suspected of murder committed in the course of a robbery, the ECtHR found that the use of means such as deceit or entrapment may also violate the privilege. Since the suspect chose to remain silent, the police used technical devices in the detention centre where he was held and an informant to obtain incriminating evidence. Such means would undermine a person's freedom of choosing silence during questioning if they were tricked by authorities into confessing or making otherwise incriminating statements, which they would not have been able to obtain otherwise.[124]

In the case of *Jalloh*, which concerned a suspected drug dealer, the ECtHR succinctly outlined four factors to be considered, but it underlined that a violation of the privilege would not immediately lead to a violation of the right to a fair trial under Article 6(1). As regards the first factor of 'the nature and degree of compulsion' used to obtain the evidence, it found that 'forcing the applicant to regurgitate the drugs significantly interfered with his physical and mental integrity', amounting to a violation of the prohibition against torture in Article 3. The Court held that the second factor of 'the weight of the public interest in using the evidence to secure the applicant's conviction' (he was selling drugs on a relatively small scale for which he was given a six-month suspended prison sentence and probation) could not justify 'such a grave interference with this physical and mental integrity'. As regards the third factor of 'the existence of relevant safeguards in the procedure', it found that the applicant was not able to make use of the safeguards generally provided for in domestic legislation because authorities had subjected him to the procedure without properly examining 'his physical aptitude to withstand it', despite the obvious language barriers. The fourth factor, which concerns 'the use to which the evidence obtained was put', the Court recognised the decisiveness of the evidence to secure a conviction for drug trafficking. In the light of all factors, a violation of the right against self-incrimination was considered to have rendered his trial unfair, leading to a violation of Article 6(1).[125] As Choo has explained, the ECtHR thus first assesses whether the privilege is 'engaged' and will then, in a further step, undertake a balancing act and examine whether the 'essence' of the privilege has been destroyed, as a result violating Article 6(1).[126]

Therefore, the protection of the integrity of an accused person, human dignity, is the threshold when considering a possible violation. There is a legal consequence attached to a violation of the privilege against self-incrimination and the right to silence. Domestic law must ensure that illegally obtained statements or confessions are excluded from the evidence, except if such material is used as evidence for torture or other ill-treatment, and the burden to prove that statements made by

[123] Trechsel (n 23) 353–354; *Saunders v UK* (n 113) para 69.

[124] *Allan v UK* App No 48539/99 (ECtHR, 5 February 2003) para 50; Trechsel (n 24) 351.

[125] Choo (n 114) 62–65; *Jalloh v Germany* App No 54810/00 (ECtHR, 11 July 2006) paras 97, 101 and 122.

[126] Choo (n 109) 64–65.

the accused have been given voluntarily is on the state.[127] However, the extent to which evidence must be excluded is a matter of domestic law. A contentious issue that could arise in this contest is how torture should be defined and what behaviour should fall under the definition of torture under domestic law.

Both protection against self-incrimination and silence are normative considerations logically flowing from the burden of proof in accordance with the presumption of innocence. The presumption of innocence itself does not explain this connection. The nexus between the presumption of innocence and the privilege against self-incrimination is the common root of human dignity; both are based on various epistemic and non-epistemic considerations, including the non-epistemic consideration of the principle of dignity.[128] Even if the privilege against self-incrimination and the right to silence could be considered in isolation from the presumption of innocence, their denial would render the presumption of innocence meaningless. This is, therefore, the rule dimension of presumption of innocence.

## C. The Principle Dimension

This section argues that the presumption of innocence is a moral legal principle manifesting the rule of law. Accepting the presumption of innocence as a principle means that it applies in all phases of criminal proceedings, including pre-trial proceedings. However, the question is why such a broad approach remains contested. We may first consider the precise meaning and function of a principle. In a Dworkinian sense, a principle is

> a standard that is to be observed, because it is a requirement of justice or fairness or some other dimension of morality.[129]

A principle argues or points in one direction, but it does not command a decision. Principles exist, regardless of whether they can be applied in a particular case or not. In contrast to rules, principles cannot determine consequences and exceptions; they compete with each other and must always be weighed and balanced against conflicting considerations.[130] Viewed in this way, the presumption of innocence operates as a principle of fairness and sets limits to the state's power.[131] The principle dimension of presumption of innocence is supported by the ethical and political underpinnings of the concept of human rights and a liberal rule of law, as outlined in the previous sections. The historical context supports a broader reading of the presumption of innocence. Even if Enlightenment thinkers like Hobbes,

[127] CAT, art 15; GC No. 32 para 41.
[128] Choo (n 109) 6–8.
[129] Dworkin (n 101) 23.
[130] Ibid 22–29.
[131] Ashworth (n 6) 243–245.

Montesquieu, Beccaria or Voltaire, who criticised the practices of the inquisitorial procedure, did not explicitly mention the presumption of innocence, they believed that the power of the state must be limited and that law should guarantee individual liberty. Beccaria emphasised the different legal status of an accused person and a convicted criminal and rejected the use of judicial torture, requiring the legitimate imposition of punishment. His formulation ('No man may be called guilty before the judge has reached his verdict') is widely understood as the establishment of the presumption of innocence.[132] The presumption of innocence was later incorporated into the *Déclaration des Droits de l'Homme et du Citoyen* of 1789 in the context of protection of personal liberty.[133] And, as already discussed, the Universal Declaration as well as the European Human Rights Convention link it to the right to a fair trial more widely.[134] The point is, it is reasonable to view the presumption of innocence as a principle of fairness.

However, scholars have voiced concerns as to such a broad reading of the guarantee. Schwikkard has held that the presumption of innocence and the concept of legal guilt should not be confused, as it would cause too many difficulties in reality. The 'rule' of presumption of innocence (ie, the requirement of proof beyond reasonable doubt) could not be applied to proceedings other than such proceedings being concerned with the determination of guilt – the trial itself – because investigation authorities were not required to meet this high standard of proof.[135] Schwikkard thus views the presumption of innocence in its narrowest sense as a common law rule of evidence. Conversely, Ho has pointed out that the presumption of innocence – as a human right – cannot be restricted to a common law rule of evidence that is not necessarily applied in other legal systems. Indeed, as a human right, the presumption of innocence must mean more than this.[136] In fact, the Human Rights Committee has also criticised such a restrictive interpretation of the presumption of innocence, as not only the courts were bound by it but also other authorities.[137] Limiting the presumption of innocence to the trial itself would, in fact, diminish its authority in the other phases of criminal proceedings.

Lippke has also been sceptical of a pre-trial presumption of innocence but for different reasons. He believes that such an approach would be too contested to establish a universal theory of the presumption of innocence. Presumably bearing

[132] Stuckenberg (n 80) 25–30; Cesare Beccaria, *On Crimes and Punishments and Other Writings*, 4th edn (Cambridge, Cambridge University Press, 2003) 39.

[133] *Déclaration des Droits de l'Homme et du Citoyen* (Paris, 26 August 1789), art 9.

[134] UDHR, art 11(1); ECHR, art 6 (2).

[135] Schwikkard (n 75) 396–404.

[136] Hock Lai Ho, 'The Presumption of Innocence as a Human Right' in Paul Roberts and Jill Hunter (eds), *Criminal Evidence and Human Rights, Reimagining Common Law Procedural Traditions* (Oxford, Hart Publishing, 2012) 261–262.

[137] Human Rights Committee, 'Summary Record of the 205th Meeting, UN Doc. CCPR/C/SR.205 (27 March 1980)' para 30.

in mind systemic differences, he believes that a universal concept of presumption of innocence could be established only with respect to its role in the trial context, while questioning the usefulness of a pre-trial presumption of innocence. He argues that other 'moral constructs' would be more sensible to protect the accused in the pre-trial proceedings.[138] The presumption of innocence would not be related to pre-trial detention or the privilege against self-incrimination. Limits to the use of pre-trial detention would not be grounded in any presumptions but rather in the fact that the guilt of such persons has not (yet) been established. Lippke rejects the idea of a pre-trial presumption of innocence as prescribing a certain behaviour that must be observed by authorities vis-à-vis the accused. Here, the use of 'probative innocence' (ie, legal innocence) would not be sensible, because police and prosecutors would investigate alleged crimes based on the conviction that they can prove the accused's guilt.[139]

On the other hand, a presumption of factual ('material') innocence would be problematic, since police and prosecutors do not operate on the assumption of such sort of innocence (eg, arrest, detention, search, etc.). After all, a 'non-presumption of probative guilt' would be more appropriate, meaning neither proven guilty nor presumed innocent, because it would remind the state authorities of the possibility of error or negligence on their part. Lippke thus argues that, if a fair trial is fully guaranteed, there is no need for a pre-trial presumption of innocence or non-presumption of guilt.[140] A reason for his scepticism towards a too broad presumption of innocence appears to lie in the risk of putting too many safeguards under the label of presumption of innocence. This brings us back to the earlier mentioned criticism of a 'super-presumption of innocence' that may create problems of redundancy.

However, the question is what happens if such a general fair trial commitment is lacking. Lippke seems to take the presumption of innocence in the pre-trial context too literally, asking how such a presumption of what sort of innocence could be rebutted. In my view, the only way in which the presumption of innocence in its narrowest sense could be rebutted in the pre-trial phase would be by an admission of guilt. Yet, as discussed, waiving the right to presumption of innocence does not affect its procedural function; the other two dimensions of rule and principle remain intact. The point is the principle of presumption of innocence cannot be rebutted because it exists irrespective of the specific circumstances of a case and must be applied as the underlying principle in the operation of criminal proceedings. Rather, it sets a behavioural standard to be observed by state authorities.

[138] Lippke (n 76) 130; Lippke (n 102) 159.

[139] As we will see in the chapters to follow, this has been one of the main arguments for rejecting the principle of presumption of innocence in the Chinese context.

[140] Lippke (n 76) 131–152.

Going back to the ECtHR and the Human Rights Committee, both of which do support a broader approach to the presumption of innocence. According to the authoritative interpretation of Article 14(2) ICCPR, the presumption of innocence

> is fundamental to the protection to human rights, imposes on the prosecution the burden of proving the charge, guarantees that no guilt can be presumed until the charge has been proved beyond reasonable doubt, ensures that the accused has the benefit of doubt, and requires that persons accused of a criminal act must be treated in accordance with this principle.[141]

This demonstrates that the broader concept aims to suppress any prejudice on the part of the state authorities, and it goes beyond the narrow reading of Article 14(2), which would – strictly speaking – only be applicable from the moment the accused is criminally 'charged'.[142] Trechsel, who is also supportive of a pre-trial presumption of innocence, has distinguished between its 'outcome-related aspect' and 'reputation-related aspect'. While the former relates to a fair outcome of the process and concerns procedural aspects such as the burden of proof, the latter particularly addresses reputational concerns of an accused person, aiming to protect the image of innocence. Trechsel argues that the case law of the ECtHR would emphasise the understanding of the presumption of innocence as a principle of the rule of law.[143] What Trechsel characterises as the 'reputation-related aspect' of the presumption of innocence relates to the dimension of principle, which binds all state authorities.

In a similar vein, Weigend suggests that the presumption of innocence is a 'procedural rule', regulating the behaviour of officials involved in the criminal process vis-à-vis the accused throughout the entire criminal process.[144] Weigend shows that the presumption of innocence functions as an important 'counterweight' because it can restrain the power of the state vis-à-vis the accused. Any interference with the rights of the accused cannot be grounded on the assumption of guilt. Therefore, for instance, the use of remand custody is justifiable *only* based on grounds other than the suspect or defendant's anticipated conviction.[145] It is true that not every system follows such a broad approach. The question therefore arises as to how domestic systems can deviate from such an approach without undermining the essence of the presumption of innocence; here, international law sets the benchmark.

Especially personal liberty can serve as an important indicator for the operation of the principle of presumption of innocence. Article 9(1) ICCPR protects the right

[141] GC No. 32 para 30.

[142] The notions 'criminal charge' and 'charged' in art 9(2) ICCPR must be autonomously defined, see Trechsel (n 23) 155.

[143] ibid 154–164.

[144] Weigend (n 91) 289.

[145] Thomas Weigend, 'There Is Only One Presumption of Innocence' (2013) 42 *Netherlands Journal of Legal Philosophy* 193, 196.

to both security and liberty of person[146] and prohibits arbitrary and unlawful arrest and detention, which is a right recognised in all major international and regional human rights treaties.[147] Article 9 ICCPR distinguishes the arbitrary deprivation of liberty from its unlawful deprivation. Unlawful deprivation of liberty refers to 'deprivation of liberty that is not imposed on such grounds and in accordance with such procedure as are established by law'.[148] While 'arbitrariness' is associated with 'inappropriateness, injustice, lack of predictability and due process of law, as well as elements of reasonableness, necessity and proportionality'.[149] For example, the detention of a person may be deemed arbitrary if it 'would lead to the violation of another human right or is the result of a violation of another human right'.[150]

According to the broader presumption of innocence, pre-trial detention is only justified if there is at least 'reasonable suspicion' that the accused person has committed a criminal offence.[151] The use of any coercive measures must conform to the assumption of the innocence of the criminal suspect or defendant, and the length of pre-trial detention should generally not be used as an indicator of guilt and its degree.[152] For this reason, the use of pre-trial detention as punishment, or unlawful and arbitrary detention, would also violate the presumption of innocence under Article 14(2) ICCPR. Therefore, presumed guilt cannot be the basis for pre-trial detention, even if the Covenant provides no precise legally binding definition of the scope of 'lawful detention'[153] and specific thresholds for deprivation of personal liberty are thus lacking.[154] Again, it is mostly the task of national law to determine the grounds of legitimate detention.[155]

Article 9(4) ICCPR, known as the habeas corpus guarantee or the writ of habeas corpus, moreover entitles anyone to a review by a court of the lawfulness of their detention.[156] Whether that person is released – for example, by considering less intensive coercive measures – depends on the balancing of principles such as

[146] Liberty and security of person in accordance with art 9 ICCPR has a narrow scope, and concerns freedom from confinement of the body – not a general freedom of action, see General comment No. 35, Article 9 (Liberty and security of person) (GC No. 35) 2014 (UN Doc CCPR/C/GC/35) para 3.

[147] See also art 6 of the African Charter on Human and Peoples' Rights; art 7(1) of the American Convention on Rights; art 5(1) ECHR.

[148] GC No. 35 para 11.

[149] ibid para 12.

[150] Sangeeta Shah, 'Detention and Trial' in Daniel Moeckli and others (eds), *International Human Rights Law*, 3rd edn (Oxford, Oxford University Press, 2017) 257.

[151] Trechsel (n 23) 323–328.

[152] GC No. 32 para 30.

[153] Rhona KM Smith, *International Human Rights Law*, 8th edn (Oxford, Oxford University Press, 2018) 263.

[154] Richard Vogler and Shahrzad Foulavand, 'Standards for Making Factual Determination in Arrest and Pre-Trial Detention' in Jacqueline E Ross and Stephen C Thaman (eds), *Comparative Criminal Procedure* (Cheltenham, Edward Elgar, 2018) 193.

[155] 'Professional Training Series No. 9/Add. 1, Human Rights in the Administration of Justice: A Manual on Human Rights for Judges, Prosecutors and Lawyers' (Office of the High Commissioner for Human Rights 2003) 263 digitallibrary.un.org/record/619913 accessed 5 June 2019.

[156] Brian R Farrell, *Habeas Corpus in International Law* (Cambridge, Cambridge University Press, 2016) 3–5.

dignity, the presumption of innocence against the state's obligation to protect society, and measures such as effective crime prevention. It is assumed that individuals continue to enjoy their human rights despite their imprisonment.[157]

Detainees are extremely vulnerable to abuse, as they are completely at the mercy of the state authorities in their search for information or a confession.[158] The use of pre-trial detention may lead to a violation of other human rights, notably Article 10 (human dignity), Article 7 (torture), or Article 14 (fair trial) of the ICCPR. Article 10(1) has implications for both the treatment of the individual as well as the conditions of detention, and it protects against attacks on dignity that do not reach the severity of the suffering threshold required under Article 7.[159] Because an accused person has the right to choose silence, they cannot be arrested on the grounds of refusing cooperation. Using pre-trial detention as a means of obtaining evidence violates the right to a fair trial. Moreover, a denial of habeas corpus may pose a substantial threat to all the other rights a detained person is entitled to. An important function of habeas corpus is, therefore, to protect other substantial rights, such as the right to protection from torture and other forms of maltreatment.[160]

It may be worth noting that, where the ECtHR has found a violation of Article 5(3) (the habeas corpus guarantee), the question of whether the presumption of innocence has been violated has not been subject to any further consideration.[161] Indeed, this would be in support of the claim that there is no need for a pre-trial presumption of innocence, but as a principle, it sets out a standard to be observed in order to uphold fairness and thus the overarching principle of the rule of law. The Human Rights Committee has addressed how the interdependence of fair trial guarantees and the erosion of individual safeguards will affect the overall fairness. For example, with respect to preventive detention, it held that it would be tantamount to presumption of guilt, as it applied a prediction about the dangerousness of a person.[162] Similarly, in another case, it found that more than nine years of excessive preventive detention affect the right to presumption of innocence and seriously compromises the overall fairness of the trial.[163] Therefore, even though the system of pre-trial detention may vary among jurisdictions, systems must meet the basic requirements of Articles 9, 10, 14 ICCPR, including the presumption of innocence in paragraph 2 of Article 14. Consequently, the principle of presumption of innocence cannot be set aside when, for example, taking coercive measures against the accused person during criminal proceedings. As a principle, it can be

[157] Shah (n 151) 258.

[158] Piet Hein van Kempen, *Pre-Trial Detention: Human Rights, Criminal Procedure Law and Penitentiary Law Comparative Law* (Cambridge, Intersentia, 2012) 3–4.

[159] Shah (n 151) 258–259.

[160] Farrell (n 157) 181–182.

[161] Trechsel (n 23) 180.

[162] *Rameka et al v New Zealand*, Human Rights Committee, Communication No 1090/2002, CCPR/C/79/D/1090/2002 (15 December 2003) para 19.

[163] GC NO. 32 para 30; *Cagas et al v The Philippines*, Human Rights Committee, Communication No 788/1997, CCPR/C/73/D/788/1997 (23 October 2001) paras 7.3 and 7.4.

weighed against other principles when assessing interferences such as deprivation of personal liberty, especially proportionality and necessity.[164]

From this it follows that there are further arguments for a pre-trial presumption of innocence. Since presumption of innocence aims to counterbalance the vulnerability of the accused, in a way, the evidential dimension expands to the early phases of proceedings in the sense that the state's duty of proving the guilt of the accused starts with the initiation of the criminal procedure and the gathering of evidence. Whereas the trial itself only represents the showdown between prosecution and defence and deals with the standard of proof required for reaching a guilty verdict – not with questions as to the treatment of the accused in accordance with the presumption of innocence.[165] The evidential dimension of the presumption of innocence requires the formulation of a set of evidence rules that connect to procedural safeguards, including the right to silence or the privilege against self-incrimination. Without taking principles of fairness into consideration, no decision as to whether a trial was indeed fair or not can be made. The most important factor for fairness is equality; this is not merely a question of law but first and foremost of morality.[166]

An underlying principle of the right to a fair trial, without which the presumption of innocence cannot be realised, is the principle of equality. Equality is a requirement that is guaranteed through the principle of equality of arms, as well as other principles and rules of criminal justice. The right to defence is a manifestation of the principle of equality of arms. It is not limited to the trial itself; it means that the accused should be informed 'promptly' and in detail of the 'nature and cause of the charges' against them,[167] that they must have 'adequate time and facilities' to prepare their defence and should have the right to communicate with a counsel of their own choosing.[168] To ensure the right to defence and thus the principle of equality of arms, lawyers should be able to advise and represent persons charged with a criminal offence without restrictions, influence, pressure or unlawful interference from any parties.[169]

Access to legal counsel must in particular be guaranteed if the accused person is deprived of their liberty, most notably through pre-trial detention. A serious violation of the right to prepare for defence may result, for example, from incommunicado detention and forced disappearances.[170] In the case of pre-trial detention, the ECtHR has emphasised that the principle of equality of arms requires the review of pre-trial detention in an oral hearing at which all parties are

[164] UN Standard Minimum Rules for Non-Custodial Measures (The Tokyo Rules) [UNGA Res 45/110 (14 December 1990)].
[165] Weigend (n 91) 291–292.
[166] Nowak (n 27) 321.
[167] ICCPR, art 14 (3) lit. (a).
[168] ICCPR, art 14 (3) lit. (b). 'Adequacy' must be determined in the light of the circumstances and complexity of the case', but a few days are usually considered insufficient, see Nowak (n 27) 332.
[169] GC No. 32 para 34.
[170] Nowak (n 27) 333.

present and can express their views. A prerequisite for the oral hearing to constitute adversarial proceedings is that legal counsel is called in and that the counsel can inspect the files and cross-examine witnesses.[171]

At trial, to ensure effective defence, all parties – prosecution and defence – should have the right to compel the attendance of witnesses, even though there may be limitations to this right. While the determination of the admissibility of evidence and its evaluation by the courts should be primarily governed by domestic legislation, it should be observed that Article 7 ICCPR sets certain limits to the use of statements, confessions and other evidence.[172] In the case of *Minelli*, the ECtHR recognised that a denial of the right to defence may also lead to a violation of the presumption of innocence.[173] Since such international standards of equality of arms are a fundamental principle of a decent criminal justice system, states parties have little room for manoeuvre for a flexible implementation, as otherwise the very purpose of a fair trial would be compromised.

Therefore, as a principle of fairness, the presumption of innocence remains invisible, but it justifies a standard that must be observed throughout the criminal process. In other words, the presumption of innocence as a principle of fairness need not be codified in legislation, but the law must explain how it protects fairness and how it relates to other rules and principles in criminal proceedings. From a holistic perspective, the presumption of innocence should be regarded as a normative conception containing all three dimensions.

## VI. Conclusions

The discussion in this chapter has shown that a broad approach to presumption of innocence is not only needed but also defensible. It has illuminated the bottom-up conception of the right to a fair trial under international law, being derived from the fundamental value of human dignity, and demonstrated the non-derogable nature of the presumption of innocence as a central aspect of fairness. The presumption of innocence has three different dimensions. The dimension of the right to presumption of innocence empowers the individual and imposes the duty on the state to guarantee this right. It is, moreover, a general principle of fairness that underpins the entire proceedings but is of particular importance in the pre-trial phases and possesses a moral force that cannot be replaced because it makes a claim about what ought to be decent. At the trial stage, its evidential dimension comes to the fore. The 'flexible or variable universalism' of fair trial rights supports such a broad

[171] Office of the High Commissioner for Human Rights, 'Human Rights in the Administration of Justice: A Manual on Human Rights for Judges, Prosecutors and Lawyers' (2003) Professional Training Series No 9 203.

[172] GC No. 32 paras 6, 39.

[173] *Minelli v Switzerland* App No 8660/79 (ECtHR, 25 March 1983) para 37.

approach. Although the right to a fair trial with the presumption of innocence allows for flexible implementation, there are some key requirements that maintain the *essence* of fairness, which ultimately aim to protect the integrity and dignity of the accused. Of course, this illustrates the interdependent relationship of fair trial guarantees that give substance to the presumption of innocence. Therefore, going beyond normative considerations and a narrow reading of the presumption of innocence as a rule of evidence, moral and political considerations highlight the principle of presumption of innocence as a manifestation of the rule of law.

# 3

# The Emergence of Presumption of Innocence in China

This chapter illuminates the emergence of the presumption of innocence in the 1950s in the Mao era and the second phase of discourse in the early years of the reform era. It sets out in the early years of the PRC. At the time, two views circulated, with the view of rejecting dominating the discourse. As explained in chapter one, while Mao was an anti-legalist, the Party very early on abandoned the idea that law would wither away; some regularisation was considered necessary, even if it had to be flexible enough to accommodate the needs of revolution and Party policies. Everything 'bourgeois' was officially condemned, but Mao also warned not to blindly copy the Soviet model, and the idea of a 'sinicisation', ie, 'Chinese characteristics', became the guiding mantra, also for scholars working on criminal justice. Being opposed to both the feudalist presumption of guilt and the 'bourgeois' presumption of innocence, the principle of 'taking facts as the basis, and the law as the yardstick' (*yi shishi wei genju, yi falü wei zhunsheng*, 'seeking truth from facts'), which was put forward by the Party leaders in the mid-1950s, appeared to be an appropriate choice to guide the determination of guilt and ensure accurate outcomes. When the focus shifted to economic development, there was a short period of commitment to socialist legality during which efforts were made to draft a criminal procedure law. The more liberal atmosphere facilitated the first round of academic discourse on the presumption of innocence in China in the mid-1950s. Especially this short period gives a glimpse into different ideas of criminal justice and shows that they were more diverse than one may perhaps expect.

The second phase of presumption of innocence discourses began in the late 1970s, after the Cultural Revolution (1966–76) that coincided with the end of the Mao era. The decision of the Third Plenum in 1978 under the leadership of Deng Xiaoping to foster the development of a socialist legal system had encouraged official and academic discourses on human rights and criminal justice. In 1979, China's first Criminal Procedure law (CPL 1979) was enacted. At the time, the official view was not to presume anything. Rather, one should stick to the principle of seeking truth from facts – many scholars followed this stance. Against the backdrop of this new law, certain scholars were eager to compare this law and to study whether it showed signs of presumption of innocence. To this end, they argued that it contains both 'reasonable' and 'unscientific' elements. While the ostensible differences were rooted in misconceptions, they laid a very important foundation for the path of a presumption of innocence 'with Chinese characteristics'. This chapter concludes that the CPL 1979 was far from meeting presumption of innocence standards, but the enthusiasm with which some scholars read it may be understandable in the light of the context. Indeed, because at this point a lot appeared possible for the future development of criminal justice in China, scholars arguably put a lot of hope into CPL 1979, albeit with all the shortcomings.

## I. The Mao Era: The Feudal Presumption of Guilt, the Bourgeois Presumption of Innocence and Seeking Truth from Facts

At the beginning of the twentieth century, when the Qing Dynasty (1644–1912) was already in decline, late Qing reformers ambitiously aimed to reform the law and the judicial system and, to this end, largely borrowed from continental legal systems. Under the guidance of Shen Jiaben and Wu Tingfang, a draft criminal procedure law was compiled. Even if there was yet to be a Chinese term for the notion of 'due process', the reformers addressed issues that touched upon the idea of it. However, the integration of procedural safeguards relating to legal representation was met with resistance. Officials considered such safeguards as obstruction of justice, and it was never formally enacted, even though the institution of judicial torture was rendered illegal normatively and the practice of indefinite detention before trial was aimed to be rectified through time limits for processing cases. Reforms nonetheless continued throughout the Republican era (1912–49), following the basic strategy of adopting norms and institutions based on western models while accommodating national conditions.[1] Interestingly, in her January 1901 edict, Empress Dowager Cixi had already suggested 'to blend together the best of what is Chinese and what is foreign' and consider carefully 'what should be kept and what abolished'.[2] Therefore, the mantra of not blindly copying foreign norms and institutions was already preached, and dynastic institutions and norms were not simply to be abandoned.[3] This sounds all too familiar when thinking of Mao's warning to not just blindly copy the Soviet model.

After the founding of the PRC in 1949, the Party had proclaimed to follow a Socialist path and followed the ideology of Marxism-Leninism. The communist leadership officially abandoned all laws and institutions of the Nationalists (GMD) and made efforts to build a socialist legal system based on the Soviet

[1] Xiaoqun Xu, *Heaven Has Eyes: Law and Justice in Chinese History* (Oxford, Oxford University Press, 2020) 108–115, 144.

[2] ibid 107–108.

[3] It may be worth noting that the late Qing reformers primarily attacked the two absolute duties of loyalty to the ruler and filial piety to one's parents, because they had symbolised an absolute authority that needed to be overthrown; Confucian morality as a cultural or society-regulating mechanism was less attacked, see Gungwu Wang, 'Power, Rights and Duties in Chinese History' [1980] *The Australian Journal of Chinese Affairs* 1, 5–6.

model.[4] The sanctioning apparatus of the CCP was greatly built on experiences of the communist-controlled areas before 1949. Law was now part of the 'political-legal work' and crucially linked to the mass line. At the time of consolidation, the Communist leadership style focused on mass mobilisation. Although the Party considered some regularisation indispensable, law and regulation were expected to be flexible and responsive to policy, and law enforcement was concerned with mass mobilisation.[5]

Maoism sees conflict as an inevitable part of the revolution to achieve social and political progress, and law was expected to be flexible, especially when dealing with enemies.[6] The ideology of revolution emphasises social and legal discontinuity because each revolution marks an overthrow of the old order and a new beginning. In this sense, law is understood as a transitional means only.[7] In the light of the class-based society, the friend-enemy distinction was omnipresent, expressed through Mao's distinction between antagonistic and non-antagonistic contradictions, which he had proclaimed in 1957 and which guided law enforcement. It may thus not be surprising that such few existing laws and regulations primarily centred on political offences to suppress counterrevolutionaries.[8]

The police dominated the sanctioning apparatus and administered an array of sanctions, including administrative sanctions as well as confinement in the notorious labour camps or even the death penalty, while formal trials were rare, unless they were considered a valuable didactical exercise for educating the 'masses'.[9] It should be observed that there was a lack of formal institutions as well as trained personnel at the time. However, the sanctioning apparatus of the PRC immediately after 1949 initially treated 'counterrevolutionaries' relatively lenient in comparison to similar crimes in the ensuing anti-counterrevolutionary campaigns. GMD judicial officials who had officially committed to the CPP were retained and had leeway in case handling due to a lack of law; they were expected to use their 'common sense'. Yet, it was plausible that their decisions were based on the abolished laws of the Nationalists with which they were familiar. However, soon Party leaders demanded harsher penalties for political crimes, and the first anti-counterrevolutionary campaign in July 1950 replaced leniency with harshness.[10]

[4] Shao-Chuan Leng, *Justice in Communist China: A Survey of the Judicial System of the Chinese People's Republic* (New York, Oceana Publications, 1967) 27.

[5] Stanley B Lubman, *Bird in a Cage* (Redwood, Stanford University Press, 1999) 72–73.

[6] ibid 67.

[7] Alice Erh-Soon Tay and Eugene Kamenka, 'Marxism and the Problem of Legal Continuity – Recent Trens in Communist Legal Theory' [1980] *Bulletin of the Australian Society of Legal Philosophy* 31, 32.

[8] The categories of 'the people' and 'the enemy' were defined in very broad terms. Whereas non-antagonistic contradictions were to be handled in accordance with the 'method of democracy' to draw 'a clear distinction between right and wrong', that is, preferably with 'discussion, criticism, persuasion and education', enemies had to be dealt with the measures of dictatorship and severe punishments, see Leng (n 4) 154–169.

[9] Lubman (n 5) 72–74.

[10] Qiang Fang, *The Communist Judicial System in China, 1927-1976* (Amsterdam, Amsterdam University Press, 2021) 111–113, 129–130.

Indeed, a real purge did not take place before 1952, when legally trained personnel that had worked under the Nationalists were replaced by politically loyal cadres whose primary task was to carry out campaigns and use the law to persecute class enemies.[11]

The leadership under Mao, of course, consciously opposed the old order. Confucianism, as part of the old order, was attacked fiercely during the Cultural Revolution.[12] Scholars have nonetheless illuminated how Confucianism resonates in Socialism,[13] and we may indeed find that certain elements of the traditional attitude towards law, influenced by Confucianism and Legalism, correspond to Socialist ethics or attitudes towards law, which may explain the felt familiarity with some aspects of the political-legal system after 1949, most notably informal mechanisms of dispute resolution,[14] the idea of virtuous governance,[15] the punitive and authoritarian nature of positive law,[16] the educational function (eg, institutionally reflected in the reform through labour (*laogai*) system), the contingency of rights or the emphasis on collectivism;[17] whether such elements were consciously accommodated remains debatable. While traditional legal culture may have reinforced the CCP's approach toward criminal justice, it is debatable whether these elements can be treated as genuine continuities. Lubman has shown in a more nuanced way how such apparently continuing features, such as mediation as an informal means of dispute settlement, had been transformed under the CCP and thus differed in many respects from traditional China.[18] Therefore, too simplistic conclusions as to continuities and discontinuities may not be sensible.

The period between 1954 and 1957 has been viewed as relatively liberal and marked by genuine efforts to establish a more stable legal system.[19] The initial phase of internal power consolidation was completed by 1953, and the Party hence shifted its focus to economic development. As part of this new policy, some ordinance and discipline, which was associated with stability, was needed. The efforts resulted in the passage of the Constitution of 1954, rules on arrest and detention, as well as organisational legislation for the courts and procuratorates, which first structured the judicial system. To support their implementation, institutional capacities were expanded through the set-up of law schools, procuratorial offices

[11] Lubman (n 5) 72–73.

[12] See, eg, Merle Goldman, 'China's Anti-Confucian Campaign, 1973-74' [1975] *The China Quarterly* 435.

[13] See, eg, P Chao, 'Socialism in Confucianism' (1971) 9 *Asian Studies: Journal of Critical Perspectives on Asia* 328.

[14] Shao-Chuan Leng and Hungdah Chiu, *Criminal Justice in Post-Mao China* (New York, State University of New York Press, 1985) 7–8.

[15] Derk Bodde and Clarence Morris, *Law in Imperial China: Exemplified by 190 Ch'ing Dynasty Cases (Translated from the Hsing-an Hui-Lan), With Historical, Social, and Juridical Commentaries* (Cambridge, MA, Harvard University Press, 1967) 19–30.

[16] Lubman (n 5) 15–16, 23.

[17] See ch 1, I and II.

[18] Lubman (n 5) 68–69.

[19] Leng (n 4) 27–44, 54–63.

and courts, lawyers' offices modelled after the Soviet system, and the training of cadres.[20] During this period, attempts were also made to draft a code of criminal procedure, and even though they were never adopted, they allow a glimpse into early contestations as to the underlying values of criminal justice in China.

The literature from the 1950s and 1960s on criminal justice predominately focused on questions of evidence and proof and on the status and rights of the accused in criminal proceedings,[21] as well as the right to criminal defence,[22] thereby indirectly touching upon the question of presumption of innocence.[23] Chinese legal scholars studied the works of Soviet legal scholars, most notably Vyshinsky or Strogovic.[24] Moreover, in the absence of a code on criminal procedure, the Constitution of 1954, as well as the other few existing laws and regulations, served as important sources for discussions on the scope of procedural rights.[25] Besides some personal liberty safeguards, the right to defence was one of those few safeguards explicitly provided for by the law; scholars especially highlighted it as the key safeguard to ensure fairness.[26]

Even if this tentative commitment to socialist legality did not last long and was far from complete, the more liberal atmosphere facilitated the first round of academic discourse on the presumption of innocence in China in the mid-1950s. Despite a general hostility towards bourgeois law, there was some space for academic discourses as regards the question of how and if elements of such law could be applied in the Chinese context.[27] At the time, scholars focused on the presumption of innocence and its supposed counterpart, the presumption of guilt, as prevalent in feudal societies. The two diametrically opposed views of advocacy and rejection dominated this early discourse. However, it should be borne in mind that, regardless of whether they were an advocate or not, scholars seriously

[20] Lubman (n 5) 74–75.

[21] It should be observed that this early scholarship did not distinguish between suspects and defendants.

[22] Chen Qiwu, '"Shishi shi genju, falü shi zhunsheng" shi woguo xingshi susong de jiben zhidao yuanze ("Taking Facts as the Basis, and Law as the Yardstick" is the Basic Guiding Principle of Criminal Proceedings in China)' [1958] *Law Science* 37, 37–38.

[23] Gelatt made similar observations, see Timothy Gelatt, 'The People's Republic of China and the Presumption of Innocence' (1982) 73 *The Journal of Criminal Law & Criminology* 259, 269.

[24] For a summary of Strogovic's position, see Carl-Friedrich Stuckenberg, *Untersuchungen Zur Unschuldsvermutung* (Berlin, De Gruyter, 1998) 376–387.

[25] Constitution 1954; Court Organisation Law 1954 (COL 1954); Procuratorates Organisation Law 1954 (POL 1954); Detention and Arrest Regulation 1954 (DAR 1954).

[26] Constitution 1954, arts 76 and 89; COL, art 7; Zhou Xiangyuan, 'Lun woguo xingshi susong zhong beigaoren de bianhuquan (On the Defedant's Right to Defence in the Chinese Criminal Proceedings)' [1956] *Chinese Journal of Law* 51; Luo Rong, 'Shi lun xingshi susong zhong de beigaoren (On the Defendant in the Criminal Procedure' [1957] *Law Science* 56; Wu Lei, 'Guanyu woguo xingshi susong zhong bianhuren susong diwei de yanjiu (Research on the Procedural Status of the Defender in the Chinese Criminal Procedure)' [1957] *Chinese Journal of Law*.

[27] Xie Youping, 'Wuzui tuiding yuanze pinglun (A Comment on the Principle of Presumption of Innocence)' [1993] *Law Science* 34, 36; Tianlong Jiang, 'The Development and Evaluation of "Presumption of Innocence in China' in Wei Zhang (ed), *Human Rights and Good Governance* (Leiden, Brill Nijhoff, 2016) 238.

discussed the scope of procedural safeguards in view of establishing a functioning criminal justice system. While the notion of presumption of innocence itself was contested, many scholars nonetheless advocated the adoption of procedural guarantees such as the right to defence or evidence rules for the determination of legal guilt. This section discusses the evolving discourse on the 'bourgeois' presumption of innocence in the mid-1950s and examines the two opposing views of advocacy and rejection of the presumption of innocence.

## A. Opponents of Presumption of Innocence

In the light of the revolutionary atmosphere, it may not come as a surprise that the view of rejection dominated in the early years of the PRC. Scholars criticised the 'bourgeois' presumption of innocence as 'reactionary'. As the argument usually goes, it is a 'subjective assumption', lacking any factual basis and giving counter-revolutionaries, as well as other criminals, basically the opportunity to escape criminal punishment. Zhang Zipei was an outspoken critic of the application of presumption of innocence in the Chinese context.[28] Evidently, scholars were aware that, when criticising the feudalist presumption of guilt and trying to distance themselves from 'feudalist' and 'bourgeois' practices, they had to propose alternative principles of criminal justice. As an alternative to the feudalist presumption of guilt and the bourgeois presumption of innocence, the principle of 'seeking truth from facts' appeared to be an appropriate choice to guide the determination of guilt and ensure accurate outcomes in the criminal justice process.[29]

At the 3rd National Judicial Congress in February 1956, Peng Zhen established a principle of criminal justice that would henceforth guide theorists and practitioners – the principle of 'taking facts as the basis, and the law as the yardstick' (*yi shishi wei genju, yi falü wei zhunsheng*, 'seeking truth from facts').[30] The claim that this principle developed from China's practical experience echoes the Maoist doctrine of practice and theory. Mao interpreted the principle of 'seeking truth from facts' in accordance with the dialectical-materialist theory of knowledge as follows:

> We are Marxists, and Marxism teaches that in our approach to a problem we should start from objective facts, not from abstract definitions, and that we should derive our guiding principles, policies and measures from an analysis of these facts.[31]

[28] Zhang Zipei, 'Bo zichanjieji de "wuzui tuiding" yuanze (Reject the Bourgeois Principle of "Presumption of Innocence")' [1958] *Law Science* 37; see also Wu Lei and Wang Shunhua, 'Bo "wuzui tuiding lun" (Rejecting the Presumption of Innocence)' *Guang Ming Daily* (13 December 1957).

[29] Chen Qiwu (n 22) 37.

[30] Zhu Linyu and Lin Hongjiao, '"Shishi shi genju, falü shi zhunsheng" yuanze de xingcheng he fazhan (Formation and Development of the Principle of "Taking Facts as the Basis, and Law as the Yardstick")' [2013] *Journal of Law Application* 42, 42.

[31] Zedong Mao, 'Talks at the Yenan Forum on Literature and Art, May 1942', vol III. (Peking, Foreign Language Press, 1965) 74.

It should be observed that the Soviet theory of truth often uses the term 'truth' in the same meaning as 'knowledge', according to which truth is understood as the 'correspondence of a concept, an idea, to an object'.[32] True knowledge of man should coincide with, or reflect, objective reality; this is what makes it objective.[33] Putting the dialectical-materialist theory of knowledge into context with the theory of base and superstructure, because rational knowledge consists of concepts and theories, it should belong to the superstructure. Knowledge is hence conditioned, even if not exclusively, by the reality of the economic base.[34]

Mao thus understood knowledge to develop gradually from practice. More specifically, it develops dialectically through a two-tier process. The process begins with the first stage of perceptual knowledge that develops into rational knowledge (the conceptual stage). Concepts that develop in the stage of rational knowledge can capture the essence, the whole of relationships of things. At this stage, logical conclusions can be drawn by means of judging and inferring. This rational knowledge can then be used to alter both the subjective and the objective world. This process is, however, an infinite circle of practice – knowledge – practice – knowledge. Therefore, social practice is of utmost significance to discover knowledge or truth. Since knowledge cannot be isolated from practice, and because theory must be based on practice, subjective ideas and so forth are considered incompatible with the theory of objective truth; practice is the source of knowledge.[35]

There is thus an interdependence of perceptual and rational knowledge; the latter should, then, guide practice. By applying knowledge, theory can be further developed. However, Mao was aware of the problem of determining whether theory (theoretical knowledge) correlates with objective reality. Therefore, as a solution, he suggested that theoretical knowledge that has been acquired through practice must be applied to practice. Only practice could determine the accuracy of any knowledge, and practice is hence the criterion for truth.[36] By achieving rational knowledge and through further practice, one could 'create ideas, theories, plans or programmes which correspond in general to the laws of that objective process'.[37] However, in the view of Mao, knowledge in the form of ideas, theories, etc, is never static and must be reviewed continuously because it is often erroneous in the sense that it does not yield the predicted objective and thus does not correctly reflect reality. Practice must be repeated until all failures have been eradicated. The development of knowledge is thus a dialectical

[32] Karl G Ballestrem, 'The Soviet Concept of Truth' (1964) 4 *Studies in Soviet Thought* 1, 1.

[33] ibid 1–5.

[34] Valentin Petev, *Kritik Der Marxistisch-Sozialistischen Rechts- Und Staatsphilosophie* (Berlin, Duncker & Humbolt, 1989) 15–18.

[35] Mao Zedong, 'On Practice, July 1937' in Foreign Language Press (ed), *Selected Works of Mao Tse-Tung*, vol I. (Peking, Foreign Language Press, 1965) 296–299.

[36] ibid 299–305.

[37] ibid 305.

process; that is, knowledge may reflect objective reality at a certain stage of the process, but it must progress with changing realities. In this sense, it is an infinite process.[38]

In the context of criminal justice, the principle of seeking truth from facts reflects the noble aim to search for the objective truth. The notion of 'objectivity' (eg, in the sense of objective facts) thus carries a particular meaning, which must be interpreted within the above-mentioned socialist theory of knowledge and which has occupied a prominent place in Chinese criminal justice. The criminal justice process itself is a reflection of dialectical materialism and not related to historical materialism.[39] Accordingly, Chen Qiwu, an early advocate of seeking truth from facts and opponent of presumption of innocence, argued that seeking truth from facts was a fundamental principle of investigation, prosecution and adjudication work and that it was developed based on the experiences of China's judicial practice.[40] Based on the theory of knowledge, Chen has held that the true circumstances of a case would exist objectively; that is, they would exist independently from the will of judicial personnel. Therefore, the discovery of criminal facts, the determination of the true circumstances of a case, would be the major task in every procedural phase. While rejecting the alleged agnostic approach of bourgeois theorists – the presumption of innocence – Chen has claimed that, because crimes are a social phenomenon, dialectical materialism would be the only 'scientific' method to discover the truth, including the motive, time and location, etc, of a crime. The essence of things should thus be seen through social phenomena. Not surprisingly, problems had to be considered from a firm class stance to protect the interests of 'the people', broadly speaking, supporters of socialism, rather than from the perspective of alleged criminals. In criminal cases, this distinction, which was defined in very broad terms, was crucial to determine the proper handling of a case.[41]

Therefore, according to Chen, the 'idealist theory' of the principle of presumption of innocence would contradict the principle of 'seeking truth from facts'. Chen thus condemned those 'rightists' or 'counterrevolutionaries' that were trying to propagate the 'bourgeois' principle, as they would help criminals to escape punishment and give them a reason not to cooperate by remaining silent. In such cases, the policy of 'leniency for those who confess, severity for those who resist' ('*tanbai congkuang, kangju congyan*'; hereafter 'combining leniency with severity') could not be applied, the accused could not be held criminally liable for false

[38] ibid 305–308.

[39] Yi Yanyou, 'Lun wuzui tuiding de hanyi yu xingshi susongfa de wanshan (On the Implications of the Presumption of Innocence and the Improvement of the Criminal Procedure Law)' [2012] *Tribune of Political Science and Law* 10, 17.

[40] Chen Qiwu (n 22) 37.

[41] The principle of 'relying on the masses' (*yikao qunzhong*) reflects the 'mass line', see CPL 1979, art 4.

statements or slander, and a 'bad attitude' towards law enforcement authorities could not be seen as an indication of the accused's guilt.[42]

Opponents of the presumption of innocence did not engage with the question of what safeguards the system should contain in the event of violation of the principle of seeking truth from facts, and it was lacking guidance on how to understand and implement it in reality. At the time, the presumption of guilt dominated in practice, as there was no equality of arms between the prosecution and defence and no functioning criminal justice system.[43] Indeed, the system and the legal framework were still in a rudimentary stage and highly fragmented.[44] The next section outlines the scholarly arguments in favour of presumption of innocence.

## B. Advocates of Presumption of Innocence

In the light of the official condemnation of 'bourgeois' elements, only a few scholars in China dared to openly advocate the presumption of innocence in the early years of the PRC. But those few who did believed it could ensure objectivity and fairness in criminal proceedings while being critical of the prevalence of subjectivism and prejudices amongst judges, which would lead to wrongfully decided cases. Indeed, the popular press also criticised 'subjectivism', as it would not follow the mass line, and emphasised the function of the principle of presumption of innocence to guarantee objectivity in the phase of criminal investigation.[45] Since such pieces appeared in the popular press, it can be presumed that the party-state had tolerated such views. However, it should be observed that Party leaders like Liu Shaoqi did not openly advocate the presumption of innocence but rather aimed to 'combat subjectivism' by deepening the understanding of Marxism-Leninism amongst Party cadres.[46]

The view of advocacy nonetheless invoked the presumption of innocence as a guiding principle of criminal justice to ensure proper case handling and thus 100 per cent accurate outcomes. The work of scholars who openly supported the presumption of innocence was less politicised, as they did not reject the idea of presumption of innocence or other fair trial safeguards in the abstract based on allegedly competing socialist principles. For them the question of how to build a functioning criminal justice system, which cannot be built on political slogans

[42] Chen Qiwu seems to refer to Huang (1957), see Chen Qiwu (n 22) 39.

[43] Jerome A Cohen, *Criminal Process in the People's Republic of China, 1949-1963* (Cambridge, MA, Harvard University Press, 1966) 15–16; Gelatt (n 23) 271; Leng (n 4) 27–44, 154–169.

[44] Leng (n 4) 27–44, 54–63; Cohen (n 43) 22, 298–317.

[45] Xiong De, 'Cong yi jian cuo'an tanqi (A Case of Wrongful Conviction' *Guang Ming Daily* (29 January 1957).

[46] 'Liu Shaoqi zuo zhengzhi baogao (Liu Shaoqi's Political Report), delivered to the Eighth CCP National Congress on 15 September 1956' cpc.people.com.cn/GB/64162/64168/64560/65452/4526551.html accessed 7 June 2019.

alone, had priority. For example, Qu Fu believed that the presumption of innocence could ensure the 'objectivity' and raised the question of the rights of criminally accused persons as subjects of proceedings. The presumption of innocence would be needed to justify procedural safeguards, as otherwise an accused person would be entirely at the mercy of state officials, who were eager to obtain an admission of guilt at any cost. To this end, Qu considered the right to defence a centrally important safeguard, as could be found in Soviet law as well, even though he did not immediately derive it from the presumption of innocence. As part of the right to defence and because the burden of proof would be on the prosecution, a suspect in the pre-trial phases could choose silence. A violation of this rule would compromise the right to defence and contradict with the principle of 'stressing evidence, do not readily believing confessions'.[47]

By recognising the status of the accused as a subject of proceedings, Qu thus justifies other procedural safeguards, notably the right to defence. He engages with the idea of presumption of innocence, embracing a broader approach that reflects the principle dimension. Even if not treating such fair trial guarantees as consistent (in the sense of interchangeable) with the presumption of innocence, Qu recognises that it explains why an accused should have a set of certain procedural safeguards. Qu's interpretation of the presumption of innocence may have been inspired by the formulation of the Universal Declaration that links it more evidently to a general right to a fair trial.

Huang Dao was another prominent and early advocate of the presumption of innocence. In contrast to those rejecting it as a bourgeois legal principle or arguing that the principle of objective truth would render the principle of presumption of innocence obsolete, Huang concludes that it could be useful for Chinese criminal proceedings and compatible with the socialist legal system. According to Huang, the presumption of innocence would provide better protection for the procedural rights of the accused. Because the search for the objective truth would be complex, the presumption of innocence should be applied, as it would provide a protective function to guarantee the lawful rights of the accused. Therefore, in Huang's view, the principles of seeking truth from facts and presumption of innocence could run in parallel, as they would not be in conflict. Huang developed three procedural principles arising from the presumption of innocence. First, an accused person would have the right to remain silent; thus the policy of combining leniency with severity could not be applied against them. Second, the accused could not be held criminally liable for false statements or slander, and, third, a 'bad attitude' towards law enforcement authorities would not be an indication of guilt. The policy of

[47] Qu Fu, 'Lüe tan xingshi susong zhong beigaoren de susong diwei (On the Procedural Position of the Defendant in the Criminal Process)' [1957] *Chinese Journal of Law* 22, 24–25. This principle was written into the CPL 1979, see art 35. In traditional China, it was understood to be the other way around, namely, 'stressing confessions, not evidence' (*zhong kougong, bu zhong zhengju*). The Tang Code is often mentioned as having established the presumption of guilt in Chinese criminal justice, see Lin Xin, '"Wuzui tuiding" haishi "wuzui jiadong"? ("Presumption of Innocence" or "Assumption of Innocence"?' [1983] *Social Sciences in China* 173, 173.

combining leniency with severity was irrelevant in the process of determining guilt; rather, it would be a factor to be considered in sentencing.[48] In practice, of course, choosing silence was not an option.[49]

Some events would soon end this early engagement with presumption of innocence and academic discourses on criminal justice more widely. The Hundred Flowers Campaign (1956–57) was a liberal policy to encourage intellectuals and other people to engage with the Party. Once the silence broke, the Party faced more criticism than initially anticipated. Considering the discrepancy between the idea of justice and the reality, it is not surprising that scholars criticised the Party leaders for their failure to establish even the most fundamental laws and institutions necessary for the administration of justice.[50] Fearing a threat to its leadership role, it soon launched the Anti-Rightist Campaign (1957–58). As a result, in 1957, the presumption of innocence, as well as other liberal values, was officially denounced as a 'reactionary' and 'bourgeois' principle,[51] and liberal-minded scholars were persecuted and often sent to re-education camps. Law journals no longer appeared, the legal education of judicial cadres was halted, and the establishment of a legal system was interrupted.[52] Indeed, Qu Fu and Huang Dao both withdrew their previous support for the presumption of innocence.[53] For example, before Huang started working as a university lecturer in 1953, he was a judge at a court in Xiamen. Motivated by Zhou Enlai's Report on the Question of Intellectuals (1956), Huang published the earlier discussed article on the presumption of innocence.[54] In the midst of the campaign, Li Baomin, who was a critic of the presumption of innocence, criticised Huang.[55] Even if Huang was not denounced as a 'rightist', he openly withdrew his commitment to presumption of innocence in a symposium held at the Law School of the East China University of Political Science and Law on 26 December 1957 and published a self-criticism of his previous paper.[56]

[48] Huang Dao, 'Lüe lun xingshi susong zhong de wuzui tuiding yuanze (A Brief Discussion on Principle of the Presumption of Innocence in Criminal Procedure' [1957] *Law Science* 49, 50 and 52.

[49] Cohen (n 43) 30, 369–370.

[50] Leng (n 4) 27–44, 54–63; Cohen (n 43) 22, 298–317.

[51] Huang Dao and Tie Li, 'Wuzui tuiding zai xin zhongguo de mingyun – jianguo yilai faxuejie zhongda shijian yanjiu (er) (The Fate of the Presumption of Innocence in New China: A Study of Major Events in Jurisprudence since the Founding of the People's Republic of China (II))' [1997] *Law Science* 2, 2.

[52] GV Thieme, 'The Debate on the Presumption of Innocence in the People's Republic of China' [1984] *Review of Socialist Law* 277, 280–283.

[53] Zhang Hui, Li Changchun and Zhang Zipei, 'Zhe bu shi woguo xingshi susong de jiben yuanze — ping Qu Fu "lüe tan xingshi susong zhong beigaoren de susong diwei (This is not a Fundamental Principle of China's Criminal Proceedings – Comment on Qu Fu's Discussion on the Procedural Position of the Defendant in Criminal Proceedings)' [1958] *Law Science* 76.

[54] ibid.

[55] Li Baomin, '"Wuzui Tuiding" Bu Ying Zuowei Woguo Xingshi Susong de Yuanze (The "Presumption of Innocence" Should not to be a Principle of Chinese Criminal Procedure)' [1958] *Law Science* 45.

[56] Huang Dao, 'Yinggai chedi pipan "wuzui tuiding" de miulun (The Fallacy of the "Presumption of Innocence" Should be Thoroughly Criticised)' [1958] *Law Science*; Law School of the East China University of Political Science and Law, 'Donghua zhengfa xueyuan juxing kexue taolunhui – pibo

Fang Qiang has observed that courts often treated 'rightists', who were basically equated to counterrevolutionaries, more leniently or even rehabilitated formerly convicted 'rightists' at the beginning of the campaign but resorted to harshness from late 1957 onwards and especially in 1958 due to the fear of receiving such a label themselves. This fear was not unfounded. The campaign had indeed led to another purge of the judicial system.[57] Cohen nonetheless believed that the developments after 1957 did not mean a complete return to the underregulated period in the early years of the PRC, as the Party could rely on a relatively systematic set of punishments to persecute alleged 'rightists'.[58] This is, of course, not to suggest that they received a fair trial (or even a trial at all). The changing attitude towards 'rightists', of course, illustrates the responsiveness of the judicial system to Party directives, as well as the early tension between legal stability and political exigencies. The emphasis on politics continued throughout the 1960s, and legal issues were largely discussed through a political-ideological lens. As will be shown in the next section, this changing political atmosphere is reflected in the Criminal Procedure Law draft proposals of the mid-1950s and again in the early 1960s.

## C. The Presumption of Innocence in the 1957 and the 1960s Criminal Procedure Law Drafts

This section is particularly interested in comparing early Criminal Procedure Law draft proposals against the backdrop of domestic developments. Domestic developments show that despite the political atmosphere, the discourse on criminal justice has not been linear. While the CPL 1957 (draft) reflects the more open period before the Anti-Rightist Campaign, as discussed in the previous section, the drafts from the 1960s are an expression of the more illiberal climate that prevailed until the end of the Cultural Revolution. The CPL 1957 (draft) enshrined an explicit provision on presumption of innocence, which was absent in the 1960s drafts. Despite the general scepticism towards the presumption of innocence, Article 5 of the CPL 1957 (draft) had codified a general provision on the presumption of innocence, which reads:

> The defendant shall be assumed innocent until the judgment has become legally effective.
>
> 被告人在有判决发生法律效力以前，应当假定是无罪的人.[59]

wuzui tuiding lun (Law School of the East China University of Political Science and Law holds an Academic Seminar – Rebuttal of the Presumption of Innocence)' [1958] *Law Science* 48.

[57] Fang (n 10) 220–224.

[58] Cohen (n 43) 18.

[59] Wu Hongyao and Zhong Songzhi, *Zhongguo Xingshi Susong Fadian Bainian 1906 Nian – 2012 Nian (Zhongce) (100 Years of the Chinese Criminal Procedure Law Codes (1906-2012) (Middle Volume))* (Beijing, China University of Political Science and Law Press, 2012) 458 (CPL (draft) 1957, art 5).

This is an explicit provision on presumption of innocence, but the introduction of such a provision was contested. Studying the draft shows that other proposals suggested similar formulations, while one proposal was not to adopt such a provision.[60]

Interestingly, the CPL (draft) 1957 makes no mention of the principle of 'taking facts as the basis, and law as the yardstick', nor does it anywhere else emphasise objective truth (factual guilt).[61] It refers to seeking truth from facts only in the context of assessing the authenticity of evidence, requiring the collection of both inculpatory and exculpatory evidence, but this provision also contains safeguards that are necessary to realise the presumption of innocence, such as the privilege against self-incrimination and the burden of proof, thus implicitly recognising the right to silence.[62] Overall, the CPL (draft) 1957 appears relatively comprehensive in terms of procedural safeguards.

As already mentioned, the Anti-Rightist Movement brought legislative efforts to a halt, and it was only between 1960 and 1963 when deliberations on a criminal procedure law were resumed. Between March and April 1963, several draft codes of criminal procedure were produced. However, the 1960s drafts had abandoned most of the language of the more liberal CPL (draft) 1957. The CPL (draft) 1962 did not mention a presumption of innocence in its general provisions, and it was also missing in the CPL (drafts) 1963. The CPL (draft) 1962 first established the principle that all facts proving the established 'true circumstances' of a case should be considered as evidence.[63] Furthermore, according to the CPL (drafts) 1963, the collection of evidential materials by the investigating authorities was to be based on the principle of seeking truth from facts.[64] For example, during criminal interrogation, the accused had to make truthful statements as to the questions of the investigators and was not allowed to 'exaggerate or hide criminal facts'.[65] Unlike the CPL (draft) 1957, the CPL (draft) 1962 and the CPL (drafts) 1963 (nos 3–6) did not contain a privilege against self-incrimination or right to silence, even if it was prohibited to obtain evidential materials by unlawful means.[66] The introduction of the theory of objective truth may have been considered incompatible with certain fair trial safeguards such as the right to silence, but the omission or denial of such safeguards may also be explained by the overall more illiberal atmosphere at the time.

However, all pre-CPL 1979 drafts contained some fair trial safeguards that can be seen as an expression of the idea of presumption of innocence. For example,

[60] ibid.

[61] See, eg, CPL 1979, art 31.

[62] Wu Hongyao and Zhong Songzhi (n 59) 463 (CPL (draft) 1957, art 48).

[63] Wu Hongyao and Zhong Songzhi (n 61) 514 (CPL (draft) 1962, art 44); ibid see, eg, 567 (CPL (third draft) 1963, art 44), 637 (CPL (fourth draft) 1963, art 28).

[64] Wu Hongyao and Zhong Songzhi (n 59) 515 (CPL (draft) 1962, art 49), 567–568 (CPL (third draft) 1963, art 44), 667 (CPL (fifth draft) 1963, art 33), 701 (CPL (sixth draft) 1963, art 33).

[65] ibid 583 (CPL (draft) 1962, art 95).

[66] ibid. See, eg, 569 (CPL (third draft) 1963, art 47(2)), 637 (CPL (fourth draft) 1963, art 29(2)).

they all enshrined a right to defence,[67] and the drafts all contained some personal liberty safeguards. In the early years of the Mao era (1954–57), efforts were made to limit the omnipotence of the police.[68] The Constitution of 1954 protected citizens from arbitrary detention (*juliu*), a form of provisional police custody, and arrest (*daibu*), which leads to custody pending trial,[69] and the Regulation on Arrests and Detentions of 1954 (DAR 1954) stipulated rudimentary rules for these two measures.[70] The CPL (draft) 1957 contained comparatively comprehensive provisions on these custodial measures. For example, like the DAR 1954,[71] the draft stipulated a relatively tight window of 48 hours for the procuratorial organs to decide on the arrest after detention.[72] However, unlike the DAR 1954, it required an arrest warrant and stipulated that it should include personal information, place of detention, and the reasons for arrest.[73] It set a maximum of three months of custody in the phase of criminal investigation.[74]

Conversely, the CPL (draft) 1962 vaguely defined the conditions for these custodial measures. It removed formal requirements, such as the previously required information along an arrest warrant. It also removed the explicit time limit of custody in the phase of investigation. It allowed for the use of coercive measures, including custodial measures, to facilitate the smooth and swift clarification of case facts.[75] Other provisions in the CPL (draft) 1962 supported this instrumental purpose of coercive measures. For example, the measure of arrest was permitted where the main criminal facts had been established, which clearly stresses the need to determine guilt or innocence at an early stage of proceedings.[76] Therefore, the CPL drafts from the 1960s contained less comprehensive and clear provisions and emphasised efficient crime control.

These different drafts illustrate that the development of criminal justice between 1949 and 1979 had not been linear. The CPL (draft) 1957, reflecting the spirit of a more liberal period, was more moderate and contained a comparatively comprehensive set of procedural safeguards. In contrast, the CPL (drafts) 1962 and 1963 integrated the theory of objective truth and abandoned most of those safeguards provided by the previous draft. Overall, the language of the CPL (draft) 1957 appears more moderate and less ideology-ridden than that of the 1960s drafts on which the CPL 1979 was later based. These early discourses on presumption of

[67] ibid 462–463 (CPL (draft) 1957, arts 43 to 46), 512–513 (CPL (draft) 1962, arts 38 to 42), 566–567 (CPL (third draft) 1963, arts 38 to 43), 636–637 (CPL (fourth draft) 1963, arts 24 to 27), 666 (CPL (fifth draft) 1963, arts 26 to 29), 700 (CPL (sixth draft) 1963, arts 26 to 29).

[68] Leng (n 4) 120.

[69] Constitution 1954, art 89. The differences between these measures will be discussed below, see V.

[70] Detention and Arrest Regulation (DAR 1954) (Adopted at the Third Session of the Standing Committee of the National People's Congress on 20 December 1954).

[71] DAR 1954, art 7.

[72] Wu Hongyao and Zhong Songzhi (n 59) 466 (CPL (draft) 1957, art 65).

[73] ibid 465 (CPL (draft) 1957, art 63).

[74] ibid 466–67 (CPL (draft) 1957, art 71).

[75] ibid 517 (CPL (draft) 1962, art 59); 571 (CPL (third draft) 1963, art 59).

[76] ibid 517 (CPL (draft) 1962, art 61).

innocence and criminal justice, more widely, and legislative efforts show that there were already tensions between liberal rights ideas, as advanced by few scholars at the time, on the one hand and the Party's official commitment to class struggle, on the other, as well as the reality of criminal justice, which was greatly impacted by it. The Mao era coincided with the end of the Cultural Revolution (1966–76).

## II. The Early Reform Era: Presumption of Innocence in the CPL 1979

The second phase of presumption of innocence discourses began in the late 1970s. In the wake of developing a socialist legal system, debates about procedural safeguards resumed, and the question was whether the presumption of innocence should be adopted, which elements of it should be recognised, and whether reasonable limits were justifiable. These questions were partly triggered by the CPL 1979 not containing an explicit provision on presumption of innocence. As discussed in chapter two, this is not necessarily significant for its realisation, nor does it necessarily mean that the CPL 1979 was rejected in the abstract.[77] In other words, even if the CPL 1979 had included an explicit provision on presumption of innocence, its actual realisation would depend on the protection of associated procedural safeguards.

Whereas western scholars have found that two diametrically opposing views of rejection and full advocacy dominated the discourse on the presumption of innocence,[78] Chinese scholars have pointed to the three different views of rejection, full endorsement and partial advocacy; the latter refers to a 'critical attitude' towards it.[79] For example, many scholars still rejected the application of presumption of innocence in the Chinese context due to a presumed ideological conflict. Scholars like Xu Yichu or Wang Bingxin argued that the bourgeoisie would embrace the presumption of innocence only to create an illusion of democracy but would apply the presumption of guilt in reality to realise its own class interests. Such a hypocritical presumption of innocence could not be applied in a socialist society.[80] Moreover, misconceptions of the presumption of innocence as establishing a factual legal fiction had also led to its rejection. The presumption of innocence was considered to contradict the empirical reality of criminal justice. It was still seen to represent subjective idealism, thus contradicting objective materialism.[81] However, as we will see, the discourse was more diverse than this.

[77] Gelatt (n 23) 262, 284.

[78] Thieme (n 52) 283.

[79] Xie Youping (n 27); Chen Guangzhong, 'Yingdang pipan de jicheng wuzui tuiding yuanze (We Should Critically Inherit the Principle of Presumption of Innocence' [1980] *Chinese Journal of Law* 34.

[80] Xu Yichu, *Xingshi susong faxue yanjiu gaishu (An Account of the Research on Criminal Procedure Law)* (Tianjin, Tianjin Education Publishing House, 1989) 86; Wang Bingxin, 'Guanyu "wuzui tuiding" yuanze de tantao (On the Principle of "Presumption of Innocence"' [1979] *Modern Law Science* 10, 10–11.

[81] Thieme (n 52) 288.

It should be borne in mind that the academic discourse was just re-emerging in the late 1970s and the question of human rights protection in criminal proceedings had not yet gained much attention. Chinese scholars nonetheless acknowledged the triumph of the presumption of innocence in the then evolving international human rights regime,[82] and, studying international law and other jurisdictions, they often read the presumption of innocence as consisting of a set of rules and principles,[83] even if the usage of the label of 'presumption' remained contested. Even though Chinese legal scholars recognised that the rationale of presumption of innocence goes beyond its evidential dimension, their focus remained on rules of evidence that would give substance to the premise of assuming innocence. In this context, scholars particularly stressed evidence-based judgments, the standard of proof, the prohibition against torture, the exclusive adjudication power of courts, and the designation of the accused as 'defendant' before a guilty verdict is passed.[84]

The two other dimensions of right and principle received less attention. Scholars in China did not discuss the dimension of the presumption of innocence as a right on its own, as enshrined in both the Universal Declaration and the Covenant. The principle dimension of presumption of innocence was also not at the centre of attention, and few scholars took a broader approach to presumption of innocence.[85] For example, there has been little discussion of the application of presumption of innocence in the context of pre-trial detention as an indicator for the treatment of a person in accordance with this principle. Moreover, while the right to defence was amongst the most uncontested procedural safeguards, at least in theory, it was not necessarily seen as flowing from the presumption of innocence or being associated with it.

The sections to follow address the question of whether the CPL 1979 had shown signs of presumption of innocence. It will be helpful to first look at the official view.

## A. The Official View of not Presuming Anything

We may use the trial against the 'Gang of Four' (*sirenbang*) as a starting point for analysing a new chapter in the history of Chinese criminal justice. The trial in the late 1980s was *the* event after the Cultural Revolution. Even if the party-state touted it as a landmark case, the first under the new legal framework, it was a

[82] Luo Xinmin, 'Wuzui tuiding bu shi shehui zhuyi de susong yuanze (The Presumption of Innocence is not a Socialist Procedural Principle)' [1982] *Modern Law Science* 27, 28.

[83] Zhao Guangyu, 'Guanyu "wuzui tuiding" yuanze de lijie he shiyong (On the Understanding and Application of the Principle of the Presumption of Innocence)' [1981] *Chinese Journal of Law* 23, 23; Zhang Jinjie, Zhang Tao and Wang Minyuan, 'Lun wuzui tuiding yuanze (On the Principle of the Presumption of Innocence)' (1991) 13 *Chinese Journal of Law* 34, 37–38.

[84] Wang Xiaohua and Ma Qingguo, '"Wuzui tuiding" bian (Defending the Presumption of Innocence)' [1980] *Chinese Journal of Law* 63, 63–64; Xie Youping (n 27) 34–38; Zhao Guangyu (n 83) 25; Ning Hanlin, 'Lun wuzui tuiding (On the Presumption of Innocence)' [1982] *Social Sciences in China* 65, 78; Lin Xin (n 47) 176.

[85] Zhang Jinjie, Zhang Tao and Wang Minyuan (n 83).

showcase, and the question of guilt or innocence was not seriously at issue; the defendants were neither presented nor treated as innocent people. The press left no doubt as to the guilt of the defendants; the only question to be negotiated was that of punishment. The alleged gang leader Jiang Qing was labelled a 'traitor' (*panzei*) and reports provided detailed accounts of the 'savage' crimes of the gang.[86] Leaving aside the political dimensions of the trial, and even though the few existing legal safeguards were largely ignored or violated, the party-state asserted that the case was handled in strict compliance with domestic legislation. However, it is important to consider the historical context. The fact that there was a formal legal process at all was already significant.[87] At the time, China's legal system barely had the capacity to carry out such a mega trial. Therefore, it is debatable whether one could have seriously expected this trial to meet fair trial standards. One may nonetheless wonder why the party-state used this political showcase to demonstrate a new era of legal governance. Indeed, merely looking at the trial from a legal perspective would fail to grasp its magnitude. It not only symbolised the new relationship between law and politics,[88] it was also used to communicate to Chinese society that there were new rules to be observed by both the government and its citizens.[89]

In 1980, Zhang Youyu, deputy director of the then Legislative Commission of the Standing Committee of the National People's Congress (SCNPC),[90] addressed the foreign observers' criticism of the trial against the Gang of Four in terms of presumption of innocence, arguing that the underlying principles of criminal justice had been misinterpreted. China would adhere to the principle of 'taking facts as the basis, and law as the yardstick'. According to Zhang, '[t]he defendant's guilt is neither affirmed nor the innocence of the defendant denied before the court has pronounced a judgment'.[91] Therefore, in his view, criminal proceedings are not based on presumptions but on facts. Even if not explicitly, Zhang implicitly rejected the presumption of innocence by rejecting the use of presumptions.

Without mentioning the presumption of innocence, Peng Zhen, who then headed the SCNPC Legislative Commission, suggested that the integration of the

[86] See, eg, 'Jiang Qing yu Xiao Jinzhuang – chedi qingsuan pantu Jiang Qing zai Xiao Jinzhuang de fangeming zuixing (Jiang Qing and Xiao Jinzhuang – Thoroughly liquidate the Counter-Revolutionary Crimes committed by the Traitor Jiang Qing in Xiao Jinzhuang)' *People's Daily* (12 January 1978).

[87] Alexander C Cook, *The Cultural Revolution on Trial: Mao and the Gang of Four* (Cambridge, Cambridge University Press, 2016) 35.

[88] James C Hsiung, 'Introduction' in James C Hsiung (ed), *Symposium: The Trial of the "Gang of Four" and Its Implications in China* (1981) 40(3) Occasional papers/reprints series in *Contemporary Asian Studies*1–4.

[89] Jerome A Cohen, 'Criminal Justice in China: From the Gang of Four to the Trial of Bo Xila' (Human Rights Watch 2013) www.hrw.org/news/2013/07/25/criminal-justice-china-gang-four-bo-xilai accessed 8 May 2021.

[90] The NPCSC Legislative Commission (*fazhi weiyuanhui*) was established in 1979 and, in 1983, renamed as NPCSC Legislative Affairs Commission (*fazhi gongzuo weiyuanhui*).

[91] 'Jiu shenpan Lin Jiang fangeming jituan an de sige falü wenti – zhuming faxuejia zhang youyu da jizhe wen (Four Legal Issues in the Trial of the Lin Jiang Counter-Revolutionary Group – Prominent Jurist Zhang Youyu Answers Reporters' Questions)' *People's Daily* (22 November 1980).

right to defence would be sufficient to protect the rights of the accused and avoid errors in sentencing. Peng further elaborated that the integrity of the accused could be protected by evidence rules and that guilt could only be established in accordance with the prescribed procedure.[92] The legality of criminal proceedings and the accuracy of the outcome were thus of major concern. Therefore, the official stance was that the defence system provided for by law could ensure fairness, whereas the use of the presumption of innocence would be superfluous. Indeed, the presumption of innocence was perhaps also considered ideologically incompatible with the law.

The fact that the legislator decided to base the CPL 1979 on the CPL (drafts) 1963, more specifically on the 33rd CPL (draft) 1963,[93] rather than on the more moderate CPL (draft) 1957, indicates a deliberate decision not to adopt a presumption of innocence. It has been suggested that the SCNPC Legislative Commission under the direction of Peng Zhen enjoyed relatively broad discretion in drafting the CPL 1979 without receiving instructions from the Party centre.[94] Of course, it is difficult to assess to what extent the drafters indeed enjoyed freedom in the law-making. It is also difficult to say why the drafters relied upon the illiberal CPL (drafts) 1963 rather than on the CPL (draft) 1957, which contained far more fair trial safeguards, including a provision on presumption of innocence. Peng Zhen's comments are too scarce to allow any definite conclusions, but the denial of the presumption of innocence appears to have echoed the official stance at the time.

Perhaps because the CPL 1979 lacked a provision on presumption of innocence in expressive terms, and since the official discourse was still open to interpretation, whether the law had implicitly integrated it became a controversially discussed issue amongst Chinese legal scholars. In a way, therefore, the absence of an explicit provision on presumption of innocence, as well as the general vagueness of the law itself, had facilitated pluralistic views on the matter. The different scholarly views that emerged in response to the CPL 1979 reflected divergent ideas as to the underlying values of criminal justice.

## B. Scholarly Views on the Question of Presumption of Innocence

In the early phase of the reform era, many scholars in China still reject the presumption of innocence for different reasons. As already mentioned, some scholars were opposed to the presumption of innocence because of its alleged

[92] Wu Hongyao and Zhong Songzhi (n 59) 863–864 (Peng Zhen's Explanations to the CPL draft (1979), 26 June 1979).

[93] ibid 860 (Peng Zhen's Explanations to the CPL draft (1979), 26 June 1979).

[94] Wang Liwan, 'Lifa guanliao: lijie zhongguo lifa guocheng de xin jiaodu (Legislative Bureaucracy: New Perspectives on Understanding Legislative Processes in China)' [2016] *China Law Review* 114, 129.

class nature, which meant it was incompatible with the socialist legal system. In their eyes, the slogan of human rights was just as hypocritical as the slogan of presumption of innocence.[95] However, it is important to note that this view no longer represented the mainstream view. While the line of reasoning was similar to the tentative engagement in the 1950s, scholars could now invoke the CPL 1979 as the basis for their arguments.

In line with the official position, Zhang Zipei, a prominent critic of the presumption of innocence, argued that the CPL 1979 did not adopt the presumption of innocence. Although the CPL (draft) 1957 contained a provision on presumption of innocence, this would have led to the adverse practice of 'favouring the accused' from 1958 onwards, causing 'contradictions' in investigation, prosecution and adjudication practices, as well as 'contradictory knowledge' among case-handling personnel. Therefore, the CPL drafts from the 1960s would not have included such a provision. Moreover, when the CPL 1979 was drafted, no views were put forward in favour of introducing a provision on presumption of innocence, which would show that the CPL 1979 did neither adopt an explicit provision nor would the law reflect the idea of it.[96] Therefore, the presumption of innocence was 'subjective idealism' (ie, one-sided) and could not reflect the objective reality of criminal justice, which would tell us that most accused persons are guilty.[97] Critics like Zhang Zipei or Wang Guiwu have argued that, despite the absence of presumption of innocence in Chinese criminal justice, the law could protect the rights of accused persons. In their view, the criminal justice process ensures objectivity, as state agencies would have to observe legal provisions, including the principle of seeking truth from facts and the rules on evidence, as codified in the 1979 CPL.[98] These critics thus believed that the legislator had no intention to codify the presumption of innocence.

Other scholars expressed concerns as regards the compatibility of the presumption of innocence with the declared tasks and principles of the CPL 1979.[99] Certain scholars argued that the law's dual aim of rights protection and crime control was irreconcilable with the presumption of innocence.[100] Other scholars followed the official view and considered it obsolete in the light of the principle of seeking truth from facts which could ensure fairness of the

[95] Wang Guiwu, 'Ping "wuzui tuiding" de susong yuanze (A Comment on the Procedural Principle of the "Presumption of Innocence"' [1984] *Legal Forum* 1, 1; Xu Yichu (n 80) 87–92.

[96] Zhang Zipei, 'Ping "wuzui tuiding" (Critique of the "Presumption of Innocence")' [1983] *Tribune of Political Science and Law* 14, 19.

[97] Zhang Zipei, '"Wuzui tuiding" yuanze pouxi (An Analysis of the Principle of the "Presumption of Innocence")' [1980] *Chinese Journal of Law* 30; Zhang Zipei (n 96).

[98] CPL 1979, arts 31, 32, 33 and 35. Zhang Zipei (n 96); Wang Guiwu (n 95).

[99] Tang Guanda, 'Dui "wuzui tuiding" yao juti fenxi (A Detailed Analysis on the "Presumption of Innocence")' [1980] *Chinese Journal of Law* 64, 28, 64.

[100] Xiao Hua, '"Wuzui tuiding" yuanze yu woguo xingshi susong shijian gegeburu (The Principle of "Presumption of Innocence" is incompatible with the Practice of Chinese Criminal Proceedings)' [1980] *Chinese Journal of Law* 62, 62–63.

criminal justice process, even if not necessarily being hostile to the idea of presumption of innocence as such.[101]

At the other end of the spectrum was the view of endorsement of presumption of innocence, though to differing degrees. Those either fully or partially supporting the presumption of innocence argued that the principle was compatible with the socialist legal system, sometimes referring to Soviet law in support of this claim.[102] Although it had become a hypocritical slogan in 'bourgeois' legal systems, it could be realised in the Chinese context and ensure fairness and prevent wrongful convictions,[103] thus not supporting the view that it would obstruct the dual aim of rights protection and crime control. However, this view recognised the rationale of presumption of innocence as a standard of fairness, which also ensures the integrity of the proceedings and is an important guarantee to protect an accused vis-à-vis the omnipotent state. Some proponents even went as far as to suggest the integration of the presumption of innocence provision into the constitution to protect the citizens' fundamental rights and personal freedoms.[104]

Wang Bingxin advocated the presumption of innocence as a universally recognised 'value' and 'principle' of criminal justice. Considering the atrocities committed by the 'Gang of Four' and the rehabilitation of the presumption of guilt during that period, China should establish a presumption of innocence to overcome the presumption of guilt, prevent subjectivism and guarantee fairness.[105] Wang held that a 'socialist presumption of innocence' would already be in usage as a means to protect the socialist system and 'the rights and interests of all working people'.[106] Therefore, the notion of 'socialist democracy', as enshrined in the CPL 1979,[107] was used in support of a socialist presumption of innocence. In accordance with the principle of seeking truth from facts, an open 'democratic debate' between the prosecution and the defence was needed to clarify the case facts, which was the primary objective of criminal proceedings. To ensure such a debate, there should be equality of arms between prosecution and defence, and, to this end, the status of the accused as subject of proceedings should be recognised. Therefore, the accused should have the right to a defence.[108]

Moreover, Ning Hanlin, who believed that the hypothesis of innocence could not be interpreted in isolation from the presumption of innocence, argued that elements of the presumption of innocence could be found in the Chinese legal culture. Ning argues that the ideas that an innocent person should not be punished, that guilt must be based on evidence, or the maxim of *in dubio pro reo* were not

[101] See, eg, Wang Guiwu (n 95); Luo Xinmin (n 82) 27.
[102] Zhang Jinjie, Zhang Tao and Wang Minyuan (n 83) 43–44.
[103] Ning Hanlin (n 84) 65; Zhao Guangyu (n 83) 24; Wang Bingxin (n 80) 12.
[104] Li Jingbing, 'Jiang wuzui tuiding yuanze zairu woguo xianfa (Write the Principle of the Presumption of innocence into the Chinese Constitution)' [1989] *Law Science* 4, 4–5.
[105] Wang Bingxin (n 80) 11–12.
[106] ibid 11–14.
[107] See CPL 1979, arts 1 and 2.
[108] Wang Bingxin (n 80) 12–13.

completely alien to China.[109] Therefore, these scholars believed that the presumption of innocence could theoretically operate in a socialist context and that some underlying values, principles and rules following from it were not completely alien to Chinese criminal justice.

Besides the views of rejection and advocacy, there was a third view, which called for a 'critical attitude' towards the presumption of innocence. According to Wang Xinqing, who supported the view of taking a 'critical attitude', the 'positive elements' of presumption of innocence were anchored in the fundamental principles of criminal justice; this includes the right to defence or the right to appeal. However, because the philosophical foundation of presumption of innocence was 'subjective idealism' and 'metaphysics', as opposed to dialectical materialism, it would be incompatible with the 'guiding thought and fundamental principles' of the Chinese criminal procedure, especially the principle of seeking truth from facts. Indeed, Wang believed that this would be the only right choice to establish a criminal justice system 'with Chinese characteristics'. Rights protection under the presumption of innocence, eg, right to refuse cooperation or *in dubio pro reo*, was too far reaching in the view of Wang, as the Chinese criminal justice would prioritise the interests of society and thus only protect the 'lawful rights' of accused persons, while he or she also had to bear 'procedural duties'.[110]

The next section examines this third view of assuming a 'critical attitude' towards the presumption of innocence, which increasingly gained prominence among legal scholars in China.

## C. 'Reasonable' and 'Unscientific' Elements of Presumption of Innocence

To maintain a 'critical attitude' towards the 'bourgeois' legal principle of presumption of innocence became a prominent slogan amongst Chinese academics in the late 1970s. As shown in the previous section, this view suggested the adoption of presumption of innocence, albeit with qualifications, as it would contain both some 'reasonable' and some 'unscientific' elements. To understand the scope of 'reasonable' elements, this section engages with the understanding of the notions of 'presumption' and 'innocence' in Chinese academic discourses. This section largely draws on Chen Guangzhong, who had also supported such a partial adoption of 'reasonable' elements of presumption of innocence and provided an early analysis of the different formulations of presumption of innocence. He examined three different expressions of presumption of innocence – Article 11(1) UDHR, Beccaria's formulation, and Article 14(2) ICCPR – arguing that those

[109] Ning Hanlin (n 84) 69–73.

[110] Wang Xinqing, 'Woguo xingshi susongfa buyi caiyong "wuzui tuiding" yuanze (The Incompatibility of the Principle of the "Presumption of Innocence" in our Criminal Procedure Law)' [1987] *Legal Studies & Research* 58, 59–60.

different formulations of presumption of innocence would contain both 'reasonable' and 'unscientific' elements. The socialist criminal justice system should adopt the 'spirit and essence', while rejecting the 'dregs'. In other words, only those elements that suit China's conditions should be adopted. At the time, Chen argued that only Beccaria's formulation is compatible with the Chinese criminal justice system. Although he was not against the idea of presumption of innocence, Chen was amongst those who took a 'critical attitude' towards presumption of innocence.[111]

Article 11(1) UDHR was controversially discussed because of the element of 'presumption', which – as already mentioned – was partly deemed 'subjective idealism', while others considered it to ensure objectivity in the criminal process:

> Everyone charged with a criminal offence shall have the right to be presumed innocent until proved guilty according to law in a public trial at which he has had all the guarantees necessary for his defence.
>
> 凡受刑事控告者，在未经获得辩护上所需的一切保证的公开审判而依法证实有罪以前，有权被视为无罪.[112]

According to Chen, this expression of presumption of innocence in Article 11(1) UDHR was theoretically and practically 'unscientific' and 'contradictory',[113] as the suspicion of the presumed guilt would be the starting point for the initiation of criminal proceedings. In China, a criminal case would have already gone through the pre-trial phases (ie, case opening, investigation, and public prosecution) before it formally enters the trial stage. In the pre-trial stages, the police and procuratorial organs would undertake enormous efforts to ascertain the case facts and determine whether the defendant is actually guilty. This would be reflected in CPL provisions, which require the establishment of main criminal facts for both the arrest (*daibu*) and prosecution of a person.[114] Put differently, Huang Huoqing, then Procurator-General of the SPP (1978–83), stressed that accuracy of case handling would amount to more than 95 per cent.[115] However, to put this into context, it should be observed that the percentage of suspects being held in custody under the measure of arrest at the time frequently exceeded 100 per cent because the percentage of persons being arrested was higher than the percentage of persons being prosecuted. For example, the figure stood at 138 per cent in 1986, meaning 355,603 people were arrested, but only 257,219 were formally prosecuted.[116] This clearly weakens the claim of accuracy. At the time, Chen nonetheless believed that the expression of presumption of innocence, as enshrined in the Universal Declaration, deviates from the empirical realities of the criminal

[111] Chen Guangzhong (n 79).
[112] See ibid 34.
[113] See also Art 9 of the French Human Rights Declaration.
[114] CPL 1979, arts 40 and 100.
[115] Chen Guangzhong (n 79) 34–35.
[116] *1987 Zhongguo falü nianjian (1987 China Law Yearbook)* (Beijing, Law Press China, 1987) 884.

justice process and hence conflicts with Chinese legislation.[117] The assumption that the use of compulsory measures was in conflict with the presumption of innocence had been made frequently.[118] On this basis, many scholars had rejected the presumption of innocence. In other words, those who are arrested and prosecuted are eventually found guilty, so how could they be presumed innocent? Indeed, this reveals a common misperception of the presumption at the time.

To explain this, it is necessary to go back to the arguments brought forward by the view of advocacy. Zhang, Zhang and Wang, who supported full endorsement, argued that it is precisely the 'presumption' of innocence that ensures objectivity in criminal proceedings. The presumption of innocence would be a means to counterbalance the presumed guilt and protect falsely accused persons. Furthermore, they emphasised that the 'lawful rights and interests' of the accused persons, including those caught red-handed, must be protected, regardless of whether they are guilty or not; and they argue that guilt must be determined in a legal process in accordance with the presumption of innocence.[119] Therefore, while Chen focused on the meaning of 'presumption', Zhang, Zhang and Wang tried to grasp the rationale of the presumption of innocence, ie, the broader principle dimension.

In the view of Chen, Beccaria's formulation of the presumption of innocence would be 'reasonable' and correspond to the reality of criminal justice. In *On Crimes and Punishments* (1764), Beccaria famously wrote:

> No man may be called guilty before the judge has reached his verdict.[120]
> 在没有作出有罪判决以前，任何人都不能称为犯罪.[121]

According to Chen, this expression of presumption of innocence indicates that, before a court has passed a guilty verdict, a person should not be considered a criminal. This formulation, which could also be found in Soviet law, would thus be 'reasonable', as it would imply that an accused person should not be *treated* as a criminal, nor that they be *assumed* innocent. From a legal perspective, this would be 'reasonable' because the courts, as the judicial organs of the state, would have the sole authority of adjudication. Chen believed that it would be a 'reasonable' expression of presumption of innocence not to regard a person as a criminal (in a legal sense) until a court has found that person guilty.[122] Chen was not the only scholar who thought that this formulation was less drastic. In a similar vein, Xu Yichu held that Beccaria's formulation of presumption of innocence was compatible with the Chinese criminal justice system.[123] The omission of the notion of 'presumption'

[117] Chen Guangzhong (n 79) 34–35.
[118] See also Zhao Guangyu (n 83) 24.
[119] Zhang Jinjie, Zhang Tao and Wang Minyuan (n 83) 39.
[120] Cesare Beccaria, *On Crimes and Punishments and Other Writings*, 4th edn (Cambridge, Cambridge University Press, 2003) 39.
[121] I use the Chinese translation as quoted by Chen Guangzhong (n 79) 35.
[122] Constitution 1982, art 127; CPL 1979, art 3; ibid.
[123] Xu Yichu (n 80) 87–92.

appears to have the decisive element. Beccaria's formulation might be described as what Stuckenberg has called 'innocence as the negation of a conviction of a criminal offence' in the absence of all conditions needed for legitimising the imposition of punishment.[124] The absence of the notion 'presumption' in Beccaria's formulation seems to have made this formulation more suitable for the Chinese context, at least in the view of scholars, as no recognition of a 'presumption' of innocence was needed. The denial of the use of a presumption indeed reflected the official position.

Chen Guangzhong also discussed Article 14(2) ICCPR with respect to the question of legal guilt and innocence:

> Everyone charged with a criminal offence shall have the right to be presumed innocent until proved guilty according to law.
>
> 受刑事控告之人，未经依法确定有罪以前，应假定其无罪.

Chen rightly found that this expression would suggest a person's *right* to be presumed innocent until proved guilty according to law, but he suggested that it was distinct from the expression in Article 11(1) UDHR. The ICCPR expression would not require that a person must be regarded as innocent until found guilty by a court; rather, it would emphasise that the criminal charges against a person must be proven, ie, legal guilt. This would mean that guilt must be proved 'beyond reasonable doubt' (*paichu heli huaiyi*) and that doubts must be 'in favour of the accused' (*in dubio pro reo*). Chen thus advocates the rules and principles flowing from the presumption of innocence.[125] In his view, the differences between Article 11(1) UDHR and Article 14(2) ICCPR appear to lie in the question of legal guilt. While he seems to view the formulation in the Universal Declaration as a factual legal fiction, the ICCPR expression appears to concern the issue of legal guilt.

However, it is important to mention that Chen's understanding of the different expressions of presumption of innocence is not in line with the thinking of the UDHR and the ICCPR. Even though he tries to highlight differences between Article 11(1) UDHR and Article 14(2) ICCPR, and whilst his understanding of the latter appears to lie in the question of legal guilt, the difference to Article 11(1) appears to be rather forced. In fact, the latter also speaks of 'proved guilty' and of 'charged with a penal offence'. Notwithstanding these consistent formulations referring to legal guilt in both the UDHR and the ICCPR, he believed that the UDHR expression of presumption of innocence created a presumption based on facts, which reflects a misperception of the presumption of innocence. As shown in chapter two, the presumption of innocence is not established on a factual basis, and it is not empirically based. The presumption of innocence is a foundational but rebuttable presumption, meaning a court must

[124] Carl-Friedrich Stuckenberg, 'Who Is Presumed Innocent of What by Whom?' (2014) 8 *Criminal Law and Philosophy* 301, 303–304.
[125] Chen Guangzhong (n 79) 36.

initially accept a certain proposition (proposition X) without requiring proof for that proposition.[126] The assumption of the presumption as a fiction or hypothesis is inconclusive, as criminal proceedings are indeed conducted based on the hypothesis that the defendant might be guilty. Recalling the principle dimension of presumption of innocence, the treatment of a person should be compatible with the possibility that this person might be innocent according to law (legal innocence).[127] For example, Article 9 of the French Declaration of 1789 suggests a broad approach to presumption of innocence by linking it to the protection of personal liberty.

Furthermore, it is difficult to grasp the rationale of presumption of innocence if insisting on what appear to be literal differences without applying a teleological interpretation. Besides, the purpose of comparing Beccaria's early formulation of 1764 with the formulations of the presumption in the UDHR (1948) and the ICCPR (1976) might also be debatable. In order to understand the moral underpinnings of presumption of innocence, the drafting and historical context of those provisions should be considered. However, it is equally important to bear in mind the Chinese backdrop against which Chen's discussion took place. Indeed, Chen did not reject the presumption of innocence in the abstract, and his analysis may also indicate a mediating approach to support the presumption of innocence without challenging the official discourse of not presuming anything.

The next section further elaborates on how the misperception of presumption of innocence as a factually based presumption has led to its rejection or narrowed its scope down to doubtful cases.

## D. Presuming Innocence but Only in Doubtful Cases?

This section deals with a more abstract academic discourse of what sort of 'innocence' ought to be 'presumed' in accordance with presumption of innocence. This question occupied a prominent place among legal scholars in the late 1970s, and it can shed light on common misperceptions at the time. As already mentioned in the previous section, many scholars construed the 'presumption' of innocence as a legal fiction – a 'presumption' (*tuiding*) of factual innocence – which contradicts the objective reality of criminal justice and thus ought to be rejected.[128] However, the recognition of *a* presumption in doubtful cases was popular among Chinese legal scholars because it was the only exit strategy to avoid being trapped in the infinite search for objective truth. Therefore, the misperception of the presumption of

[126] Pamela R Ferguson, 'The Presumption of Innocence and Its Role in the Criminal Process' (2016) 27 *Criminal Law Forum* 131, 135–137.

[127] Stefan Trechsel, *Human Rights in Criminal Proceedings* (Oxford, Oxford University Press, 2005) 154–156.

[128] See, eg, Luo Xinmin (n 82); Wang Guiwu (n 95).

innocence as a factual presumption narrowed the scope of application of presumption of innocence to 'doubtful cases' (*zui yi cong wu*).[129]

The notion of 'presumption' has given rise to controversies not only in the Chinese context. As shown in chapter two, we can find similar debates on the presumption of innocence in other systems, especially when expanding the scope of it to the pre-trial context. For example, a similar discussion had developed in the Soviet context about the precise meaning of the notion 'presumption'; the inaccurate translation of it, it was argued, had led to the rejection of presumption of innocence.[130] In China, since scholars focused on the literal meaning of 'presumption', the prevailing view regarded the 'presumption' as a legal fiction, a 'hypothesis' or 'assumption' (*jiading* or *jiashe*) as to the guilt or innocence of the accused. In the Chinese context, the understanding of the notion 'presumption' (*tuiding*) is thus of particular significance.[131]

According to Ning, a 'presumption' (*tuiding*) describes a condition where the law establishes a 'fiction of facts'. Ning apparently did not consider the conception of 'fiction' to be equivalent to the description of objective things; it would rather indicate that the law establishes a hypothesis applicable 'if the true circumstances of objective things or their conditions of existence are unclear'. The presumption of innocence was thus understood to establish a rebuttable legal fiction in cases of unclear objective truth, ie, a presumption of innocence in doubtful cases. In such cases, the accused would not be obligated to prove their own guilt or innocence. Where the innocence of the accused could not be proved, they should be acquitted, or the case should be sent back for supplementary investigation, in accordance with the principles of 'in favour of the accused' and '*in dubio pro reo*' that would flow from the presumption of innocence. Yet, the presumption of innocence would not preclude the use of coercive measures against an accused; as Ning points out, the 'presumption' (*tuiding*) of innocence should not be confused with the 'determination' (*rending*) of innocence.[132]

In the view of Ning, the fiction of presumption of innocence could not be used where criminals were caught red-handed.[133] Consequently, the presumption of innocence was not applicable in the case of the Gang of Four because innocence was incontestable. In other words, there was no doubt that a court, when examining the evidence, would reach the same epistemological conclusion regarding their

[129] Wang Guiwu (n 95) 2–3.

[130] George P Fletcher, 'The Presumption of Innocence in the Soviet Union' 15 *UCLA Law Review* 1203, 1211–1212.

[131] It might be worth noting that the Chinese word for 'presumption of innocence' (*wuzui tuiding*') was translated from the Japanese word '*muzainosuitei*', see Zhang Jinjie, Zhang Tao and Wang Minyuan (n 83) 34.

[132] Ning Hanlin (n 84) 65–68.

[133] Similarly, Zhao has argued that no 'presumption' is needed when a criminal is caught red-handed, or when the presumption is otherwise rebutted, because in such cases the evidence facts were clear. Therefore, at this point, the hypothesis of innocence would have been rebutted, see Zhao Guangyu (n 83) 23.

factual guilt and apply the law accordingly.[134] Therefore, if facts clearly point to the accused's guilt, the law cannot create a fiction of facts at the same time. Indeed, in a flawless system this would mean that factual guilt would correspond to legal guilt. Ning's presumption of innocence thus refers to a condition where the guilt or innocence of a person cannot be determined. However, it is not clear if Ning speaks of 'factual' innocence/guilt or of 'legal' guilt/innocence, even if here Ning seems to presume that factual innocence/guilt corresponds to legal guilt/innocence. The problem is that legal guilt/innocence must not necessarily correspond to real guilt/innocence, even if a criminal process aims to achieve the concurrence of legal guilt and factual guilt or legal innocence and factual innocence.[135]

The misperception of the presumption of innocence as a factually based presumption has been partly attributed to the Chinese translation of 'presumption'. Scholars have criticised the use of the word *tuiding* (presumption) instead of *jiading* (assumption). The use of *tuiding* would be misleading as it refers to a method of proof. A 'presumption' (*tuiding*) is factually based and thus is accurate in most circumstances; *jiading*, conversely, is not based on facts.[136] From this perspective, it would be unreasonable for a court to 'presume' (*tuiding*) the accused innocent, as there is both the possibility of guilt and innocence, not just the possibility of innocence. According to Lin, this is the main reason for the misconception of presumption of innocence in theory and practice because such a strong law was considered detrimental to fighting crime. Therefore, *tuiding* should be replaced by *jiading* (assumption), and an 'assumption of innocence' (*wuzui jiading*) should be included in the CPL as a fundamental principle of criminal proceedings. The '*wuzui jiading*' would be consistent with the meaning of the presumption of innocence, namely that the accused must be *assumed* innocent until proved guilty according to law.[137]

As for other reasons, the emphasis of the CPL 1979 on objective truth compromised the idea of legal guilt as it indicated that a judgment corresponds to 'real' (or 'material') guilt. In other words, the law equated 'real' ('factual') guilt with 'procedural' (or 'formal') guilt.[138] The misperception of the presumption of innocence as fact-based was also because the presumption of innocence was understood as the opposite of the presumption of guilt, which is not true. As Packer points out, the two presumptions have different rationales:

> [The presumption of innocence] means that until there has been an adjudication of guilt by an authority legally competent to make such an adjudication, the suspect is to be treated, for reasons that have nothing whatever to do with the probable outcome of

[134] Ning Hanlin (n 84) 65–68.
[135] Stuckenberg (n 124) 304.
[136] Xifen Lin and Casey Watters, 'Understanding the Presumption of Innocence in China: Institution and Practice' in Yun Zhao and Michael Ng (eds), *Chinese Legal Reform and the Global Legal Order: Adoption and Adaptation* (Cambridge, Cambridge University Press, 2018) 50–51.
[137] Lin Xin (n 47) 175–176.
[138] Stuckenberg (n 24) 441.

> the case, as if his guilt is an open question. The presumption of innocence is a direction of officials how they are to proceed, not a prediction of outcome. The presumption of guilt is basically a prediction of outcome. [...] The presumption of guilt is descriptive and factual; the presumption of innocence is normative and legal.[139]

Therefore, the presumption of innocence is not the opposite of the presumption of guilt. As shown in chapter two, the presumption of innocence applies to persons charged (or accused) of a criminal offence. It thus cannot be denied that a person is *presumed* to have committed a criminal offence, as reflected in such terms like 'suspicion'. Therefore, we are faced with a contradiction in terms because the person who is presumed guilty still has the right to be presumed innocent. However, as discussed, 'suspicion' merely implies that a person might be guilty – not that they are guilty.[140] This is further underlined by Packer's reference to the dimension of the principle of presumption of innocence as a guide for state officials, an invisible standard that underpins the entire proceedings and not a prediction of outcome.[141]

While it is not sensible to limit the presumption of innocence to doubtful cases, as it would mean that, in all other cases, factual guilt would correspond to legal guilt, it may be seen as a product of the time. Scholars seem to have confused 'factual' guilt with 'legal' guilt. Suppose a person surrenders themselves or is caught red-handed and confesses at the scene; this does not affect the validity of the principle of presumption of innocence, although it would be absurd to claim that this person could be innocent.[142] As outlined in chapter two, innocence can appear in different forms. It can describe a condition where a person is really innocent in the sense that they did not engage in the wrongful conduct or that their behaviour is in some way justified, or it can refer to the absence of a conviction. It may, moreover, refer to a condition where a person has been proven innocent ('proven innocence') or where it has not been possible to reach the standard of proof necessary to establish guilt ('failed proof of guilt' or 'formal innocence'). On a normative level, the latter two forms of innocence can be treated equally.[143]

The misleading notion of 'presumption' (*tuiding*) may be one explanation to explain the scepticism towards the presumption of innocence, but this issue received little attention in the academic discourses of the 1990s. The idea of legal guilt was moreover undermined by the CPL 1979 itself, which had emphasised objective truth. However, certain scholars believed that especially the evidence rules of the new law had enshrined the essence of the presumption of innocence. This view largely treated the presumption of innocence as synonymous with a rule of evidence.

[139] Herbert L Packer, 'Two Models of the Criminal Process' (1964) 113 *University of Pennsylvania Law Review* 1, 12.
[140] Trechsel (n 127) 154.
[141] Packer (n 139) 12.
[142] ibid.
[143] Stuckenberg (n 124) 303–304.

## III. Evidence Rules as an Expression of Presumption of Innocence

Many scholars in China took a narrow approach to presumption of innocence as a rule of evidence regardless of whether being an advocate or not. First, the burden of proof is to be placed on the prosecution. Second, guilt can only be determined if proof reaches the statutory standard required for conviction, meaning any doubts should be in favour of the accused ('*in dubio pro reo*'). Third, the accused should have the right to silence. Beyond this, however, there was no consensus among scholars on a set of rules and principles flowing from the presumption of innocence. These three elements indicate a strong focus on the evidential dimension, as outlined in chapter two, which is often confined to the trial setting. Interestingly, some scholars in China expanded this dimension to pre-trial proceedings.

Supporters of the presumption of innocence have pointed out that the CPL 1979 has not included an explicit provision on presumption of innocence but that the general sense of it could be found in the law. Early mentioned, Ning Hanlin suggested that the CPL 1979 evidence rules manifested the essence of presumption of innocence. This would include the rule of evidence-based judgments.[144] In a similar vein, Wang and Ma argued that this rule embodies the presumption of innocence, as it would focus on the issue of proof, and because evidence was an expression of objective facts, it would reflect materialism in criminal proceedings.[145]

However, it is important to note that some of them viewed the new evidence rules as being independent from presumption of innocence, thus not putting them under the label of presumption of innocence. One explanation for this approach is that it allowed supporting certain elements while rejecting other elements of the presumption of innocence. In other words, it was not necessary to position oneself with respect to the question of presumption of innocence while still being able to advocate certain evidential standards required for a guilty verdict. While the court is the last line of defence, and since the rule of evidence-based judgements and the court's exclusive adjudication power was not contested, the question is how these evidential elements would have expanded to pre-trial phases and provided for sufficient protection, especially in the phase of police investigation. For example, Zhang, Zhang and Wang were sceptical whether these rules can provide sufficient protection. They attributed the misuse of CPL 1979 provisions to the lack of an explicit provision on presumption of innocence, saying that coerced confessions and other unlawful means to obtain evidence would be rooted in the belief that evidence

[144] Ning Hanlin (n 84) 78–79.
[145] Wang Xiaohua and Ma Qingguo (n 84) 63–64.

must correspond with the 'objective case facts', neglecting the integrity of proceedings.[146]

The following sections examine the three evidential aspects in the CPL 1979 and the scholarly arguments for and against a manifestation of presumption of innocence. While the reality of criminal justice shall not be the main concern of the sections to follow, it should be observed that written law in China does not necessarily correspond to practice, and I will occasionally refer to practice.

## A. Burden of Proof

In academic discourse, the burden of proof has been identified as an element of the presumption of innocence. Indeed, it was relatively uncontested that the prosecution should generally bear the burden of proof in criminal cases.[147] Certain scholars invoked the presumption of innocence to justify this rule. According to Lin Xin, the evidentiary standard required for prosecution in Article 100 implicitly established the rule that the burden of proof rests on prosecution, which was required to reach the standard of 'clear facts and hard evidence' (*shishi qingchu, zhengju queshi, chongfen*) for public prosecution.[148] However, it should be observed that the CPL 1979 used the same evidentiary standard for the closure of criminal investigations, even though – strictly speaking – these two evidentiary standards do not fall within the scope of the standard of proof, which primarily applies to the trial procedure.[149]

Moreover, according to Xie Youping, to realise the burden of proof, the CPL 1979 established the prohibition against extortion of confessions by torture and the collection of evidence by unlawful means (Article 32) and emphasises the principle of 'stressing evidence, do not readily believe confessions' (Article 35), while any doubts about the guilt of the accused should be in favour of the accused.[150] These provisions were thus understood to emphasise the prosecution's duty to gather evidence. It is debatable whether those provisions implicitly established the burden of proof in criminal cases only on the basis that the accused could not be forced to make a confession (*argumentum e contrario*). They may also be read as rules regarding the means of producing evidence, as suggested by the wording of Article 32, which required the collection of both incriminating and exculpatory evidential materials.

Whether the CPL 1979 had fully placed the burden of proof on the prosecution remained indeed contested. For example, Wang Guiwu has argued that an accused

[146] Zhang Jinjie, Zhang Tao and Wang Minyuan (n 83) 44–45.

[147] Zheng Chengliang, 'Wuzui tuiding lun (On the Presumption of Innocence)' [1988] *Jilin University Social Sciences* 58, 63.

[148] See also CPL 1979, art 96 no 1; Lin Xin (n 47) 177–178.

[149] Chen Ruihua, *Xingshi zhengju faxue (Criminal Evidence Law)* (Peking, Peking University Press, 2014) 303.

[150] Xie Youping (n 27) 34.

has the right to a defence and to present evidence and that they thus have a certain duty to provide evidence.[151] Such a partial burden of proof has indeed often been found to stem from the duty to make truthful statements under Article 64(2). Regarding the rationale of the duty to make truthful statements, Luo Xinmin, who rejected the presumption of innocence, explained that it aims to facilitate the clarification of the true circumstances of a case. At the same time, the law would observe the right to testify and the right to defence, which Luo understands as a manifestation of socialist democracy in the criminal process.[152]

Others agreed that the accused must actively cooperate. According to Tang, in the pre-trial phase, a suspect is obliged to make a truthful confession or statement about the circumstances of the case,[153] while it is prohibited to falsify, conceal or destroy evidence.[154] In fact, at the investigation stage, the law required every unit and individual to hand over, upon the request by the police or prosecution, material or documentary evidence that could prove the guilt or innocence of the accused.[155] In case of refusal to cooperate, the investigatory organs could use measures such as searches and seizures to obtain such evidence.[156] By imposing a duty on the accused to cooperate with the investigation authorities, Tang appears to deny the accused the right to take such a passive role, which compromises the presumption of innocence but is consistent with the maxim of pursuing objective truth, which emphasises substantive fairness.

The duty of the suspect to answer truthfully relevant questions of the interrogators therefore indicates that the prosecution bears only an initial burden of proof.[157] Once the presumption of innocence was rebutted, the accused could decide whether to challenge the evidence presented by the prosecution.[158] Indeed, a 'false' burden of proof at trial is not uncommon. If the prosecution presents conclusive evidence at trial, the defendant may be implicitly required to challenge the evidence and thus present evidence at trial; such a scenario is not necessarily a violation of the presumption of innocence.[159] The crucial question is whether the burden of proof had shifted to the accused or whether the accused only had to bear an evidential burden of proof.[160]

However, the obligation of the accused to cooperate with the police to help them uncover the objective truth contradicts the very idea of presumption of innocence.

[151] Wang Guiwu (n 95) 2–3.
[152] Luo Xinmin (n 82) 30.
[153] CPL 1979, art 64.
[154] CPL 1979, art 34(3).
[155] CPL 1979, art 80.
[156] Tang Congyao, *Xingshi beigaoren de susong quanli he yiwu (The Procedural Rights and Duties of the Criminal Defendant)* (Fujian, Fujian Renmin University Press, 1982) 70.
[157] Zhao Guangyu (n 83) 23.
[158] Zheng Chengliang (n 147) 63.
[159] Magnus Ulväng, 'Presumption of Innocence Versus a Principle of Fairness, A Response to Duff' (2013) 42 *Netherlands Journal of Legal Philosophy* 205, 208.
[160] The evidential burden means 'adducing sufficient evidence on a point to make it a live issue', which is common when challenging the evidence presented by the prosecution, for instance, see Andrew Ashworth, 'Four Threats to the Presumption of Innocence' (2006) 10 *The International Journal of Evidence & Proof* 241, 269.

Under such circumstances, an accused person cannot choose to remain passive. Therefore, the claim that the law established the burden of proof in line with the presumption of innocence was weakened by requiring the accused to make truthful statements, despite slogans such as 'do not readily believe confessions'. As we will see in the next section, the duty to make truthful statements was especially contested in the context of the right to silence.

## B. A Right to Silence?

Another element to realise the burden of proof, scholars identified the right to silence. Even if accepting that the prosecution bears the burden of proof, the consequences of this rule were contested, as it raised the question of whether an accused should have a right to silence and a privilege against self-incrimination. I refer to a right or a privilege to emphasise that the scope of these safeguards was controversially discussed in the Chinese context. Ambiguous provisions in the CPL 1979 further triggered such controversies. As already indicated in the previous section, scholars in China argued that the duty to make truthful statements in Article 64(2) undermined any claims as regards a right to silence and a privilege against self-incrimination.[161] The duty had moreover generated controversies as regards its relationship with other CPL provisions, notably the earlier mentioned prohibition against extorted confessions.[162]

Competing values and interests obviously shaped arguments for and against the right to silence. While scholars like Long Zongzhi unconditionally advocated the inclusion of a right to silence,[163] Wang Bingxin took a more utilitarian approach, arguing that rules and principles flowing from presumption of innocence should be adopted only to the extent that they can facilitate police investigation. For example, it would be unreasonable to grant a suspect a 'right to lie', implying criminal non-liability for false statements, as this would not concern their 'lawful rights and interests'.[164] Such a middle ground seems to be reflected in these two seemingly contradictory CPL 1979 provisions that require cooperation while prohibiting coerced confessions.

Common argument choosing silence would violate the interests of the (innocent) 'people'[165] and only encourage suspects to refuse cooperation and thus obstruct the case handling, which was considered unacceptable in view of the unity of rights and duties. A right to silence would thus not only undermine the interests of society, but it would also, moreover, compromise the unity of rights and duties. Therefore, once factual guilt was established, in the view of the police,

[161] See, eg, Song Yinghui, *Xingshi susong mudi lun (Objective Theory of Criminal Proceedings)* (China Police University Publishing House, 1995) 117–120.

[162] CPL 1979, art 32.

[163] Long Zongzhi, 'Dui "wuzui tuiding" de xin siwei (New Thoughts on the 'Presumption of Innocence)' [1989] *Modern Law Science* 17, 17–19.

[164] Wang Bingxin (n 80) 11.

[165] CPL 1979, art 1.

a suspect was understood to be morally obliged to a duty to right their wrongs. Since Article 64(2) does not entail legal consequences, it was seen as a kind of expectation of cooperation rather than a legal obligation to do so. However, there was a legal consequence to silence in practice. While it was argued that a defendant could not be convicted based on their silence in the absence of incriminating evidence, the defendant's silence in the light of incriminating evidence would most certainly mean harsher punishment.[166] In fact, the CPL 1979 prohibited the conviction of a person solely on the basis of a confession, so a confession alone could not be considered to meet the statutory standard of proof for conviction.[167] However, in an interview with foreign scholars in the late 1970s (apparently before the passage of the 1979 CPL), a Chinese judge mentioned two conditions that were to be assessed in sentencing, meaning the seriousness of a crime and the willingness to make a confession.[168]

Leaving aside the evidential value and utility of a confession, recalling classical socialist attitudes towards law, a confession has an educational function with the aim of modelling a particular conception of man and the moral obligation of cooperation reflects the element of social involvement. These attitudes illustrate the ideological significance of a confession beyond its evidential value. Therefore, discourses about rights and duties should be considered in the context of broader moral and political discourses.[169] The understanding of rights and duties, or the qualities of the ideal socialist prototype, is moreover not static but may vary dependent upon the stage of development, as notably demonstrated by the class-consciousness. A relatively static attribute is the subordination to collective interests, which is enforced through coercion.[170] The duty to make truthful statements is an expression of all of this. The idea is that a person that is really innocent (ie, factually innocent) has nothing to hide, while a person that is factually guilty is expected to amend their wrongs to ensure a smooth processing of the case,[171] and a criminal is eventually to be reintegrated into the socialist society. This, of course, is irreconcilable with the prohibition against self-incrimination.

The point is that an admission of guilt in a socialist society has an educational function. It is seen as a tool to correct antisocial, ie, anti-socialist behaviour. From an ideological perspective, a confession is a form of 'exculpation' and a pledge of commitment to the socialist cause; it thus legitimises the Communist regime. This educational function of a confession is reflected in policies of the party-state,

[166] Zheng Chengliang (n 147) 63–64.
[167] CPL 1979, art 35.
[168] Angelika Glöckner and Sylvia Seelig, 'Falldarstellungen Und Ausführungen Zum Chinesischen Rechtssystem: Gespräch mit einem Richter Am Oberen Volksgericht in Shanghai' in Hans-Dieter Schwind and Konrad Wegmann (eds), *Studien zum chinesischen Recht* (Bochum, Studienverlag Dr N Brockmeyer, 1979) 9–13.
[169] Alan Hunt, 'Marxist Theory of Law' in Dennis Patterson (ed), *A Companion to Philosophy of Law and Legal Theory*, 2nd edn (Chichester, Blackwell Publishing, 2010) 352.
[170] Petev (n 34) 137–139.
[171] Song Yinghui (n 161) 118.

which have been partly translated into legislation. In fact, the entire sanctioning mechanism builds on the criminal policy of combining leniency with severity, which stresses the willingness to cooperate.[172] The duty to make truthful statements presupposes a hypothetical scenario in which both sides (investigation personnel and suspects) are honest and law-abiding persons. This explains why silence can never be in favour of the accused and why false statements were seen as unacceptable. A false statement violates the interests of society, the masses, as well as socialist policies and laws.

It should be borne in mind that voluntary cooperation does not violate the presumption of innocence. Regarding the question of voluntariness of confessions in the Chinese context, the prosecuting organs were obligated to review the lawfulness of the investigation activities when examining an arrest request or a case for prosecution.[173] However, the interrogation procedure was only rudimentarily regulated and largely in the hands of the police without external supervision, which made detecting unlawful behaviour difficult.[174] The CPL 1979 granted the right to bring accusations against the investigatory, prosecuting and judicial personnel for rights violations,[175] but apart from this, the law did not provide for a mechanism to exclude illegally obtained evidence.

In this context, it is important to note that advocates of presumption of innocence have viewed the right to defence as the 'mother' of all procedural safeguards to ensure the principle of equality of arms.[176] However, in the absence of a right to counsel in pre-trial proceedings, the suspect was in a weak position, especially in the phase of police investigation.[177] Even though the CPL 1979 did not explicitly prohibit such an early involvement, it indirectly did so by stipulating that a 'defendant' (meaning excluding suspects) has the right to defence.[178] Indeed, defence lawyers obtained access to the defendants only when a case reached the trial phase, granting them a few days to prepare for trial.[179] Furthermore, a defence counsel was obligated to ensure that the views of the defence were consistent with the facts of a case, that is, those facts established by the investigation authorities. As state employees, they were expected to seek truth from facts and to serve the socialist cause.[180] Given the imbalance of power between prosecution and defence, it is not surprising that the role of defence lawyers was marginalised in practice.[181]

[172] Chen Ruihua (n 149) 59.
[173] CPL 1979, arts 52 and 96(5).
[174] CPL 1979, art 62.
[175] CPL 1979, art 10(2).
[176] Zheng Chengliang (n 147) 62.
[177] Zhang Jinjie, Zhang Tao and Wang Minyuan (n 83) 44–45.
[178] CPL 1979, art 8.
[179] CPL 1979, art 110.
[180] Provisional Regulations of the People's Republic of China on Lawyers (adopted by the NPC Standing Committee on 26 August 1980, No. 5 [1980]) arts 1 and 3.
[181] Sida Liu and Terence Halliday, *Criminal Defense in China, The Politics of Lawyers at Work* (Cambridge, Cambridge University Press, 2016) 23.

The duty to make truthful statements was widely interpreted as a denial of silence and the prohibition against self-incrimination. Even if agreeing that cooperation was only a moral duty, in the absence of mechanisms to enforce silence, procedural safeguards, such as 'do not readily believe confessions', were largely empty promises. In reality, choosing silence was barely an option.

## C. The Maxim of 'in Favour of the Accused'

As a third evidential requirement required under the presumption of innocence, scholars have argued that guilt can only be established if the statutory standard of proof is met; otherwise, the maxim of 'in favour of the accused' ('*in dubio pro reo*') should be applied. When speaking of 'in favour of the accused' (*youliyu beigao*), the mainstream view at the time did not refer exclusively to *in dubio pro reo*. It was used more broadly to indicate that proceedings at the different procedural stages should be dropped in favour of the accused (*yi zui congwu*) if the evidentiary standard to proceed with a case could not be met. I will therefore use the broader notion 'in favour of the accused' or 'to favour the accused' when discussing issues related to the maxim in the pre-trial context. Chen Guangzhong believed that a presumption of innocence in doubtful cases would be in line with the Party's policy of the handling of contradictions, that is, the handling of a case in accordance with 'non-antagonistic contradictions', ie, 'contradictions among the people'.[182] Similarly others held that doubts should be dealt with based on the principle of seeking truth from facts. Echoing the official stance, doubtful cases should be first dealt with according to 'internal contradictions among the people', which would represent the fundamental interests of the people and 'favour the masses' (not the individual).[183]

While the CPL 1979 evidently required the existence of criminal facts to open a case,[184] the question arose of how to proceed with doubtful cases where the evidentiary standard for closing a criminal investigation and public prosecution could not be met; in such cases, the issue of 'in favour of the accused' became relevant. As already mentioned, the CPL 1979 established the evidentiary standard of clear facts and reliable and sufficient evidence for public prosecution without specifying this standard.[185] According to a commentary, this evidentiary standard requires that the criminal facts (including such facts as the time, place, execution, means, motive and aim of the crime) are established and that sufficient and reliable evidence can prove the guilt of the accused.[186] The law thus required the police and prosecution personnel to determine the factual guilt of a person (the

[182] Chen Guangzhong (n 79) 36; Cohen (n 43) 22–23.
[183] Xu Yichu (n 80) 87–92; Wang Bingxin (n 80) 11; Luo Xinmin (n 82) 29.
[184] CPL 1979, art 61.
[185] CPL 1979, arts 96(1) and 100.
[186] Fan Fenglin, *Xingshi susong fa (Criminal Procedure Law)* (China Police University Publishing House 1988) 195–196.

'true circumstances of a case') at the pre-trial stages.[187] In other words, the law required the investigation and prosecuting organs to reach the same standard of proof required for conviction.

To prevent pending cases, under the CPL 1979, the police and prosecuting organs were allowed to dismiss cases if the criminal investigation did not produce the statutory evidentiary standard needed to proceed with a case.[188] When examining a case for prosecution, the procuratorial organ was moreover competent to request supplementary investigation, ie, to send a case back to the police for further investigation.[189] However, the CPL 1979 did not explain how to proceed with a case if the supplementary investigation did not produce the evidentiary standard necessary for public prosecution. At the trial stage, courts were allowed to pass a verdict of not guilty due to doubts to prevent endless supplementary investigations.[190] Instead, it established the system of 'exemption from prosecution', which empowered the people's procuratorates to find a person guilty at the pre-trial stage and to exempt criminal punishment.[191] The pre-trial determination of guilt was an evident violation of the presumption of innocence. Moreover, it is debatable whether this provision was compatible with the exclusive adjudication power of the courts.[192] There may have been an agreement that doubts should be in favour of the accused, but the CPL 1979 lacked clear guidance on the handling of doubtful cases. The institution of exemption from prosecution was a convenient mechanism to deal with doubtful cases, but it was not 'in favour of the accused'. The pre-trial determination of guilt by the prosecuting organs undermines claims as to the application of presumption of innocence in Chinese criminal justice. Therefore, the maxim of 'in favour of the accused' remained a subjective and arbitrary standard at the discretion of the investigation and prosecution authorities.

Overall, it is debatable whether the CPL 1979 evidence rules could manifest the rule dimension of presumption of innocence. Owing to the absence of an explicit provision on the burden of proof in criminal cases, the right to silence, access to counsel in the pre-trial phases, and given the duty to make truthful statements, the few existing safeguards could not provide sufficient protection for suspects and defendants.

[187] CPL 1979, arts 96 and 100.

[188] CPL 1979, art 94.

[189] CPL 1979, art 99.

[190] Notice of the Supreme People's Court on Issuing Detailed Provisions Regarding the Procedure for Adjudication of Criminal Cases (21 March 1994, No. 4 [1994]) art 127; Reply of the Supreme People's Court on the Question of How to Apply the Law in Cases of Public Prosecution of First Instance Acquittals (Judicial Interpretation issued by the Supreme People's Court on 4 November 1989) para 3; Timothy A Gelatt, *Opening to Reform? An Analysis of China's Revised Criminal Procedure Law* (New York, Lawyers Committee for Human Rights, 1996) 64; Chen Guangzhong, Chen Ruihua and Tang Weijian, 'Shichang jingji yu xingshi susong faxue de zhangwang (Perspectives on Market Economy and Criminal Procedure Studies)' [1993] *China Legal Science* 3, 6.

[191] CPL 1979, arts 93 and 94.

[192] COL 1979, see art 1; Zhang Zetao, 'Zui cong panding yu wuzui tuiding (No Guilt without Judgment and the Presumption of Innocence)' [1999] *Journal of Xinjiang Police College* 34, 35.

## IV. Seeking Truth from Facts and the Presumption of Innocence

It is an inherent claim of the official doctrine of national conditions that the application of dialectical materialism ought to be a national condition. The introduction of the principle of seeking truth from facts was seen as a specification of the materialistic worldview. The CPL 1979 codified the principle of seeking truth from facts. It was understood as a basic principle of Chinese criminal proceedings, which had developed based on China's judicial practice and experience.[193] As the previous discussions have shown, many scholars believed that this principle would compromise or be incompatible with the principle of presumption of innocence.

However, Thieme has argued that the principle of seeking truth from facts could contribute to rising awareness among state officials of the fundamental difference between an accused and a convicted person. Thieme writes:

> [T]he fierce rejection of the "endless investigations" and the "groundless accusations" which had been the stock trade of the "Gang of Four" and the guarantees granted by the Code of Criminal Procedure which strengthen the position of the accused strongly indicate the tendency to discontinue the situation in which an accused was entirely at the mercy of the prosecution and the judiciary. Consequently, the nature of the information on the criminal process in China renders only one concluding statement possible, namely that the principle "The facts are the basis, the law is a yardstick" may prove to be of the same "real" significance in the practice of criminal law as the presumption of innocence. Or in other words, that the judicial cadres will remain aware of the fundamental difference between an accused and a convicted person, and guarantee that the accused is free to make his statements and never forced to incriminate himself. Let us hope so.[194]

Indeed, the inclusion of this guiding principle into the law has caused many debates as to its compatibility with the principle of presumption of innocence. Some have denied the compatibility of the two principles in the context of criminal justice in the abstract. Others saw no need for any presumptions. Luo Xinmin critically asked why China could choose only between the 'feudal' presumption of guilt and the 'bourgeois' presumption of innocence instead of introducing a new socialist principle, namely the principle of seeking truth from facts. Luo considered this socialist principle to be an immediate denial of both the presumption of guilt as well as the presumption of innocence.[195] The rejection of both in favour of the principle of seeking truth from facts was a dominant position among Chinese scholars in the late 1970s.

[193] CPL 1979, art 1. Wu Hongyao and Zhong Songzhi (n 59) 863 (Peng Zhen's Explanations to the CPL draft (1979), 26 June 1979); Xu Yichu (n 80) 12–14.
[194] Thieme (n 52) 289.
[195] Luo Xinmin (n 82) 27.

However, a minority view argued that these two principles are not per se incompatible or even called for the adoption of the presumption of innocence to implement the principle of seeking truth from facts.[196] The question is whether these two principles, indeed, do exclude each other or whether they can co-exist in the same system. In my view, they can co-exist, but the search for objective truth, as understood by official and scholarly discourses and which is an intrinsic part of the principle of seeking truth from facts, compromises the idea of legal truth if procedural safeguards are sacrificed to facilitate a search for the supposed objective truth. It is therefore necessary to explain the emphasis on objective truth in the CPL 1979.

## A. The Emphasis on Objective Truth in the CPL 1979

While the conception of criminal justice is understood to be derived from practical experience, the criminal justice process itself connects to dialectical materialism.[197] According to the epistemology of dialectical materialism, the question of guilt can only be resolved through a process of knowing that begins with the opening of a case and continues through all stages of the criminal justice process until the final judgment is announced – it is a process from perceptual to rational knowledge.[198] Scholars have described the emphasis on objective truth as a socialist characteristic of the criminal justice process, as materialism places great emphasis on uncovering the objective truth in criminal proceedings.[199] The CPL 1979 established an inquisitorial-style criminal trial that reinforces the goal of pursuing objective truth in criminal cases by emphasising the establishment of factual guilt.[200] Moreover, the idea of objective truth can be found throughout the CPL 1979, as notably stressed by the principle of seeking truth from facts ('taking facts as the basis, and law as the yardstick').[201]

According to a commentary to the 1979 CPL, the first part, 'taking facts as the basis', means that only objective facts can be used to decide a case. This interpretation is in line with Mao's understanding of objective truth based on the dialectical-materialist theory of knowledge. The objective existence of criminal facts was therefore seen as a demand of the theory of reflection in dialectical materialism. In the context of criminal justice, it has been argued that the use of evidence is the only appropriate means to establish case facts. Therefore, the main task of all procedural stages formally initiated with the filing of a criminal case was

[196] Zhang Jinjie, Zhang Tao and Wang Minyuan (n 83) 40–41; Ning Hanlin (n 84) 77–82.
[197] See CPL 1979, art 1.
[198] Xu Yichu (n 80) 13.
[199] Yin Bo and Peter Duff, 'Criminal Procedure in Contemporary China: Socialist, Civilian, or Traditional?' (2010) 59 *International & Comparative Law Quarterly* 1099, 1117.
[200] Alexander Shytov and Peter Duff, 'Truth and Procedural Fairness in Chinese Criminal Procedure Law' (2019) 23 *The International Journal of Evidence & Proof* 299, 300.
[201] CPL 1979, art 3.

to gather, examine, and use evidence to ascertain the facts of a case.[202] In order to uncover the true circumstances of a case, one must resort to evidence; scholars thus emphasised the need for a comprehensive investigation.[203]

The second part, 'taking the law as the yardstick', is understood to require the three agencies, meaning the police, the procuratorates, and the courts, to strictly abide by the law when establishing the criminal facts and deciding on how to handle a case.[204] On the basis of the established facts, therefore, the law was expected to be used as the yardstick to distinguish crimes from non-crimes, to determine the nature of a crime, to decide on criminal punishment, and so forth. It was thus understood to ensure a unified and correct application of the law.[205]

The aim to uncover the true circumstances of a criminal case was reflected in various provisions on evidence in the CPL 1979. For example, the law stressed that 'all facts that prove the *true* circumstances of a case' can be used as evidence.[206] Furthermore, it required the collection of various kinds of evidence to ensure objectivity, and it prohibited the collection of evidence by torture and coercion;[207] a false confession would have hindered the search for objective truth. As already mentioned, to reduce the evidential value of confessions, the CPL 1979 warned against the reliability of confessions and prohibited the conviction of the defendant in the absence of other evidence to prove their guilt.[208] Unsurprisingly, deliberate concealment of facts was strictly prohibited, while state officials were obliged to 'be loyal to the facts'.[209] To decide on a case, evidence must be assessed and facts must be proved; with objective facts as the standard, the facts must be clear and evidence must be reliable and sufficient. Chinese scholars therefore placed great emphasis on the theory of proof.[210] However, the CPL 1979 contained only a few provisions on evidence and no provisions on the procedural aspect of evidence collection, even if it prohibited extorted confessions and unlawful obtainment of evidence.[211]

Moreover, the CPL 1979 stipulated the need to determine and review the objective truth at every stage of the proceedings, stressing a prompt and correct ascertainment of the criminal facts.[212] Against this backdrop, state agencies focused on establishing the factual guilt of the accused as early as possible. In

[202] Filing a criminal case is the first stage of Chinese criminal justice, which is followed by the stages of criminal investigation, public prosecution, and the trial stages.
[203] Wu Lei, 'Xingshi susong fa de jiben yuanze (Fundamental Principles of the Criminal Procedure Law)' in Central Political-Legal Cadres School (ed), *Xingshi susongfa jiangyi (Handouts on Criminal Procedure Law)* (Beijing, Renmin University, 1981) 35–36.
[204] Xu Yichu (n 80) 12–14.
[205] Wu Lei (n 203) 36.
[206] CPL 1979, art 31.
[207] CPL 1979, art 32.
[208] CPL 1979, art 35.
[209] CPL 1979, art 33.
[210] Xu Yichu (n 80) 12.
[211] CPL 1979, arts 31 to 37.
[212] CPL 1979, art 2.

the phase of case opening, ie, the stage of initiation of criminal proceedings, the law referred to the accused as 'criminal suspect'; it also used this notion in the context of detention (*juliu*), a form of police custody that usually precedes pre-trial custody.[213] The interrogation of a suspect within 24 hours of their detention and arrest (*daibu*) was also aimed at clarifying whether there was a reasonable basis for presuming guilt.[214] In the subsequent pre-trial phases, however, the law referred to a criminal suspect as 'defendant'[215] or even as 'offender' (*renfan*),[216] indicating that the factual guilt of the accused was already ascertained at that point. The use of the custodial measure of arrest against an 'offender' presupposed that the main facts of a crime had been established,[217] which once again indicates that the determination of guilt was necessary to justify the arrest of an accused. In other words, the establishment of factual guilt was a precondition for arrest, which violates the principle of presumption of innocence. However, the reference to 'defendant' in the provisions on the interrogation procedure in the investigation phase was justified insofar as their guilt was already established, at least according to the logic of the law. In view of these provisions, Yi Xiaozhong rightly questioned the applicability and compatibility of presumption of innocence with China's criminal justice system, as, for example, the indication of 'offender' would be incompatible with the very idea of presumption of innocence.[218] It should be noted, however, that some Chinese scholars considered the terminology of the law appropriate, as the CPL 1979 would have separated 'defendants' from convicted 'criminals' and from ordinary citizens.[219]

Following the dialectical process of knowledge, knowledge must be studied again and again in order to exclude any possibility of errors. Therefore, a case can only move to the next stage if the true circumstances of a case have been determined;[220] otherwise, it must be dropped. To ensure that the knowledge of the case-handling authorities is consistent with the true circumstances of a case, the law requires that both the possibility of guilt and of innocence must be weighed.[221] Therefore, the police would only transfer a case to the procuratorial organs for prosecution if the investigation led to the conclusion that the suspect is guilty and should be prosecuted under the law.[222] As already mentioned, the CPL 1979 established the evidentiary standard of 'clear facts and reliable and sufficient

[213] CPL 1979, arts 41 and 59.
[214] CPL 1979, arts 44 and 51.
[215] CPL 1979, see especially arts 26 to 30, 32, 35, 36, 38 and arts 62 to 66.
[216] CPL 1979, arts 40, 45 and 79; Gelatt (n 23) 285–286.
[217] CPL 1979, art 40.
[218] Yi Xiaozhong, '"Wuzui tuiding" yuanze he woguo "daibu juliu tiaoli" daxiangjingting (The Gap between the Principle of the "Presumption of Innocence" and China's "Detention and Arrest Regulation")' [1980] *Chinese Journal of Law* 63, 63.
[219] Wang Xinqing (n 110) 60.
[220] CPL 1979, arts 96(1), 100 and 108. The law allowed for one appeal against the judgment of first instance, the second instance judgment is final, see CPL 1979, arts 129 to 143.
[221] CPL 1979, art 32.
[222] CPL 1979, art 93.

evidence' for prosecution.[223] Therefore, when handing over a case to the prosecuting authorities, the police had to make sure that the case facts were clear and the evidence conclusive. If the procurator found that this evidentiary standard had not been met, the investigation authorities could be asked to conduct a supplementary investigation.[224] This explains why the option of supplementary investigation had been included in the CPL 1979. Moreover, exemption from prosecution was a possible exit in doubtful cases, without suggesting any errors on the part of the state.

Against this backdrop, it makes sense that the defence was expected to support the search for the objective truth. A defence lawyer was required to 'prove' the innocence of the defendant in accordance with the *facts*, which seems to refer to 'real' innocence and undermines the right to defence.[225] However, according to Wang Bingxin, the accuracy of the dialectical criminal process is ensured by 'arguing back and forth' (*fanfu bianlun*), i.e. the prosecution and the defence could mutually expose the contradictions and examine materials and evidence to establish the facts on a reliable basis, which could gradually be further clarified to determine the proper handling of a case.[226] The supposed cooperation between the prosecution and the defence undermines the idea of adversarial criminal proceedings. However, following Mao's understanding of the dialectical-materialist theory of knowledge, failures are not taboo; they are part of the process – the phases of conception, judgment and inference – and can lead to success; failures can be remedied through further practical experience, provided the knowledge corresponds to objective reality.[227] To ensure that cases are handled correctly, the law has established an appeal system and a mechanism for trial supervision to rectify possible errors in the determination of objective truth.[228] Here the element of 'taking the law as the yardstick' serves as a corrective means.

Given the requirement to determine guilt in pre-trial proceedings, the principle of presumption of innocence could have counterbalanced the prosecution's pre-trial evaluation of evidence. It nonetheless remains problematic to require a standard of 'reliable evidence' before trial. In other words, it might be challenging to accept the presumption of innocence in a criminal justice system in which

> [...] the indictment is supposed to be based not merely on probable cause but on an inner conviction of guilt reached by the investigator and the procurator after an objective examination of all the evidence.[229]

[223] CPL 1979, arts 96(1) and 100.

[224] CPL 1979, art 99.

[225] CPL 1979, art 28. The reference to 'proving' (*zhengming*) the innocence of the accused was removed from the law in 2012.

[226] Wang Bingxin (n 80) 11.

[227] Mao Zedong (n 35) 306.

[228] CPL 1979, arts 148 to 150.

[229] Harold J Berman and John B Quigley, Jr., 'Comment on the Presumption of Innocence under Soviet Law' (1968) 15 *UCLA Law Review* 1230, 1236–1237.

This describes well the expectation imposed on state agencies in pre-trial proceedings. Leaving aside the empirical reality of criminal justice, the CPL 1979 itself already showed that the question of guilt was no longer seriously at issue at the trial stage. The investigation and the prosecuting organs had already determined guilt in the pre-trial proceedings. However, the question of whether the presumption of innocence can operate along the principle of seeking truth from facts has not yet been answered.

## B. The Question of Compatibility of the Two Principles

Regarding the compatibility of the two principles, Gelatt concluded in the early 1980s that the emphasis on objective truth in Chinese criminal procedure seems to deny presumption of innocence.[230] Yet, Chinese scholars were divided on this issue. Those scholars who supported a critical attitude towards the 'bourgeois' presumption of innocence did not question the legitimacy of the principle of seeking truth from facts in the criminal process, but they tried to reconcile these two principles. For example, Zhao Guangyu argued that the principle of seeking truth from facts was no 'panacea'. While the CPL 1979 only emphasised the need to furnish 'evidence',[231] it would not specify who should be obliged to do so, and the principle of seeking truth from facts was of no help in this regard. As a solution, the presumption of innocence would imply a set of underlying principles and rules on evidence in criminal proceedings.[232] Here, Zhao stresses the complementary function of presumption of innocence. Indeed, the presumption of innocence was seen as a solution to the question of how to deal with doubtful cases. In the view of Chen Guangzhong, the dilemma is that the principle of seeking truth from facts was rather abstract with limited practicability. The presumption of innocence would be a useful tool to curb the infinite search for objective truth, as it implied a rule on how to deal with doubtful cases.[233]

The aim of objective truth faced several practical problems. When the epistemological process had reached an impasse, in the sense that the case had entered an infinite process of truth-seeking because it was impossible to reach a definitive conclusion regarding guilt or innocence, cases were pending infinitely. Indeed, critics who rejected the presumption of innocence because of the principle of seeking truth from facts faced the dilemma that an acquittal due to reasonable doubts would have violated the latter.[234] The goal of absolute accuracy and thus objective truth is reflected in the traditional slogan 'do not wrong a good person, do not free a bad person' (*bu wang bu zong*'), which is hostile to the maxim of *in*

[230] Gelatt (n 23) 259–316.
[231] CPL 1979, art 35.
[232] Zhao Guangyu (n 83) 24.
[233] Chen Guangzhong (n 79) 36.
[234] Zheng Chengliang (n 147) 58–59.

*dubio pro reo*.[235] However, the CPL 1979 did not, at least in theory, allow for an infinite search for the objective truth, as it set time limits for various stages of the criminal proceedings, including investigation and prosecution.[236] In a sense, by setting time limits, it restricted the search for the true circumstances of a case, and it could therefore be argued that the law itself compromised the principle of seeking truth from facts. This may explain why scholars advocated the presumption of innocence, as well as other safeguards, to fill the gap if seeking truth from facts no longer worked. The principle of presumption of innocence was thus not understood as a substitute for the principle of seeking truth from facts but as a complement.[237]

However, not all scholars embraced the compatibility of the two principles. As already mentioned, for certain scholars, both the presumption of guilt and the presumption of innocence would lead to subjectivism, implying either the guilt or the innocence of a person, and were thus no solution. Instead, it would be crucial to maintain an objective attitude in criminal proceedings.[238] It was emphasised that the principle of presumption of innocence was fundamentally different from the principle of seeking truth from facts in that it operated on the basis of facts rather than assumptions.[239] This view underlines an important point: the principle of seeking truth from facts aims to establish the real guilt/innocence of a person, while it is not concerned with legal guilt or innocence. The search for the objective truth implies that substantive fairness or truth is more important than procedural fairness or truth. The CPL 1979 had placed great emphasis on objective truth, which seemed to leave no room for legal guilt and thus a presumption of legal (procedural) innocence. Here, tensions between the two principles become tangible.

As the previous discussions have shown, one view rejected the presumption of innocence based on a supposed contradiction with the empirical reality of criminal justice, as they had interpreted it as a presumption of 'real' innocence.[240] However, if one takes the maxim of seeking truth from facts seriously, it would imply an objective procedure based on facts that exist independently, and through a dialectical process these facts are discovered. This process would then continue until the knowledge corresponds with the objective reality; this process is reflected in the different stages of the criminal proceedings. The uncovering of objective truth thus leads to the resolution of criminal cases. Therefore, the rationale of this maxim is to ensure accurate outcomes by taking an objective attitude towards criminal cases and leaving the question of guilt or innocence open, which indicates the

[235] Tian Wenchang, 'Zouchu xingshi susong linian de shi da wuqu (Overcoming Ten Major Misconceptions of Criminal Justice)' (*Caixin*, 15 September 2020) opinion.caixin.com/2020-09-15/101605412.html accessed 4 May 2020.

[236] CPL 1979, arts 92 and 97.

[237] Chen Guangzhong (n 79) 36; Zhao Guangyu (n 83) 24; Ning Hanlin (n 84) 77–82; Zheng Chengliang (n 147) 59–61.

[238] Wang Guiwu (n 95) 1–5.

[239] Xu Yichu (n 80) 13.

[240] Wang Guiwu (n 95) 2–3.

denial of presuming both guilt and innocence. However, this illustrates the fallacy of the ivory tower of objectivity and objective truth, even if it may be a noble undertaking.

Of course, every criminal case is a search for the truth. This is reflected in the claim that no innocent person should be punished. The question is what that truth is supposed to be, whether it ought to be objective truth or legal truth. If a trial was merely a search for the truth, the defendant could not be acquitted if guilt could not be proven beyond reasonable doubt, because then it would fail to achieve its objective.[241] There are different approaches to 'truth'. While inquisitorial systems are more outcome-oriented, that is, a judgment is accepted as true if it is believed to correspond to reality. Adversarial systems, on the other hand, view the criminal process as a competition. What is accepted as truth is agreed upon through discourse between the parties – a process governed by rules to ensure fairness. Legal systems, however, are much more complex than this, and it would be wrong to claim that adversarial systems do not strive for objective truth and inquisitorial systems respect the limits of objective truth-finding by, eg, respecting the right to silence.[242]

Moreover, producing fair and just outcomes is not just about fact-finding. While the investigation phase is primarily concerned with fact-finding, the presumption of innocence must also be applied at the trial stage – especially the evidential dimension of it – and the defendant must be presumed innocent until proven guilty according to law.[243] As Ho has noted:

> The presumption of innocence is not a statement of probability but a statement of political conviction. If the criminal trial is to stay true to its function as a check on the executive, the starting point cannot be one of prima facie credence to the prosecutor's allegations.[244]

Theoretically, the presumption of innocence could operate in parallel to the principle of seeking truth from facts, because it functions as a moral legal principle that explains the conditions under which a person can be found guilty. The supposed national condition of applying the materialistic principle of seeking truth from facts does not prevent the application of the presumption of innocence. However, on a normative level, the aim to find the objective truth in every criminal case to establish factual guilt seems difficult to reconcile with the presumption of innocence, which is about legal guilt and accepts it as truth. In other words, the presumption of innocence sets limits to the search for objective truth. Therefore, although these

[241] Hock Lai Ho, 'The Presumption of Innocence as a Human Right' in Paul Roberts and Jill Hunter (eds), *Criminal Evidence and Human Rights, Reimagining Common Law Procedural Traditions* (Oxford, Hart Publishing, 2012) 272.

[242] Thomas Weigend, 'Should We Search for the Truth, and Who Should Do It?' (2011) 36 *North Carolina Journal of International Law and Commercial Regulation* 388, 393–395.

[243] Ho (n 241) 272–273.

[244] ibid 273.

two principles are not conceptually in conflict, there may be tensions at the normative level that affect the underlying values of the criminal justice system.

Therefore, Chinese scholars have invoked the alleged incompatibility between these two principles, which manifest the two different conceptions of legal guilt and factual guilt. The alleged incompatibility has served as a powerful defensive justification for the denial of the moral authority of the presumption of innocence, ie, the recognition of the principle of presumption of innocence and its related positivistic conception of the conditions under which a person can be considered legally guilty. We should thus recognise that tensions might arise between the presumption of innocence and the aim of pursuing objective truth when the law sacrifices individual safeguards to facilitate the search for the objective truth, especially in cases where factual guilt (and thus supposed objective truth) is established at an early stage. In such a scenario, the criminal process is no longer subject to the constraints imposed by the presumption of innocence to ensure that punishments are imposed legitimately.

## V. Personal Liberty and the Assumption of Factual Guilt

In the early reform era, the protection of personal liberty was of particular concern in light of the rampant rights violations, especially the arbitrary and unlawful deprivations of personal liberty that had occurred during the Cultural Revolution (1966–76), and the Party leaders made genuine efforts to ensure better safeguards.[245] However, scholars were less concerned with the application of the presumption of innocence in this context as an indicator of the treatment of a person in accordance with this principle, even if many scholars recognised that the presumption of innocence regulates the legal status of the accused in criminal proceedings. As has been explained in chapter two, the interference with personal liberty, most notably in the form of pre-trial detention, can serve as an indicator for the operation of the presumption of innocence in any criminal justice system, as the use of such coercive measures against an accused person must be consistent with the assumption of innocence.[246] This section discusses the normative framework for interferences with personal liberty under the CPL 1979, focusing on the most intrusive measures of criminal detention (*xingshi juliu*), 'detention' and arrest (*daibu*), which lead to pre-trial custody to examine whether deprivations of personal liberty were based on the assumption of innocence.

Shortly after the passage of the CPL 1979, the Constitution of 1982 was enacted, which enshrined the fundamental right to personal liberty. This was an important

[245] Qianfan Zhang, *The Constitution of China: A Contextual Analysis* (Oxford, Hart Publishing, 2012) 197.

[246] Thomas Weigend, 'Assuming the Defendant Is Not Guilty: The Presumption of Innocence in the German System of Criminal Justice' (2014) 8 *Criminal Law and Philosophy* 285, 287–288.

moment. Before discussing the CPL 1979 provisions in detail, some observations should be made on the fundamental right of personal liberty. Article 37(1) of the Constitution is a general provision providing that personal liberty is 'inviolable'. Paragraphs 2 and 3 of Article 37 stipulate the following safeguards and limitations of personal liberty:

> No citizen may be arrested [*daibu*] except with the approval or by decision of a people's procuratorate or by decision of a people's court, and a public security organ must make arrest. Unlawful detention [*jujin*] or deprivation or restriction of citizens' freedom of the person by other means is prohibited, and unlawful search of the person of citizens is prohibited.

In the Chinese context, 'arrest' (*daibu*) is a term with a very narrow meaning. It does not involve the deprivation of personal liberty by the state power in non-criminal cases or administrative detention. Therefore, it excludes safeguards against other forms of deprivation of personal liberty, such as administrative and criminal detention or forced drug rehabilitation, even if paragraph 3 prohibits unlawful detention (*jujin*) or the deprivation or restriction of personal liberty in general.[247]

Paragraph 2 does not provide a 'positive requirement of release';[248] that is, it does not contain the idea that the deprivation of personal liberty should be the exception by, for example, granting a constitutional right to bail. It stipulates the formal requirement that an arrest must be lawful, both substantially and procedurally, with the approval or by the decision of a procuratorate or court.[249]

It should be observed that the CPL 1979 established a system of mutual coordination and mutual restraints (*huxiang peihe, huxiang zhiyue*) among the three agencies[250] that ought to ensure checks and balances.[251] Mutual restraint is reflected in the supervision powers of the procuratorial organs to oversee the legality of criminal investigations,[252] the courts at the corresponding level, and their power to protest judgements and the legality of judgments.[253] In the context of compulsory measures, the supervisory power to oversee the legality of investigation should

247 Chen Guangzhong, *'Gongmin quanli he zhengzhi quanli guoji gongyue yu woguo xingshi susong' (International Covenant on Civil and Political Rights and Criminal Process in China)* (Beijing, The Commercial Press, 2005) 134.

248 Body Principles for the Protection of All Persons under Any Form of Detention or Imprisonment 1988 [UNGA res. 43/173] Principle 39.

249 CPL 1979, art 3.

250 Constitution 1982, art 135; CPL 1979, art 5.

251 Xie Youping, 'Lun gongmin renshen ziyouquan de xianfa baozhang yu sifa baohu – yi xingshi sifa wei zhongxin (On the Constitutional Guarantees and Judicial Protection of Citizens' Right to Personal Liberty – with a Focus on Criminal Justice)' (2013) 11 *Shanghai Jiaotong Journal* 10, 13–16.

252 CPL 1979, art 96, no 5; Detailed Rules for the Criminal Prosecution Work of the People's Procuratorate (for Trial Implementation) (issued by the Supreme People's Court on 10 December 1991) art 4, no 4.

253 CPL 1979, arts 130 and 149; Elisa Nesossi and Susan Trevaskes, *Procedural Justice and the Fair Trial in Contemporary Chinese Criminal Justice System* (Leiden, Brill, 2018) 34.

serve as an effective means of limiting the powers of the public security organs in the absence of judicial oversight.

The CPL 1979 divided the criminal process into three separate stages: investigation, prosecution and trial. The police almost monopolise the phase of investigation, during which compulsory measures against suspects may be applied.[254] It moreover established five different types of compulsory measures that can be employed by the three agencies: summons and forced appearances (*chuanhuan, juchuan*),[255] release on guarantee (*qubao houshen*, 'bail'),[256] residential surveillance (*jianshi juzhu*),[257] criminal detention (*xingshi juliu*), and arrest (*daibu*).[258] The law did not establish pre-trial detention as an independent measure. Even though the CPL 1979 does not use the term 'remand custody', the word 'custody' (*jiya*) itself occurs many times in the code and refers to the compulsory measures of detention or arrest that might be applied against a criminal suspect or defendant during criminal proceedings.[259] However, custody is not an independent measure. In China, it is understood to be the consequence of detention and arrest.[260] At the pre-trial stages, the procuratorial organs are authorised to approve arrest. At the stage of formally charging a criminal suspect or at the trial stage, procuratorates and courts decide on arrest.[261]

Regarding less intrusive measures, the CPL 1979 empowered the police to summon (or compel the appearance of) a suspect, as well as to enforce the measure of detention in criminal investigations. However, the law did not regulate time limits for summonses, it merely stated that a person may be summoned to a designated place for questioning or may be questioned in their residence.[262]

[254] CPL 1979, arts 3 and 58, no 1.

[255] CPL 1979, art 38.

[256] CPL 1979, art 38.

[257] ibid; it may be worth noting that house arrest has generally been qualified as a measure depriving personal liberty, see Sangeeta Shah, 'Detention and Trial' in Daniel Moeckli and others (eds), *International Human Rights Law*, 3rd edn (Oxford, Oxford University Press, 2017) 254.

[258] The Guomindang government (GMD) produced the authentic Chinese language versions of the ICCPR, as adopted by the UN General Assembly in 1966, whereas the PRC's version has not been formally adopted thus far, see James D Seymour and Patrick Wong, 'China and the International Human Rights Covenants' (2015) 47 *Critical Asian Studies* 514, 514–515. According to the ICCPR, 'arrest' is an action and only temporarily, whereas 'detention' is a condition. In both Chinese versions of the UDHR and the ICCPR 'arrest' is translated as '*daibu*', detention as '*jujin*'; while in the GC No. 35 detention is translated as '*juliu*'. The Chinese version of the GC No. 35 defines 'arrest' (*daibu*) as 'any apprehension of a person that commences a deprivation of liberty', the term 'detention' (*juliu*) is understood to mean 'the deprivation of liberty that begins with the arrest and continues in time from apprehension until release', see General comment No. 35, Article 9 (Liberty and security of person) (GC No. 35) 2014 (UN Doc CCPR/C/GC/35) para 13.

[259] Guo Bing, 'Jiya biyaoxing shencha zhidu shijian yunxing shenshi (Examination on the Practical Operation of the Custody Necessity Examination System)' [2016] *Criminal Science* 61, 62.

[260] Lu Jin, 'Qianxi gongmin ji zhengzhi quanli guoji gongyue zhong "arrest" yu woguo daibu zhidu de chayi – jian yi "arrest" de fanyi (Research on the Differences between "Arrest" under the ICCPR and the Chinese System of "Arrest")' [2012] *Law Science* 124, 135.

[261] CPL 1979, arts 3 and 39.

[262] CPL 1979, art 63.

The law authorised the police to enforce the measure of detention in the phase of criminal investigation without external (judicial) supervision.[263] The requirement of producing warrants was new. Under the 1954 and 1979 DAR, the police were not required to do this when detaining a suspect, and detention was permissible under exigent circumstances.[264] In contrast to the DAR of 1954 and 1979, the CPL 1979 first established the requirement to produce a detention warrant,[265] but it integrated the time limits and the scope of criminal detention as provided for by the DAR 1979.[266] The CPL 1979, moreover, regulated the conditions under which an initial detention of an 'active criminal deserving arrest' was permissible. Targets could be divided into three broader categories: (1) active criminals/major suspects, (2) (quasi-) flagrant criminals, and (3) people who may obstruct the investigation.[267]

Under the 1979 CPL, the police were required to submit a request to the procuratorial organ for arrest upon detention within three days; this time limit could be expanded to four days. The procuratorate then had to decide on arrest within three days whether to approve it, resulting in a total of ten days of criminal detention. The law provided that the detainee or his family could demand the release of a person if the police exceeded the time limit of ten days,[268] but it did not provide for an appeal mechanism to a judicial authority if such a request was denied.[269] However, these time limits were more generous than those stipulated under the DAR 1954, which required the police to inform the procuratorate at the same level of the facts of the case and the reasons for the detention within 24 hours of the detention of a person. The procuratorial organ had to decide on the arrest within 48 hours of receiving the notification, without specifying the arrest conditions.[270]

While the DAR 1954 did not contain any evidentiary conditions of arrest, the CPL 1979 established three conditions that had to be cumulatively met in order to justify an arrest: the establishment of 'main criminal facts' (*requirement of evidence*), a possible prison sentence (*requirement of sentence*), and the necessity of arrest because of a danger to society (*requirement of necessity*).[271] In other words, in cases of non-social danger, the measures of bail or residential surveillance could be applied. In addition, the law stipulated that 'criminals' who are ill or women who are pregnant or breastfeeding, or if the evidence was not sufficient to justify an arrest, should

[263] CPL 1979, art 50.
[264] DAR 1954, art 5; DAR 1979, art 6.
[265] CPL 1979, art 43.
[266] DAR 1979, arts 6 and 8.
[267] CPL 1979, art 41 No. 1 to 7.
[268] CPL 1979, art 48.
[269] Timothy A Gelatt, *Criminal Justice with Chinese Characteristics: China's Criminal Process and Violations of Human Rights* (New York, Lawyers Committee for Human Rights, 1993) 16.
[270] DAR 1954, art 11.
[271] CPL 1979, art 40; DAR 1979, art 3.

be placed under the less intrusive measures of bail or residential surveillance.[272] However, neither the CPL 1979 nor any other relevant regulations contained formal requirements for the measures of bail and residential surveillance.

Regarding the time limits of arrest, the CPL 1979 stipulated a maximum period of two months for 'investigation custody', but allowed a possible extension of one month in 'major and complex cases'.[273] The law did not explicitly refer to the time limits of custody in the later phases of proceedings, but it can be assumed that they are identical with the time limits for the prosecution in the first instance and second instance, each of which shall not exceed one month, though extensions in these phases of up to one month were also possible.[274]

Indeed, the CPL 1979 regime of compulsory measures soon encountered several issues in practice. The provisions on arrest generated controversy regarding their compatibility with the presumption of innocence, as the establishment of factual guilt was a precondition for arrest. Scholars have held that the evidentiary standard of 'clear main facts' to get an arrest approved was too high to be met in practice.[275] The police, moreover, suggested that the maximum period of ten days to request the arrest of a detainee under the CPL 1979 was too tight in practice.[276] The police frequently circumvented the CPL time limits and instead applied extra-judicial detention measures, such as the administrative measure of 'detention for investigation' (*shourong shencha*).[277] It should be kept in mind that there was a shortage of trained personnel at the time and the implementation of these new provisions had just begun.[278] It is therefore hardly surprising that the vague provisions and legal loopholes, combined with lacking external supervision, provided a fertile ground for abusing measures or even ignoring the prescribed procedure altogether in order to meet the expectation of efficient crime control. In fact, the Supplementary Regulations on Deadline in Handling Criminal Cases of 1984, issued shortly after the CPL 1979, soon provided for extensions and recalculation of the time limit for custody in criminal proceedings.[279]

In the 1990s, the problem of custody became increasingly visible. The measures of detention and arrest had formed a symbiotic relationship between them due to

[272] CPL 1979, arts 40 and 44.

[273] CPL 1979, art 92.

[274] CPL 1979, arts 97, 99, 125 and 142; Central Political-Legal Cadre School, Department of Criminal Law and Criminal Procedure Law, *Zhonghua Renmin Gongheguo xingshi susong fa jiangyi (PRC Criminal Procedure Law Handout)* (Amherst, Mass Publishing House, 1981) 162.

[275] see CPL 1979, art 40; Gelatt (n 269) 13–14; Yang Yi, 'Yi shehui weixianxing shencha wei hexin de daibu tiaojian chonggou – jiyu jingyan shishi de lilun fansi (Reconstruction of Arrest Conditions centred on the Examination of Social Danger – a Theoretical Reflection based on Empirical Facts)' [2018] *Journal of Comparative Law* 130, 131.

[276] Gelatt (n 269) 13–14; Mike McConville and (with Satnam Choongh, Pinky Choy, Dick Wan, Eric Chui, Wing Hong, Ian Dobinson and Carol Jones), *Criminal Justice in China: An Empirical Inquiry* (Cheltenhman, Edward Elgar, 2011) 5.

[277] Yang Yi (n 275) 131.

[278] Leng and Chiu (n 14) 215.

[279] Supplementary Provisions on Time Limits for the Handling of Criminal Cases (Adopted by the NPC Standing Committee on 7 July 1984, No. 15 [1984]).

the absence of proper checks and balances. The procuratorial organs remain the most important actors as regards arrest approvals.[280] Although courts can decide on arrest, this was and is rarely the case in practice. Research on the ground has shown that most persons are taken into custody at the pre-trial stage after being initially criminally detained.[281] The CPL 1979 did not provide a legal basis for effectively challenging deprivations of personal liberty in criminal proceedings but stated that a criminal suspect could only demand their release if the time limit of provisional criminal detention had been exceeded.[282]

Despite all these shortcomings, unlike other fair trial safeguards, the right to personal liberty was not contested, meaning the idea that a person should not be arbitrarily and unlawfully deprived of their personal liberty. The right to personal liberty was enshrined in the Constitution, and the law established some minimum personal liberty safeguards. Admittedly, the interpretation of the right to liberty, the concrete conditions under which a person (an 'ordinary' criminal suspect) should be lawfully deprived of their liberty in criminal proceedings, remained controversially discussed among theorists and practitioners. As shown, it was widely acknowledged that these few safeguards were not observed in reality.[283] Chapter four will show that personal liberty safeguards became one of the main concerns in the 1990s.

Simply looking at the 1979 CPL, the high evidentiary standards required for an arrest indicate that the law intended to prevent the arrest of an innocent person, even if these requirements were not met in reality. It could be argued the evidentiary standard for arrest and other CPL provisions establishing some personal liberty safeguards reflect the idea that deprivations of personal liberty should be constrained by certain legal conditions in order to prevent arbitrary and unlawful inference with this right.[284] From this point of view, it could be argued that the evidentiary standard as well as other conditions reflects an aspect of the principle of presumption of innocence. However, the dimension of the principle of presumption of innocence was insufficiently manifested in other CPL 1979 provisions to maintain the claim that the law reflected the presumption of innocence in relation to the right to personal liberty in the sense that the use of coercive measures must be consistent with the assumption of the innocence of the accused person. The conditions for deprivations of personal liberty remained vaguely contoured, and the law did not provide for a legal remedy to challenge deprivations of personal liberty. This imbalance of powers between the prosecution and the defence was exacerbated by the absence of other safeguards, such as a right to silence or access to legal counsel, in the phase of the criminal investigation.

280 CPL 1979, art 39.

281 Chen Guangzhong (n 247) 136; Xie Xiaojian, 'Lun woguo xingshi juliu de jinjixing yaojian (On the Requirement of Exigency of Criminal Detention in China' [2016] *Modern Law Science* 110, 113.

282 CPL 1979, art 48(2).

283 Gelatt (n 269) 12–13.

284 Leng and Chiu (n 14) 87.

## VI. Conclusion

The tentative discourses on presumption of innocence in the Mao era were largely politicised and short-lived, and only few scholars dared to openly show support for such 'bourgeois' safeguards. The early reform commended the second phase of presumption of innocence discourses in China. Even if initially still being confronted with the two opposing views of acceptance and rejection in academic circles, and even though the official discourse was opposed to using any presumptions, academic discourses would soon become more pluralistic and nuanced against the backdrop of constructing a legal system and in the light of the CPL 1979. As shown, some scholars proposed a critical engagement with presumption of innocence, some saying that especially the new rules on evidence were an expression of presumption of innocence, even if the law had not adopted the label of presumption of innocence. The latter was still met with scepticism, partly due to misconceptions of the presumption of innocence as factual legal fiction. Yet, it is fair to say that the scholars, who were also recovering from the Mao era, showed great interest in and fascination for the presumption of innocence.

However, the CPL 1979 was far from meeting presumption of innocence standards, and the reality of criminal justice was in stark contrast to the thin legal promises of the CPL 1979. After the law was put into effect in 1980, the three agencies reported to the National People's Congress the state of implementation, and it was anticipated that nationwide implementation could be achieved by the end of the following year.[285] However, earlier that year and again in September 1981, it authorised the people's congresses at the provincial level to extend the statutory time limits for case-handling,[286] leading to major regional discrepancies in the handling of criminal cases.[287] Indeed, in contrast to orthodox Marxian thinking that crime will disappear with the development of the economic base, socio-economic changes in China had led to growing crimes, and the threat of social instability soon became the overriding concern of the Party leaders. In July 1983, Liu Fuzhi, then Minister of Public Security, criticised the lenient treatment of criminals and voiced concerns that the party-state would need to harshly and swiftly fight crime, asking, 'Why can we not organise one, two or three campaigns against criminal activities?'[288]

[285] Resolution of the NPC Standing Committee on the Plan for Implementing the Criminal Procedure Law (Adopted at the 14th Meeting of the Standing Committee of the Fifth National People's Congress on 16 April 1980).

[286] Decision of the NPC Standing Committee Regarding the Implementation of the Criminal Procedure Law (Adopted at the 13th Meeting of the Standing Committee of the Fifth National People's Congress on 12 February 1980); Decision of the NPC Standing Committee regarding the Question on Time Limits for the Handling of Criminal Cases (Adopted at the 20th Meeting of the Standing Committee of the Fifth National People's Congress on 10 September 1981).

[287] Jianfu Chen, *Criminal and Criminal Procedure Law in the People's Republic of China* (Brill, Nijhoff, 2013) 56–57.

[288] Hu Yue, "83 yanli daji xingshi fanzui huodong ('83 Crack Down on Criminal Activities)' *People's Police*, 24 October 1999.

His calls were heard. On 25 August 1983, the Party Central issued an important document, which set the task of three campaigns in three years and thus launched the first anti-crime campaign (*yanda*), during which legal safeguards were largely put aside. Even if Liu had stressed that campaigns should be conducted by strict observance of the law, Tanner has described the first campaign from 1983–86 as the 'bloodiest chapter in post-Mao Chinese politics'.[289] The *yanda* campaigns were not only used to restore public morals but also revived the tradition of public denunciation of guilt, which had already existed in imperial and Mao China, including mass rallies and public executions.[290] Research into the causes of wrongful convictions, which were exposed from the late 2000s onwards, has shown that these campaigns provided a fertile ground.[291] Because the socialist attitude towards law deemphasises legal continuity and follows the logic that law cannot go beyond national conditions – in the view of the Party – such measures were arguably justified and thus legitimate to regain control and facilitate effective law enforcement, even if it meant sacrificing individual safeguards, especially as regards personal liberty. After 1984, no further (formal) modifications to the CPL 1979 were made.[292] However, the damage was done. From the early 1990s, the many shortcomings of the law came to light, and theorists and practitioners began to discuss how to improve the criminal justice system.

[289] Murray Scot Tanner, 'State Coercion and the Balance of Awe: The 1983-1986 "Stern Blows" Anti-Crime Campaign' [2000] *The China Journal* 93, 93.

[290] ibid 98.

[291] Xiong Moulin and Michelle Miao, 'Miscarriage of Justice in Capital Cases in China' (2018) 41 *Hastings International & Comparative Law Review* 273, 318–320.

[292] Gelatt (n 190) 3–5.

# 4

# Deepening the Discourse of 'Reasonable' Elements of Presumption of Innocence

Chapter four illustrates the merger of the discourses on criminal justice and human rights and the rise of the view of a presumption of innocence 'with Chinese characteristics'. Chapter three has shown that the view of adopting only the 'reasonable elements' of the presumption of innocence ('the reasonable' elements discourse) first emerged in the late 1970s. At the core of this discourse was the idea of a presumption of innocence 'with Chinese characteristics', echoing the official doctrine of national conditions. This position was increasingly met with approval from the 1990s onwards. In this context, the issuance of the 1991 White Paper had marked an important momentum because the official recognition of shortcomings of human rights protection in the criminal justice process merged the previously separately evolving discourses on criminal justice and human rights. This convergence brought new dynamics into criminal justice discourses and coincided with the beginning of the third phase of presumption of innocence in China. Academic discourses were constrained by the official doctrine of national conditions, and the convergence of the two discourses exacerbated the conflicts between human rights claims, on the one hand, and national conditions claims, on the other. This chapter examines whether the CPL 1996 made improvements in terms of presumption of innocence standards. Despite an unsuccessful lobbying for the presumption of innocence, the view that domestic legislation had adopted a presumption of innocence 'with Chinese characteristics' resonated in official and academic discourses. This chapter reviews this claim. The chapter sets out by looking at the state of academic discourses in the early 1990s as regards the presumption of innocence against the backdrop of the merger of the two discourses. It then turns to contrasting the scholarly CPL draft proposal with the CPL 1996 amendments before analysing specific areas of the revised law in relation to the presumption of innocence. This chapter concludes that the official doctrine of national conditions has triumphed over international presumption of innocence standards in the process of revising the law, and the claim of a partial acceptance of the presumption of innocence stands on very fragile grounds.

# I. Human Rights 'with Chinese Characteristics' in the Sphere of Criminal Justice

The previous discussions have shown that, as part of the legal reforms in the reform era, the establishment of a criminal justice system 'with Chinese characteristics', based on Marxism-Leninism and Maoism, was high on the political agenda.[1] In the early years of the reform era, the domestic human rights discourse did not extend to the sphere of criminal justice and vice versa. Of course, it should be borne in mind that academia was just remerging and recovering from the Cultural Revolution (1996–76). In the early 1990s, a wave of domestic scholarship on 'improving human rights' (*wanshan renquan*) in the criminal justice process gradually emerged.[2] There were various reasons for the growing reference to human rights in the context of criminal justice.

The 1991 White Paper clearly marked a crucial moment for the recognition of human rights protection in criminal proceedings, which first acknowledged the protection of human rights as an objective of criminal justice.[3] The recognition that China had deficits in human rights protection – or that there was 'still room for improvements' – was the green light for academia to push ahead with human rights research and examine the situation in the context of criminal justice.[4] The 1991 White Paper thus provided a substantial link between human rights and criminal justice and thereby also merged the two discourses. It had moreover and perhaps more importantly, given scholars in China the green light to do research on these themes and perhaps provide constructive criticism. For scholars, human rights arguably offered a more abstract conception or ideal aspiration and superior aim of how the criminal process should operate. As the considerations in these sections will demonstrate, international human rights law had become the most important source for scholars to formulate reform goals. Therefore, the previously separately evolving discourses on human rights and criminal justice had merged.

Another explanation for the growing interest in human rights in the context of criminal justice was the party-state's increasingly proactive participation in the international human rights regime, which had led to more articulated and growing concern for human rights protection in the criminal process in Chinese scholarship. Between 1949 and 1971, the PRC was not yet a member of the United Nations, and the party-state was not at the global standard and rather operated outside

[1] Fan Fenglin, *Xingshi susong fa (Criminal Procedure Law)* (China Police University Publishing House, 1988) 5.

[2] This observation is based on personal research.

[3] Song Yinghui, *Xingshi susong mudi lun (Objective Theory of Criminal Proceedings)* (China Police University Publishing House, 1995) 102.

[4] Chen Guangzhong, Chen Ruihua and Tang Weijian, 'Shichang jingji yu xingshi susong faxue de zhangwang (Perspectives on Market Economy and Criminal Procedure Studies)' [1993] *China Legal Science* 3, 6.

the international human rights system. However, this isolated status substantially changed after 1971 when the PRC became the sole representative of China in the UN and diplomatic relations normalised. At the time, the party-state pursued a rather selective approach to international human rights treaties. It joined certain international human rights treaties, most notably the Convention Against Torture (CAT) in 1988.[5] Moreover, the PRC first became a member of the UN Commission on Human Rights in 1982 or, for example, engaged in the formulation of the UN Declaration on the Right to Development of 1986.[6] Both domestic legislation and practices were now under scrutiny.

In the early 1990s, outside observers criticised the party-state's failure to fulfil international human rights obligations with respect to fair trial, pointing to flagrant violations of the prohibition against torture or personal liberty.[7] Domestically, there was a consensus amongst legal scholars that the CPL 1979 could no longer meet the demands of the developing market economy, even if the ideological footing was not necessarily questioned.[8] In 1988, the legislator put the question of an overhaul of the 1979 CPL on the agenda. In January 1991, the SCNPC Legislative Affairs Commission arranged the first roundtable in Beijing to discuss the revision, which was followed by a report to the Central Committee of the CPC and various local seminars.[9] Theorists and practitioners agreed that the law was outdated, and genuine efforts were made to improve the law, albeit different ideas were proposed.

In 1991, the Procedural Law Research Association of the China Law Society (*zhongguo faxuehui susongfaxue yanjiuhui*), which was founded in 1984 and rebranded as China Association of Criminal Procedure Law (*zhongguo xingshisusongfaxue yanjiuhui*) in 2006 (I will consistently refer to it as 'Criminal Procedure Association'),[10] emphasised the need to revise the law as part of an effort to improve the socialist legal system. It should be observed that the delegates

[5] Katrin Kinzelbach, 'Human Rights in Chinese Foreign Policy: A Battle for Global Public Opinion' in Sarah Biddulph and Joshua Rosenzweig (eds), *Handbook on Human Rights in China* (Cheltenham, Edward Elgar, 2019) 85–87.

[6] Yu-Jie Chen, 'China's Challenge to the International Human Rights Regime' (2019) 51 *NYU Journal of International Law and Politics* 1179, 1184–1187.

[7] Donald C Clarke and James V Feinerman, 'Antagonistic Contradictions: Criminal Law and Human Rights in China' [1995] *The China Quarterly* 136, 144–149, 153.

[8] Chen Guangzhong and Bian Jianlin, 'Xingshi susong faxue yanjiu xianzhuang yu fazhan qushi (The Present State and the Trend of Development of Criminal Procedure Law Research' [1996] *The Jurist* 34, 37; Chen Guangzhong, 'Lun xingshi susongfa xiugai de zhidao sixiang (On the Guiding Thought of the Revision of the Criminal Procedure Law' [1995] *Law and Social Development* 43, 43.

[9] Jianfu Chen, *Criminal and Criminal Procedure Law in the People's Republic of China* (Brill, Nijhoff, 2013) 59.

[10] It is a branch of the 'China Law Society' (*zhongguo faxue hui*). There is no information about the composition of the delegates at that time. The current composition, however, shows that the association is composed not only of academics but also, eg, of Party secretaries and delegates from national and public security organs. From 1984, Professor Chen Guangzhong, a leading scholar of criminal procedure at CUPL, was the President of the China Association of Criminal Procedure Law for four consecutive terms, see 'China Association of Criminal Procedure Law' cacpl.chinalaw.org.cn/portal/page/index/id/6.html accessed 18 August 2018.

participating in the meetings are not exclusively theorists, meaning scholars, but also include practitioners, notably from the three agencies. The CPL 1979 was criticised for containing too general, partly contradictory, as well as vague provisions. Further, economic reforms had facilitated new types of crimes and growing crime rates; a modified law was therefore considered to ensure greater social stability. Moreover, it should be borne in mind that the CPL 1979 had predated the Constitution of 1982, which introduced fundamental rights; the alignment of the law with the Constitution was thus widely supported and uncontested. Although the Chinese Constitution does not know a general right to a fair trial, it contains relevant guarantees such as equality before the law, personal liberty, personal dignity, and inviolability of residences.[11] It moreover enshrines such guarantees as the principle of openness, the right to defence,[12] and the independence of courts and procuratorates.[13] In line with the idea of combining theory with practice, the delegates suggested that reforms should focus on the experiences under the CPL 1979 to improve the criminal process, especially as it relates to criminal defence or personal liberty, as well as with respect to external supervision over investigation proceedings and the contested institution of exemption from prosecution, and thus at least implicitly touching upon the question of presumption of innocence.[14]

With the theme of human rights protection gradually entering the official and academic discourses on criminal justice, in 1992, Chen Guangzhong of China University of Political Science and Law called for better human rights protection in criminal proceedings in the light of the socio-economic changes.[15] However, in the light of Deng's vision of a socialist legal system 'with Chinese characteristics', Chen Guangzhong and Bian Jianlin stressed that some scholars voiced concerns, saying that more time was needed to study foreign legal systems and international fair trial standards and review domestic legislation and judicial practice.[16] During his Southern Tour in 1992, Deng had stressed the idea of adopting only valuable achievements of the bourgeoisie.[17] This idea should indeed become an important premise for scholars studying the adoption of the presumption of innocence.

The recognition of human rights in the criminal justice system led to more pluralistic academic discourses on the question of presumption of innocence.

[11] Constitution 1982, arts 33(2), 37, 38 and 39.

[12] Constitution 1982 (2018 Amendment), art 130.

[13] Constitution 1982 (2018 Amendment), arts 131, 133, 136, and 138.

[14] Hong Daode, 'Zhongguo faxuehui susongfaxue yanjiuhui 1991 nian nianhui (The 1991 Annual Meeting of the China Law Society Procedural Law Research Association' in Institute of Law at CASS (ed), *Zhongguo faxue yanjiu nianjian (China Law Research Yearbook)* (Beijing, China University of Political Science and Law Press, 1991) 597–598.

[15] Chen Guangzhong, 'Jiaqiang renquan baozhang shi gaige kaifang de xuyao (Strengthening the Protection of Human Rights is a Demand for Reform and Opening-up)' [1992] *China Legal Science* 18, 18–19.

[16] Chen Guangzhong and Bian Jianlin (n 8) 36.

[17] The slogan to 'critically inherit [it], abandon [its] dregs, absorb [its] spirit' is derived from Lenin's comment on Marxism's attitude towards the achievements of the bourgeoisie, see Lin Xin, '"Wuzui tuiding" haishi "wuzui jiadong"? ("Presumption of Innocence" or "Assumption of Innocence"?' [1983] *Social Sciences in China* 173, 177.

Assuming a more rights-based language in their writings, scholars in China reviewed the hostility with which the presumption of innocence was met largely on ideological and political grounds in the Mao era and early years of the reform era. For reform-minded scholars, the adoption of the presumption of innocence was no longer seen as conflicting with supposed national conditions, most fundamentally China still being in the primary stage of socialism. In contrast to the prevailing view in the 1970s, which condemned the presumption of innocence as 'unscientific', it was now claimed that this principle could guarantee fairness. With a growing attention to human rights, the question of how to strike a proper balance between crime control and rights protection, as enshrined in the CPL 1979, became a controversial issue in the process of revising the law. Although the Party leaders now emphasised the need to protect individuals' rights, political reports reflected the position that anything deemed a potential threat to its leadership role must be suppressed – or, as Jiang Zemin had put it, 'hostile forces', suggesting the instrumentalist view towards law.[18]

While leading criminal procedure scholar Chen Guangzhong did not challenge the official position of national conditions, he used official parlance to argue in favour of better rights protections, saying that because the Criminal Procedure Law belongs to the superstructure, it must serve the economic base. To this end, he argued, the revised law should ensure crime control and social stability, on the one hand, and procedural safeguards, on the other, to strengthen human rights protection. In his view, crime control was a legitimate aim, as the state has the responsibility to protect society, but these objectives, as well as the state's power to impose punishment, would not compete with the aim of human rights protection. Chen proposed that the law should become more 'scientific' in the sense of modifying the terminology of the law and removing or revising outdated provisions. Furthermore, because China is a socialist democracy, it should become more 'democratic' by improving fair trial standards.[19] The latter manifests the idea of democratic centralism, as explained in chapter one. The point is, despite his acknowledgement of national conditions and without fundamentally questioning the official stance, Chen invoked the theory of base and superstructure, ie, socio-economic changes, to advocate international fair trial safeguards while criticising shortcomings, as acknowledged in the 1991 White Paper, saying that the Chinese government should fulfil its international human rights obligations, including moral obligations coming from soft law.[20]

The party-state's goal of developing a socialist legal system, as first put forward at the Third Plenum of 1978, had opened room for academic discourses, which were broadened by the 1991 White Paper. Many reform-minded scholars

[18] Jiang Zemin, 'Jiakuai gaige kaifang he xiandaihua jianshe bufa duoqu you zhongge tese shehui zhuyi shiye de geng da shengli (Accelerating the Reform, the Opening to the Outside World and the Drive for Modernisation to Achieve Greater Successes in Building Socialism with Chinese Characteristics)' (1992) Report to the 14th National Congress II, s 6.

[19] Chen Guangzhong, 'On the Guiding Thought of the Revision of the Criminal Procedure Law' (n 8) 44–47.

[20] Chen Guangzhong, 'Lun xingshi susongfa xiugai de zhidao sixiang (On the Guiding Thought of the Revision of the Criminal Procedure Law' (n 8) 47–48. (1996) (n 8) 27.

took a more moderate and a more cautious approach to the official doctrine of national conditions. By not challenging the official doctrine, scholars could make more constructive criticism and possibly have greater influence on the outcome. As shown, Chen interpreted the official doctrine of national conditions differently. His position may be described as moderate, advocating the adoption of international human rights standards while not challenging the party-state as such. Such a mediating position arguably represented the mainstream approach at the time. Therefore, many scholars held that the CPL 1979 should be amended in accordance with national conditions and thus have 'Chinese characteristics.'

## II. The Scholarly Criminal Procedure Law Draft Proposal

In autumn 1993, the China Law Society submitted a report on the revision of the Criminal Procedure Law, including views of academics, to central Party authorities. This has been interpreted to indicate support for a reform from the highest level.[21] In 1993, a first overhaul of the CPL 1979 was formally put on the legislative agenda.[22] In October of the same year, the SCNPC Legislative Affairs Commission assigned Professor Chen Guangzhong the drafting work. To this end, he organised a group of researchers ('the drafters') and, by July 1994, they had produced a CPL draft and submitted it to the legislator for deliberation. The draft aimed to accommodate the socio-economic changes. The drafters produced a comprehensive draft, altogether containing 329 provisions. Regarding pre-trial proceedings, the draft integrated provisions on access to legal counsel at all stages of the proceedings, as well as more detailed provisions on interrogations,[23] evidence,[24] and compulsory measures. Overall, it de-emphasised the requirement of objective truth (ie, factual guilt), while laying greater weight on legal guilt and therefore procedural justice.[25]

Although the inclusion of an explicit presumption of innocence provision was controversially discussed,[26] the drafters eventually supported such a provision. They made the following two proposals:

> Anyone who has not convicted by a judicial organ in accordance with the prescribed procedure shall be presumed innocent.

[21] Chongyi Fan, 'The Process of Revising "The Criminal Procedure Law of the People's Republic of China" 1996' law.unimelb.edu.au/__data/assets/pdf_file/0006/1546260/The_Process_of_Revising_The_Criminal_Procedure_Law_of_the_Peoples_Republic_of_China_19961.pdf accessed 2 October 2023.

[22] 'Legislative Plan of the Standing Committee of the 8th NPC (152 Items)' npcobserver.com/wp-content/uploads/2024/10/8th-NPCSC-Legislative-Plan.pdf accessed 2 January 2018.

[23] Chen Guangzhong and Yan Duan, *Zhonghua Renmin Gongheguo xingshi susongfa xiugai jianyigao yu lunzheng (Draft for Amendment to the PRC Criminal Procedure Law and Its Annotations)* (Beijing, China Zhengzhou Publishing House, 1995) 30–31 (arts 135 to 138).

[24] ibid 14–18 (arts 57 to 81).

[25] For example, art 2 CPL 1979 used the phrase 'clarify criminal *case* facts' instead 'clarifying *crime* facts', see Chen Guangzhong and Yan Duan (n 23).

[26] Cui Min, 'Guanyu xingshi susong fa xiugai yu wanshan de ruogan jianyi (Some Suggestions on the Revision and Improvement of the Criminal Procedure Law)' [1996] *The Jurist* 86, 88.

任何人未经司法机关依照法定程序判定有罪以前，都应当假定为无罪的人.

No one shall be considered a criminal until [he or she] has been convicted by a judicial organ in accordance with the prescribed procedure.

任何人未经司法机关依照法定程序判定有罪以前，都不应当视为罪犯.[27]

The universal recognition of the presumption of innocence as a fundamental human right was seen as an indicator for a 'civilised' criminal justice system, a label that reform-minded scholars were eager to achieve for China as well. The drafters emphasised the function of presumption of innocence in clarifying the status of the accused as a procedural subject. In other words, state agencies should 'assume' (*jiading*) or 'presume' (*tuiding*) the legal innocence of an accused person until they are proved guilty according to law to protect the human rights of suspects and defendants in the criminal process.[28]

While the first proposal uses the notion of presumed innocence, the second, though similarly phrased, refers to not presuming guilt, which seems to resemble Beccaria's formulation, as discussed in chapter three.[29] Whether this makes a difference may be debatable. Yet, the emphasis of the first formulation on innocence may have given such a presumption of innocence greater significance. While different translations of different expressions of the presumption of innocence at international and domestic levels have been understood to have led to divergent interpretations in Chinese academic discourses, there was no longer doubt that it was a universally recognised principle of fair trial. The rationale of the presumption of innocence was therefore considered more important than the literal differences between the various manifestations of the presumption of innocence at the international level and in the various legal systems.

Against the backdrop of international law obligations, the drafters invoked especially China's accession to CAT and CRC as justification for strengthening the protection of human rights in the criminal process. The CRC explicitly protects the presumption of innocence in the context of juvenile justice, with the minimum requirements being comparable to that of the ICCPR.[30] As shown in chapter two, the CAT is of particular importance with respect to evidence rules in the criminal process. It not only requires the criminalisation of the use of torture and other forms of ill-treatment in criminal proceedings but also bans the use of illegally obtained evidence. Minimum guarantees such as, notably, the privilege against self-incrimination and the right to silence logically follow from it.[31] In the light of these legal obligations under international law, it is not surprising that the drafters

[27] Chen Guangzhong and Yan Duan (n 23) 5 (art 10), 106–107.

[28] ibid 102–107 (comment by Bian Jianlin, who was part of the research team).

[29] See ch 3, II.C.

[30] Convention on the Rights of the Child (CRC) (New York, 20 November 1989) art 40; General Comment No. 10, Children's rights in juvenile justice (GC No. 10) 2007 (UN Doc CRC/C/GC/10) para 40.

[31] CAT, arts 13 and 15.

supported the adoption of minimum guarantees, including the presumption of innocence and the right to silence or access to counsel.[32] They attributed systematic shortcomings, including prejudices and subjectivism, to the absence of the presumption of innocence in Chinese legislation and the prevalence of presumption of guilt in reality. The latter would have led to the flagrant disregard for the rights of the accused and the occurrence of coerced confessions. However, this is not to say that there was always a consensus amongst scholars on how to rectify the system. Undoubtedly, the drafters considered a functioning defence system as the very precondition for the realisation of presumption of innocence. To this end, it was relatively uncontested that an earlier involvement of lawyers would be needed to guarantee the right to defence to realise equality of arms between prosecution and defence. It was recognised that safeguards like the right to silence were difficult to implement without proper external supervisors like lawyers, who play a key role in ensuring that the rights of the accused are protected. With a rising legal profession and changing socio-economic conditions, meaning more capacities, the expansion of lawyers' rights was seriously discussed, not just by the drafters but by legal scholars in general.[33]

As part of an effort to improve the defence system, the scholarly draft partly incorporated more detailed provisions than those that had been issued to supplement the CPL 1979.[34] It contained a general right to defence and access to legal counsel at all stages of the proceedings without restrictions.[35] The draft aimed at prompt access to legal counsel for suspects and defendants being held under detention (*juliu*) or arrest (*daibu*) (ie, not later than 24 hours from the time of arrest detention or arrest).[36] The inclusion of these safeguards was generally understood to bring Chinese legislation closer to international standards, for example, the UN Basic Principles on the Role of Lawyers of 1990.[37] And even if these principles fall within the category of UN soft law, they were an important point of reference.

However, even if there was a consensus amongst the drafters that an earlier involvement of lawyers was necessary, the precise stage at which *defence* lawyers should enter the process, as well as the scope of such involvement, remained a

[32] Chen Guangzhong and Yan Duan (n 23) 106.

[33] ibid 145–149; Hong Daode, 'Zhongguo Faxuehui Susongfaxue Yanjiuhui 1991 Nian Nianhui (The 1991 Annual Meeting of the China Law Society Procedural Law Research Association' in Institute of Law at CASS (ed), *Zhongguo faxue yanjiu nianjian (China Law Research Yearbook)* (Beijing, China University of Political Science and Law Press, 1991) 597–598; Cui Min (n 11) 87–88.

[34] See, eg, Several Supplementary Provisions of the Supreme People's Court, the Supreme People's Procuratorate, the Ministry of Justice and the Ministry of Public Security on the Participation of Lawyers in Litigation (Adopted on 26 June 1986).

[35] Chen Guangzhong and Yan Duan (n 23) arts 9 and 45 to 56.

[36] ibid 12–13 (arts 48 and 51), 150.

[37] All accused persons should have access to a lawyer in all stages of criminal proceedings (Principle 1), and those being arrested or detained shall have such access promptly (Principle 7), see Basic Principles on the Role of Lawyers (Adopted by the Eighth United Nations Congress on the Prevention of Crime and the Treatment of Offenders, Havana, Cuba, 27 August to 7 September 1990) 1990.

point of controversy. While some of the drafters supported an early involvement of defence lawyers in the phase of investigation, others were against such a proposal. Those being against it argued that it would be too heavy a burden for the system, as it could hinder smooth criminal investigations; this view proposed an involvement of defence lawyers from the moment a case is reviewed for prosecution, meaning the prosecution stage. For them, only in exceptional cases involving minors, for example, should a suspect have the right to entrust a defence lawyer in the earlier phases.[38] There was therefore disagreement among scholars as to whether an earlier involvement of defence lawyers was possible, as it was feared that this would overburden the system.

Moreover, the scholarly draft aimed at expanding the evidential dimension of presumption of innocence, which, following the view of the drafters, the CPL 1979, as well as other rules and regulations, had already been partly recognised by implicitly allocating the burden of proof, establishing a high standard of proof needed for conviction, and adopting the maxim of *in dubio pro reo*.[39] All that was needed, so the drafters said, was further clarifying the evidential burden in criminal cases. To this end, the drafters proposed allocating the burden of proof by stating that 'a criminal suspect or defendant does not bear the burden of proving his or her own guilt' (*xianyiren, beigaoren bu chengdan zhengming ziji you zui de zeren*).[40] This formulation undoubtedly would have placed the burden of proof on the prosecution and would have codified a privilege against self-incrimination. In the light of China's obligations under international law and because the CPL 1979 had adopted the prohibition against extortion of confession and unlawful obtainment of evidence, the question of exclusionary rules was also on the agenda. While there was an agreement that statements extorted through torture from suspects and defendants should be excluded, as required by Article 15 CAT,[41] whether all types of illegally obtained evidential materials should be excluded remained contested. Some believed that the exclusion of illegally obtained evidence should indeed be limited to such illegally obtained statements, as it was the most pressing issue in practice to be addressed by legislation. Here, again, the drafters raised the issue of feasibility, and it was understood that the limits of the system, the actual conditions, should be considered instead of pursuing too high expectations. Arguably as a compromise, the drafters proposed exceptions from the non-admissibility of illegally obtained evidence as a basis for deciding a case with respect to behaviour endangering national security or the interests of society; an exception to this exception was statements extorted from suspects and defendants under torture or duress.[42]

In this context, the duty to make truthful statements was reviewed against the backdrop of the internationally recognised right to silence. The question was

[38] Chen Guangzhong and Yan Duan (n 23) 11 (art 45), 149–150.
[39] ibid 105–106. On the evidence rules in the 1979 CPL, see ch 4, III.
[40] ibid 15 (art 59).
[41] See CAT, art 15.
[42] Chen Guangzhong and Yan Duan (n 23) 15 (art 60), 171.

whether it should be maintained or whether suspects and/or defendants should have a right to silence. Beyond the drafters, three views (advocacy, rejection and compromise) dominated the debate on a right to silence among legal scholars in China. One view was in favour of an implicit right to silence by codifying a right to testify. Formulated as a right, a suspect or defendant could choose to make a statement voluntarily and thus waive their right to silence or choose to remain silent without bearing any consequences; the duty to make truthful statements should be abandoned. Another view rejected the incorporation of a right to silence, be it implicitly or explicitly, on the grounds that the duty to make truthful statements would facilitate the resolution of cases. The latter view reflects the dual objective of crime control and human rights protection, albeit with a tendency towards crime control. This view held that, even if the right to silence was universally recognised, China was not obliged to adopt it. Finally, there was the view of compromise. While it was acknowledged that the duty to make truthful statements undermines the goal of changing the culture of coerced confessions, an explicit right to silence was also seen as potentially interfering with the investigation procedure. The revised law should therefore simply bypass this issue.[43]

The scholarly draft contained three different proposals, reflecting these three different positions: (1) suspects and defendants' duty to truthfully answer the questions of interrogating, prosecuting and judicial personnel; (2) suspects and defendants' right to make a statement; (3) no provision. The first proposal held that the duty would facilitate the declared objective of crime control, as enshrined in the 1979 CPL, and it was considered almost natural that an accused person was expected to cooperate, whether guilty or not, to ensure smooth proceedings. A right to silence, on the other hand, would at best be an open invitation to resistance. The second proposal was understood to affirm the suspect or defendant's right to silence without using the notion of silence, as they would have the freedom to choose silence, which could restrain the powers of investigation authorities. The view of omission, in contrast, recognised the risk inherent in the duty in terms of rights violations but did not advocate a right to silence either, as such a guarantee would be a heavy burden for the system.[44] The draft, moreover, contained a provision stipulating that the credibility of suspects and defendants' statements should be assessed in the light of the other evidence.[45] Therefore, even if partly advocating to retain the duty of truthfulness, this provision aimed to address the subjectivism of investigation personnel by providing for more objective standards to assess the credibility of statements.

This concern was not unfounded. Wrongful convictions dating back to the 1990s had later shown that the confession(s) of the alleged perpetrator often

[43] Sun Changyong, 'Chenmoquan yu zhongguo xingshi susong (The Right to Silence and the Chinese Criminal Process)' (2000) 22 *Modern Law Science* 18, 18; Yi Yanyou, 'Lun fandui ziwo guizui de tequan (On the Privilege Against Committing Self-Incrimination)' [1999] *Journal of Comparative Law* 273, 273.

[44] Chen Guangzhong and Yan Duan (n 24) 17 (art 72), 183–187.

[45] ibid 17 (art 73).

did not add up with the facts or other evidence in the case, or exculpatory evidence that would have raised questions as to their credibility was deliberately concealed. In other words, coerced confessions were later found to be the major cause of wrongful convictions in China.[46]

## III. Response of the Legislator

In October 1995, the SCNPC Legislative Affairs Commission issued a Criminal Procedure Law Draft Revision ('legislator's draft') and the Explanations on Several Major Issues Concerning the Revision of the CPL ('CPL Explanations'), which was sent to relevant departments at all levels to seek opinions.[47] The NPC Standing Committee discussed the draft revision twice.[48] At the meeting of the Criminal Procedure Association in 1995, at which scholars and implementing agencies participated, the legislator's draft was discussed. Commentators found that the draft amendments generally received positive feedback, as they were considered to strike a proper balance between the duality of crime control and human rights protection. While many scholars believed that it had laid a more 'scientific' and 'democratic' foundation for criminal justice in light of the socio-economic changes. A more critical view contended that the revisions were too marginal. In their view, the draft had retained not only 'poor' language but also many contradictory provisions and had failed to address important issues. Fearing that a too rushed reform would not be sensible in the long run, a minority view suggested postponing it, until the actual impacts of the economic reforms were clearer.[49]

Interestingly, the presumption of innocence was not among the controversial issues, nor was the inclusion of a provision on the presumption of innocence recommended. Nevertheless, issues relating to presumption of innocence were on the agenda, especially the strengthening of personal liberty safeguards, the reform of the system of exemption from prosecution, and improvements to the defence system. Some delegates criticised the many restrictions lawyers would face under

[46] See, eg, Xiong Moulin and Michelle Miao, 'Miscarriage of Justice in Capital Cases in China' (2018) 41 *Hastings International & Comparative Law Review* 273; He Jiahong, 'Miscarriage of Justice and Malpractice in Criminal Investigations in China' (2016) 16 *The China Review* 65.

[47] Criminal Procedure Law of the PRC (Draft for Soliciting Public Opinions), Issued by the SCNPC Legislative Affairs Commission on 24 October 1995; Wei Tong, 'Guanyu xiugai xingshi susong fa wenti de qingkuang fanying – zhongguo faxuehui susongfaxue yanjiuhui 1995 nian nianhui zongshu zhiyi (Some Reflections on the Issue of Revising the Criminal Procedure Law – A Summary of the 1995 Annual Meeting of the China Law Society Procedural Law Research Association)' [1996] *Journal of CUPL* 89, 89.

[48] Chen (n 9) 59.

[49] Wei Tong (n 47) 89; Chen Guangzhong, '"Jianchi chengzhi fanzui yu baozhang renquan xiang jiehe lizu guoqing yu jiejian waiguo xiang jiehe" (Adhering to the Combination of Punishing Crimes and Safeguarding Human Rights, Being based on National Conditions and Drawing on Foreign Countries)' [1996] *Tribune of Political Science and Law (Journal of CUPL)* 25, 25–27.

the legislator's draft, including the omission of a right to have a lawyer present during criminal interrogations or the proposed requirement to obtain the investigation organ's approval to meet with clients in custody. Regarding the issue of prolonged custody, it was suggested to set a clear time limit for the maximum period of custody pending trial. Moreover, some delegates suggested including a provision on the exclusion of illegally obtained confessions to rectify the practice of coerced confessions and meet CAT standards.[50]

In theory, both the scholarly draft and the legislator's draft of 1995 showed efforts to adopt more elements prevalent in adversarial systems by improving equality of arms between prosecution and defence,[51] the details of which will be discussed in the sections to follow. However, the lengthy process of negotiations indicates a lack of consensus on central issues. A fundamental issue concerned the value orientation of the law. As discussed in chapter three, the CPL 1979 established an inquisitorial-style criminal process. While the investigation and prosecution organs possessed great powers, the defence was put in a weak position, especially in the investigation and prosecution phases. Considering the relatively weak checks and balances, the relationship between the three agencies has been described as the 'iron triangle', rendering the trial itself a mere formality. Indeed, as regards the scholarly draft, a point of criticism was ostensibly structural issues of the proposed draft. Some commentators believed that the scholarly draft contained 'inner contradictions', as the drafters sought to establish an adversarial trial structure, or at least integrate some procedural aspects of it, while retaining elements of the traditional 'authority-ism' (*zhiquan zhuyi*) structure, as reflected in the CPL 1979. For example, the scholarly draft retained most of the provisions on criminal investigation, without allowing for an active involvement of the parties, which would have been crucial for the realisation of an adversarial trial pattern. Although the draft strengthened the access to counsel at the phase of criminal investigation, the investigation organs (the police) would have maintained the final say as to the place and date of meetings. In the view of critics, this constellation would have facilitated 'investigation advantage-ism' (*zhencha bianyi zhuyi*), meaning the investigation authorities would have been in a better position than the accused. Therefore, it was argued that the scholarly draft, if adopted in this form, would have reinforced the goal of efficient crime control, while it would have been difficult to integrate more adversarial elements.[52]

[50] Wei Tong (n 47) 90–92; Chen Guangzhong and Yan Duan (n 23) 17, 183–187.

[51] Cui Min (n 26) 90; Jennifer Smith and Michael Gompers, 'Realizing Justice: The Development of Fair Trial in China' (2006) 2 *Chinese Law & Policy Review* 108, 111–112; Wang Minyuan, 'Woguo xingshi susongfa xiugai shu ping (Review of China's Criminal Procedure Law Revision)' [1996] *The Jurist* 41, 45–46; Xie Youping, '"hunhexing" xingshi susong moshi pinglun – «xingshi susongfa xiugai jueding» suixiang (Review of the "Hybrid" Model of Criminal Procedure – Reflections on the 'Decision on Amendments to the Criminal Procedure Law")' [1996] *Law Science* 10, 10–12.

[52] Long Zongzhi, 'Susong jizhi de chongtu yu xietiao – ping xingshi susongfa xiugai de xuezhe jianyigao (Conflict and Coordination of Procedural Mechanisms – Comment on the Scholars' Draft Proposal for the Revision of the Criminal Procedure Law)' [1995] *Modern Law Science* 54, 55.

Overall, 65 per cent of the scholarly draft was reportedly incorporated into the Criminal Procedure Law of 1996 (CPL 1996), as adopted by the NPC in March 1996.[53] In comparison to the CPL 1979, the law had made significant improvements in terms of rights protections. However, important fair trial guarantees were not adopted. Gu Angran, then Director of the SCNPC Legislative Affairs Commission, made the following comment on the revised CPL 1996:

> Judicial practice has shown that the tasks and fundamental principles of the Criminal Procedure Law are appropriate. Over the last sixteen years, China's socialist democracy and the construction of the legal system have continuously developed. Social conditions have changed. In judicial practice, experiences have accumulated, and some problems have emerged. The practical experience must be reviewed and put into context with the contemporary development of the legal system.[54]

This statement echoed the official mantra of learning from practice, reflecting the dialectical process of knowledge. Gu added an interesting point by indicating that the 1996 CPL had to adjust to practice becoming legitimate, not that practice should be changed or rectified by amending the law; this reflects the official doctrine of national conditions. Put differently, law ought to track socio-economic change (ie, China's changing realities or conditions) and must be adjusted accordingly.

However, notwithstanding the improvements, this suggests that modifications to the Criminal Procedure Law must not automatically go hand in hand with improvements. In the light of Gu's statement, this may indicate that such practices – no matter how illiberal or suppressive they are – may be considered more compatible with the realities of the criminal justice process in China. Of course, the party-state had never strictly followed the tenet that law can never be higher than the base, as the wave of codification meant that law increasingly predefined the economic base. In other words, the official doctrine of national conditions does not make a value claim in the sense that law has to align to widely recognised moral principles and values such as fairness and thus sets a limit to rights interferences. At the time, scholars played a critical role, as they could provide a counterbalance, but the tensions between the official doctrine of national conditions and broader human rights claims steadily grew.

Amongst the centrally important fair trial safeguards that were not adopted was the presumption of innocence. While it was the aim of the scholarly draft to include a presumption of innocence provision as a fundamental principle in the revised law,[55] none of the proposals were met with approval, and no explicit

[53] '"Zhonghua Renmin Gongheguo xingshi susongfa xiugai jianyigao yu lunzheng" jianjie (Introduction to the "Draft for Amendment to the PRC Criminal Procedure Law and Its Annotations")' *Guangming Daily* (2 July 1997) www.gmw.cn/01gmrb/1999-07/02/GB/18105^GM8-0210.HTM accessed 5 February 2018.

[54] Wu Hongyao and Zhong Songzhi, *Zhongguo xingshi susong fadian bainian 1906 nian – 2012 nian (zhongce) (100 Years of the Chinese Criminal Procedure Law Codes (1906-2012) (middle volume))* (Beijing, China University of Political Science and Law Press, 2012) 868 (Gu Angran's Explanations on the Draft Amendments (1996)).

[55] Zhao Shunrong, 'Chuyi wuzui tuiding yuanze (Some Suggestions on the Principle of the Presumption of Innocence)' [1999] *Hebei Law Science* 110, 110–111.

provision was incorporated into the legislator's draft of 1995 or in the CPL 1996. Although the presumption of innocence was not explicitly included, the CPL 1996 triggered debates as to whether the law had implicitly shown signs of it. Certain scholars, like Yi Yanyou, claimed that, unlike the CPL 1979, which did not show any acceptance of the presumption of innocence, the CPL 1996 would promise great improvements in terms of human rights protection and fair trial.[56] This optimism had not been shared by all observers, especially not by those outside of China, who suggested that the CPL 1996 showed no acceptance of presumption of innocence at all;[57] others saw 'little movement towards a full acceptance of the presumption of innocence', as key elements of it were either severely restricted or missing.[58]

Indeed, after the CPL 1996 was put into effect, many scholars in China shared the view that the CPL 1996 showed signs of acceptance of presumption of innocence by embracing its 'essence' or some 'reasonable elements' of it. In other words, the law had embraced a presumption of innocence 'with Chinese characteristics'. Chen Guangzhong, who had guided the law-making of the CPL 1996, argued that the law had not adopted the label of presumption of innocence, for example, as enshrined in the Universal Declaration, or associated safeguards such as the right to silence. Chen argued that the label would have led to confusion in practice as state agencies would operate on the basis of presuming guilt. The right to silence, on the other hand, would conflict with the policy of combining leniency with severity and give the accused too much power – the power of silence.[59] Of course, this justification is not new. As discussed in chapter three, the discourse on 'reasonable elements' of the presumption of innocence reflects the doctrine of national conditions, as it supports the idea of adopting those elements of the presumption of innocence that ought to suit China's conditions. Amongst those scholars advocating such an approach, there was not necessarily a consensus on the scope of 'reasonable' elements.[60]

Leaving aside the question of an explicit presumption of innocence provision, the CPL 1996 showed improvements. Most fundamentally, the language of the law was modified and de-ideologised. References to 'Marxism-Leninism-Mao Zedong Thought' as guiding ideology or to the 'people's democratic dictatorship' and 'the enemy' were removed from the law. This de-ideologisation was favourable to a broadening of individual safeguards.[61] And, as also proposed by the scholarly draft, the CPL 1996 clearly distinguished between 'criminal suspects'

[56] Yi Yanyou, 'Lun wuzui tuiding de hanyi yu xingshi susongfa de wanshan (On the Implications of the Presumption of Innocence and the Improvement of the Criminal Procedure Law)' [2012] *Tribune of Political Science and Law* 10, 19.

[57] Amanda Whitfort, 'The Right to a Fair Trial in China: The Criminal Procedure Law of 1996' (2006) 2 *Chinese Law & Policy Review* 141, 141–151.

[58] Timothy A Gelatt, 'Opening to Reform? An Analysis of China's Revised Criminal Procedure Law' (Lawyers Committee for Human Rights, 1996) 63.

[59] Chen Guangzhong (n 49) 29.

[60] See below, IV.A.

[61] CPL 1996, art 1.

(*fanzui xianyiren*) and 'defendants' (*beigaoren*), depending on the procedural stage, and removed all mention of 'criminals' (*renfan*).[62] Moreover, the CPL 1996 comprehensively modified the provisions on legal representation and defence. However, there were also areas that showed few signs of improvement, notably the investigation procedure or the rules on evidence. And while some of the CPL 1979 provisions were abolished, other newly introduced provisions gave rise to concerns about the acceptance of the presumption of innocence in the Chinese criminal justice process.

The question is whether the CPL 1996 could be read as an implicit recognition of the presumption of innocence. The CPL 1996 adopted one particular provision, Article 12, which scholars invoked to claim that the law had adopted an expression of presumption of innocence, which may be understood to manifest Beccaria's formulation that was seen as more compatible with the Chinese criminal justice system. The sections to follow examine whether a presumption of innocence 'with Chinese characteristics' can be maintained, starting with said Article 12.

## IV. The Rule of Exclusive Adjudication Power as Establishment of Presumption of Innocence?

According to Wang Junmin, Chinese legislation, most prominently the CPL 1979, had never completely abandoned the presumption of innocence, regardless of the official rejection of the use of any presumption in the criminal procedure. The CPL 1996 would have confirmed the acceptance of presumption of innocence.[63] Indeed, a provision introduced as part of the CPL 1996 reform sparked scholarly debates as regards the acceptance of presumption of innocence. The revised law introduced Article 12, which was praised for abandoning the traditional notion of presumption of guilt and ending decades of academic debates over the question of presumption of innocence,[64] marking only 'the beginning for the acceptance of presumption of innocence in China'.[65] Article 12 reads as follows:

> No person shall be found guilty without being judged as such by a people's court in accordance with the law.
>
> 未经人民法院依法判决，对任何人都不得确定有罪.

In Chinese academic discourses, both the specific meaning and the possible implications of this provision were under scrutiny. As already mentioned, many

[62] See Chen Guangzhong and Yan Duan (n 23) 5 (art 15).

[63] Especially the CPL evidence rules, see Wang Junmin, '"Wu cong panding" yu wuzui tuiding ("No Guilt without Punishment" and the "Presumption of Innocence")' [1996] *Law Science* 13, 14–15.

[64] Zhang Zetao, 'Zui cong panding yu wuzui tuiding (No Guilt without Judgment and the Presumption of Innocence)' [1999] *Journal of Xinjiang Police College* 34, 36; Wang Junmin (n 63) 13.

[65] Zhu Zongjie, 'Zai renquan baozhang shiye xia lun wuzui tuiding yuanze (On the Principle of the Presumption of Innocence from the Perspective of Human Rights Protection' [2011] *Human Rights* 23, 26.

scholars argued that Article 12 integrated the 'essence' and 'reasonable elements' of the presumption of innocence, even though it had avoided using the label of presumption of innocence in expressive terms, meaning an explicit reference to *tuiding* or *jiading*.[66] In academic circles, it has been widely argued that this provision established 'a presumption of innocence that accords with China's national conditions' (a presumption of innocence 'with Chinese characteristics').[67] Revisiting the presumed incompatibility with the principle of seeking truth from facts, Lü argued that these two were mutually reinforcing rather than competing principles. While the principle of seeking truth from facts would require case handling based on objective facts at the different stages of criminal proceedings, evidence should be used to establish the case facts, as already reflected under the CPL 1979.[68] Therefore, Lü connected the two elements of the principle of seeking truth from facts ('taking facts as the basis, and the law as the yardstick') to argue that the presumption of innocence, as part of the latter, was in line with China's national conditions. The view of compatibility was shared by many scholars from the 2000s onwards.

In the view of certain scholars, this 'formal establishment' of presumption of innocence in Chinese criminal procedure would imply that the power of adjudication rests with the judiciary and that a conviction must be based on evidence. Therefore, until a court finds a person guilty in accordance with a prescribed procedure, they cannot be considered a criminal.[69] The wording of Article 12 CPL shows resemblance to Beccaria's maxim. In fact, this provision was modelled after the Italian Constitution, which states, 'A defendant shall be considered not guilty until a final sentence has been passed.'[70] This view was not new. As shown in chapter three, a similar discourse had occurred in Soviet discourses,[71] and it was also present in Chinese discourses in the 1950s and again in the 1970s based on the court's adjudication power in accordance with organisational legislation for the courts.[72]

Many scholars at the time therefore supported the idea that Article 12 adopted the 'basic spirit' or 'essence' of the presumption of innocence by stating that 'no

[66] Zhang Zetao (n 64) 34; Chen Guangzhong, *'Gongmin quanli he zhengzhi quanli guoji gongyue yu woguo xingshi susong' (International Covenant on Civil and Political Rights and Criminal Process in China)* (The Commercial Press 2005) 31; Chen Ruihua, *Xingshi zhengju faxue (Criminal Evidence Law)* (Beijing, Peking University Press, 2014) 44.

[67] Lü Zhongya, 'Xin xingshi susongfa jiangou qi shihe guoqing de "wuzui tuiding" yuanze (The New Criminal Procedure Law Established the Principle of Presumption of Innocence in Accordance with National Conditions)' [1996] *Law Science* 17, 17. See also Huang Yansheng, 'Wuzui tuiding yu shishi qiushi (The Presumption of Innocence and Seek Truth from Facts)' [1997] *People's Procuratorate* 13, 13–14.

[68] CPL 1979, art 35; Lü Zhongya (n 67) 18.

[69] Xiu Ke, 'Xin xingshi susongfa zhong de wuzui tuiding yuanze (The Principle of the Presumption of Innocence in the New Criminal Procedure Law)' *Guangming Daily* (6 June 1996).

[70] See art 27(2) of the Italian Constitution 1947; Chen Guangzhong (n 49) 29.

[71] Timothy Gelatt, 'The People's Republic of China and the Presumption of Innocence' (1982) 73 *The Journal of Criminal Law & Criminology* 259, 285.

[72] COL 1979, art 1.

person shall be found guilty' in the absence of a guilty verdict, although it would depart from international presumption of innocence standards, more precisely, the guarantee under Article 14(2) ICCPR regarding the implications of procedural safeguards of the accused.[73] Chen Guangzhong, who had guided the work of the scholarly draft, which proposed an explicit presumption of innocence provision in the revised law, also supported this view. Chen argued that Article 12 contained two fundamental requirements. First, it would regulate the courts' exclusive power to adjudication, and second, the requirement of lawfulness of the outcome, meaning guilt must be established in accordance with the prescribed procedure.[74] In other words, Article 12 introduced the concept of legal guilt and, together with evidential requirements, thus manifests the 'essence' of the presumption of innocence. The question is whether this is sufficient enough to realise the presumption of innocence.

Indeed, scholars have pointed to normative differences between Article 12 and Article 14(2) ICCPR. As discussed in chapter two, Article 14(2) gives everyone charged with a criminal offence the *right* to be presumed innocent until proven guilty according to law and thus regulates the legal status of the accused in criminal proceedings. This is precisely what Article 12 does *not* do – it does not refer to a *right* that would have placed a duty on the state to guarantee the right to presumption of innocence. It first and foremost establishes the courts' exclusive power of adjudication.[75] Therefore, some scholars have claimed that this provision primarily regulates the courts' exclusive adjudication power, or the principle of 'no guilt without judgment' (*zui cong panding*), and thus only incorporated *one* 'reasonable element' of the presumption of innocence.[76] Similarly, others have held that Article 12 could be interpreted to mean that the police or prosecuting organs cannot decide on the guilt of a suspect or defendant unless a court has passed a guilty verdict. Put differently, a person should be *treated* as if they were innocent, which would constitute at least one element of the presumption of innocence under Article 14(2) ICCPR.[77] More critical observers rejected the claim that Article 12 could be interpreted to manifest the presumption of innocence, as there was a too evident gap between this provision and international standards.[78]

[73] Chen Guangzhong (n 66) 31; Chen Ruihua (n 66) 44; Yue Liling, *Xingshi shenpan yu renquan baozhang (Criminal Trial and Human Rights Protection)* (Beijing, Law Press China, 2010) 132.

[74] Chen Guangzhong, *Xingshi susong fa (Criminal Procedure Law)* (Peking, Peking University Press, 2013) 108.

[75] Zhang Xiaohai, *Wuzui tuiding quanli lun (On the Right to Presumption of Innocence)* (Beijing, China Democracy Legislative Publishing House, 2015) 185; Tianlong Jiang, 'The Development and Evaluation of "Presumption of Innocence in China' in Wei Zhang (ed), *Human Rights and Good Governance* (Leiden, Brill Nijhoff, 2016) 242–243; Chen Guangzhong, Jiang Jiahua and Xiao Peiquan, 'Lun wuzui tuiding jiqi zai zhongguo de shiyong (On the Presumption of Innocence and its Application in China)' [2013] *Law Science Magazine* 1, 5–6.

[76] Zhang Zetao (n 64) 36; Chen Guangzhong, Jiang Jiahua and Xiao Peiquan (n 75) 5–6.

[77] Jiang (n 75) 45.

[78] Xi Danni, *Lun wuzui tuiding (On the Presumption of Innocence)* (Beijing, People's Court Press, 2015) 208.

A look at the legislator's stance might shed some further light on this dispute. At the 4th Plenary Session of the Eighth National Congress in March 1996, Gu Angran, then head of the SCNPC Legislative Affairs Commission, elaborated on the CPL 1996 with explicit reference to presumption of innocence:

> We are firmly opposed to the presumption of guilt, but [we] also do not [advocate] the presumption of innocence as prevalent in Western countries; rather, [our criminal process is based on the principle of] taking facts as the basis and the law as the yardstick. In fact, the CPL provisions and the present amendments have incorporated the reasonable elements of presumption of innocence, such as the prosecution's burden of proof [*see Article 43*], [or the provision that] no person shall be found guilty without this being decided by a people's court in accordance with the law [*see Article 12*]; if the evidence at trial is insufficient and the guilt of the defendant cannot be established, an acquittal shall be rendered on the ground that there is insufficient evidence and the alleged offence cannot be established [*see Article 162(3)*]. However, there is no provision for the presumption of innocence before the court's judgment of guilt. Because if there were such a provision, a presumption of innocence before the court's judgement, then why should the investigating authorities carry out an investigation? Why take coercive measures? [...] We adhere to the principle of taking facts as the basis; before a court has reached a guilty verdict, one cannot say that [a person] is guilty, but also not that [a person] is not a crime suspect, rather [we] seek truth from facts, [meaning] during investigation various kinds of evidence of guilt, innocence, seriousness, negligibility of a crime is collected objectively in accordance with law; whether [the accused] committed a crime is ultimately to be determined by the court based on facts at trial.[79]

As Gu makes very clear, the CPL 1996 did not embrace the label of 'presumption', indicating that this was considered incompatible with the basic principle of seeking truth from facts.[80] The fact that the legislator rejected the label of presumption of innocence, moreover, indicates that it was not seen as a guiding thought of the revised law.[81] This implies a denial of the principle dimension of presumption of innocence. Looking at the formulation in Article 12, it was arguably more acceptable for the legislator to refer to 'no guilt' than to use the term 'innocence'. The provision stipulating the court's adjudication power was not new, but under the CPL 1979 it was undermined by the prosecutor's power to exempt from prosecution.[82] However, Gu Angran's comments reflect the view that the revised law adopted 'reasonable elements' of the presumption of innocence, including the rule of 'no guilt without judgment', as enshrined in Article 12. In other words, the legislator approved certain elements of the rule dimension of presumption of innocence, such as the burden of proof or the maxim *in dubio pro reo*. Gu's statement reflects the official stance of not blindly copying other systems but rather combining national conditions with foreign experience.

[79] Own translation, original quote cited in Yue Liling (n 73) 132–133.
[80] CPL 1996, art 6.
[81] Xi Danni (n 78) 208.
[82] CPL 1979, art 3.

Elaborating on the scope of such 'reasonable elements' of the presumption of innocence. Zhang, who largely considers the presumption of innocence as a rule of evidence, rejects the right to silence but accepts some other evidential elements, as integrated into Article 12, as well as other provisions in the CPL 1996, as 'reasonable'. Although this provision would suggest a certain treatment towards suspects and defendants, and even if the state would be obliged to guarantee certain procedural safeguards, Zhang believed that Article 12 was distinct from the presumption of innocence. The objective existence of guilt or innocence would conflict with the 'intrinsic epistemological limitations' of presumption of innocence.[83] Therefore Zhang understood it as a factual presumption and followed the old view that believed the application of presumption of innocence would conflict with the reality of criminal justice. And while this understanding of presumption of innocence was no longer the dominant view in the 1990s, it was perhaps the idealism residing in the principle of presumption of innocence that continued to cause unease among scholars in China.

Regarding the question of a presumption of innocence 'with Chinese characteristics', Article 12 established only one rule: no guilt without judgment. Indeed, the practical significance of Article 12 alone can only be limited. This rule would need to be specified and supplemented by other rules and principles to realise presumption of innocence. As for the broader dimension of presumption of innocence as a principle of fairness, the wording of Article 12 does not clearly prescribe any particular behaviour on the part of state agencies that must be observed vis-à-vis suspects and defendants in criminal proceedings, notably in the context of compulsory measures, even if it could be understood to mean that state officials should refrain from making any statements that could indicate the guilt of a suspect or defendant. For example, the provision is silent on how pre-trial errors like unlawful and arbitrary deprivations of personal liberty or coerced confessions can be remedied. Rather, the provision aims to specify the separation of powers in criminal proceedings, ie, the court's exclusive power of adjudication, which is supported by the abolition of exemption from prosecution.[84] This assumption is shared by scholars who believe that the primary purpose of Article 12 was to bring the CPL 1996 in line with the Constitution, while the legislator had no intention to establish the presumption of innocence due to the many ambiguities underlying the 'western' presumption of innocence.[85]

In other words, Article 12 implies that guilt must be established through formal legal proceedings, as indicated by Gu Angran, but it is silent on the nature of these

[83] Zhang Zetao (n 64) 34–36.
[84] Wu Hongyao and Zhong Songzhi (n 54) 871–872 (Gu Angran's Explanations on the Draft Amendments (1996)).
[85] Zhao Shunrong (n 55) 111.

proceedings.[86] Therefore, it is fair to say that Article 12 introduced the concept of legal guilt.[87] However, the revised law reaffirmed the principle of seeking truth from facts.[88] Even if overall the language of the CPL 1996 was de-politicised, it reiterated the need to establish factual guilt at an early stage of criminal proceedings and introduced new mechanisms to facilitate the establishment of factual guilt. Indeed, a major shortcoming of the CPL 1996 was its emphasis on ascertaining the factual guilt (or innocence) of the suspects in the pre-trial phases. The CPL 1996 reiterated the need to clarify the criminal facts (*fanzui shishi*) accurately and swiftly, which indicates that the law still equated case facts with criminal facts.[89] The CPL 1996 thus created a critical conflict between the concepts of legal and factual guilt.

In hindsight, observers criticised the overemphasis on Article 12 when examining the existence of the presumption of innocence in China.[90] Indeed, as shown above, the argument that Article 12 can be seen as a manifestation, or reflection of the 'essence' of the presumption of innocence in China stands on fragile grounds, but it may have been a strategic choice. For scholars, the motive behind advocating this view may have been hope for a gradual expansion. As shown in chapter three, the party-state had endorsed the principle of law-based governance in 1997 and wrote the 'construction of a Socialist rule of law state' into the Chinese Constitution in 1999. This has nurtured reform-minded scholars' hopes that China will eventually transform into a rule-of-law state and thus ultimately embrace the presumption of innocence as a central pillar of rule of law. The next section will show, however, that the revised law, from a more holistic perspective, had maintained old and adopted new provisions that must be seen as eroding the presumption of innocence.

## V. (Missing) Elements of the Presumption of Innocence

As discussed in the previous section, Article 12 alone cannot be considered as an establishment of the presumption of innocence in China. In order to examine the overall acceptance of presumption of innocence elements in the CPL 1996, this provision must indeed be examined in conjunction with other new provisions.[91]

[86] Wu Hongyao and Zhong Songzhi (n 54) 870 (Gu Angran's Explanations on the Draft Amendments (1996)).
[87] 'Yijiujiuliu nian Zhongguo renquan shiye de jinzhan (Progress of human rights in China in 1996)' www.gov.cn/zhengce/2005-05/26/content_2615745.htm accessed 27 March 2020.
[88] CPL 1996, art 6.
[89] CPL 1996, art 2; Chen Guangzhong (n 66) 35.
[90] Xifen Lin and Casey Watters, 'Understanding the Presumption of Innocence in China: Institution and Practice' in Yun Zhao and Michael Ng (eds), *Chinese Legal Reform and the Global Legal Order: Adoption and Adaptation* (Cambridge, Cambridge University Press, 2018) 52.
[91] Zhang Xiaohai (n 75) 118; Yi Yanyou (n 56) 19; Yue Liling (n 73) 132–133.

In the 1990s, Chinese scholars continued to focus on the evidential dimension of presumption of innocence, which entails that the burden of proof is on the prosecution and proof must be beyond reasonable doubt, as well as the application of the maxim of *in dubio pro reo*. As the previous discussions have shown, Article 12 established the concept of legal guilt, and the official stance was that the burden of proof was clearly placed on the prosecution when reading Article 162(3) (*in dubio pro reo* at trial) and Article 43 (prosecution's burden of proof) in conjunction with the newly added Article 12 (exclusive adjudication power).[92] Therefore, the legislator did not follow the scholar's proposal to allocate the burden of proof in expressive terms. Furthermore, it was suggested that Article 43 provides for an implicit privilege against self-incrimination by prohibiting the use of force to obtain evidential materials. It was assumed that the general acceptance of the self-incrimination privilege was due to the signing of the ICCPR by China in 1998.[93] Whether the law indeed endorsed such an implicit privilege will be analysed in the next section.

As proposed in the scholarly draft,[94] the CPL 1996 introduced provisions on the handling of doubtful cases at the pre-trial stages and the trial stage, reflecting the idea of the maxim of the *in dubio pro reo*.[95] As shown in chapter three, the CPL 1979 was silent on that matter, which had led to the widespread practice of pending cases – a heavy burden for the system. According to Gu Angran, the scope of non-prosecution powers was expanded, while the institution of exemption from prosecution was abolished. The intention was to protect innocent persons from being basically labelled criminals.[96]

The CPL 1996 established a regime of compulsory and optional non-prosecution and non-prosecution due to insufficient evidence.[97] Under the revised law, if the evidentiary standard of clear facts and reliable and sufficient evidence, as required to close a criminal investigation and initiate prosecution, could not be reached, the prosecuting agencies were allowed to order the police to provide further evidence by conducting supplementary investigation or simply decide not to prosecute due to insufficient evidence. Where supplementary investigation could not produce the required evidentiary standard for prosecution, which had remained unchanged, the prosecutor could now decide to drop a case.[98]

[92] CPL 1979, art 32, requiring the collection of all kinds of evidence (inculpatory and exculpatory) and prohibiting the extortion of confessions and illegal obtainment of evidence, was renumbered as CPL 1996, art 43 but not revised; Yue Liling (n 73) 134.

[93] Zhou Shimin, 'Shou xingshi kongzhizhe de chenmoquan (The Right to Silence of the Criminal Accused)' in Chen Guangzhong (ed), *Gongmin quanli he zhengzhi quanli guoji gongyue pizhun yu shishi wenti yanjiu (Study on the ratification and implementation of the International Covenant on Civil and Political Rights)* (Beijing, China Legal Publishing House, 2002) 289.

[94] Chen Guangzhong and Yan Duan (n 23) 16 (art 65(2)), 26–27 (art 119), 37–38 (arts 171 and 172).

[95] CPL 1996, art 162(3).

[96] Wu Hongyao and Zhong Songzhi (n 54) 871–872 (Gu Angran's Explanations on the Draft Amendments (1996)).

[97] Chen Guangzhong (n 74) 325–327.

[98] CPL 1996, arts 129, 137, 140 and 141.

The revision nonetheless enabled the possibility of prosecution at a later stage.[99] Therefore, an initial decision of non-prosecution did not necessarily mean finality.

Non-prosecution was now mandatory in cases not falling in the scope of criminal behaviour due to pettiness, where the time limits for prosecution had and in a few other exceptional cases.[100] In minor cases, the prosecutor could now decide not to prosecute but instead suggest that the suspect should receive administrative punishment. This effectively amounts to an exemption from prosecution, since the determination of their guilt was required to transfer the case for administrative punishment, and the accused had no chance to defend themselves; letting an allegedly guilty person escape punishment was out of the question.[101] And even if, unlike the CPL 1979, the CPL 1996 granted a person the right to challenge the decision of non-prosecution, the review of such a decision remained in the hands of the prosecuting organs.[102] In other words, the law did not install a judicial review by a court. Although the powers of non-prosecution in doubtful cases were strengthened, it was still possible to dismiss a case after it had formally entered the trial stage, meaning after public prosecution had already been initiated.[103]

Interestingly, these evidence rules, used in official and academic discourses to demonstrate the existence of presumption of innocence standards, were understood to function without a legally guaranteed right to silence and privilege against self-incrimination. Conversely, under the revised law, the suspects' duty to make truthful statements was retained. Observers therefore asked how to rationalise this duty in the light of a greater commitment to meet fair trial standards.

## A. Rationalising the Absence of Silence

As shown in the previous chapter, the CPL 1979 established the prohibition to extort confessions by torture and the unlawful obtainment of evidence.[104] While this prohibition was seen as an expression of the prohibition against self-incrimination, the law had also stipulated the duty to make truthful statements during interrogation, which was widely viewed as conflicting with the presumption of innocence.[105] As already mentioned, this duty was maintained, but, due to the overall adjustment of the terminology of the law, it was now explicitly limited

[99] Mike McConville (with Satnam Choongh, Pinky Choy, Dick Wan, Eric Chui, Wing Hong, Ian Dobinson and Carol Jones), *Criminal Justice in China: An Empirical Inquiry* (Cheltenham, Edward Elgar, 2011) 108; Criminal Procedure Rules of the People's Procuratorate (Amended by the Supreme People's Procuratorate on 21 September 1999, No. 1 [1999]) art 287.

[100] CPL 1996, arts 15, 142(1).

[101] CPL 1996, art 142(2); McConville et al (n 99) 109–110.

[102] CPL 1996, art 146.

[103] Chen Guangzhong (n 66) 33.

[104] CPL 1979, art 32.

[105] Chen Guangzhong (n 66) 31.

to suspects.[106] Although there has been a debate as to whether the CPL 1996 at least implicitly introduced a right to silence, the prevailing view is that the view of denial triumphed, as the law neither abandoned the duty of truthful statements nor introduced a right to silence.[107] With the right to silence gaining more recognition among legal scholars in China, especially through the accession to CAT in 1988 and the signing of the ICCPR in 1998, scholars discussed how this duty, as well as other provisions in the CPL 1996, could be rationalised and possibly harmonised.

Here it may be worth noting that Chinese scholars often appear to use the right to silence and the privilege against self-incrimination interchangeably, though some nuances were recognised. Yi Yanyou, for example, believes that, functionally speaking, the right to silence, partly being a 'defence right', is closely intertwined with the privilege not to commit self-incrimination because both allow the accused person to remain silent.[108] Yi does not necessarily indicate that the two are the same, but he points to the interrelated nature between them. In a similar vein, Chen Ruihua has held that the right to silence is a procedural rule, whereas the privilege against self-incrimination would constitute a principle, allowing a person to remain silent or voluntarily make a statement. Since the former would follow from the privilege, silence would be a form of exercising the privilege. Moreover, the privilege was broader in scope and would require further normative considerations in terms of exclusion of illegally obtained evidence or deprivations of personal liberty.[109]

Since the ICCPR only explicitly refers to the privilege against self-incrimination, certain scholars have argued that China would not undermine the Covenant if it did not adopt a right to silence. To make such a claim, one would have to consider the two guarantees completely independent from each other. For example, Liu Genju, who suggested that both suspects and defendants should have a right to silence that binds the three agencies,[110] recognises the interrelated nature of the two guarantees but holds that they are two different guarantees. In his view, the privilege against self-incrimination would predate the right to silence, and the two would carry different expressions and implications because the right to silence would be limited to verbal communication; some national system would thus stipulate them separately. For example, the prohibition against extortion of confessions and unlawful obtainment of evidence in Article 43 would reflect the privilege against self-incrimination, but whether a suspect or defendant has a right to silence was a different question. In the light of the suspect's duty to make truthful statements, Liu holds that the CPL 1996 had denied a right to silence.[111]

[106] The CPL 1979 did not distinguish between suspects and defendants and used 'defendants' (*beigaoren*) throughout the law.

[107] Liu Genju, 'Zai woguo queding chenmoquan yuanze jige wenti zhi yantao (Discussing Some Issues Regarding China's Establishment of the Principle of Right to Silence)' [2000] *China Legal Science* 43, 52–54.

[108] Yi Yanyou (n 43) 280–282.

[109] Chen Ruihua (n 66) 57–59.

[110] Liu Genju (n 107) 47.

[111] ibid 49–54.

Yi Yanyou, an advocate of the right to silence and critic of the duty to make truthful statements, discussed the absence of an explicit right to silence against the backdrop of Article 12, which would manifest the presumption of innocence. He voiced concerns regarding the view that such a guarantee would not suit national conditions due to the rise in crime and the overall limited capacities and backward methods of investigations; this was not an argument against it but one for it. In his view, the presumption of innocence and the right to silence are interdependent guarantees, and the duty to make truthful statements runs counter to Article 12 because it would be associated with the presumption of guilt and thus compromise the burden of proof. Yi rejected the claim that a right to silence was not in line with national conditions as baseless; the acceptance of such a guarantee was a question of willingness. In his view, extorted confessions were a national condition that ought to be addressed.[112] Yi believed that the prohibition against extortion of confession or obtaining evidence in Article 43 recognised an implicit privilege against self-incrimination of suspects and defendants. The CPL 1996 would thus have enshrined an explicit but narrow right to silence, namely, the right to refuse to answer questions that are 'irrelevant' to the case, albeit with no clear guidance on what ought to fall within the scope of irrelevance.[113] Earlier mentioned Liu Genju criticised this interpretation, as the right to refuse to answer irrelevant questions would not fall within the scope of the right to silence.[114]

In the light of the policy of combining leniency with severity, as reflected in the suspects' duty to make truthful statements, some scholars rejected a right to silence, as it would vest suspects with too much power. Considering the reliance on statements (and confessions), silence would not only hinder efficient crime control but also fair outcomes.[115] Leading scholars like Chen Guangzhong voiced concerns as regards the compatibility of this guarantee with this policy, as it would provide the accused with a 'shield of non-cooperation', leading to significant obstacles in reality.[116] However, others have argued that this policy is irrelevant in the pre-trial context but applies in the trial context at sentencing.[117]

Although a violation of the duty to make truthful statements is not explicitly followed by legal consequences, as already mentioned, it was widely agreed that courts would impose a heavier punishment on defendants in the event of silence.[118] Even if it was only a moral obligation, there was thus an agreement that it entailed consequences. However, policies requiring full clearance of criminal

[112] Yi Yanyou (n 43) 277–279.
[113] Yi Yanyou (n 56) 20–21; Song Yinghui (n 3) 118–119.
[114] Liu Genju (n 107) 52–54.
[115] Zhang Zetao (n 64) 34.
[116] Chen Guangzhong (n 49) 29.
[117] Huang Dao and Tie Li, 'Wuzui tuiding zai xin zhongguo de mingyun – jianguo yilai faxuejie zhongda shijian yanjiu (er) (The Fate of the Presumption of Innocence in New China: A Study of Major Events in Jurisprudence since the Founding of the People's Republic of China (II))' [1997] *Law Science* 2, 3.
[118] Yue Liling, *Gongmin quanli he zhengzhi quanli guoji gongyue yu zhongguo xingshi sifa (International Covenant on Civil and Political Rights and Criminal Justice in China)* (Beijing, Law Press China, 2007) 114; Liu Genju (n 107) 52–54.

cases further exacerbated the issue of confession reliance,[119] made even worse by provisions of the Ministry of Public Security of 1998 formally emphasising the function of criminal investigations as a tool to solve cases.[120]

In the view of He Jiahong, many scholars in China had understood the implications of the right to silence in the late 1990s; the most critical question was whether China should adopt a right to silence in the phase of police investigation versus the duty to make truthful statements. Based on anecdotal evidence, He stressed that the opposition rate coming from the police was more than 80 per cent in the late 1990s. His empirical evidence showed that the overall opposition rate remained very high, even if the overall acceptance had increased. The usual pros and cons brought forward by both sides have already been discussed. In the view of He, amongst them, the problem of striking a balance between crime control and human rights protection would be the most complex issue. He concedes that a right to silence would certainly have a huge impact on the work of the police that were confronted with issues resulting from the socio-economic changes, such as vagabond criminals. In the light of the many factors contributing to extorted confessions, it would indeed take more efforts than simply stipulating a right to silence. He believed that a shift from substantive to procedural justice was needed. To this end, the quality and capabilities of case-handling personnel should be improved, and a shift away from confession reliance towards scientific evidence and scientific and technological means would be needed; a strengthening of supervision over interrogations and exclusionary rules was also indispensable. Recalling the debate as to whether a right to silence was needed to meet international standards, He believes that domestic legislation would not need to adopt an explicit right to silence; it would be enough to make sure that no coercion is applied to suspects. The fact that a suspect does not have the right to silence when being questioned is not tantamount to saying that they are forced to incriminate themselves, nor is it tantamount to a presumption of guilt but would only imply that they may choose to answer truthfully. He raised concerns as regards blindly copying other systems and underlined criminal justice 'with Chinese characteristics'.[121]

Sun Chanyong, who rejected the claim that Article 12 manifests the presumption of innocence, believed that the view of denial of the right to silence had won in the making of the CPL 1996 for various political, procedural, societal, and cultural reasons. Politically speaking, the mantra 'stability overrides everything' had successfully suppressed calls for individual rights. Procedurally speaking, the law was not rigid enough but rather used by the three agencies to handle the

[119] Chen Zexian and Xiong Qiuhong, *Xingshi susong fa xiugai jianyi gao yu lunzheng – yi bei kongzhi ren de quanli baohu wei hexin (Draft Proposal for Amendments to the Criminal Procedure Law and Argumentation – Centred on the Protection of the Rights of Accused Persons* (Beijing, China Social Sciences Press, 2009) 62.

[120] Provisions on Handling of Criminal Cases by the Public Security Organs (14 May 1998, No. 35 of Ministry of Public Security) art 186.

[121] He Jiahong, 'Chenmoquan zhidu ji xingshi sifa de jiazhi quxiang (Right to Silence Regime and the Value Orientation of Criminal Justice)' (2000) 8 *Journal of National Prosecutors College* 32, 41–44.

'formalities'. Owing to the absence of independent and impartial courts, lacking legislation for excluding evidence and the absence of presumption of innocence, it was impossible to effectively limit state power. From a social perspective, the socio-economic changes would have led to growing crime rates, putting a lot of pressure on the police to maintain social order, which would render any debate about such a guarantee superfluous. From a cultural perspective, Su believes that the traditional de-emphasis on the individual has contributed to greater acceptance of using compulsion, at least if a person is considered factually guilty.[122]

Therefore, to meet CAT and ICCPR standards and to realise the presumption of innocence, Sun suggested establishing a right to silence regime, even if it should accommodate national conditions. Sun criticises the many 'myths' surrounding the right to silence, including the claim that it could not curb the occurrence of extorted confessions. While he agrees that it would not be a panacea, it would obviously be a starting point and an important preventive measure. In terms of costs, Sun is sceptical of the claim that a right to silence would be a heavy burden for the system. While the difficulty and cost of investigating and solving crimes would increase, it would be a necessary commitment to protect the human rights of criminal suspects and defendants. The idea that criminals may escape would also be erroneous in the sense that no system could ensure 100 per cent accuracy or fairness. The claim that the duty meets national conditions and is based on 'social morality' would be untenable and beneficial only for the police. Such a moral duty was not unique to China, and precisely because it exerts a lot of pressure and may lead to abuse, the right to silence has been codified in many systems. However, it could not be ignored that the system would be struggling with the impact of the socio-economic changes. For example, besides an overall improvement of pre-trial proceedings in terms of interrogations, access to counsel, etc, and independent and impartial courts, a solution would lie in expanding the system of mitigated punishment or allowing courts to draw inferences from silence under certain circumstances.[123] Therefore, scholars like He or Sun recognised that the codification of a right to silence alone could not rectify the problem of coerced confessions.

## B. The Zero Confession Rules

To address the problem of confession reliance, some localities nonetheless tried new ways to change the culture and change the mode of criminal investigation. In August 2000, the Shuncheng District People's Procuratorate of Fushun City, Liaoning Province, issued the Rules on Zero Confession in Criminal Cases ('Zero Confession Rules') to suppress the occurrence of coerced confessions. Yet, the scope of silence was understood to be different from that applied in western

[122] Sun Changyong (n 43) 18–19.
[123] ibid 18–23.

countries. The Zero Confession Rules were applicable only in the investigation stage and only intended to serve as an *internal* standard for case handling authorities.[124] However, these rules were not unanimously embraced. Observers criticised that they would compromise the Criminal Procedure Law provisions, which explicitly allow for the use of confessions as evidence.[125] In addition, according to these critics, there would be no absolute rights and no absolute duties. Even if suspects and defendants should be considered legally innocent until found guilty by a court, they were not necessarily factually innocent and should therefore be able to make a confession.[126] Indeed, as shown in chapter two, Article 14 ICCPR does not exclude the possibility of conviction solely based on a confession. Yet, it should also be borne in mind that the principle of presumption of innocence remains intact, even if a confession of guilt has been made.[127] While this criticism is thus not unfounded, the Zero Confessions Rules should be interpreted as an attempt to change the culture of confession reliance, even if such a complete ban seems rather extreme and not sensible in practice.

In fact, the Zero Confession Rules were subsequently amended five times and gradually relaxed. 'Allowing [the suspect] to remain silent' was modified, stating that they should be 'encouraged to make a truthful statement without being forced to make an unfavourable statement', thus emphasising the element of voluntariness. Although these modifications no longer banned confessions outright, the case-handling authorities were encouraged to carefully review the reliability of confessions and not to establish criminal facts solely based on a confession, thereby reducing the probative value of confessions. Echoing the critics, it was suggested that the rules were modified due to the absence of a legal basis for enforcing zero-confessions and because they would indeed conflict with Criminal Procedure Law provisions. According to a spokesperson of the Shuncheng District People's Procuratorate, the main purpose of the Zero Confessions Rules was to improve the ability of investigation authorities to use evidence, not to clarify the issue of a right to silence. Within ten months, they were reportedly only applied in 20 out of 200 cases. As an explanation, it was said that they could not be applied in all criminal cases, including corruption or homicides, or where a confession would be necessary to resolve a case.[128] While the Zero Confessions Rules aimed at limiting the importance of confessions and raising the reliability of evidence obtained in the investigation phase, thereby also improving the competences of the case-handling authorities without directly addressing the question of a right to silence, the figures indicate that they only played a marginal role in practice and were arguably not well received by practitioners.

[124] Liu Tieshan, '"Ling kougong" bu zai "yunxu baochi chenmo" ("Zero Confessions" no longer "Permission to Remain Silent")' *China Judge* (30 March 2001) www.china-judge.com/fzhm/fzhm461.htm accessed 4 January 2020.

[125] CPL 1996, art 42, No. 4.

[126] Fang Zhongbing, 'Zhiyi "ling kougong guize" (Questioning the "Zero Confessions Rules")' *China Judge* www.china-judge.com/fnsx3/fnsx2057.htm accessed 30 April 2021.

[127] See ch 2, III.B.

[128] Liu Tieshan (n 124).

## C. Voluntariness without Lawyers

The previous discussion raises the question of how the voluntariness of a confession made in the phase of an investigation can be guaranteed if choosing silence is not really an option. The involvement of lawyers at pre-trial proceedings can be an effective control mechanism to ensure the integrity of the accused and the voluntariness of a confession, especially in the absence of other safeguards such as audio-visual recordings of interrogations, etc. Although the Chinese government had ratified the CAT in 1988 and even if the scholarly draft proposed the adoption of provisions on the admissibility of evidence, the CPL 1996 did not address this issue.[129]

In 1996, the Lawyers Law (LL) first reorganised the legal profession and specified the rights and obligations of lawyers. The legal profession was no longer part of the state apparatus, and lawyers were no longer state legal workers.[130] Regarding representation and defence,[131] the law thus clarified that lawyers acting as criminal defenders should represent the interests of suspects or defendants.[132] And lawyers involved in the proceedings were now entitled to gather and consult case materials and to communicate with clients who are in custody, albeit under the CPL limitations.[133] However, the CPL 1996 and other legislation set further limits to the pre-trial involvement of lawyers in criminal cases.

Regarding criminal defence, Gu Angran claimed that the rights of the defence have been sufficiently strengthened, especially an earlier involvement of lawyers in criminal proceedings.[134] The CPL 1996 indeed signalled some progress in this regard. For example, a suspect was allowed access to counsel in the phase of investigation, meaning after the first interrogation or from the day a coercive measure was taken against them. In cases involving state secrets, the appointment of a lawyer was to be approved by the relevant investigating authorities. However, lawyers were not given the status of a defender at this point.[135]

Under the CPL 1996, a suspect had the right to entrust a *defence* lawyer from the date the case was transferred for examination of prosecution.[136] Furthermore, it added that defence lawyers are allowed to collect their own evidence, although they needed the witness's consent and, for testimony from the victim's witnesses,

[129] Gelatt (n 58) 69.

[130] LL 1996, art 1 (see also CPL 1996, art 35). As part of this reform, licensed lawyers today are governed by the All China Lawyers Association (ACLA), which is organised under the Ministry of Justice, see Sida Liu and Terence Halliday, *Criminal Defense in China, The Politics of Lawyers at Work* (Cambridge, Cambridge University Press, 2016) 21.

[131] CPL 1996, arts 32 and 82 No. (3).

[132] LL 1996, art 28.

[133] LL 1996, art 30.

[134] Wu Hongyao and Zhong Songzhi (n 54) 870 (Gu Angran's Explanations on the Draft Amendments to the CPL (1996)).

[135] CPL 1996, art 96.

[136] CPL 1996, art 33(1).

the approval from the procuracy or the court.[137] Moreover, the investigation authorities were authorised to decide whether to be present at the meeting.[138] Therefore, the CPL 1996 did not protect the *right* of a suspect to have a lawyer present during interrogations, including the first interrogation, which would have been crucial in ensuring their integrity, as well as the voluntariness of a confession. As already mentioned, lawyers largely only indirectly participated in the revision process through representatives of the Ministry of Justice, which had less power than representatives of the Ministry of Public Security. These power struggles are reflected in the CPL 1996, which partly gave lawyers more procedural rights, but it retained crime control elements by making them conditional through approval requirements, etc.[139]

Regulations issued by the Supreme People's Procuratorate set further limits to the pre-trial involvement of lawyers in criminal cases involving state secrets, including the right of a suspect being held in custody to entrust or communicate with a lawyer.[140] Regarding the defence, the CPL 1996 had provided for defence lawyers to have access to the case files and to meet and communicate with their clients in custody only from the moment the procuratorate examines a case with a view to prosecution.[141] Overall, the involvement of lawyers in the early stages of proceedings, especially criminal investigation, remained very limited. Without the presence of a lawyer during questioning and in the absence of additional safeguards to enforce silence, a suspect could hardly choose to remain silent, even if the CPL 1996 had contained fundamental fair trial safeguards such as a right to silence or a privilege against self-incrimination. As part of an effective right to defence, the principle of equality of arms requires access to legal counsel and the opportunity to prepare for defence, among others.[142] There was a lack of effective checks on investigation powers. In the light of these many normative shortcomings, it becomes clearer why the earlier discussed Article 12 may not be seen as more than a small screw in a defective mechanism.

Since the CPL 1996 was put into practice, supplementary regulations further regulated the involvement of lawyers in the stage of investigation without granting them a right to be present during interrogations. While the All China Lawyers Association issued provisions to provide clearer guidance on criminal defence work, they are of no relevance for the behaviour of the three agencies.[143] However, overall, law-making activities by implementing agencies had become more frequent in the 1990s, though it was not necessarily helpful as many inconsistent or contradictory provisions emerged, reflecting these agencies' own and sometimes creative

[137] CPL 1996, art 37.
[138] CPL 1996, art 96(2).
[139] Liu and Halliday (n 130) 26.
[140] Criminal Procedure Rules of the People's Procuratorate (1999) arts 146, 148 and 152.
[141] CPL 1996, art 36.
[142] ICCPR, art 14(3)(b); see also ch 2, V.C.
[143] Liu and Halliday (n 130) 29.

interpretation of the CPL 1996 provisions.[144] For example, a regulation of the Ministry of Public Security stipulated that meetings with clients must be approved by the public security organs and that the date and place are to be decided by that organ.[145] This provision compromised the lawyer's right to meet with clients in the phase of investigation, as granted under the CPL 1996. To harmonise the conflicting provisions, a joint regulation by the three agencies and other departments stipulated that no approval for meeting with suspects is needed unless state secrets were involved. The Supreme People's Court and Supreme People's Procuratorate adjusted their interpretations to the Criminal Procedure Law accordingly, but the Ministry of Public Security did not.[146] As will be discussed in chapter five, although the revised LL 2007 aimed to strengthen the rights of criminal defence lawyers beyond those provided for in the CPL 1996,[147] research on the ground showed that these reforms had not significantly improved the situation of criminal defence lawyers in China in reality.[148]

## VI. Insufficient Legal Protection of Personal Liberty

In the 1990s, legal scholars in China held different views regarding compliance with personal liberty safeguards under the CPL 1979, especially with respect to the custodial measures of detention (*juliu*) and arrest (*daibu*). While some scholars suggested that the police comply with the legal provisions in most criminal cases, others argued that they are largely ignored.[149] As the previous discussions have shown, many practitioners and theorists agreed that the system of compulsory measures needs to be improved. Going back to the scholarly draft proposal, it suggested retaining the five compulsory measures of the CPL 1979 but reordered them.[150] It enumerated them in a sequential order ranging from less intrusive (forced appearance, bail, residential surveillance, detention) to the most intrusive measure of arrest resulting in remand custody.[151] It, moreover, established basic principles that law enforcement and judicial organs should observe when using

[144] ibid 27.

[145] Provisions on the Lawyer's Involvement in Criminal Proceedings in the Investigation Phase (Issued by the Ministry of Public Security on 20 December 1996) arts 8, 11 and 12.

[146] Liu and Halliday (n 130) 28–29; Provisions Concerning Several Issues in the Implementation of the Criminal Procedure Law (Jointly adopted by the SCNPC Legislative Affairs Commission, the Supreme People's Court, the Supreme People's Procuratorate, the Ministry of Public Security, the Ministry of State Security, and the Ministry of Justice on 19 January 1998) arts 9 and 11.

[147] The Law on Lawyers of 1996 was first amended in 2001, but the changes were marginal. 2007 LL, art 33 (meetings with clients shall not be monitored), art 34 (expanded access to 'all relevant' case files), and art 37 (protection of lawyers' personal rights); Liu and Halliday (n 130) 39.

[148] McConville et al (n 99) 68.

[149] Timothy A Gelatt, 'Criminal Justice with Chinese Characteristics: China's Criminal Process and Violations of Human Rights' (Lawyers Committee for Human Rights, 1993) 12–13.

[150] See ch 3, V.

[151] Chen Guangzhong and Yan Duan (n 23) 18–19 (art 82).

compulsory measures against a criminal suspect or defendant, encompassing concepts such as proportionality, necessity or reasonableness of compulsory measures.[152]

The scholarly draft further set out the requirements for the compulsory measures by following the sequential order. It provided for an expansion of the provisions on summons and established time spans and limits for forced appearances.[153] It included a provision that would have entitled a suspect to apply for bail.[154] The drafters proposed maintaining the time limits for detention, as established in the CPL 1979, even if they acknowledged that they were comparatively long.[155] With respect to the measure of arrest, the drafters recommended relaxing the evidentiary standard but clarifying the time limits at different stages of criminal proceedings in a single provision.[156] Whether the revised law should retain the measure of residential surveillance was more controversially discussed. Although some of the drafters proposed the abolition of this measure, the draft eventually retained but restricted the location to the residence of the suspect or defendant to prevent potential misuse.[157]

The question is whether the CPL 1996 has brought about significant changes in terms of personal liberty safeguards. Since Article 12 introduced the concept of legal guilt, and because it was the official interpretation that a person should not be regarded as a criminal until found guilty according to law, it may be understood to imply that compulsory measures against an accused person must be taken based on the assumption of innocence, which underlines requirements such as proportionality or necessity of deprivation of personal liberty.

As regards non-custodial measures, the CPL 1996 specified the conditions for bail and residential surveillance (which were previously identical) and first introduced time limits for these measures.[158] It added a provision, stipulating that residential surveillance can be enforced at a designated location if the suspect or defendant has no fixed residence.[159] It included a provision on the right of a suspect or denfendant in custody to apply for bail and moreover provided that a suspect or defendant 'may' (*keyi*) be released on bail or placed under residential surveillance if the statutory time limits of a procedural stage (ie, criminal investigation, examination for prosecution, first or second instance proceedings) are exceeded.[160] However, the wording indicates that this remained optional.

While the CPL 1996 did not provide for specific conditions of bail, the three agencies had issued judicial interpretations and regulations providing clearer

[152] ibid 19, 195.

[153] ibid 19 (art 84).

[154] ibid 14 (art 58(2)) and 19 (art 85), 198–199.

[155] Art 48 of the 1979 CPL stipulated a maximum of ten days for requesting the arrest of a detainee; ibid 21–22 (art 96).

[156] ibid arts 98 and 105.

[157] ibid 20 (art 90), 200–201.

[158] CPL 1996, arts 51 and 58(1).

[159] CPL 1996, art 57(2).

[160] CPL 1996, arts 52 and 74.

guidance on circumstances under which bail should be applied in the different stages of the proceedings. These provisions stipulated that a suspect or defendant may be released on bail if they cannot be incarcerated due to serious health conditions or because she was either pregnant or nursing an infant or if the case could be concluded within the statutory time limits. While the Ministry of Public Security and the Supreme People's Procuratorate additionally stressed the use of bail if the conditions for arrest cannot be met and a consideration of the possible sentence, the Supreme People's Court listed instances of compulsory bail (*yingdang*) for defendants who had already been sentenced to control (*guanzhi*) or independent supplementary punishment (*duli shiyong fujiaxing*), by the court of first instance or if the period of custody had already amounted to or exceeded the term of punishment imposed by the court of first instance or where the statutory time limits of case handling had already been exceeded but the case was still ongoing. None of these provisions elaborated on how to assess the requirement of 'social danger' in this context, though they made clear under which conditions bail should be denied.[161]

The CPL 1996 modified the targets of detention. In addition to those regulated in the CPL 1979, the scope was extended to suspects who conceal their true name and address and who are suspected of gang crimes or are alleged repeat offenders.[162] The scope of detention was thus expanded to former targets of 'detention for investigation' (*shourong shencha*), ie, persons concealing their identity or who are unknown, vagabond criminals.[163] Therefore, this measure was incorporated into the CPL 1996 and thus now belonged to the supervision powers of the procuratorial organs. To compensate for the abolition of this measure, the CPL 1996 extended the time limits for submitting a request for arrest. Even though the regular time limit for it was three days and 'under special circumstances' seven days, in cases involving major suspects suspected of having committed crimes in different places, repeatedly or in a gang, the revised law allowed an extension of up to 30 days, making a total maximum of 37 days.[164]

The requirements as to the notification of the reasons for detention were not modified.[165] Although the reasons should be included in the detention warrant, they still usually only mentioned the offence for which the suspect is suspected. The CPL 1996 introduced no requirement on the part of the police that the reasons should be communicated orally at the time of detention in a language that the

[161] The Supreme People's Court's Interpretation on Several Issues regarding the Application of the Criminal Procedure Law of the PRC 1998 (Adopted on 29 June 1998, No. 23 [1998]) arts 80, 81 and 82; Criminal Procedure Rules of the People's Procuratorate (1999) arts 37 and 38; Provisions on Handling of Criminal Cases by the Public Security Organs (1998) arts 63 and 64.

[162] CPL 1996, art 61; Provisions on Handling of Criminal Cases by the Public Security Organs (1998) art 110.

[163] Chen Guangzhong (n 66) 33; Cui Min (n 26) 87.

[164] CPL 1996, art 69.

[165] CPL 1996, arts 64 and 65 (renumbered).

suspect understands.[166] This appears particularly problematic when considering that there is no judicial oversight by courts over pre-trial proceedings, which would be the next line of defence to enable a suspect to understand the reasons for their deprivation of liberty. In this regard, the CPL 1996 made no improvements.

Furthermore, the CPL 1996 lowered the evidentiary requirements for arrest to address arbitrary deprivations of liberty and the circumvention of the statutory provisions.[167] It stipulated that a suspect or defendant should be arrested if there is *evidence* to *prove* (or *support*) the facts of a crime and if the suspect or defendant could be sentenced to a term of at least imprisonment and if measures such as the possibility of providing them with a guarantor pending trial or placing them under residential surveillance would be insufficient to prevent a danger to society, so that their arrest is necessary. The CPL 1996 therefore no longer required that the *main* facts of a crime had to be established to justify an arrest.[168] Yi Yanyou has argued that this evidential requirement could effectively ban the use of preventive detention in the criminal justice system.[169] This evidentiary standard is met if there is evidence of the existence of a crime, evidence that the suspect committed the crime, and the evidence of the suspect's criminal behaviour has been verified.[170] It does not mean that all criminal facts must be verified, but that one criminal fact or one criminal fact among multiple criminal acts is sufficient.[171]

However, the evidence needed to close a criminal investigation remained the standard of clear facts and reliable and sufficient evidence.[172] This did not reduce the pressure put on the case-handling organs to reach this evidentiary standard during the criminal investigation phase. The procuratorial organs were still to review whether this standard has been met when examining a case for prosecution in accordance with the CPL 1996.[173] While the law was silent on the conditions for meeting this evidentiary standard, the Supreme People's Procuratorate clarified this standard by stating that the *criminal* facts (the *corpus delicti*) may be considered clear if, for example, they are sufficient to support a conviction and sentence.[174] In other words, it does not reach the standard of proof needed for conviction.

[166] Yue Liling (n 119) 63.

[167] Wu Hongyao and Zhong Songzhi (n 54) 869–870 (Gu Angran's Explanations on Draft Amendments to the CPL (1996).

[168] CPL 1996, art 60.

[169] Yanyou Yi, 'Arrest as Punishment: The Abuse of Arrest in the People's Republic of China' (2008) 10 *Punishment and Society* 9, 10.

[170] Criminal Procedure Rules of the People's Procuratorate (1999) art 86; Provisions Concerning Several Issues in the Implementation of the Criminal Procedure Law (1998) art 26.

[171] Criminal Procedure Rules of the People's Procuratorate (1999) art 87; Provisions of the Supreme People's Procuratorate and Ministry of Public Security on Issues relating to the Application of the Measure of Arrest in accordance with the Law (6 August 2001, No. 10 [2001] of the Supreme People's Procuratorate) s 1, para 1; Quality Standards for the Examination of Arrest Requests by the People's Procuratorates (Adopted by the Supreme People's Procuratorate on 25 August 2010) art 2.

[172] CPL 1996, art 129; Criminal Procedure Rules of the People's Procuratorate (1999) art 234.

[173] ibid art 250.

[174] ibid art 279, No. (1).

However, as already mentioned, the chances of acquittal after prosecution are extremely low, which suggests that the pre-trial determination of guilt is thus barely challenged at trial.

However, the CPL 1996 itself was silent on how other conditions such as 'necessity' should be understood. Implementing agencies drew up provisions specifying the conditions under which 'necessity of arrest' should be affirmed in accordance with Article 60 CPL 1996. In addition, more vague conditions such as a potential 'danger to society', the likelihood of the suspect fleeing to avoid trial, and the nature of the offence (crimes related to organised crime, violent crimes) should also be relevant for the assessment of social danger.[175] Interestingly, this provision deemphasised the evidential requirement as grounds for justifying the necessity of arrest.[176] While the CPL 1996 was silent on whether the procuratorial organ should interrogate a suspect during the arrest examination upon request by the police, the Supreme People's Procuratorate vaguely stipulated optional interrogation during arrest examination if the procuratorial organs had doubts regarding the evidence in the case.[177]

The CPL 1996 introduced the requirement that the procuratorate only must explain the reasons for disapproving an arrest (not for its approval).[178] Moreover, in case of disapproval and if the police consider that decision to be erroneous, the law now enabled them to file for reconsideration, even to the next higher prosecuting organ. Interestingly, the suspect or defendant was not granted such a possibility of review.[179]

The CPL 1996 relaxed the three months' time limits of 'investigation custody' (meaning arrest (*daibu*) in the phase of investigation) and stipulated that it may be extended for up to seven months or even recalculated under certain circumstances.[180] The time limits for the prosecution's first and second trial stages were also expanded.[181] For example, at the prosecution stage, a case could now be sent back for supplementary investigation twice, effectively meaning another one-month extension.[182] The CPL 1996 exacerbated the already existing problem of excessive and prolonged incarceration. If different compulsory measures are subsequently applied at the pre-trial stage, suspects may be deprived of their liberty for many months or even years before a public prosecution decision is made.

[175] Provisions on Issues relating to the Application of the Measure of Arrest in accordance with the Law (2001) s 1, para 2.

[176] Yi (n 169) 11.

[177] Criminal Procedure Rules of the People's Procuratorate (1999) art 97.

[178] CPL 1996, art 68; Provisions on Issues relating to the Application of the Measure of Arrest in accordance with the Law (2001) s 5, para 3.

[179] CPL 1996, art 70; Zhang Zetao, 'Goujian zhongguoshi de tingzheng shencha daibu chengxu (Constructing the Hearing Procedure of Examination of Criminal Arrest with Chinese Characteristics)' (2018) 36 *Tribune of Political Science and Law* 18, 20–21.

[180] CPL 1996, arts 124 to 128. These time limits have been maintained (CPL 2018, arts 156 to 159).

[181] CPL 1996, arts 168 and 196.

[182] CPL 1996, art 140.

Overall, the CPL 1979 system of compulsory custodial measures was largely maintained. The imbalance of powers between the prosecution and the defence was not addressed. The CPL 1996 provisions on custodial compulsory measures did not reflect the principle of presumption of innocence. Owing to the absence of effective separation of powers and checks and balances and given the weak oversight of the detention powers of the police and the lack of judicial oversight of pre-trial proceedings.

Considering the ambiguous and vague conditions for the two custodial measures, as well as potentially indefinite remand custody, the lack of mechanisms to challenge deprivations of personal liberty under the CPL 1996 appears even more worrisome. In this context, the limited effect of Article 12 becomes particularly clear, because this provision, understood as an expression of the essence of the presumption of innocence, does not have much to say in the context of compulsory measures. In other words, Article 12 cannot prescribe a certain treatment to be followed vis-à-vis the accused in the absence of certain personal liberty safeguards such as habeas corpus.

Although the CPL 1996 established time limits of 12 hours for interrogations by summons forced appearances and mandated that suspects should not be held in de facto custody through successive summonses and forced appearances (*lianxu chuanhuan, juchuan*),[183] the Police Law 1995 (PL 1995) undermined these new provisions, as it had empowered the police to hold a person for interrogation and then again for 'further interrogation' (*jixu panwen*) for up to 48 hours.[184] And even if the legislator had followed the scholarly draft and lowered the evidentiary standard for arrest and modified the conditions for detention, the law considerably relaxed the time limits for the latter. In the view of Chen Guangzhong, the relaxation of the conditions, targets and time limits for detention and arrest would facilitate efficient crime control, but the principle of proportionality would be reflected in the CPL 1996, as prosecutors were obliged to consider alternative measures (such as bail or residential surveillance) when examining arrest.[185] Yet, as the next chapter will demonstrate, the reform of the alternative measures of bail and residential surveillance had very limited impact. Bail was still barely used in practice, and even if there may have been a genuine intention to curb the use of residential surveillance as a form of de facto confinement, there is indication that the police often abused it against migrant suspects as a means of maintaining social control, even if the use of it remained comparatively infrequent.[186]

[183] CPL 1996, art 92(2).
[184] Police Law 1995 (PL 1995), art 9.
[185] Chen Guangzhong (n 66) 137.
[186] Joshua Rosenzweig, 'Residential Surveillance: Evolution of a Janus-Faced Measure' in Elisa Nesossi and others (eds), *Legal Reforms and Deprivation of Liberty in Contemporary China* (Abingdon, Routledge, 2016) 82–83.

The provisions of the scholarly draft reflected the idea that deprivations of liberty in the criminal process should not be the rule; although it did not provide for a habeas corpus guarantee, it endorsed the ideas of necessity and proportionality of compulsory measures and aimed to integrate a right to challenge compulsory measures.[187] In terms of feasibility, some of the proposed changes, such as the principle of proportionality in relation to the deprivation of personal liberty, would have required far-reaching institutional reforms ensuring effective external control in order not to be just a promise on paper. Overall, and compared to other areas, the revised CPL 1996 did indeed make significant changes to the provisions on compulsory measures, even if they remained incomplete and did not follow the scholarly proposal to reorganise this system. However, official figures for the period 1986 to 2002 seem to indicate that the gap between the number of people held in custody under the measure of arrest and those who were formally prosecuted within one year remained over 90 per cent. Even after the 1996 reform, the percentage remained high and sometimes still exceeded 100 per cent because the percentage of persons being arrested was higher than the percentage of persons being prosecuted; the gap began to widen after 2001.[188] This indicates that arrest requirements under the CPL 1996 were not strictly observed, leading to excessive custody rates.

## VII. Conclusions

Overall, the CPL 1996 marked a crucial value shift away from a pure crime control model. After the reform, observers were of the opinion that the CPL 1996 provided a basic structure for fair trial but criticised the weak implementation of the revised law;[189] others were more sceptical, believing that the revised law was still far from being in conformity with international fair trial standards.[190] In comparison to the CPL 1979, the CPL 1996 had indeed made considerable improvements in terms of rights protections. The question is whether the claim of a partial acceptance of the presumption of innocence is sound. Scholars may have chosen this view in the hope that a partial adoption of presumption of innocence would lead to its full acceptance. In other words, cautious lobbying and patience will pay off. While the argument of full acceptance was indeed not brought forward, there are weaknesses in the claim of an adoption of the 'essence' of the presumption of innocence, as enshrined under international law, in light of centrally important safeguards

[187] Chen Guangzhong and Yan Duan (n 23) 197–210 (arts 83, 105, 107 and 108).

[188] These statistics do not include other compulsory measures that deprive a suspect or defendant of liberty. They pertain only to the measure of arrest (*daibu*).

[189] See, eg, Rongjie Lan, 'A False Promise of Fair Trials: A Case Study of China's Malleable Criminal Procedure Law' (2010) 27 *Pacific Basin Law Journal* 153.

[190] See, eg, Whitfort (n 57).

being absent and many conflicting or inconsistent provisions in the CPL 1996. A partial acceptance of the presumption of innocence is, however, not possible if it challenges or undermines the principle of fairness as a whole and denying the imperative nature of human dignity, which was the case with respect to the CPL 1996. What scholars hoping for a gradual transformation of the criminal justice system could not anticipate at the time was the fate of liberal values such as presumption of innocence. The 'reasonable elements' view not only triumphed over the competing human rights discourse; it had even led to a strengthening of the official discourse of national conditions. Therefore, it could only be argued that it had enshrined a presumption of innocence 'with Chinese characteristics', but this would be a false label.

In the late 1990s and early 2000s, a series of events facilitated domestic research on human rights in the criminal justice process, and another revision of the Criminal Procedure Law was soon discussed. The party-state initially endorsed the principle of law-based governance as a basic strategy of governance at the 15th Party Congress in 1997. Jiang Zemin, moreover, put forward the goal of establishing a socialist legal system 'with Chinese characteristics' by 2010. In October 1998, the Chinese government signed the ICCPR – a momentum for legal scholars in China. And in 1999, the principle of law-based governance was written into the Constitution.[191] Four years after the reform, in 2000, the Law Enforcement Inspection Group of the Standing Committee of the NPC assessed the status of implementation of the CPL 1996. According to the report, the areas of prolonged custody, coerced confessions, and the obstacles for lawyers remained of serious concern.[192]

At the 16th Party Congress in 2002, the commitment to human rights protection was first included in a political document.[193] In other words, the protection of human rights had explicitly become a policy goal of the Party. On this occasion, Jiang also emphasised that further legal reforms were needed.[194] In 2003, the 10th NPC put a second overhaul of the Criminal Procedure Law on the legislative agenda.[195] In 2004, the principle of human rights protection ('The state respects and protects human rights') was written into the Constitution, albeit underlying the

[191] Constitution 1982 (1999 Amendment), art 5.

[192] 'Report of the Law Enforcement Inspection Group of the NPC Standing Committee on the Status of Implementation of the PRC Criminal Procedure Law, Presented by Hou Zongbin at the 19th Meeting of the Standing Committee of the Ninth National People's Congress on 27 December 2000'.

[193] Jiang Zemin, 'Quanmian jianshe xiaokang shehui, kaichuang zhongguo tese shehui zhuyi shiye xin jumian (Build a Well-off Society in an All-Round Way and Create a New Situation in Building Socialism with Chinese Characteristics), Report delivered to the 16th CCP National Congress on 8 November 2002' (2002) s 5, para 1 www.moe.gov.cn/jyb_sjzl/moe_364/moe_258/moe_44/tnull_5009.html accessed 20 March 2017.

[194] Jiang Zemin (n 197) s 5, para 6.

[195] 'Legislative Plan of the Standing Committee of the 10th NPC' www.chinacourt.org/article/detail/2003/12/id/96741.shtml accessed 15 May 2019.

constraints of the legal system;[196] it was also introduced into the CCP Constitution in 2007 in the exact same wording.[197] However, as we will see in the next chapter, due to power struggles and disagreements among theorists and practitioners, it would indeed almost take ten years before the law-making of the 2012 CPL was completed, and the outcome was arguably not what reform-minded scholars had hoped for.

[196] Constitution 1982 (2004 Amendment), art 33(3). The idea that the 2004 constitutional principle of human rights protection established a basis for improving human rights in the criminal justice system reinforces the Party-state's legalist top-down approach to human rights implementation.

[197] See General Programme of the Charter of the Communist Party of China, Adopted at the 12th CCP National Congress on 6 August 1982, Amendments adopted at the 17th National Congress of the CCP on 21 October 2007.

# 5

# The Rise of a Competing Discourse: The Presumption of Innocence as a Human Right

China's ICCPR signature in 1998 was seen as a major vehicle through which presumption of innocence standards could be incorporated into the Chinese legislation. For scholars advocating rights and freedoms associated with liberal values, in the 2000s, international law became the most important source of reference. Since the decision of a second overhaul of the law was already made in 2003, scholars had begun to prepare comprehensive Criminal Procedure Law draft proposals, resulting in an extensive body of literature during the almost ten years until the revision was finalised in 2012. To be clear, none of them was appointed by the legislator. This chapter will pay particular but not exclusive attention to these drafts that emerged throughout the 2000s. Overall, the drafts supported the adoption of safeguards that can be associated with liberal-democratic values, and they provided constructive criticism on how the system could be improved, even if they remained moderate in the sense that they did not aim at turning the entire system upside down. Indeed, many Chinese scholars did not unconditionally embrace the presumption of innocence. Nonetheless, the academic discourse increasingly oriented itself towards the broader conception of the presumption of innocence, as outlined in chapter two. Well into the reform era, scholars had fully grasped the rationale of presumption of innocence. Therefore, it may not be surprising that the tensions between the official doctrine of national conditions and broader human rights claims steadily grew, even if the period after the 1996 CPL until the late 2000s was relatively stable in terms of space and freedoms for expressing pluralistic views. As this chapter will argue, the continued insistence on the official doctrine of national conditions had forced the destruction of the human right to presumption of innocence into various elements, leading to a fragile presumption of innocence in the CPL 2012, as, again, compromises had led to some improvements in terms of procedural safeguards and key safeguards were not adopted. However, the 2012 reform marked a more fundamental turning point; it suggested an illiberal shift, which would have more far-reaching implications than perhaps initially expected, as cemented during the 2018 Criminal Procedure Law reform.

## I. A Critical Discourse of 'National Conditions' in the Light of Competing Human Rights Claims

The 2003 decision of a second overhaul of the Criminal Procedure Law prompted the delegates of the Criminal Procedure Association to discuss the matter at the meeting in December 2003. More than 300 delegates took part in the meeting and discussed more than 200 submitted proposals. As regards the timing of another revision, three different views were advanced. Supporters of the 'necessity' view held that the law should be revised to address major shortcomings and to bring domestic legislation closer to international human rights standards. Proponents of the 'defer' view, however, believed that the conditions were too premature for another reform. The Criminal Procedure Law should be considered in the broader context of judicial reforms, whose outcome would depend on the outcome of political reforms. Moreover, the value choice between substantive and procedural justice remained controversially discussed. From an institutional perspective, the division of powers between investigation, prosecution and adjudication organs had not yet been clarified. In their view, the success or failure of the CPL 1996 could not yet be judged as not enough time had passed to see the impact of the revised law. The extent to which the revised law should 'draw on foreign experience' remained an area of contestation due to a proper understanding of the practice and development of other legal systems. Finally, the 'motion' view held that because an overhaul of the law had already been put on the legislative agenda and thus been approved by the central government, the question was not whether but how the law should be revised.[1]

A significant proportion of the discussion concerned the question of the fundamental values underlying the criminal justice system, the improvement of the system of compulsory measures, including time limits and conditions of custodial measures, and the criminal defence system. In terms of the value orientation, the difficult question was how to strike a proper balance between the official stance of combining human rights protection with crime control, as well as fairness with efficiency ('justice is prioritised, efficiency is taken into account', *gongzheng youxian, jiangu xiaolü*).[2] The party-state portrays the principles of efficiency and justice and the dual objectives of human rights protection and crime control as running in two parallel strands, although they are indeed competing values, which strained the negotiations between practitioners and theorists. Scholars especially

[1] Li Zhongcheng, 'Zhongguo faxuehui susong faxue yanjiuhui 2003 nian nianhui zongshu (Summary of the 2003 Annual Meeting of the China Law Society Procedural Law Research Association)' [2004] *China Legal Science* 186, 186–187.

[2] ibid.

criticised the CPL 1996's dual objective of crime control and rights protection, which was not conducive to the implementation of fair trial guarantees.[3]

In the process of law-making, a central question concerned the implementation of the 2004 constitutional human rights protection clause into the law. The introduction of this clause had facilitated a new wave of scholarship examining the realisation of this constitutional promise with respect to criminal justice. Indeed, it had made the abstract conception of human rights in the Chinese context more tangible. The Criminal Procedure Law was seen as a vehicle through which human rights can be codified. While the Party leadership tried to maintain control over the official narrative, the party-state's promise of human rights protection meant a threat to the official doctrine of national conditions because more outspoken scholars used the former to challenge the latter. As we will see, the making of the CPL 2012 was characterised by a critical discourse of national conditions in the light of human rights claims.

An initially planned deliberation on the reform of the Criminal Procedure Law, supposed to take place in October 2007, had to be postponed because scholars and law enforcement agencies held different opinions and due to power struggles between two powerful stakeholders – the police and the prosecuting organs.[4] However, the academic discourse continued nonetheless. While many scholars agreed that procedural safeguards should be strengthened, the exact scope of such safeguards was controversially discussed.[5]

A controversial question was whether the constitutional human rights protection principle should be integrated in the revised Criminal Procedure Law. The group of scholars working on draft proposals largely supported the adoption of the phrase 'safeguarding human rights' (*baozhang renquan*), instead of the politicised notion of 'protecting the people' (*baohu renmin*), into Article 1 of the revised law, which outlines the guiding ideology and objectives of the law. However, at the same time, they retained the objective of crime control.[6] Being concerned about a potential backlash, Chen Weidong also advocated such a more mediating approach. Since greater human rights protection would have meant a pushback for the powers of the law enforcement agencies, most notably the police as the main investigation authority, which traditionally emphasise crime control, it is not surprising that such proposals were met with resistance. In the light of the

[3] Chen Guangzhong, *'Gongmin quanli he zhengzhi quanli guoji gongyue yu woguo xingshi susong' (International Covenant on Civil and Political Rights and Criminal Process in China)* (Beijing, The Commercial Press, 2005) 35.

[4] Jianfu Chen, *Criminal and Criminal Procedure Law in the People's Republic of China* (Brill, Nijhoff, 2013) 60–61.

[5] 'Guanzhu xingshi susong fa xiugai de lizudian zhongdian nandian (Focusing on the Foothold, Main Issues and Difficulties of the Revision of the Criminal Procedure Law)' *Legal Daily* (13 April 2008) news.sina.com.cn/o/2008-04-13/110213729449s.shtml accessed 20 November 2020.

[6] Chen Guangzhong, *Zhonghua Renmin Gongheguo Xingshi Susongfa Zai Xiugai Zhuanjia Jianyigao Yu Lunzheng (Expert Draft for Re-Amendment to the PRC Criminal Procedure Law and Annotations)* (Beijing, China Legal Publishing House, 2006) 1 (art 1), 2–3.

disagreements that had already caused the suspension of the revision work, Chen Weidong thus believed that 'frontal attacks' would not be helpful in achieving the desired goals.[7]

The reasonableness of claims of national conditions was nonetheless increasingly questioned. For example, Xie Youping and Chen Weidong voiced concerns as to an overemphasis on national conditions, arguing that international fair trial standards (ie, the ICCPR standards) should guide criminal justice reforms. In their view, any country could insist on national particularities, and overemphasising national conditions would only hamper criminal justice reforms.[8] In a similar vein, Bian Jianlin has suggested that the introduction of both the principle of law-based governance in 1999 and the human rights protection clause in 2004, respectively, were important catalysts for another round of criminal justice reform. Although Bian did not challenge the official position in the abstract, he suggested that the Criminal Procedure Law should first and foremost meet international human rights standards.[9] For these scholars, the fact that the party-state was legally obligated to fulfil certain human rights obligations seemed to have played a subsidiary role; nor did they address the issue of the relativistic tendencies of the official doctrine of national conditions, which relativise international fair trial standards and diminish their moral foundations.

However, there was opposition. The main theme of the annual China Association of Criminal Procedure Law meeting in 2008 therefore centred on the 'scientific construction' of a criminal justice system. Echoing the political agenda of 'scientific' legislation as part of the broader aim of legal governance,[10] 'scientific' here relates to the distribution of powers, the relationship between justice, efficiency, and authority, and the question of how to 'balance severe punishment and leniency'. While it was generally held that China should fulfil minimum standards of international criminal justice, the delegates agreed that national conditions could not be ignored.[11]

[7] Chen Weidong, *Mofan xingshi susong fadian (Model Code of Criminal Procedure)* (Beijing, Renmin University Press, 2011) 3 (Art 1), 111; 'Guanzhu xingshi susong fa xiugai de lizudian zhongdian nandian (Focusing on the Foothold, Main Issues and Difficulties of the Revision of the Criminal Procedure Law)' (n 5).

[8] 'Guanzhu xingshi susong fa xiugai de lizudian zhongdian nandian (Focusing on the Foothold, Main Issues and Difficulties of the Revision of the Criminal Procedure Law)' (n 5).

[9] ibid.

[10] Hu Jintao, 'Gaoju zhongguo tese shehuizhuyi weida qizhi wei duoqu quanmian jianshe xiaokangshehui xin shengli er fendou (Hold High the Great Banner of Socialism with Chinese Characteristics and Strive for New Victories in Building a Moderately Prosperous Society in all Respects), 15 October 2007, Report to the 17th National Congress of the CCP' (2007) s 6, para 3 cpc.people.com.cn/GB/64162/134580/141428/index.html accessed 14 April 2017.

[11] Ye Qing and Xu Meijun, 'Zhongguo faxuehui xingshi susong faxue yanjiuhui 2008 nian nianhui zongshu (Summary of the 2008 Annual Meeting of the China Association of Criminal Procedure Law of the China Law Society)' [2008] *ECUPL Journal* 154, 154–158.

In November 2008, the Opinion of Central Party Committee Political-Legal Commission on Several Issues Concerning Deepening Reform of the Judicial System and Working Mechanisms set central reform goals for the criminal justice system, including the transfer of the management powers over detention centres from the Ministry of Public Security to the Ministry of Justice to achieve a greater separation between investigation and custodial powers to address the issue of coerced confessions, as well as greater standardisation of proceedings through the shift of the power to decide on re-education through labour to courts, or the implementation of the criminal policy of combining leniency with severity, among others.[12] Chen Zexian argued that the 2008 Decision, although being part of the efforts to strengthen the protection of human rights in the criminal process, emphasised 'the orientation of socialism with Chinese characteristics'. China's supposed national conditions were hence seen to remain the starting point for legal reforms. Put differently, even if judicial systems should be studied and the 'achievements of civilised rule of law countries' should be adopted, such systems should not be blindly copied.[13] The 2008 Decision was nonetheless widely considered to have crucially facilitated the reform of the 1996 CPL,[14] and in the same year a revision of the Criminal Procedure Law was again put on the legislative agenda.[15] In 2009, the SCNPC Legislative Affairs Commission was instructed to begin with the revision work.[16]

In the view of Xiong Qiuhong, the making of the CPL 2012 was dominated by two opposing views. Whereas one view would have suggested predominantly drawing on foreign experience, adhering to international standards, and strengthening human rights protection to pursue judicial fairness. Another view would have proposed that the revised law should rely on national conditions, ie, recognise the reality of rampant crime, increase the intensity of cracking down on crimes, and safeguard national security and stability, thus stressing the value of crime control.[17] In the process of law-making, the combination of the arguments of these two opposing views essentially represented the prevailing view of relying on national conditions while accommodating foreign experience. Recalling the previous discussions, this 'mediating' view was already prevalent in the making of the CPL 1996.

[12] 'Opinion of the Central Party Committee Political-Legal Commission on Several Issues Concerning Deepening the Reform of the Judicial System and Working Mechanisms, Issued on 28 November 2008.' ss 4–6.

[13] Chen Zexian and Xiong Qiuhong, *Xingshi susong fa xiugai jianyi gao yu lunzheng – yi renquan baozhang wei shijiao (Draft Proposal for Amendments to the Criminal Procedure Law and Argumentation – from the Perspective of Human Rights Protection)* (Beijing, China Social Sciences Press, 2012) 1–2.

[14] Chen (n 4) 60–61.

[15] 'Legislative Plan of the Standing Committee of the 11th NPC' (30 March 2019) www.npc.gov.cn/zgrdw/wxzl/gongbao/2008-12/26/content_1467452.htm accessed 17 April 2019.

[16] Wu Hongyao and Zhong Songzhi, *Zhongguo xingshi susong fadian bainian 1906 nian – 2012 nian (zhongce) (100 Years of the Chinese Criminal Procedure Law Codes (1906-2012) (middle volume))* (Beijing, China University of Political Science and Law Press, 2012) 874 (Wang Zhaoguo's Explanations on the Draft Amendments to the CPL (2012)).

[17] Xiong Qiuhong, 'Xiugai xingshi susongfa ying yi baozhang renquan wei hexin (Revision of the Criminal Procedure Law should be centred on the Protection of Human Rights)' (*China Legal Science*) www.iolaw.org.cn/showArticle.aspx?id=1691 accessed 9 January 2020.

Bian Jianlin has summarised the guiding thoughts of the CPL 2012 reform that reflect such a mediating view: First, China should proceed from its actual conditions (obviously open to interpretation) and thus improve the criminal justice system gradually. Second, a balance between punishing crimes and protecting human rights should be maintained. Lastly, efforts to resolve major issues with respect to the punishment of crimes while safeguarding judicial fairness should be upheld. That way, he believes, a 'major development and healthy improvement' of the socialist system of criminal jurisdiction 'with Chinese characteristics' can be realised.[18] The latter implies the need to balance efficiency against individual due process rights; similarly, the second principle indicates that restrictions to individual safeguards might be sacrificed to ensure combating crimes and thereby protect the interests of the state and the society, ie, the collective. The first principle evidently refers to the need to pursue a gradual development according to national conditions. Other scholars have expressed similar views.[19] Moreover, it should be observed that Chen Weidong's earlier discussed scepticism does not necessarily represent a denial of the official doctrine of national conditions. I believe it suggests treating the latter with caution rather than implying an outright rejection of it. The problem with such a mediating view may be that it aims to find a compromise between international human rights standards and a purportedly Chinese path of criminal justice, which may result in sacrificing certain human rights protections to achieve this goal.

In August 2011, the legislator published a draft for public consultation (CPL draft August 2011) before discussing the revised draft, which had reportedly considered several recommendations, in December 2011. The legislator eventually adopted the final draft in March 2012.[20] The CPL 2012 law has been understood to represent another trade-off, trying to satisfy all sides involved, namely, scholars, the legislator and state agencies.[21] In the view of the legislator, the revised law was going in the right direction and had properly implemented the directives of the party-state. While it would have reinforced the duality of crime control and rights protection, it also emphasised social harmony and stability. The legislator highlighted that the reform observed the maxim of achieving a gradual transformation of the criminal justice system based on national conditions. Echoing the official position, the determination of China still being in the primary stage of socialism would not only be a 'fundamental condition' but also represent a

[18] Bian Jianlin, 'Zhongguo tese shehui zhuyi xingshi sifa zhidu de zhongda fazhan – quanguo renmin daibiaodahui guanyu xiugai zhonghua renmin gongheguo xingshi susongfa de jueding gailan (Major Developments in China's Socialist Criminal Justice System – Overview of the Decision by the National People's Congress to amend the PRC Criminal Procedure Law)' *Procuratorate Daily* (15 March 2012) www.npc.gov.cn/npc/c221/201203/276ffcb6c80e4057b419a30a39da983.shtml accessed 9 May 2017.

[19] Dai Yuzhong, 'Jianshe zhongguo tese shehui zhuyi xingshi susong zhidu (Building a Socialist Criminal Justice System with Chinese Characteristics)' *People's Procuratorate Monthly* (2007) 7.

[20] Wu Hongyao and Zhong Songzhi (n 16) 874 (Wang Zhaoguo's Explanations on the Draft Amendments to the CPL (2012)); Decision of the NPC Standing Committee to Amend the Criminal Procedure Law of the PRC (Adopted at the Fifth Meeting of the Standing Committee of the Eleventh National People's Congress on 14 March 2012).

[21] Chen (n 4) 60–61.

'periodic characteristic', and the law could not overstep the actual conditions of this stage by blindly adopting 'foreign standards' of criminal justice.[22]

The principle of the protection and respect of human rights was eventually introduced into Article 2 CPL 2012 as one of the tasks of the law. Even if not fully satisfying, at least it brought the concept of human rights into the realm of criminal justice. The official view was that the incorporation of the human rights protection clause into the CPL 2012 would be beneficial for the socialist legal system and would emphasise that the three agencies should observe and implement this constitutional principle.[23] Chen Guangzhong, who had advocated the introduction of human rights protection into Article 1, nevertheless called this 'the greatest highlight' of the 2012 reform. It was the first time that a law had incorporated the constitutional human rights protection clause. Since it is regulated in Article 2, it would entail the guidance of the fundamental principles, system and procedures of the criminal procedure. Under the guiding thought of human rights protection, the rights of the criminal suspect or defendant with respect to defence, coercive measures, etc, could be further strengthened.[24] Bian Jianlin has referred to various new and modified provisions in the CPL 2012 in terms of voluntariness of confessions, exclusionary rules, personal liberty, criminal defence or criminal interrogations to demonstrate that the constitutional human rights protection clause had been translated into the revised law, comparing the scholarly draft and discourses, more widely. The remainder of this chapter asks whether this had been the case.[25]

## II. The Question of an Explicit Presumption of Innocence Provision

Following the ICCPR signature by the Chinese government in 1998, government representatives had on numerous occasions expressed the intention to ratify the covenant as soon as domestic legislation was in line with these standards.[26] At the time, for many scholars the question was therefore no longer *if* but merely *when* China would ratify the treaty. For example, Chen Guangzhong was convinced that ratification and implementation of the Covenant was only a matter of time.[27]

[22] Wu Hongyao and Zhong Songzhi (n 16) 873–875 (Wang Zhaoguo's Explanations on the Draft Amendments to the CPL (2012)).

[23] ibid 873–875 (Wang Zhaoguo's Explanations on the Draft Amendments to the CPL (2012)).

[24] Chen Guangzhong, Zeng Xinhua and Liu Linna, 'Xingshi susong fazhi jianshe de zhongda jinbu (Significant Progress in the Development of the Criminal Procedure Legal System)' (2012) 6 *Tsinghua Law Journal* 7, 16.

[25] Bian Jianlin (n 18).

[26] Katie Lee, 'China and the International Covenant on Civil and Political Rights: Prospects and Challenges' (2007) 6 *Chinese Journal of International Law* 445, 457; Wan Qianhui, 'Zhongguo tese renquanguan de lishi fazhan yu neizai luoji (Historical Development and Internal Logic of the View of Human Rights with Chinese Characteristics)' [2017] *Human Rights* 33, 741; UNHRC, 'National Report Submitted in Accordance with Paragraph 5 of the Annex to Human Rights Council Resolution 16/21 – China' (2018) UN Doc A/HRC/WG.6/31/CHN/1.

[27] Chen Guangzhong (n 3) 1–3.

Especially from the mid-2000s onwards, scholars began to carefully examine the gap between Chinese legislation and the ICCPR standards. As shown in chapter four, many scholars argued that the CPL 1996, more specifically, Article 12, had embraced the 'essence' of the presumption of innocence, while a full endorsement was lacking.[28] For scholars in China, a pressing issue was therefore the question of an explicit presumption of innocence provision, which they considered to secure full recognition of the principle.

Scholars working on draft proposals made different proposals for a presumption of innocence provision:

> Xu Jingcun:
>
> Anyone shall be considered innocent until a people's court has passed a final judgment finding [that person] guilty.
>
> If the guilt of a criminal suspect or a defendant cannot be ascertained, [that person] shall be considered innocent. If the pettiness or seriousness of a crime cannot be ascertained, [it] shall be dealt with according to the pettiness of the crime.
>
> 任何人在未经人民法院生效裁判确定有罪之前，应当被视为无罪.
>
> 不能确定犯罪嫌疑人，被告人犯罪的，应当做无罪处理；罪轻罪重不能确定的，应当做罪轻处理.[29]
>
> Chen Weidong:
>
> Anyone subject to prosecution shall be presumed innocent until a people's court has passed a final judgment finding [that person] guilty in accordance with law.
>
> 任何受到追诉的人, 在被人民法院依法最终判决有罪之前, 推定其无罪.[30]
>
> Chen Guangzhong:
>
> Anyone shall be presumed innocent until a people's court has passed a final judgment finding [that person] guilty.
>
> If the guilt or innocence of a criminal suspect or a defendant cannot be established, [that person] shall be considered innocent. If the pettiness or seriousness of a crime of a criminal suspect or a defendant cannot be established, [it] shall be dealt with in accordance with the pettiness of the crime.
>
> 在人民法院依法作出生效裁判确定有罪之前, 任何人应当被推定无罪.
>
> 不能认定犯罪嫌疑人，被告人有罪或无罪的，按无罪处理；不能认定犯罪嫌疑人，被告人罪重或罪轻的, 按罪轻处理.[31]
>
> Yi Yanyou:
>
> Anyone charged with a criminal offence shall be presumed innocent until proven guilty by a people's court in a public and fair hearing at which the defendant has been given all the guarantees necessary for his defence.

[28] Chen Guangzhong (n 6) 257; Chen Weidong (n 7) 112–113.

[29] Xu Jingcun, *Zhongguo xingshi susongfa (dier xiuzhengan) xuezhe nizhigao ji lifa liyou (China Criminal Procedure Law (Second Amendment) Scholarly Draft and Legislative Rationale)* (Beijing, Law Press China, 2005) 7–9.

[30] Chen Weidong (n 7) 3 (art 4, General Principles).

[31] Chen Guangzhong (n 6) 4 (art 10).

> 任何受刑事指控者，未经人民法院在公开，公正的，对被告人赋予一切辩护所需之保障的法庭上被证实有罪之前，都应当推无罪.[32]

None of these formulations spoke of a *right* to presumption of innocence, at least not explicitly. Except for Yi Yanyou, the proposed provisions were all formulated based on Article 12 CPL 1996, ie, on the second half of the sentence, 'No person shall be found guilty.'[33] Xu Jingcun suggested changing this wording to 'Anyone shall be considered innocent' in order to de-emphasise the notion of guilt and establish a broader normative conception of presumption of innocence consistent with, for example, Article 11(1) UDHR or Article 9 of the French Human Rights Declaration; the second paragraph of his proposed provision introduced the maxim of *in dubio pro reo*. The wording of his proposed provision shows that the maxim was not limited to the trial itself but was understood to regulate the handling of doubtful cases at all stages of the proceedings where the question of guilt or the seriousness of a criminal offence could not be resolved.[34] Xu's draft, moreover, integrated a set of guarantees, such as the burden of proof or the right to silence to realise the presumption of innocence.[35]

Although Chen Guangzhong's provision does not speak of a right, he understood the presumption of innocence as a right of accused persons. In his view, it was the duty of the state, and therefore of state agencies, to guarantee this right. Therefore Chen advocated the inclusion of an explicit provision. Chen supported a broad approach to presumption of innocence and expanded the scope of application to the pre-trial stages to ensure that suspects and defendants would be treated in accordance with this principle.[36] The presumption of innocence would thus not be an epistemological presumption, with the aim of truth-finding, while the principle of seeking truth from facts would imply that case-handling authorities should proceed from the reality that the accused has not (yet) been convicted.[37] In other words, the two can coexist in the same system. Chen, moreover, proposed the adoption of additional safeguards deriving from presumption of innocence, including the principle of in favour of the accused.[38]

Yi Yanyou's formulation of presumption of innocence aimed to embody both the rule and the principle of presumption of innocence.[39] Indeed, Yi's formulation of the presumption of innocence is almost consistent with Article 11(1) UDHR,

[32] Yi Yanyou, 'Lun wuzui tuiding de hanyi yu xingshi susongfa de wanshan (On the Implications of the Presumption of Innocence and the Improvement of the Criminal Procedure Law)' [2012] *Tribune of Political Science and Law* 10, 20.

[33] See ch 4, IV.

[34] Xu Jingcun (n 29) 7–8.

[35] Art 97 (burden of proof), art 5 (privilege against self-incrimination), art 147 ('voluntariness of statements' of criminal suspects, defendants), art 215 ('freedom of statements' of criminal suspects, defendants), see ibid 8–9.

[36] Chen Guangzhong (n 3) 27–28.

[37] ibid 28–30.

[38] Chen Guangzhong (n 6) 257.

[39] Yi Yanyou (n 32) 20.

which links the presumption of innocence much more closely to the general right to a fair trial than Article 14(2) ICCPR. Yi thus interprets the presumption of innocence as a comprehensive guarantee that includes procedural conditions. In his view, it is a value choice, regardless of facts. Like Chen, he understands the presumption of innocence as conferring a behavioural standard. Although Yi believes that the presumption of guilt prevails in the sense that law enforcement authorities inevitably had to presume a person's guilt when, for example, in the context of coercive measures, they were obliged to observe the legal procedure through which the guilt or innocence of a person was determined. Yi has called this the parallelism of a 'factual presumption of guilt' and a 'procedural presumption of innocence'.[40]

Drawing on Article 14(2) ICCPR, the Russian and French Codes of Criminal Procedure,[41] Chen Weidong supported the full acceptance of presumption of innocence as a general principle in the revised law. The evidential requirements, such as the burden of proof, and the treatment of the accused should be regulated separately. In contrast to Yi, Chen did not formulate the presumption of innocence as a comprehensive guarantee.[42]

Overall, the proposed provisions read consistently, albeit with slightly different formulations. They all require a final (or effective) guilty verdict by a court. Except for Chen Weidong's proposal, all these provisions link the presumption of innocence to either specific substantive and/or procedural conditions. Regardless of the concrete formulation, it was uncontested that additional safeguards were needed to fully realise the presumption of innocence. For these reform-oriented scholars, national conditions (be they economic, social, or cultural conditions) were not seen as an obstacle to the implementation of the label of presumption of innocence.

However, the CPL 2012 did not include an explicit provision on presumption of innocence. Therefore, a similar debate about whether certain aspects of the revised law could be used as an indicator for further acceptance of the presumption of innocence in the Chinese criminal procedure arose, not least because the revised law incorporated the constitutional human rights protection clause into Article 2. As already indicated, the introduction of the constitutional human rights protection clause provided a legal basis for demanding greater human rights protection in the criminal justice process. Scholars have argued that especially the inclusion of a privilege against self-incrimination, the adoption of exclusionary rules, the improvement of the defence system, and the strengthening of personal liberty safeguards in the revised law signalled efforts to implement the constitutional

[40] ibid 17–19.

[41] While the Russian Code speaks of 'non-guilt' before conviction and codifies the evidential aspects, the French Code uses the notion of 'presumed innocence' and provides for a catalogue of procedural safeguards, see Article 14 of the Criminal Procedure Code of the Russian Federation of 18 December 2001 (as of 2012), Preliminary Article III of the French Criminal Procedure Code (Code de procédure pénale) of 23 December 1958 (2020 Amendment).

[42] Chen Weidong (n 7) 112–113.

human rights protection clause.[43] If adopted, these safeguards would have been important for the realisation of presumption of innocence in the Chinese criminal justice system. The sections to follow discuss these in detail to assess whether it can be argued that CPL 2012 has strengthened the presumption of innocence in the Chinese criminal justice process as compared to the scholarly proposals.

## III. Expanding the Evidential Dimension of Presumption of Innocence

Recalling that the evidential dimension of presumption of innocence was relatively uncontested, scholars discussed how the already adopted 'reasonable elements' could be expanded. Although the CPL 1996 did not explicitly allocate the burden of proof, nor did it adopt a privilege against self-incrimination or a right to silence, it was commonly argued that the evidence provisions *implicitly* allocated the burden of proof in criminal prosecutions. Notwithstanding such an implicit allocation of the burden of proof, the absence of a right to silence and the lack of rules on the admissibility of evidence were at the centre of academic debates, partly also because a substantial corpus of legislation was issued to clarify the vague CPL 1996 provisions.[44] These provisions, in particular, served as an important source for scholarly claims because they were more detailed.

A related issue concerned the relationship between objective and legal truth.[45] While the former relates to the idea of substantive justice, the latter refers to the idea of procedural justice. As discussed in chapter three, the CPL 1979 emphasised the need to discover the objective truth while deemphasising the concept of legal truth. Chapter four has shown that the idea of legal truth was first introduced by the courts' exclusive adjudication power, as enshrined in Article 12 CPL 1996.[46] Therefore, scholarly CPL drafts of the 2000s aimed to strengthen the principle of evidence-based judgements, which had not yet been addressed by CPL 1996, even if it was said to be already implicitly manifested in some provisions.[47]

In academic discourses, it was undisputed that the law should *explicitly* place the evidential burden on the prosecution, and the law should also clarify which methods fall within the scope of illegal means of obtaining evidence. While the scholarly drafts largely supported the concept of 'burden of proof' (*zhengming zeren*),[48] Chen Guangzhong proposed integrating the broader concept of the 'burden of producing evidence' (*juzheng zeren*), which was not limited to the trial

[43] Chen Guangzhong, Zeng Xinhua and Liu Linna (n 24) 17.

[44] Chen Guangzhong, *Xingshi susong fa (Criminal Procedure Law)* (Peking, Peking University Press, 2013) 55.

[45] Chen Guangzhong (n 6) 6–7.

[46] See ch 4, IV.

[47] CPL 1996, art 42; Chen Weidong (n 7) 169; Xu Jingcun (n 29) 75.

[48] Chen Weidong (n 7) 219 (art 178); Xu Jingcun (n 29) 79 (art 97).

itself, meaning claims – regardless of whether brought forward by the prosecution or defence – must be supported by evidence.[49] Although the legislator did not follow such a broad approach, the CPL 2012 did first explicitly place the burden of proof on the prosecution,[50] and it provided for a (limited) privilege against self-incrimination of the accused, which will be discussed in the next section.[51]

These changes were seen as an improvement in terms of strengthening presumption of innocence standards. Based on these new provisions, it has been suggested that the CPL 2012 established an implicit requirement of voluntariness of confessions in criminal proceedings, which would be an essential element of exclusionary rules.[52] The (limited) right against self-incrimination would hence impose minimal requirements on investigation and adjudication authorities in relation to the evidential burdens, as well as the means of obtaining evidence.[53]

Regarding the standard of proof, scholarly drafts advocated the introduction of the concept of 'beyond reasonable doubt' in accordance with the international presumption of innocence standards.[54] Indeed, the CPL 2012 first clarified the substantive and procedural conditions required to meet the standard of proof of clear facts, reliable and sufficient evidence, stating that the following three conditions must be met in order to reach this standard: 'all facts for conviction and sentencing are proved by evidence', 'all evidence used to decide a case has been verified in accordance with the legal proceedings', and 'the established facts are proven beyond reasonable doubt on the basis of the overall evidence'.[55] It should be observed that pre-trial evidentiary standards as regards the closure of criminal investigations or the initiation of prosecutions were not changed and must still amount to a standard of clear facts and reliable and sufficient evidence,[56] even if these evidentiary standards do not amount to the standard of proof needed for conviction.[57] However, the low acquittal rate has rendered the meaning of presumption of innocence in the trial context nearly meaningless, as the pre-trial determination of guilt is barely challenged at trial. This remained extremely problematic in the light of the many shortcomings of pre-trial proceedings.

However, criminal procedure scholars have emphasised that the Chinese standard of 'beyond reasonable doubt' (*paichu heli huaiyi*) was not comparable to the western standard of 'proof beyond reasonable doubt'.[58] While the western

[49] Chen Guangzhong (n 6) 40 (arts 75, 77).
[50] CPL 2012, art 49.
[51] ibid art 50.
[52] Jiahong He, *Back from the Dead: Criminal Justice and Wrongful Convictions in China* (Honolulu, University of Hawaii Press, 2016) 157–160.
[53] Chen Ruihua, *Xingshi zhengju faxue (Criminal Evidence Law)* (Peking, Peking University Press, 2014) 55.
[54] Xu Jingcun (n 29) 80 (art 98); Chen Weidong (n 7) 221 (art 180).
[55] CPL 2012, art 195, No. (1), art 53, Nos. (1) to (3); Chen Ruihua (n 53) 303.
[56] Chen Guangzhong (n 44) 306.
[57] Criminal Procedure Rules of the People's Procuratorate (Amended by the Supreme People's Procuratorate on 21 September 1999, No. 1 [1999]) art 279, No. 1. See also ch 4, VI.
[58] CPL 2012, art 53, No. (3).

standard would be tantamount to around 95 per cent certainty, the Chinese standard of beyond reasonable doubt would require that the proof of the key facts lead to a single conclusion beyond reasonable doubt, and only in this way could the requirements of epistemology and judicial practice be met and wrongful convictions be prevented to the greatest extent possible.[59] In judicial practice and in academic discourses, this standard of proof for a conviction is interpreted as objective truth.[60]

In this context, a related issue concerned the question of the handling of doubtful cases. As already mentioned, the proposed scholarly provisions largely reproduced the more detailed provisions issued to supplement the CPL 1996.[61] In 1998, the Ministry of Public Security issued provisions clarifying the conditions under which police were permitted to dismiss cases, for example, due to a lack of criminal facts or negligibility.[62] After 1999, the Supreme People's Procuratorate provided some guidance on cases eligible for non-prosecution at the prosecution stage due to insufficient evidence, negligibility or insurmountable doubts, among others.[63] The CPL 2012 amalgamated and replicated these provisions that stipulate statutory non-prosecution and non-prosecution due to insufficient evidence.[64]

It should moreover be observed that doubts still relate only to the criminal charges themselves, while it remains unclear how doubts as to facts and evidence at the different stages of criminal proceedings will be in favour of the accused. For example, during examination for prosecution, there is still the option to send doubtful cases back for further investigation, basically pending decision, which is evidently not favourable for the accused.[65] Moreover, the police may still handle cases that do not meet the threshold of criminal prosecution through other channels, most notably administrative sanctions.

While the CPL 2012 adopted some of the scholarly proposals as regards burden and standard of proof in criminal trials, the expectation of an early determination of guilt or innocence combined with this standard of proof needed for conviction remains a problematic combination. Cases of wrongful convictions show that

[59] Chen Guangzhong, Jiang Jiahua and Xiao Peiquan, 'Lun wuzui tuiding jiqi zai zhongguo de shiyong (On the Presumption of Innocence and its Application in China)' [2013] *Law Science Magazine* 1, 6–7.

[60] CPL 1996, art 162, No. (1); Yu Mou, *The Construction of Guilt in China, An Empirical Account of Routine Chinese Injustice* (Oxford, Hart Publishing, 2020) 14.

[61] Chen Weidong (n 7) 327 (art 290), 339–340 (art 311); Chen Guangzhong (n 6) 126 (art 241), 134 (art 261); Xu Jingcun (n 29) 181 (art 248). See ch 4.

[62] Criminal Procedure Rules of the People's Procuratorate (1999) art 237; Provisions on Handling of Criminal Cases by the Public Security Organs (14 May 1998, No. 35 of Ministry of Public Security) art 168.

[63] Criminal Procedure Rules of the People's Procuratorate (Amended by the Supreme People's Procuratorate on 21 September 1999, No. 1999(1)) 1999 arts 187, 189 and 286; these provisions were reproduced in the Supreme People's Procuratorate, Standards on the Quality of Handling Cases of Non-Prosecution by the People's Procuratorates (Trial Implementation) 2001.

[64] CPL 2012, arts 171(4), 173(1).

[65] CPL 2012, art 171; Chen Guangzhong (n 44) 327–328; Wen Ziyang, 'Wuzui tuiding yuanze zai woguo xianzhuang ji fazhan (Status and Development of the Principle of Presumption of innocence in China)' [2018] *Legality Vision* 26, 27.

the ostensibly flawless and superior standard of 100 per cent accuracy is not met in practice. Rather, authorities continue to routinely construct the 'truth' to build cases against accused persons, which has led to a normalisation of injustice.[66] A case of wrongful conviction that covers three versions of the CPL (1979, 1996, 2012) is a case in point. In 1994, Nie Shubin was accused of raping and murdering a woman in Shijiazhuang City, Hebei Province. Nie was convicted and executed for rape and intentional murder. Then, in 2005, Wang Shujin, who had been apprehended by the police in Henan Province and suspected of several other rapes and murders, voluntarily confessed to the crime. However, although Wang was charged with intentional murder and sentenced to death in 2007, he was not prosecuted for the Shijiazhuang murder. Wang appealed against the verdict, claiming that the Shijiazhuang case had been omitted, while the prosecutor expressed doubts that he had committed the murder due to inconsistencies between his story and the case facts. The trial of second instance was pending for six years, until in 2013, the Hebei Provincial High Court decided to reject Wang's appeal, uphold the original judgment, and send the case to the Supreme People's Court (SPC) for approval of the death penalty. In 2014, the SPC tasked the Shandong Provincial High Court with a review of the Nie case. An investigation into the case raised serious doubts as to the lawfulness of Nie's confession. In 2016, the Supreme People's Court publicly announced the innocence of Nie, citing inconsistencies between his confession and other evidence in the case. In the view of Dai Peng, the significance of the Nie case lies in the fact that he had been cleared of the murder on legal grounds. Since Wang had confessed, there were reasonable doubts as to Nie's guilt, thus applying *in dubio pro reo*. Wang, however, could not be charged with the Shijiazhuang murder, as the evidential standard for prosecution was not met, meaning non-prosecution due to doubts. From a legal point of view, neither Wang's nor Nie's guilt in the Shijiazhuang murder case could be proved beyond reasonable doubt. Dai argues that the prosecution does not interfere with the court's power of adjudication and deciding a person's innocence or guilt in the event of non-prosecution but would observe the principle of presumption of innocence.[67] However, Nie was wrongfully convicted and executed, and the actual perpetrator was never convicted.

Regarding the question of the legality of evidence, scholars criticised the absence of provisions in the CPL 1996 on substantive and procedural facts to be proved by evidence, even though the former had already been addressed in a judicial interpretation by the Supreme People's Court.[68] To this end, Chen Guangzhong's draft de-emphasised the requirement of objective truth by integrating a set of provisions

[66] Mou (n 60) 39–48.

[67] Dai Peng, 'Shishi shang de wuzui yu falü shang de wuzui – Nie Shubin'an yu Wang Shujin'an luoji fenxi (Factual and Legal Innocence – Logical Analysis of the Nie Shubin and the Wang Shujin Cases)' [2017] *Tianjin Legal Science* 86, 86–90.

[68] The SPC Interpretation 1998 contained a list of case facts to be proved by evidence, including the motive and intent of the defendant or the circumstances of the alleged offence (time, place, etc), see The Supreme People's Court's Interpretation on Several Issues Regarding the Application of the Criminal Procedure Law of the PRC 1998 (Adopted on 29 June 1998, No. 23 [1998]) art 52.

that laid greater stress on legal truth and procedural fairness. The draft required the facts of a case to be established by evidence, which was seen as an expression of the principle of evidence-based judgement, without making use of the notion of truthfulness in this context.[69] He believed that such an evidence-based approach was compatible with the factually based principle of seeking truth from facts, emphasising that criminal cases should be handled in accordance with the case facts ascertained by judicial personnel and that the objective facts of a case would be those proved by evidence, including material and procedural facts to be proven.[70]

Substantive case facts requiring proof would include, eg, facts relating to intention, motive, time, and means and facts relating to a more severe, lighter or mitigated punishment. The procedural facts requiring proof would include, eg, procedural facts related to compulsory measures and facts related to violations of legal proceedings, including proof of the legality of evidence; the latter should ensure procedural fairness.[71]

The issue of proof of procedural facts relates to questions of legality of evidence. As shown in chapter three, the Criminal Procedure Law prohibited the extortion of confessions by torture or other coercive means as early as 1979 but did not provide for mechanisms of enforcement; the revised CPL 1996 reaffirmed this prohibition and stipulated that the prosecutors should investigate cases of extorted confessions. However, it had only vaguely spoken of 'threat, enticement, deceit' as illegal means of obtaining evidence, which were not further specified in legislation.[72] From 1998 onwards, both the Supreme People's Court and the Supreme People's Procuratorate had issued regulations calling for the enforcement of the prohibition against coerced confessions.[73] In June 2010, five state agencies jointly issued two provisions that first provided for rules on the exclusion of illegally obtained oral and material evidence for the first time (Evidence Rules 2010),[74] which were replicated in a more detailed manner in the CPL 2012, establishing a regime of mandatory exclusion of oral evidence and discretionary exclusion of physical and documentary evidence.[75] While the prosecution has to prove that evidence was lawfully obtained, the defendant bears an initial burden of proof, ie,

[69] Chen Guangzhong (n 6) 36 (art 68).
[70] ibid 320.
[71] ibid 38 (art 72), 325.
[72] CPL 1996, arts 18 and 43.
[73] SPC's Interpretation on Several Issues regarding the Application of the CPL 1998, art 61; Criminal Procedure Rules of the People's Procuratorate (1999) arts 140 and 265; Notice on Strictly Prohibiting the Use of a Criminal Suspects Confession Coerced under Torture as the Basis for Conviction (Adopted by the SPP on 2 January 2001, No. 2 [2001] of the Supreme People's Procuratorate) s 3.
[74] Provisions on the Examination and Evaluation of Evidence in Capital Cases and the Provisions on the Exclusion of Illegally Obtained Evidence in Criminal Cases (No. 2 [2010] of the Supreme People's Court), both jointly issued by the Supreme People's Court, the Supreme People's Procuratorate, the Ministry of Public Security, the Ministry of State Security and Ministry of Justice on 13 June 2010.
[75] CPL 2012, arts 54 to 58; Xi Danni, *Lun wuzui tuiding (On the Presumption of Innocence)* (Beijing, People's Court Press, 2015) 208–212; Zhiyuan Guo, 'Exclusion of Illegally Obtained Confessions in China: An Empirical Perspective' (2017) 21 *The International Journal of Evidence & Proof* 30, 50.

providing 'relevant leads or materials about person(s), time, place, manner and content suspected of obtaining evidence illegally'.[76] Such an approach of mandatory and optional exclusion of evidence had also been proposed by some of the scholarly drafts.[77]

However, the scholarly drafts made different proposals as regards the burden and standard of proving the legality of obtained evidence. Chen Guangzhong also placed a minimal onus on the individual to provide 'relevant leads' that the prosecution would have been required to rebut by presenting 'reliable and sufficient evidence to prove the legality of such evidence';[78] this stance was not unanimously supported. For example, although Chen Zexian and Xiong Qiuhong did not place such a minimal onus on the defence, they considered that 'reliable and sufficient evidence' provided by the prosecution would be sufficient to prove the legality of obtained evidence.[79] Xu Jingcun proposed placing the burden to prove the legality of evidence obtained on the prosecution, which would have to meet the standard of beyond reasonable doubt, once the defence requests the exclusion of evidence on such grounds in order to put greater pressure on the authorities to obtain evidence lawfully.[80] Chen Weidong suggested placing the burden of proving the lawfulness of the investigation on the prosecution, using the common law concept of 'preponderance of evidence' (*youshi zhengju*); meaning the prosecution must prove that the probability of lawful obtainment of evidence is higher than that of unlawfulness.[81]

However, the proposed scholarly provisions were more detailed than those eventually integrated into the CPL 2012; the revised law did not clarify what constitutes 'threat, enticement, deceit'. In contrast, the scholarly drafts had proposed specifying what kind of methods (beyond corporal punishment) may go beyond lawful questioning techniques in accordance with internationally recognised standards and exclusionary rules existing in other jurisdictions, including fatigue during interrogation, hunger, the use of medication or hypnosis, among others.[82] The CPL 2012, moreover, failed to explain the degree of proof needed to show the lawfulness of obtained evidence.[83] Although prosecutors are obliged to check on the lawfulness of the evidence obtained during the police investigation, they have little incentive to do so in reality, as it would mean additional workload, and they

[76] CPL 2012, arts 56 and 57; The Supreme People's Court's Interpretation on the Application of the Criminal Procedure Law of the PRC 2012 (Adopted on 5 November 2012, No. 21 [2012]) 96 and 101; Chen Ruihua (n 53) 304–305.

[77] Chen Guangzhong (n 6) 40–42 (arts 77, 78), 333–335; Xu Jingcun (n 29) 86 (art 105).

[78] Chen Guangzhong (n 6) 42 (art 79).

[79] Chen Zexian and Xiong Qiuhong, *Xingshi susong fa xiugai jianyi gao yu lunzheng – yi bei kongzhi ren de quanli baohu wei hexin (Draft Proposal for Amendments to the Criminal Procedure Law and Argumentation Centred on the Protection of the Rights of Accused Persons* (Beijing, China Social Sciences Press, 2009) 7.

[80] Xu Jingcun (n 29) 87–88 (art 106).

[81] Chen Weidong (n 7) 314–315 (art 279).

[82] Chen Guangzhong (n 6) 332–333 (art 77); Xu Jingcun (n 29) 85 (art 104); Chen Zexian and Xiong Qiuhong (n 78) 6–7.

[83] CPL 2012, art 57.

often lack a full picture themselves of how such evidence was obtained.[84] While the CPL 2012 had avoided addressing all these issues, the explanations to the law by the Supreme People's Court clarified that 'other illegal means to extort confessions' include any 'methods that cause severe physical or mental suffering to force the defendant to confess against his will'.[85] Moreover, as part of an effort to prevent wrongful convictions, the Supreme People's Court explained what instances may be considered to fall within the scope of 'torture and other illegal means', including 'cold, hunger, sunlight, heat, and fatigue during interrogation'.[86]

However, after the CPL 2012 was put into effect, research by Guo Zhiyuan has shown that, even in those few instances in which evidence was excluded, the court did not acquit the defendant, and practitioners would lack guidance on how to understand such notions as 'severe pain or suffering' and delineate lawful from unlawful interrogation methods.[87] Vague provisions are arguably not the only problem. Although Jiang Na considers the CPL 2012 exclusionary provisions to be an improvement compared to the Evidence Rules 2010, she has demonstrated that judges have been unable to properly enforce the exclusionary rules, as they are embedded in a system that does not want acquittals. And because judges presume guilt, illegally obtained evidence was not properly excluded, and accused persons were wrongfully convicted. Without institutional reforms, especially giving the defence a more meaningful role, it would be difficult to establish the presumption of innocence. The collection of evidence would remain one-sided, and, owing to the absence of specific standards on how to apply the exclusionary rules, judges barely listen to the arguments of the defence, or they impose the full burden to prove the unlawfulness of obtained evidence on the defence. The system would indeed work against the accused, and this had not changed under the CPL 2012.[88]

Considering the many loopholes in legislation that lead to abusive practices, most notably prolonged interrogations due to the absence of lawyers, the institutionalisation of these provisions arguably remains very difficult. This imbalance of powers between prosecution and the lack of transparency, moreover, means that the threshold to trigger an investigation into allegations of torture remains very high. It should be observed that, under the CPL 2012, the police could still make full use of its monopoly over investigation activities, manipulate information and construct cases against accused persons, partly with the help of the

[84] Mou (n 60) 115–122.

[85] SPC's Interpretation on the Application of the CPL 2012, art 95.

[86] Opinions of the Supreme People's Court on Establishing and Completing Work Mechanisms for Preventing Unjust, False and Wrongly Decided Criminal Cases (Adopted on 13 August 2013, No. 11 [2013] of the Supreme People's Court) art 8.

[87] Zhiyuan Guo, 'The First Step of the Long March: Implementing the Exclusionary Rules in China' (2017) 25 *Asia Pacific Law Review* 48, 54.

[88] Na Jiang, 'The Presumption of Innocence and Illegally Obtained Evidence: Lessons from Wrongful Convictions in China' [2013] *Hong Kong Law Journal* 745, 756–761.

prosecution.[89] Indeed, investigation authorities have arguably not done this for ideological reasons, even if ideologies underlying the criminal process such as the mass line have shaped certain mentalities and their workstyle; time restrictions and mandatory case clearance demands imposed on them are not conducive to changing their mindset.[90] The persistent culture of sending cases back for supplementary investigation and the anti-acquittal attitude create an environment that is hostile to individual rights protection.

Since the party-state was not interested in the exposure of wrongful convictions and their prevention had indeed become a policy goal, the adoption of evidential rules was generally supported. However, it should be observed that even the evidential requirements of the presumption of innocence were only accepted to the extent that they did not put too much of a burden on state agencies to prove the lawfulness of their actions. In other words, the introduction of procedural safeguards like the right to silence that are closely interwoven with the presumption of innocence was less successful.

## IV. The Unresolved Relationship between Silence and Truthfulness

Following the CPL 1996, as shown in chapter four, the relationship between the provisions of the duty to cooperate and the prohibition against torture remained a point of controversy.[91] In anticipation of an overhaul of the CPL 1996, scholars made renewed efforts to strengthen the protection of procedural safeguards and especially advocated the inclusion of a right to silence and/or a privilege against self-incrimination in the revised law, saying that these safeguards were a logical consequence of the burden of proof in accordance with internationally recognised presumption of innocence standards.[92] However, it should be borne in mind that the privilege against self-incrimination is one of the most complex fair trial safeguards, and there is a lot of room for contestation, especially regarding the adverse consequences of choosing silence. The question of whether this guarantee is absolute or relative, as well as in what sense it is absolute or relative, has also haunted Chinese scholars. In this context, a critical question, again, was whether the duty should be abolished or not.

[89] Mou (n 60) ch 3.

[90] He Jiahong, 'Miscarriage of Justice and Malpractice in Criminal Investigations in China' (2016) 16 *The China Review* 65, 69–73.

[91] CPL 1996, arts 43 and 93.

[92] Zhu Zongjie, 'Zai renquan baozhang shiye xia lun wuzui tuiding yuanze (On the Principle of the Presumption of Innocence from the Perspective of Human Rights Protection' [2011] *Human Rights* 23, 27; Yi Yanyou (n 32) 21; Yue Liling, *Xingshi shenpan yu renquan baozhang (Criminal Trial and Human Rights Protection)* (Beijing, Law Press China, 2010) 219–220.

The scholarly drafts proposed the following provisions as regards a right to silence and privilege against self-incrimination:

> Chen Guangzhong:
>
> No one shall be compelled to incriminate himself or herself or to make any other statements against himself or herself.
>
> 不得强迫任何人证明自己有罪或作其他不利于自己的陈述.[93]
>
> Chen Zexian, Xiong Qiuhong:
>
> No one shall be compelled to prove his or her guilt or to make any other statements against himself or herself.
>
> 任何人不得被强迫证明自己有罪或者作其他不利于自己的陈述.[94]
>
> Yi Yanyou:
>
> Any criminal suspect or defendant subject to criminal prosecution shall have the right to remain silent during interrogation; the personnel responsible for the interrogation shall inform [that person] of his or her right to silence.
>
> 任何受刑事追诉的犯罪嫌疑人，被告人，在受讯问时应当有权保持沉默；负责讯问的人员应当告知其有权保持沉默.[95]
>
> Chen Weidong:
>
> In criminal proceedings, no one can be compelled to make statements against himself or herself.
>
> 在刑事诉讼中,任何人不受强迫作不利于自己的陈述.[96]

The formulations of Chen Weidong, Chen Guangzhong and Chen Zexian and Xiong Qiuhong are almost identical and based on international human rights norms, notably the right against self-incrimination in Article 14(3)(g) ICCPR. Since it was an open secret that criminal interrogations were used to obtain confessions, and because the investigation authorities can decide whether a suspect answered 'truthfully', if necessary, by force, Chen Zexian and Xiong Qiuhong proposed to remove this provision.[97]

In the view of Chen Guangzhong, the 'principle' against self-incrimination was enshrined in the ICCPR, and Chinese legislation should meet international standards in this regard, but he remained ambiguous as to whether his privilege covers a right to silence, saying that this ought to be 'interpreted in the light of Chinese practice'.[98] Considering all the controversies surrounding the right to silence, Chen Guangzhong was apparently reluctant to take a clear stance on the matter, even if the two guarantees are obviously linked. Bai has called this a strategic move

[93] Chen Guangzhong (n 6) 6 (art 12).
[94] Chen Zexian and Xiong Qiuhong (n 79) 6.
[95] Yi Yanyou (n 32) 21.
[96] Chen Weidong (n 7) 3 (art 5).
[97] Chen Zexian and Xiong Qiuhong (n 79) 64–65.
[98] Chen Guangzhong (n 6) art 12, 258–259; Chen Zexian and Xiong Qiuhong (n 79) 63.

to avoid a controversy.[99] As shown in chapter two, however, although the right to silence and the prohibition against self-incrimination are two different guarantees, silence is a direct consequence of the prohibition.

Chen Weidong used the overarching principle of presumption of innocence and personal dignity as justification for his privilege against self-incrimination provision, reflecting the status of the accused as the subject of the proceedings as well as the allocation of the burden of proof. Such a privilege could form the basis for introducing a right to silence, which could ensure the principle of voluntariness. Chen Weidong, while not explicitly proposing the inclusion of a right to silence, recommended the abolition of the duty to make truthful statements and instead the inclusion of a provision allowing the suspect to refuse to answer all questions during interrogation, except for those relating to basic personal information. In his view, such a provision would reflect the state of criminal investigation and thus suit the national conditions.[100] Using the same reference benchmark, Yi Yanyou supported the introduction of a right to silence for suspects and defendants in expressive terms.[101] Yi moreover proposed to oblige interrogating authorities to inform a suspect or defendant about their right to silence; any failure to do so would have led to procedural violations.

While both the rationale and value of this guarantee were generally accepted, there was no agreement amongst scholars regarding the precise scope of silence, and certain scholars referred to other jurisdictions, most notably common law systems, in which inferences have been permitted in legislation in order to argue in favour of a limited right of silence.[102] Some scholars, which may be considered to represent the compromise view, argued that national conditions in terms of investigation methods would not allow for a full right to silence, proposing exceptions regarding certain types of cases in which the obtainment of evidence was seen as particularly difficult, including corruption, bribery, organised crime, or

[99] Bai Dong, 'Rushi huida yu chenmoquan feili zhizheng – jiyu quanqiu huayu zhong "women de" difangxing zhishi" zhi zai renshi (Conflicts between the Duty to Make Truthful Statements and the Right to Silence: Reconceptualising "Our" "Local Knowledge" in Global Discourse)' [2017] *Nankai Journal* (Philosophy, Literature and Social Science Edition) 62, 64.

[100] Chen Weidong (n 7) 40 (art 222(1) No. 3), 113.

[101] Yi Yanyou (n 32) 20–21.

[102] Chen Guangzhong and Yan Duan, *Zhonghua Renmin Gongheguo xingshi susongfa xiugai jianyigao yu lunzheng (Draft for Amendment to the PRC Criminal Procedure Law and Its Annotations)* (Zhengzhou, China Zhengzhou Publishing House, 1995) 185; Andrew LT Choo, *The Privilege Against Self-Incrimination and Criminal Justice* (Oxford, Hart Publishing, 2013) 101–103; Bian Jianlin and Guo Zhiyuan, 'Yingguo dui chenmoquan de xianzhi (Restrictions on the Right to Silence in England)' [1999] *Journal of Comparative Law* 283; He Jiahong, 'Zhongguoshi chenmoquan zhidu zhi wo Jian – yi "meiguoshi" wei canzhao (My Views on the Chinese System of the Right to Silence – with Reference to the American system)' (2013) 31 *Tribune of Political Science and Law* 107; Yue Hanwei, 'Fandui ziwo guizui quan de ying mei fa suyuan yu fali fenxi – jian lun woguo xingshisusongfa xiangguan guiding de wanshan (The Legal Sources in Anglo-American Law and the Jurisprudential Analysis of Privilege against Self – incrimination: And the Improvement of relevant Regulations about Criminal Procedure Law in China)' [2016] *Journal of Comparative Law* 96.

offences relating to interference with public order, among others.[103] As shown in chapter two, inferences may be drawn from silence under certain circumstances, and silence thus contains some relativity, but it is problematic to undertake such an a priori categorisation by applying different degrees of fairness to different categories of accused criminals. This opens a backdoor for becoming a bottomless pit, and this risk appears especially high in a system that lacks genuine checks and balances. The CPL 2012 did not adopt a right to silence, but it codified a privilege against self-incrimination that co-exists with the retained duty to make truthful statements.

## A. Narrow Privilege against Self-Incrimination as Compromise

It may not come as a surprise that the 'iron triangle', meaning the three agencies (*gongjianfa*), unanimously protested the adoption of a right to silence, claiming that national conditions were too premature for such a safeguard. As a reason, the evidential value of confessions was emphasised, and such a safeguard would have obviously compromised the aim of obtaining this valuable piece of evidence.[104] Allegedly underdeveloped investigation methods were thus invoked, even if in a rather opportunistic way, using the rhetoric of national conditions to justify the denial of silence. This argument is not very sound in the light of research by scholars about the factors leading to wrongful convictions. In fact, investigation authorities regularly violate the principle of seeking truth from facts by first producing a suspect and then obtaining evidence based on their admission of guilt in a one-sided and prejudiced manner; they operate on the basis of presumption of guilt and ignore any inconsistencies in the case or even evidence of innocence.[105] In some instances, especially where the alleged victims later re-emerged, conducting DNA testing on the victims for identification would have prevented the conviction of an innocent person.[106]

[103] Xie Yong and Tang Qiyou, 'Lun xingshi beigaoren xianfa quanli de baozhang – cong wuzui tuiding jiaodu suozuo de fenxi (On the Safeguarding of the Criminal Defendant's Constitutional Rights – An Analysis from the Perspective of Presumption of Innocence' [2012] *Law Science Magazine* 99, 101; Feng Xin and Jiang Ke, 'Chenmoquan zai zhongguo de kunjing yu chulu – yi "xingshisusongfa" xiugai wei beijing (Dilemmas and Ways forward of the Right to Silence in China – against the Background of the Revision of the Criminal Procedure Law)' [2012] *Journal of Heilongjiang Administrative Cadre College of Politics and Law* 95.

[104] 'Zhuanjia xiangjie xingsufa daxiu: gongjianfa jun fandui chenmoquan ru fa (Experts explain the major overhaul of the Criminal Procedure Law: the Police, the Procuratorates and the Courts are all opposed to the Inclusion of the Right to Silence in the Law)' *Jinghua Daily* (19 September 2011) news.qq.com/a/20110919/000186.htm accessed 5 August 2018; 'Jujiao xingshisusongfa xiugai: shifou mingque "chenmoquan" cun zhengyi (Spotlight on the Revision of the Criminal Procedure Law: whether to explicitly provide for the "right to silence" is controversial)' *People's Daily* (14 September 2011) ylzy.chinacourt.gov.cn/article/detail/2011/09/id/2004057.shtml accessed 5 August 2018.

[105] He Jiahong (n 90) 76–78.

[106] Mou (n 60) 9.

The utilitarian argument in favour of stressing crime control has been challenged by scholars as being no longer appropriate against the backdrop of China's commitment to human rights, judicial fairness and the principle of legal governance.[107] This connects to the declared ideologies underlying the utilitarian argument. Both moral and utilitarian arguments in favour of a right to silence had been advanced. The close link between the protection of dignity and the right to silence was recognised in Chinese discourses in the 2000s.[108] The functional or utilitarian argument that this guarantee can enhance procedural fairness has thus been widely accepted in Chinese academic discourses.

It should nonetheless be observed that such resistance had been cultivated for over decades and that such questionable views may seem more plausible when considering the earlier mentioned pressures imposed on the investigation authorities. As shown in chapter two, neither the right to silence nor the privilege against self-incrimination prohibits the use of confessions for conviction, in principle, provided they have been made voluntarily. Undoubtedly, the requirement of voluntariness logically follows from the prohibition against compulsion. The introduction of such a requirement would have indicated more strongly that the authorities must prove the lawfulness of the obtained confession(s). In the view of authorities, such a safeguard was arguably considered a threat to the conviction culture. This fits the stability and crime control ideology underlying the criminal justice process, in which supposedly insignificant procedural irregularities could not suppress substantive justice. The Party's approved priorities vest state agencies with a powerful rhetoric to suppress procedural safeguards by using the notion of national conditions. However, justifying the reliance on confessions in this way can be interpreted as an admission of the routine use of coercion in the Chinese criminal justice process. Mou Yu has called this the 'normalisation' of 'routine injustice'.[109]

To further address the issue of coerced confessions, the legislator nonetheless partly supported scholarly proposals and introduced a prohibition of self-incrimination in Article 50 CPL 2012, stating that 'no one shall be compelled to provide evidence proving his or her own guilt' (*bu dei qiangpo renhe ren zhengshi ziji you zui*). However, it retained the duty to cooperate and make truthful statements.[110] In the view of certain scholars, the inclusion of such a narrow privilege was a way to avoid the more sensitive issue of whether suspects have a right to silence.[111] In other words, the incorporation of a narrow privilege against self-incrimination was the only way to find a compromise amongst all stakeholders.

[107] Chen Zexian and Xiong Qiuhong (n 79) 61–63.

[108] Yi Yanyou, 'Lun fandui ziwo guizui de tequan (On the Privilege Against Committing Self-Incrimination)' [1999] *Journal of Comparative Law* 273, 273–274; Bai Dong, 'Rushi huida yu chenmoquan de gongneng zhuyi fenxi yu wenhua jieshi (Functional Analysis and Cultural Interpretation to Truthful Answer and Right to Silence)' [2012] *Law Science Magazine* 113, 114.

[109] Mou (n 60) 12.

[110] Renumbered CPL 2012, art 118(2).

[111] Bai Dong (n 99) 64.

However, considering the undeniable conflict between the duty and the privilege, the question was how this duty and such a privilege against self-incrimination should co-exist and how the latter relates to silence. Indeed, while it seems that the freedom to choose silence has always been more contested than the privilege against self-incrimination, it should be borne in mind that silence is a direct effect of the prohibition against self-incrimination. As shown in chapter two, Article 14(3)(g) ICCPR itself is silent on the scope of the right against self-incrimination, and the Covenant in principle allows for exceptions to this privilege, and the scope of the privilege indeed varies across legal systems. However, the general principles of rights restrictions under the Siracusa Principles must be respected, which means that the essence of the privilege should not be undermined by limitations of rights. However, it is not clear whether China's privilege in Article 50 CPL 2012 is intended to be a broad privilege against self-incrimination, which could be aimed at ensuring equality between the suspect and law enforcement at the pre-trial stage.[112] The prevailing view remains that the CPL 2012 did not establish a right to silence.[113] Therefore, the CPL 2012 introduced a very narrow privilege against self-incrimination.

Clearly, the inclusion of this narrow privilege against self-incrimination did not resolve the contested relationship with the duty of truthfulness. The view of conflict and the view of non-conflict dominated the discourse, while a minority tried to reconcile the two conflicting provisions. In the view of the legislator and the three agencies, there was paradoxically no conflict. Following the official view, the purpose of the privilege against self-incrimination in Article 50 was twofold: curbing the practice of extorted confessions and establishing rules on the voluntariness and legality of confessions. The question of whether a suspect is willing to cooperate would exist irrespectively and be of relevance only for consideration of leniency.[114] However, this arguably simplified view has faced backlash.

Chen Guangzhong criticised that the claim of compromise would be difficult to sustain if the duty to cooperate was maintained. Considering the contested nature of the right to silence in international discourses and practices and China's state of criminal justice, he believed it was reasonable that the legislator did not include a right to silence in the CPL draft of August 2011. Chen emphasised that the three agencies opposed such a guarantee in light of the continuing reliance on confessions. As regards the view that the narrow privilege was introduced as a compromise, he emphasised that, as long as the duty to truthfulness is maintained, there will not be a substantial change in practice. In his view, there was an undeniable conflict between these two, even if law enforcement authorities argued that

[112] Thomas Weigend, 'The Suspect as a Source of Information' in Michael Lindemann and Andreas Ransiek (eds), *Interrogation, Confession, and Truth* (Baden-Baden, Nomos, 2020) 21.

[113] Chen Ruihua (n 53) 57.

[114] '2018 Legislative Work Plan of the NPC Standing Committee)' www.npc.gov.cn/npc/c30834/201804/1c1b9070eb574282b8ef6d2f33615383.shtml accessed 2 August 2020; Huang Yan, 'Lun woguo chenmoquan de lifa gouxiang (On the Legislative Conception of the Right to Silence in China)' *China Court* (20 June 2013) www.chinacourt.org/article/detail/2013/06/id/1015808.shtml accessed 7 October 2021.

there was no such conflict based on their own interpretation that a suspect should answer truthfully and if they do not, they were not forced to do so. Indeed, it was a legal duty to answer truthfully, and in the light of the policy of combining leniency with severity, resistance would be met with harshness, albeit in the absence of any legal provision stipulating consequences of silence. Instead, the law could stipulate that investigation authorities should simply inform the accused that truthful statements may lead to a lighter sentence.[115]

The 2012 CPL indeed added that a suspect should be further informed that their 'truthful' confession may lead to lenient punishment.[116] As shown in chapter two, simply urging someone to tell the truth indeed does not conflict with the right to silence, but it appears highly problematic against the backdrop of the retained duty to make truthful statements. Because the revised law clearly reinforced the policy of combining leniency and severity, maintaining the duty may even confirm interrogators' assumption that the suspect, in fact, has a moral (and de facto legal) duty to cooperate. Criminal justice policies are being applied as quasi-law in China. Even if Chinese legislation does not explicitly allow inferences to be drawn from silence or clarify under what conditions inferences may be drawn from silence, it does not prohibit them either. Indeed, the duty to make truthful statements could be interpreted to implicitly allow inferences from silence. Considering that resistance in the form of silence will lead to a heavier punishment in practice, drawing inferences from silence based on the duty appears to be established practice.

Certain scholars tried to reconcile the privilege against self-incrimination with the duty to make truthful statements. In the view of He Jiahong, Article 50, which would codify an 'implicit right to silence', reflected a compromise. Although he also supported the abolition of the suspect's duty to make truthful statements because there was an obvious conflict, since it was retained, He suggested interpreting the relationship between silence and truthfulness in the sense that a suspect may choose silence but has no right to lie.[117] A similar approach to overcoming these conflicting provisions has been suggested by Lin and Watters, arguing that the duty could be understood to require the suspect to tell the truth when voluntarily waiving their right to silence, thus implying a right against self-incrimination. They believe that a gradual implementation of the right to silence was more realistic due to the reluctance of the police and prosecuting organs to accept such an interpretation in practice.[118] This reflects the official stance that if a suspect answers the questions of the interrogators, they must truthfully answer and not lie; and if that person has indeed made truthful statements, they may be treated leniently.

[115] 'Zhuanjia xiangjie xingsufa daxiu: gongjianfa jun fandui chenmoquan ru fa (Experts explain the major overhaul of the Criminal Procedure Law: the Police, the Procuratorates and the Courts are all opposed to the Inclusion of the Right to Silence in the Law)' (n 104).

[116] CPL 2012, arts 50 and 118(2).

[117] He (n 52) 157–160.

[118] Xifen Lin and Casey Watters, 'Understanding the Presumption of Innocence in China: Institution and Practice' in Yun Zhao and Michael Ng (eds), *Chinese Legal Reform and the Global Legal Order: Adoption and Adaptation* (Cambridge, Cambridge University Press, 2018) 60–62.

In view of these conflicting standpoints, Bai Dong tried to explain the legislator's rationale behind retaining the duty. From a functional perspective, Bai argues that the right to silence and the duty to make truthful statements would both possess their own rationales but ultimately pursue conflicting values and objectives. While the duty would be associated with the presumption of guilt prevalent in inquisitorial systems, the right to silence would be linked to the presumption of innocence being prevalent in adversarial systems. Undoubtedly, the duty would weaken the procedural status of the accused and compromise the principle of equality of arms. Even if only construed as a moral duty, the duty to truthfulness denies the freedom of choosing silence. Bai believes that the absence of a tradition of individualism would have contributed to the acceptance of the duty, though he does not see this as an obstacle to the adoption of a right to silence.[119]

After the CPL 2012 was put into effect, Bai observed that the privilege against self-incrimination has not been institutionalised, and in the absence of a system protecting the freedom of silence, it would remain a very loose principle of criminal procedure.[120] Indeed, many scholars voiced concerns as to the effectiveness of the privilege in Article 50 and continued to support the abolition of the duty to make truthful statements to enforce the newly introduced privilege and meet international presumption of innocence standards.[121]

As will be discussed in the next section, Chinese scholars had recognised that an effective right to silence would have required further normative considerations, most notably a strengthening of the defence rights to prevent and detect human rights violations in the phase of investigation.

## B. Some Normative Considerations on Silence and Voluntariness

In the absence of a legal framework providing for minimum safeguards in pre-trial proceedings, it would have been challenging to enforce silence. In this context, the pre-trial involvement of lawyers remained an area of concern. As discussed in chapter four, since the CPL 1996 was put into effect, criminal defence lawyers continued to face various problems in reality, especially as regards meeting with suspects, collecting evidence, or accessing case files, as well as the threat

[119] Bai Dong (n 108) 115–116; Bai Dong (n 99) 67–68.

[120] Bai Dong (n 99) 63.

[121] ibid 62; Zhang Xiaohai, *Wuzui tuiding quanli lun (On the Right to Presumption of Innocence)* (Beijing, China Democracy Legislative Publishing House, 2015) 186; Chen Ruihua (n 53) 57–59; 'Tian Wenchang Lüshi Tan Xingsufa Daxiu: Cao'an Reng Wei Fuyu Gongmin Chenmoquan (Lawyer Tian Wenchang on the Overhaul of the CPL: The Draft Still Gives Citizens No Right to Silence)' *Legal Daily* (1 September 2011) www.chinanews.com/fz/2011/09-01/3298146.shtml accessed 18 April 2018. Xie Yong and Tang Qiyou (n 103) 100.

of being persecuted for lawyer's perjury.[122] At the annual meeting of the Criminal Procedure Law Research Association in 2003, the delegates made proposals in relation to improving the defence system. For example, it was suggested that the rights of lawyers in the investigation phase should be expanded and especially effective access to legal counsel should be ensured; the approval requirement of meetings in cases involving state secrets should thus be abolished. In addition, the right to meet with a lawyer should be guaranteed at all stages of criminal proceedings, the power of investigating authorities to dispatch personnel to be present at meetings should therefore be abolished, and access to a suspect's files should be ensured. To prevent extorted confessions and guarantee the truthfulness and voluntariness of confessions, a lawyer should have the right to be present at interrogations.[123] Therefore, the inclusion of a right to make the presence of a lawyer at interrogations mandatory was considered key to changing the traditional emphasis on confessions and to curbing the practice of extorted confessions.

While the revision of the Criminal Procedure Law was still in the making, reforms to the Lawyers Law expanded the scope of lawyers' rights. The LL 2007 went beyond the CPL 1996. In terms of meetings and access to case files, it stipulated that lawyers' meetings with suspects and defendants should not be monitored by the police,[124] and it expanded lawyers' access to case files to 'all relevant files' of the case as soon as a court had accepted a case.[125] In August 2008, the SCNPC Legislative Affairs Commission made clear that the revised LL 2007 should take precedence over the CPL 1996 in practice. Liu and Halliday have emphasised that lawyers were able to have greater influence on the revision work of the Lawyers Law than of the Criminal Procedure Law because it was mainly taken on by the Ministry of Justice.[126] However, neither the CPL 1996 nor the LL 2007 provided for a provision on the presence of lawyers during interrogations, nor did any other legislation. In the process of a third overhaul of the Criminal Procedure Law, lawyers first appeared at the stage as stakeholders and negotiators.[127]

Therefore, scholars worked on a normative framework regulating the criminal interrogation procedure that could effectively protect against torture and ill-treatment and thus strengthen international presumption of innocence standards. In their view, at the core of these normative considerations were the questions of how the law could ensure silence and protect against self-incrimination. Scholars

[122] Sida Liu and Terence Halliday, *Criminal Defense in China, The Politics of Lawyers at Work* (Cambridge, Cambridge University Press, 2016) 29–30.
[123] Li Zhongcheng (n 1) 187.
[124] LL 2007, art 33.
[125] LL 2007, art 34.
[126] Liu and Halliday (n 122) 39–40.
[127] ibid 35.

working on draft proposals aimed to integrate what they arguably considered the positive elements of the LL 2007 into the Criminal Procedure Law in order to harmonise the two laws. When looking at the proposed changes, it becomes clear that an earlier involvement of lawyers was considered a key safeguard, echoing the endeavours of lawyers as stakeholders, but not all supported an unrestricted access to counsel. Some examples will be used to illustrate proposed scholarly formulations regarding the right to have a lawyer present during interrogations:

> Chen Zexian and Xiong Qiuhong:
>
> When the investigation personnel first interrogate a criminal suspect or from the day of taking compulsory measures against a criminal suspect, [they] shall first inform the criminal suspect that he enjoys the following rights: […] (4) To request the presence of an entrusted or appointed lawyer when answering the questions of the investigation personnel during interrogation, and to request that the entire interrogation be audio-recorded and video-recorded.
>
> 侦查人员第一次讯问犯罪嫌疑人时或对犯罪嫌疑人采取强制措施之日起，首先应当告知犯罪嫌疑人享有以下权利: (…) (4) 在回答侦查人员讯问时要求所委托或者指定的律师在场，请求全程录音，录像.[128]
>
> Chen Guangzhong:
>
> In cases where a defender shall be appointed, a lawyer shall be present during the interrogation of the criminal suspect.
>
> 对于应当指定辩护的案件, 讯问犯罪嫌疑人时, 应当有律师在场.[129]
>
> Yi Yanyou:
>
> Any criminal suspect or defendant subject to criminal prosecution shall have the right to have his or her lawyer present when being questioned by investigation or supervisory authorities, or the judicial authorities; the personnel responsible for the interrogation shall inform [the criminal suspect or defendant] about his or her right to request the presence of his or her lawyer during interrogation.
>
> 任何受刑事追诉的犯罪嫌疑人, 被告人, 在接受侦查机关或监察机关, 审判机关讯问时, 均应当有权要求其律师到场; 负责讯问的人员应当告知其有权在讯问时要求其律师到场.[130]

Therefore, according to Yi Yanyou, all suspects and defendants should have the right to have a lawyer present during interrogations, including the first interrogation and regardless of the seriousness or the nature of the accusations. Xiong Qiuhong and Chen Zexian had proposed a similar provision, but they retained the ambiguous reference to 'during the first interrogation', as used in the CPL 1996.[131] Yet, read in conjunction with other proposed provisions in their draft, the presence of lawyers was to be fully implemented, without any prima facie exceptions.[132]

[128] Chen Zexian and Xiong Qiuhong (n 79) 1.
[129] Chen Guangzhong (n 6) 122 (art 231).
[130] Yi Yanyou (n 32) 21.
[131] CPL 1996, art 96.
[132] Chen Zexian and Xiong Qiuhong (n 79) 1, 27–33, 47–48.

Moreover, interrogations should be fully audio-visually recorded, and interrogation records were to be signed by the suspect and their attending defence lawyer; otherwise, such evidential materials should not be permissible as evidence at trial.[133] Since the Supreme People's Procuratorate and Supreme People's Court had already addressed the issue of audio-visual recording of criminal interrogations, provisions to this effect should be included in the revised law. However, because resources and capacities were limited, audio-visual recording should be restricted to major suspects or to cases where the lawfulness of an interrogation could be questioned at trial; this reflects the approach of a gradual expansion of audio-visual recording.[134] As shown in chapter four, while the CPL 1996 had not modified the interrogation procedure, the Supreme People's Procuratorate specified the procedure for interrogating suspects held in custody and enabled optional audio-visual recording.[135]

While scholars like Fan Chongyi or Chen Guangzhong supported the involvement of defence lawyers in the criminal investigation stage, they were reluctant to advocate a mandatory presence of lawyers during interrogation in all cases and to all suspects. Fan suggested that the scope of this guarantee should be limited to certain types of cases, including serious accusations, such as rape and bribery or joint and group crimes, and major and complex criminal cases where suspects are being held in custody, because a confession of the suspect or defendant was an important piece of evidence in these cases; it should not be applied in cases involving criminals caught red-handed and minor offences where the obtainment of evidence would be less complex.[136] In a similar vein, Chen suggested limiting the scope of the right to have a lawyer present during interrogation to cases involving mandatory defence, which largely corresponded with Fan's categories.[137]

Chen Zexian and Xiong Qiuhong suggested that additional safeguards be put in place to curb the practice of coerced confessions. Considering field research, which had suggested that the confession rate reached 90 per cent in some locations, and the issue of recanted confessions, they proposed a provision requiring the prosecution to prove the legality of interrogation procedures where inconsistencies between the confession of the prosecution and view of the defence arise at trial.[138] As the previous discussions have shown, all scholarly drafts generally supported imposing the burden to prove the legality of evidence on the prosecution, albeit to different degrees.

[133] ibid 61–63.

[134] ibid 69–70.

[135] Criminal Procedure Rules of the People's Procuratorate (1999) arts 139 and 144; Provisions of the Supreme People's Procuratorate on the Implementation of Synchronous Audio and Video Recording throughout the Whole Process of Duty-Related Suspects (for Trial Implementation) (Adopted on 15 December 2005).

[136] Fan Chongyi, *Xingshi susongfa xiugai zhuanti yanjiu baogao (Thematic report on the revision of the Code of Criminal Procedure)* (Beijing, China Police University Publishing House, 2004) 205–206.

[137] Chen Guangzhong (n 6) 23–32 (arts 49 to 60), 122 (art 231).

[138] ibid 6–7, 73.

Chen Weidong proposed adopting a principle of voluntariness of confessions and detailed rules for criminal interrogations, including permissible methods of obtaining evidence, fixed locations for questioning, time limits or rules on the production of interrogation records, among others.[139] In this context, scholars evidently believed that setting time limits for interrogations would be decisive to curb police powers. Proposals ranged from a tight four hours' time limit for interrogation of suspects and at least four hours of rest between two interrogations[140] to a more generous maximum of 12 hours and the same hours of rest between each interrogation.[141]

These scholars therefore focused on establishing a normative framework that could ensure the voluntariness of confessions and protect the integrity of the accused. Although an extension of the rights of lawyers in the stage of investigation was widely considered necessary to ensure the procedural safeguards of suspects, it is plausible that Chinese scholars were aware that the three agencies would oppose a too drastic expansion of lawyers' rights at this stage. Considering that they knew it would depend on negotiation, constructive criticism with the hope of gradual improvements was arguably more promising and sensible than frontal attacks. The official endorsement of the principle of law-based governance and the constitutional human rights clause provided useful paradigms. However, there was an undeniable discrepancy between theory and practice – or ideal and reality.

Despite scholarly proposals to specify and expand procedural safeguards for suspects, only modest efforts were made to clarify provisions on the interrogation procedure. The CPL 2012 granted lawyers the status of defender in the investigation phase, stipulating that a suspect may appoint a defence lawyer when being interrogated for the first time by the police or from the day a compulsory measure is taken against him or her,[142] which enabled defence lawyers to collect evidence for their clients during police investigation, as further outlined in other provisions.[143] The CPL 2012, moreover, integrated some of the LL 2007 provisions. For example, it stipulated that a lawyer's meeting with a suspect or defendant does not require the police's approval, and the meeting shall be arranged within 48 hours without being monitored by the police, even if allowing a few exceptions with respect to state security cases, terrorism cases, or extraordinarily significant bribery cases.[144] The CPL 2012 specified that interrogations of suspects in custody must be conducted *in the detention centre*, and that the police shall interrogate a detainee within 24 hours after detention,[145] but such requirements can be easily ignored in practice due to a lack of external supervision over investigation procedures.

[139] Chen Weidong (n 7) 27 (art 151), 39–40 (arts 119 to 127).
[140] Chen Zexian and Xiong Qiuhong (n 49) 66–68; see also Chen Weidong (n 3) 263–264.
[141] Chen Guangzhong (n 6) 118–120 (arts 222 and 223).
[142] CPL 2012, art 33.
[143] See CPL 2012, art 41. On the rights of defenders, see especially arts 36 to 41 of the CPL 2012.
[144] CPL 2012, art 37; Liu and Halliday (n 122) 39–40.
[145] CPL 2012, arts 116(2) and 84.

But the CPL 2012 did not include a right for criminal suspects to have a lawyer present during interrogations. Indeed, these reforms did not significantly improve the situation of defence lawyers on the ground.[146] Resistance as regards the defence's right to collect evidence especially came from law enforcement. For example, representatives of the Ministry of Public Security soon questioned the scope of the right to collect evidence in the phase of investigation, some saying that it should be limited to certain aspects, such as the lawfulness of obtained evidence, ie, coerced confessions or mitigating circumstances, while any interferences with the criminal investigation work could not be tolerated.[147]

Legal developments after 2012 further illustrate that, instead of fundamentally changing the power relations, the party-state made further efforts to specify the scope of mandatory and optional audio-visual recording of interrogations.[148] However, at the time, it was clear that the interrogation procedure was prone to manipulation and that the interrogation record was often prepared in a way to get a conviction without raising suspicion as to the legality of investigation activities,[149] and the enforcement of the exclusionary rules remained lacking. Even if it is fair to say the party-state has taken some steps to improve pre-trial proceedings, this has been done primarily out of self-interest to tighten control over law enforcement authorities. These mechanisms can be best understood to signal that there are some checks on authorities, but they cannot genuinely empower individuals vis-à-vis the state.

Therefore, in the absence of silence and centrally important pre-trial guarantees, it is difficult to claim that legislation had fully realised the presumption of innocence in both the dimensions of rule and principle. This begins with the question of who bears the burden of proof; the de facto legal obligation to make truthful statements comprises the burden of proof, which is worsened by the absence of centrally important safeguards such as a legal right to silence. The narrow privilege against self-incrimination is undoubtedly compromised by the duty to cooperate. Leaving aside the reality of criminal justice, ostensible legal safeguards are thus always followed by a *but*… Indeed, too many *buts* are also observable in the context of personal liberty.

[146] Liu and Halliday (n 122) 40–42.

[147] See art 41 of the CPL 2012; Tian Ye, 'Jujiao shiwu xin wenti, tuidong xingsufa guanche zhixing – zhongguo xingshi susong faxue yanjiuhui 2013 nian nianhui zongshu (Focusing on new Practical Issues and Promoting the Implementation of the Criminal Procedure Law – Summary of the 2013 Annual Meeting of the China Criminal Procedure Law Research Association)' [2013] *People's Procuratorial Semimonthly* 49, 49–50.

[148] See, eg, Provisions of the Supreme People's Procuratorate on the Implementation of Synchronous Audio and Video Recording throughout the Whole Process of Duty-Related Suspects (for Trial Implementation) (Adopted on 15 December 2005); Provisions on Audio and Video Recording Interrogation of Criminal Suspects by Public Security Organs (Issued on 5 September 2014, No. 33 [2014] of the Ministry of Public Security); Provisions on the Interrogation of Criminal Suspects in the Phase of Arrest Examination (Adopted on 11 August 2010, No. 6 [2010] of the Supreme People's Court).

[149] Mou (n 60) 42–48.

## V. Personal Liberty and the Principle of Presumption of Innocence

Chinese scholars began to consider the broader dimension of presumption of innocence in the late 1990s. As outlined in chapter two, the principle of presumption of innocence is closely linked to the rule of law and thus assumes limits on state power and consequently effective checks and balances. With the Party's official endorsement of the principle of law-based governance in the 1990s, domestic discourses on the presumption of innocence had moved away from the narrow reading as an evidential rule towards the recognition of the broader dimension of principle, especially in relation to personal liberty.[150] For example, Yi Yanyou emphasised that the principle of presumption of innocence requires effective separation of powers and checks and balances to ensure the protection of the rights of the accused. Regarding personal liberty, the lack of judicial approval and review (by a court) over deprivations of personal liberty in criminal proceedings, most notably custody pending trial, was of particular concern.[151] Yi's criticism highlights the deeper-rooted systemic problems, which would have required far more far-reaching reforms, notably breaking the police's monopoly over pre-trial proceedings, than modifying time limits.

The CPL 1996's regime of compulsory measures had faced severe criticism domestically. Media reports about instances of torture, often in police custody and in the context of criminal investigations, sometimes even leading to death, were no rarity.[152] Authorities came up with partly absurd excuses to explain the causes of death, for example, saying that persons had died while playing 'hide and seek'.[153] In academic circles, misuse of such measures was attributed to the overriding goal of crime control and the lack of proper checks and balances in the criminal justice system.[154]

Following the reform of the CPL 1979 in 1996, the police had developed their own understanding of how the investigation procedure ought to take place. As discussed in chapter four, even if the CPL 1996 had first introduced time limits for interrogations by summons, they were generous and thus opened room for misuse by holding a suspect for prolonged periods of time. Furthermore, the 1996 CPL had relaxed the time limits for detention (*juliu*) while lowering the evidentiary standard for arrest (*daibu*), which in practice had led to a symbiotic relationship

[150] Chen Weidong, 'Xingshi susong fazhi sishi nian: huigu yu zhanwang (40 Years' Development of Criminal Procedure Law: Retrospect and Prospect)' (2019) 37 *Tribune of Political Science and Law* 18, 20.

[151] Yi Yanyou (n 32) 19.

[152] Flora Sapio, *Sovereign Power and the Law in China* (Leiden, Brill, 2010) 210.

[153] 'Yunnan "duomaomao" an "laotou yu ba" zhufan bei pan wuqi tuxing (Yunnan "Hide-and-Seek" Case – "Jailbird" Main Offender Sentenced to Life Imprisonment)' *China News* (15 August 2009) www.chinanews.com.cn/gn/news/2009/08-15/1819929.shtml accessed 30 September 2019.

[154] Yanyou Yi, 'Arrest as Punishment: The Abuse of Arrest in the People's Republic of China' (2008) 10 *Punishment and Society* 9, 17–18; Yi Yanyou (n 32) 21.

between these two measures, meaning a suspect was usually first detained by the police and in almost all cases subsequently arrested. According to one field research carried out in three local police stations in Shenzhen, Guangdong province, in 2005, this was the case in 70 to 80 per cent of suspects.[155] Conversely, the less intrusive measure of bail was used only on a relatively small scale and often misused, failing its purpose as an alternative measure to protect personal liberty.[156]

The police, moreover, regularly exceeded the time limits for filing requests for arrest approval of detainees. Research on the ground had shown that even in arguably 'uncomplicated' cases, due to the lack of clear definitions of terms such as 'special circumstances', 'major criminal suspect' etc, most persons were detained for the legal maximum period of 30 days and more, or even re-detained after their release,[157] although the law prohibited the recalculation of time limits for detention.[158]

In the absence of external supervision, detention had become an instrument for resolving criminal cases. To facilitate the investigation procedure, the police adopted the modus operandi of completing the process of obtaining evidence before formally requesting the procuratorate to approve arrest. This practice is reflected in No. 2 of the so-called 'Hidden Rules' (*qian guize*), which states that 'a major part of criminal investigation must be completed before the decision to arrest is taken'.[159] Moreover, as part of the culture to publicly denounce guilt, after a case has been handed over to the procuratorate for prosecution, the police have in some cases organised so-called 'public arrest rallies' (*gongkai daibu dahui*) aimed at presenting the 'criminal facts' and the identity of the suspects to the public.[160] Clearly, the question of guilt or innocence already had to be settled before the case could be transferred to the prosecuting organs.

As for the causes of the high pre-trial custody rates and the abuse of compulsory measures, scholars have identified shortcomings in the checks and balances system, especially in the procuratorial supervisory function.[161] Scholars have criticised the CPL 1996's lack of clear guidance for understanding conditions such as 'necessity', as a condition of arrest. Considering that no interrogation will take

[155] Huang Haibo, 'Zhencha jiandu shiye zhong de xingshi juliu (Criminal Detention from the Perspective of Investigation Supervision)' [2007] *Chinese Criminal Science* 89, 89–90.

[156] Mike McConville and (with Satnam Choongh, Pinky Choy, Dick Wan, Eric Chui, Wing Hong, Ian Dobinson and Carol Jones), *Criminal Justice in China: An Empirical Inquiry* (Cheltenham, Edward Elgar, 2011) 56–58; Enshen Li, 'The Abuse of Guaranteed Pending Trial in the Chinese Criminal Process: A Violation of International Human Rights Law' (2011) 9 *Indonesian Journal of International Law* 79, 84.

[157] Huang Haibo (n 155) 89–90; McConville et al (n 156) 45, 49–51.

[158] Notice of the Supreme People's Court, Supreme People's Procuratorate and the Ministry of Public Security on Strictly Enforcing the Criminal Procedure Law and Redressing and Preventing Exceeded Custody (issued on 12 November 2003, No. 163 [2003]) art 2.

[159] Chen Ruihua, 'Zhongguo xingshi sifa de 17 ge qianguize (17 Hidden Rules of Chinese Criminal Justice)' (*Zhihu Net*, 8 August 2018) zhuanlan.zhihu.com/p/41566281 accessed 10 January 2019.

[160] Chen Ruihua (n 53) 45.

[161] Gao Jiapeng, 'Zhencha jiandu wenti de fajieshixue fenxi (Hermeneutic Analysis of Investigation Supervision Issues)' (2018) 36 *Tribune of Political Science and Law* 33.

place in most instances, prosecutors examining arrest requests in an administrative manner would usually focus on the evidential circumstances of a case rather than the potential punishment or necessity of the deprivation of liberty, which had contributed to excessive custody rates.[162] Consequently, in such cases, arrest was approved if the evidence established that the person was the major suspect, regardless of whether the offence or social harm was relatively 'minor'; such cases may include excessive self-defence or negligent crimes in which the suspect showed repentance and paid compensation, among others.[163]

Once the decision to arrest the accused was made, it inevitably affected the outcome of a case. Especially in minor cases, judges were faced with a dilemma, as in many cases the prison sentence possible under criminal law would have been shorter than the period of custody the suspects and defendants were already in. In other words, a heavier punishment had to be imposed, as the period of custody could not be shorter than the period of imprisonment.[164] Such a practice evidently runs counter to the principle of presumption of innocence, as the duration of remand custody should generally not be used as an indicator of guilt and its degree. From the late 1990s onwards, the party-state has addressed the issue of 'prolonged custody',[165] announcing policies such as 'arrest less, arrest cautiously' (*shao bu shen bu*). A substantial body of supplementary regulations has also aimed to prevent excessive and prolonged custody.[166]

In the light of all these problems and against the backdrop of promoting legal governance, the question arguably was how to restrain police powers. The

[162] Lin Xifen, 'Fenduan shencha yihuo guikou: jiya biyaoxing shencha de gaige luoji (Sectionalized or Centralized Examination: the Logic behind the Reform of Custody Necessity Examination)' [2015] *Chinese Journal of Law* 157, 157–158.

[163] Quality Standards for the Examination of Arrest Requests by the People's Procuratorates (Adopted by the Supreme People's Procuratorate on 25 August 2010) para 6.

[164] Yang Yi, 'Yi shehui weixianxing shencha wei hexin de daibu tiaojian chonggou – jiyu jingyan shishi de lilun fansi (Reconstruction of Arrest Conditions centred on the Examination of Social Danger – a Theoretical Reflection based on Empirical Facts)' [2018] *Journal of Comparative Law* 130, 132.

[165] In a Notice issued by the SPP in 2015, 'extended custody' has been defined as concerning cases where the period of custody of the criminal suspect or defendant in the stage of investigation, prosecution examination or trial exceeds the custody period prescribed by laws; 'long-period custody without conviction' refers to cases, in which the criminal suspect or defendant is held in custody for five years or more and the case is still in the stage of investigation, prosecution examination, first or second instance, see Notice of the Criminal Execution Procuratorial Department of the Supreme People's Procuratorate on Issuing the Provisions of the Criminal Execution Procuratorial Departments of the People's Procuratorates on Preventing and Redressing the Cases of Extended Custody and Long-Period Custody without Conviction (for Trial Implementation) (issued by the Supreme People's Procuratorate on 1 June 2015) art 2.

[166] See, eg, Notice of the Supreme People's Court on Strictly Controlling the Use of Custody Measures against Persons Subject to Enforcement (Adopted by the Supreme People's Court on 9 October 1996, No. 96 [1996]); Notice of the Supreme People's Court, Supreme People's Procuratorate and the Ministry of Public Security on Strictly Enforcing the Criminal Procedure Law and Redressing and Preventing Exceeded Custody (issued on 12 November 2003, No. 163 [2003]); Provisions of the Supreme People's Procuratorate and Ministry of Public Security on Issues relating to the Application of the Measure of Arrest in accordance with the Law (6 August 2001, No. 10 [2001] of the Supreme People's Procuratorate); Provisions on the Application of the Term of Criminal Custody by Public Security Organs (issued on 27 January 2006, No. 17 [2006] of the Ministry of Public Security).

Legislation Law of 2000 was the first to formally restrict the legislative powers to deprive citizens of their personal liberty in matters relating to criminal charges, stating that only the National People's Congress and its Standing Committee (not the State Council) are empowered to enact administrative regulations on matters involving the restriction of personal freedom.[167] Efforts to strengthen personal liberty safeguards have thus involved regulating the powers to deprive citizens of their personal liberty in criminal proceedings. In addition, the party-state, through the legislator, has undertaken efforts to abolish so-called extra-legal and extra-extra-legal detention measures[168] while seeking to expand alternative measures to custody. Moreover, since 2005, most administrative detention measures have been formally regulated under the Public Security Administration Punishments Law.[169] The regulation aimed to prevent the abuse of administrative detention measures in the criminal justice process.

Besides the criminal defence system, the improvement of the system of compulsory measures was a recurring theme during the meetings of the Criminal Procedure Association. For example, at the meeting in 2003, delegates made various proposals, including the clarification of the time limits, targets and location for interrogations by forced appearances; broadening the scope of bail and clarifying the six months' time limit; and clarifying conditions of arrest. Delegates voiced concerns as regards the practice of long periods of deprivations of liberty in criminal proceedings and emphasised that liberty ought to be the rule to which detention should be an exception. The question of establishing a judicial review by a court of custodial measures was fiercely discussed, but there was no consensus; different views were shared that arguably reflect the interests of law enforcement agencies, on the one hand, and human rights advocates, on the other.[170] Similar discussions regularly reoccurred during later meetings.

Against the backdrop of the Party's commitment to legal governance and the reform agenda of the Party central, the delegates (including representatives from the Supreme People's Court, the Supreme People's Procuratorate, and the Ministry of Public Security) focused on the overarching questions of proper allocation of criminal justice powers and the institutionalisation of the policy of combining leniency with severity. Some delegates proposed to reorganise the powers among the three agencies to change the practice of the 'assembly line' and make a shift towards trial-centredness. Certain delegates suggested that the allocation of powers should observe the two principles of fairness and efficiency, on the one hand, and the protection of human rights, on the other; this would mean that there should be appropriate constraints on the powers of state agencies. Indeed, a majority emphasised that judicial oversight by the courts over investigation and

[167] LL 2015, arts 7 to 9.

[168] Hualing Fu, 'The Varieties of Law in China' (*China Rights Forum*, 18 July 2011) www.hrichina.org/en/crf/article/5422 accessed 10 January 2019.

[169] Public Security Administration Punishments Law 2005.

[170] Li Zhongcheng (n 1) 186–187.

procuratorial powers should be strengthened. The latter powers had been criticised for the administrative nature of decision-making, unclear competences among the departments, and conflicts between prosecution and supervision powers. Some practitioners thus suggested bundling the supervision power over investigation in one procuratorial department. Regarding investigation powers, largely in the hands of the police, representatives of the Ministry of Public Security stressed the ongoing progress in terms of standardisation of many procedures to improve case handling, presumably not willing to give up the monopoly over criminal investigation.[171] The next section discusses scholarly proposals with respect to improving personal liberty protections and the outcomes of the reform.

## A. The Rule of Liberty

With domestic legislation under growing scrutiny in the 2000s, Chinese scholars critically examined the compliance with ICCPR standards. The prevailing view on China's compliance with Article 9 was that domestic legislation overall complies with paragraph 1 of the provision, which protects the liberty and security of persons and prohibits arbitrary deprivations of personal liberty through arrest or detention in the ICCPR sense, although the implementation of statutory provisions was lacking.[172] The question of personal liberty protection vis-à-vis apparently omnipotent state agencies also occupied scholarly drafts. As part of an effort to suggest greater limits to such power, scholarly drafts have proposed a 'principle of proportionality'. Chen Weidong's draft provided for a general principle of proportionality that should be observed throughout criminal proceedings, without specifying which authority should oversee compliance with such a principle.[173] Furthermore, drawing on such principles as the rule of law or the presumption of innocence, the law should emphasise the principle of lawfulness (legality) of the deprivation of personal liberty in order to prevent the misuse of compulsory measures as a means of imposing 'anticipated punishments'.[174]

In a similar vein, Chen Guangzhong proposed the inclusion of a principle of proportionality that state agencies should observe when using compulsory measures to reduce the risk of unlawful and arbitrary deprivations of liberty;[175] however, it was again not clear which organ should oversee the implementation of such a

[171] Ye Qing and Xu Meijun (n 11) 154–158.

[172] Chen Guangzhong (n 3) 139; Yue Liling, *Gongmin quanli he zhengzhi quanli guoji gongyue yu zhongguo xingshi sifa (International Covenant on Civil and Political Rights and Criminal Justice in China)* (Beijing, Law Press China, 2007) 60; Wei Yuening, 'Shenpan qian de jiya (Pre-trial Detention)' in Chen Guangzhong (ed), *Gongmin quanli he zhengzhi quanli guoji gongyue pizhun yu shishi wenti yanjiu (Study on the Ratification and Implementation of the International Covenant on Civil and Political Rights)* (Beijing, China Legal Publishing House, 2002) 155.

[173] Chen Weidong (n 7) 3 (art 3), 112.

[174] ibid 140–141 (art 56).

[175] Chen Guangzhong (n 6) 4 (art 11), 258.

principle. Considering China's obligations under CAT and ICCPR, Xu proposed the adoption of a principle of lawfulness of compulsory measures, prohibiting the unlawful restriction and deprivation of personal liberty of criminally accused persons. Together with his presumption of innocence provision, it could prevent the abuse of successive interrogations and the regular circumvention of statutory time limits for interrogation by summons and forced appearances and thus rectify the issue of prolonged custody.[176] However, without far-reaching institutional and political reforms, it would likely have remained a promise on paper.

Moreover, it was now widely agreed that the presumption of innocence would imply the rule that deprivation of personal liberty should be the exception, as reflected in the Tokyo Rules.[177] To realise this rule, the scholars focused primarily on clarifying the conditions and expanding the scope of alternative, less intrusive measures such as bail, while at the same time tightening the conditions for criminal detention and arrest, although there were different views on the time limits and conditions for these measures. Furthermore, many scholars agreed that the time limit of 12 hours for interrogation by forced appearances, including fixed intervals like eight hours between interrogation sessions, as well as places for forced appearances, should be clarified to prevent the use of this measure as a form of police custody.[178]

As part of the effort to strengthen the use of non-custodial measures, many scholars believed that the conditions for bail and residential surveillance under the CPL 1996, such as 'social danger' or 'possible imprisonment', were too vague, leading to their indiscriminate use. As discussed in chapter four, there was also criticism that the CPL 1996 did not provide for specific conditions for each of these measures, even if supplementary regulations provided some more guidance. The scattered nature of the provisions had an adversarial impact on the protection of suspects and defendants' personal liberty in practice. Both these measures faced similar issues: they were hardly applied in practice but often misused if applied. The measure of residential surveillance was a point of controversy amongst scholars, especially the question of whether it should be abolished. Indeed, intended as an alternative and less-intrusive measure, the lack of guidance in terms of application under the CPL 1996 and other legislation had opened room for abuse. While its application was comparatively infrequent, it was primarily applied to migrant suspects.[179]

Since the criminal justice system had not yet integrated a right to be released on bail, the question of a new bail system arose. Many of the scholars compiling drafts agreed that the right of suspects and defendants to request bail should be

[176] Xu Jingcun (n 29) 42–43.
[177] Chen Zexian and Xiong Qiuhong (n 79) 73–78.
[178] Fan Chongyi (n 135) 314; Xu Jingcun (n 29) 43–44 (art 58).
[179] Joshua Rosenzweig, 'Residential Surveillance: Evolution of a Janus-Faced Measure' in Elisa Nesossi and others (eds), *Legal Reforms and Deprivation of Liberty in Contemporary China* (Abingdon, Routledge, 2016) 82–83.

strengthened, meaning establishing a legal right, although different proposals were made on how to reform the bail system.[180] For example, Chen Weidong aimed at a bail system with a *right* to bail, as it would be a constitutional guarantee in accordance with the internationally recognised habeas corpus guarantee (*renshen baohu ling*) that could be found in many systems.[181] Chen Zexian and Xiong Qiuhong, on the other hand, believed that the percentage of suspects and defendants being held in custody pending trial could be reduced by improving the existing bail system, thus specifying instances of mandatory and optional bail. In their view, bail should be mandatory in minor cases (meaning where the anticipated sentence does not exceed three years' imprisonment) and if the suspect or defendant is a minor or first offender or if it involves negligent offences, among others.[182] As far as conditions for bail are concerned, scholarly drafts drew largely on the supplementary regulations that had been issued after the 1996 CPL reform and which had already provided some guidance.

Regarding the scope of the right to apply for bail under the 1996 CPL, the law had limited it to arrestees. Given the relatively long periods of detention and in the light of the internationally recognised right to be tried within a reasonable time or be released,[183] Chen Guangzhong argued that a detainee, ie, a suspect held in police detention, should also have the right to *apply* for bail, thus maintaining the softer language ('apply') of the 1996 CPL.[184] Another point of criticism concerned the unclear time limits for bail; ie, it was not clear whether the 12-month time limit for bail set in the 1996 CPL referred to a total period of 12 months or whether it could be applied anew at each stage of the criminal procedure. There was an agreement among scholars that the revised law should explicitly state that this time limit applies to the entire criminal proceedings.[185]

Regarding the measure of residential surveillance, Chen Guangzhong had suggested retaining it but distinguishing more clearly the conditions for residential surveillance from those for bail. Whereas residential surveillance should be applied to suspects and defendants who do not meet the conditions for arrest and have no fixed residence.[186] Bail, on the other hand, may be granted to suspects and defendants who cannot be arrested due to health issues, as well as to pregnant and breastfeeding women; and to those who may receive a lighter punishment, including criminal detention (*juyi*), control (*guanzhi*) or independent supplementary punishment (*duli shiyong fujiaxing*), or a sentence of fixed-term imprisonment but do not pose a social danger; bail may also be granted to minors

[180] Chen Weidong (n 7) 12, 13 (arts 61, 71), 146–157; Fan Chongyi (n 135) 315–316; Chen Zexian and Xiong Qiuhong (n 78) 80–83; Xu Jingcun (n 29) 54-55 (Art 69).

[181] Chen Weidong (n 7) 155.

[182] Chen Zexian and Xiong Qiuhong (n 79) 73–83 (art 51).

[183] See ICCPR, art 9.

[184] Chen Guangzhong (n 7) 50–52 (arts 98 and 100), 356; CPL 1996, art 52.

[185] Fan Chongyi (n 136) 315–316; Chen Zexian and Xiong Qiuhong (n 79) 80–83; Xu Jingcun (n 30) 54–55 (art 69).

[186] ibid 58 (art 108), 365.

and to those suspects and defendants who do not meet the conditions for arrest due to insufficient evidence or where the statutory time limits of case handling had already been exceeded but case was still ongoing; if they had already been sentenced to a lighter punishment, as outlined above, by the court of first instance, or if the period of custody had already amounted to or exceeded the term of punishment imposed by the court of first instance.[187] Chen thus merged, with marginal modifications, the supplementary regulations issued by the three agencies after the 1996 CPL reform, though giving the agencies more leeway by using 'may' (*keyi*) instead of 'shall' (*yinggai*).[188] As with bail, Chen suggested that the time limits of residential surveillance should be regulated in accordance with the procedural stages and that strict time limits should be set for each stage to prevent the authorities from circumventing the statutory time limits.[189]

Although Xu Jingcun had advocated the abolition of residential surveillance, if it had to be retained, he suggested specifying the scope of application, which was largely identical with Chen Guangzhong's bail conditions.[190] In the view of Fan Chongyi, among all compulsory measures, residential surveillance was lacking practicability the most and was barely used in practice. Owing to a lack of clear provisions, especially residential surveillance *at a designated location* had become a disguised form of confinement. As shown in chapter four, the CPL 1996 had added the option to enforce residential surveillance at a designated location to prevent the abuse of this measure as de facto confinement. Although it was intended to protect the rights of suspects and defendants, it continued to be used as de facto confinement. And because the three law enforcement agencies had all separately codified a time limit of six months, this was interpreted to mean that it can be used three times for up to six months, amounting to one and a half years of de facto confinement. Their creative interpretation evidently was that the time limits relate only to the relevant procedural stage. Considering all these issues, Fan, like many other scholars, supported the abolition of this measure. However, if this measure had to be retained, the revised law should at least clarify the six months' time limit, and its use should be limited to specified offences such as bribery and corruption and other economic crimes.[191]

Regarding the custodial compulsory measures of detention and arrest, scholars working on draft proposals agreed that more safeguards were needed to prevent abuse by law enforcement agencies, here, notably the police. For example, the CPL 1996 had already mandated police interrogation within 24 hours upon detention, but it made no mention of a notification requirement as regards the reasons and grounds of deprivation of liberty.[192] There was a general agreement amongst

[187] ibid 50 (art 98).
[188] See ch 4, VI.
[189] Chen Guangzhong (n 6) 62 (art 112), 370.
[190] Xu Jingcun (n 29) 45–49.
[191] Fan Chongyi (n 136) 323.
[192] CPL 1996, art 65.

these scholars that such a requirement should be adopted, even if certain scholars proposed exceptions where obstructions of proceedings may occur.[193]

Regarding these two measures, two controversial issues stood out. There was no consensus on if and how the controversially discussed 37-day time limit to request arrest of a detainee should be modified. As regards the measure of arrest, moreover, a point of contention was whether the authority of approval should be shifted to the courts in order to reduce the rate of persons who are taken into custody awaiting trial.[194] Chen Weidong argued that the power to decide on these two measures should rest exclusively with the courts, especially to ensure the fairness and impartiality of the arrest examination.[195] This view reflects efforts to bring the Criminal Procedure Law in line with the ICCPR, according to which a person arrested or detained (in the ICCPR sense) should be 'promptly', meaning within 48 hours, brought before a judge or other judicial officer.[196] One aim of this requirement evidently is to prevent and reduce the risk of ill-treatment arising from longer periods of detention in the custody of law enforcement officials without judicial control.[197] It should be borne in mind that, in the view of the Human Rights Committee, however, prosecutors cannot be considered eligible to decide on pre-trial detention, as they lack independence, objectivity and impartiality in this regard.[198] Indeed, the Working Group on Arbitrary Detention has criticised the procuratorial power over arrest several times and questioned whether it can fulfil the requirements of paragraph 3 of Article 9 ICCPR as regards 'the independence of an officer authorised by law to exercise judicial power'.[199]

The competing scholarly view that the arrest approval powers at the pre-trial stages should be retained in the hands of the procuratorates was based primarily on their constitutional nature as organs of legal supervision. There exist divergent views on the nature of the power of the procuratorates – either it is argued that they only possess an executive or a judicial function, or a dual function that encompasses both executive and judicial powers, or it is suggested that these organs should have only a supervisory power.[200] Leaving aside the classification of the procuratorates' powers, their threefold function is clearly enshrined in Chinese legislation. The procuratorates are state organs responsible for criminal investigation, prosecution and supervision.[201]

[193] Xu Jingcun (n 29) 58.
[194] Li Zhongcheng (n 1) 186–187.
[195] Chen Weidong (n 7) 523.
[196] ICCPR, art 9(3); General comment No. 35, Article 9 (Liberty and security of person) (GC No. 35) 2014 (UN Doc CCPR/C/GC/35) paras 32 and 33.
[197] ibid para 34.
[198] *Kulomin v Hungary*, Communication No. 521/1992, UN doc GAOR A/51/40 (22 March 1996).
[199] Human Rights Council, 'Report of the Working Group on Arbitrary Detention, Mission to China' (2004) E/CN.4/2005/6/Add.4, para 3.
[200] Yu Mou, 'Overseeing Criminal Justice: The Supervisory Role of the Public Prosecution Service in China' (2017) 44 *Journal of Law and Society* 620, 626–62.
[201] Chen Guangzhong (n 44) 66–67.

In the light of these institutional arrangements, Fan Chongyi, for example, raised the question of whether the concept of judicial oversight over arrest could be applied in China; instead, he proposed to establish personal liberty safeguards 'with Chinese characteristics', meaning an arrestee should have the right to request a judicial review by a court at a hearing, during which they should also be entitled to have a lawyer present, but the initial decision to arrest should remain in the hands of the procuratorial organs; at the same time, this would more clearly distinguish between the two custodial measures and restrain the powers of the police and prosecuting agencies.[202]

The drafts of Xu Jingcun and Chen Guangzhong also both retained this power in the hands of the procuratorates, though advancing different ideas as to how the system of custodial measures could be improved. Xu proposed to change the measure of detention (*juliu*) into the measure of arrest, in the ICCPR sense of provisional arrest, which would have been followed by pre-trial custody (*jiya houshen*). As regards the targets of this measure, the draft largely reproduced the three broad categories of active criminals/major suspects, (quasi-) flagrant criminals, and suspects who may obstruct the investigation, as outlined in the CPL 1996,[203] only abolishing the category of suspects who conceal their identity because it could be easily abused. Except for the terminology, Xu did not substantially change the three conditions of the requirement of evidence, sentence, and necessity, as stipulated under the CPL 1996, for his pre-trial custody (*jiya houshen*).[204]

Regarding the controversially long period of detention before requesting arrest, amongst those scholars retaining the arrest approval powers at the pre-trial stages in the hands of the procuratorial organs, Fan Chongyi suggested deleting the possibility of a 30-day extension altogether;[205] Xu proposed to keep the maximum time limit of 37 days but limited the scope to major criminal suspects in cases involving crimes committed in different locations, alleged repeated offences and gang-related crimes, as in these cases the evidence collection would be more complex.[206]

Chen also suggested tightening the time limits for requesting a detainee's arrest, permitting an extension of up to 14 days only.[207] He proposed maintaining the existing system of coercive measures, but he supported changing the administrative nature of arrest examination by obliging the procuratorial organs to interrogate a suspect and hear the opinion of their legal representative or defender in the process of examination. During the interrogation, the prosecutors should moreover inform a suspect about the nature of the charges and the grounds for police detention, as required under Article 9 ICCPR, as well as their procedural

[202] Fan Chongyi (n 136) 324–326.
[203] CPL 1996, art 61.
[204] Xu Jingcun (n 29) 55–67 (arts 70 to 85).
[205] Fan Chongyi (n 136) 324.
[206] Xu Jingcun (n 29) 62 (art 78).
[207] Chen Guangzhong (n 6) 70 (art 124), 382.

rights, including the right to appoint and communicate with defence counsel, the right to make statements voluntarily, or the right to challenge the decision of detention.[208]

As regards the targets of detention, Chen proposed to narrow them down to suspects who cumulatively meet three conditions: there is evidence to prove that they are suspected of a crime, the suspect may receive no less than a fixed-term prison sentence, and if there is a real possibility that they will evade arrest, obstruct the investigation or continue to endanger society. The inclusion of the social danger requirement aimed to ban the use of these measures as preventive detention.[209] Even though the detention powers remained in the hands of the police, the draft adopted the requirement of notifying the detainee of the nature of the suspected crime and the grounds for detention in order to enable them to challenge the measure. Moreover, the police should inform the prosecuting organ within 48 hours upon detention, which should then review the appropriateness of the measure as part of its legal supervision powers and make a correction opinion, if necessary. In the absence of a comparable provision in the CPL 1996, as Chen explained, the prosecuting organs often would not be informed about the detention of a suspect and thus could not effectively exert their supervision powers.[210]

Regarding the conditions for arrest leading to custody pending trial, Chen Guangzhong proposed to tighten the evidentiary standards, requiring 'reliable evidence that supports a strong suspicion that a criminal suspect or defendant has committed a crime' to prevent arrest from being used as a substitute for the investigation process. Since the prison sentence requirement would apply to almost all criminal offences provided for under the criminal law, thus precluding case-by-case decisions, Chen suggested raising the standard to '[may be] sentenced to imprisonment of three years or more' and emphasising that it should only be applied when less intrusive measures such as bail or residential surveillance were insufficient to prevent a social danger; such a provision would be in line with international presumption of innocence standards.[211]

In contrast, Chen Zexian and Xiong Qiuhong intended to increase impartiality and ensure greater separation between the powers of detention and arrest and proposed to shift the power over arrest decisions to the courts. The arrest decision should be made in a hearing, meaning all parties (including the defence lawyer of the suspect or defendant) should appear before the court to present evidence and express their opinions. In their view, an obstacle was that such a shift would have meant amending Article 37 of the Constitution, which grants the procuratorial organs the power over arrest decisions. Drawing on Article 9 ICCPR, they suggested that a request for the arrest of a detainee (in the Chinese sense) should generally be filed within 48 hours after detention to a people's court, but that it

[208] ibid 3 (art 3), 68 (art 122), 70 (art 125), 383–384.
[209] ibid 62 (art 113), 371–372.
[210] ibid 66 (arts 117, 118), 376–377.
[211] ibid 68 (art 121), 379.

could be extended up to 72 hours 'under certain circumstances' or 96 hours in cases involving suspects who are allegedly roaming, committing multiple offences, or working in a criminal gang; this would have meant a cut from 30 days to 96 hours. They proposed to make the time limits of custody pending trial in the different phases of proceedings dependent on the nature of the case, ranging from a maximum of three months in ordinary cases and up to a year in more complex or serious cases such as death penalty cases. Under their draft, an extension was only allowed by filing a new request of arrest to the relevant court that should decide in a hearing.[212] The period of detention would have been shortened considerably through these time limits. Moreover, at least theoretically, deciding on arrest in a court hearing would have given the defence the opportunity to understand the reasons and thus possibly challenge such a decision later.

Amongst all scholarly drafts, Chen Weidong's proposals went even further, aiming at a radical approach. Chen introduced the measure of arrest (*jubu*) in the sense of provisional police custody (ie, arrest within the meaning of the ICCPR), which may be followed by pre-trial detention (*jiya*). While the draft provided that an arrest (*jubu*) should be decided by a procuratorate or a court, the decision over pre-trial detention should be made only by a court in a hearing at which the criminal suspect or defendant and their defender should be heard. The draft did not adopt the targets of police detention, as enshrined under the CPL 1996; instead, it required 'evidence to prove that the suspect is suspected of having committed a crime'; it stipulated mandatory questioning immediately upon arrest (*jubu*) and a maximum duration of 72 hours for this measure.[213] The draft aimed at a 48-hour time limit upon arrest (*jubu*) for the procuratorates to file an application for pre-trial detention (*jiya*) to the court, which should then, within 24 hours, hold a hearing on the matter.[214]

Drawing on international standards, Chen suggested that arrestees (*jubu*) and detainees (*jiya*) should both be entitled to a set of rights, including the privilege against self-incrimination and the right to be informed of the reasons and grounds for arrest (*jubu*) (and, in the case of detention (*jiya*), of the criminal charges), the right to apply for bail, the right to defence and lodge complaints, and the right to counsel.[215] Detainees should moreover have the right to counsel and defence, the right to request prompt notification of their family members or other persons of the place and reasons for detention, and, in principle, the right to be visited and communicate with family members and the outside world, the right to request a physical examination or an expert opinion, the right to be compensated for wrongful detention, and the right to humane treatment.[216] As for time limits of pre-trial detention (*jiya*), it set time limits for investigation and trial proceedings,

[212] Chen Zexian and Xiong Qiuhong (n 79) 86–96.
[213] Chen Weidong (n 11) 12 (arts 58, 60), 142–144.
[214] ibid 142–149 (arts 58, 65, 66).
[215] ibid 12 (art 61), 146.
[216] ibid 13 (art 71), 154–157.

rather than one independent time limit, albeit distinguishing them from the time limits of procedural stages (investigation, prosecution, and trial).[217]

These academic discourses show that, although there was a consensus that the checks and balances should be improved to protect the personal liberty of suspects and defendants, scholars were divided as to how far reforms should go and, indeed, most of the more radical scholarly suggestions were not adopted. In terms of feasibility, the more radical proposals were indeed unlikely to be met with enthusiasm. The police would have been neither supportive of such tight time limits nor of judicial oversight, and the prosecuting organ would have been deprived of their monopoly over arrest decisions. Undoubtedly, this would have given the courts more powers vis-à-vis the other two agencies. However, whether this alone would have brought a fundamental change is disputable. There is no practice of considering alternative measures from the perspective of protection of the personal liberty of suspects and defendants. The system is hostile to acquittals, and case breaking is the utmost aim of law enforcement, which means that any risk resulting from, for example, releasing a person on bail should be avoided. For law enforcement and judicial organs, even less intrusive measures, such as residential surveillance, are seen from an instrumentalist view and are only part of their toolbox to secure the smooth progress of case handling. The sections to follow examine the outcome of the CPL 2012 in terms of personal liberty protection.

## B. The Compromise: Stricter Conditions without Institutional Reforms

On paper and especially in comparison with the earlier versions of the law, it may seem that the CPL 2012 provided more incentives for the alternative compulsory measures of bail and residential surveillance to strengthen the protection of personal liberty. It moreover added that a criminal suspect or defendant in custody should be released if a case cannot be handled within the statutory time limits in the stages of criminal investigation, examination for prosecution, etc.[218] However, despite the scholarly proposals, the CPL 2012 did not fundamentally change the regime of compulsory measures.

The CPL 2012 retained the measure of residential surveillance. As suggested by scholars like Chen Guangzhong, the CPL 2012 for the first time distinguished more clearly the conditions for residential surveillance from those for bail, though it did not limit residential surveillance to suspects and defendants without fixed residence. There is some overlap between the conditions for both measures; bail should be applied especially in minor and non-social danger cases, whereas

[217] ibid 13–14 (art 72), 157–160.
[218] CPL 1996, art 74 (amended and renumbered as CPL 2012, art 96).

residential surveillance should be used against suspects and defendants who meet the conditions for arrest but should not be taken into custody due to health or personal conditions or where the conditions for bail are met but a person cannot provide a surety or pay the bond.[219] Therefore, bail was no longer a measure for accused persons who had met the conditions for arrest but was more clearly designed as an alternative and less-intrusive measure, at least in theory.

As regards residential surveillance at a designated location, it further enabled incommunicado detention. After the amended law was adopted, it faced harsh criticism for including potential incommunicado detention with restricted access to legal counsel.[220] Under the revised law, the three agencies are allowed to enforce residential surveillance at a designated location not only in cases of suspects without a fixed residence but also in cases involving national security, terrorism or corruption for up to six months.[221] In the law-making, an initial draft proposal was publicised in August 2011 for public consultation. The envisaged changes to the measure of residential surveillance triggered many controversies. Commentators especially voiced concerns as to the possibility of incommunicado confinement by allowing to waive notification, where such notification is impossible or may interfere with the investigation work or in cases involving endangering national security or terrorism – the newly added categories.[222] In the face of public outcry, the notification waiver was removed, but the CPL 2012 retained the exception 'unless such notification is impossible', which still leaves enough room for abuse.[223] Another point of concern remains the lack of clarity as regards the precise location of a designated location, as supplementary provisions to the revised law still vaguely exclude detention facilities or other police spaces and set certain conditions for such locations as regards living or security but do not establish a clear standard; this appears to grant law enforcement authorities a great degree of flexibility.[224]

None of the scholarly suggestions with respect to summonses and forced appearances were adopted. Conversely, the CPL 2012 expanded the time limits

[219] CPL 2012, art 72; Criminal Procedure Rules of the People's Procuratorate (Amended by the Supreme People's Procuratorate in the 80th Meeting of the 11th Procuratorate Committee on 16 October 2012, No. [2] 2012) art 488.

[220] 'Quanguo Renda Changweihui Fagongwei Jiu Xingshisusongfa Xiugai Da Jizhe Wen (The NPCSC Legislative Affairs Commission Answers Questions from Reporters Regarding the Revision of the Criminal Procedure Law)' (8 March 2012) www.npc.gov.cn/zgrdw/npc/zhibo/zzzb26/node_4249.htm accessed 27 August 2020.

[221] CPL 2012, arts 73 and 77.

[222] See art 30 of the 'Xingshi susong fa Xiuzheng'an (cao'an) tiaowen ji cao'an shuoming ((Draft) Amendments to the Criminal Procedure Law, with Commentary), 30 August 2011' www.npc.gov.cn/zgrdw/npc/xinwen/lfgz/2011-08/30/content_1668503.htm accessed 27 March 2020; Rosenzweig (n 179) 84–86.

[223] CPL 2012, art 73.

[224] Rosenzweig (n 179) 86–87; Criminal Procedure Rules of the People's Procuratorate (2012) art 110; Provisions on Handling of Criminal Cases by the Public Security Organs (Adopted on 13 December 2012, No. 127 [2012] of the Ministry of Public Security) art 108.

for interrogation by summons and forced appearances in 'complicated and 'major' cases in which detention (*juliu*) and arrest (*daibu*) are deemed necessary to 24 hours. Since the definition of what counts as 'complicated' or 'major' cases in this context will remain at the discretion of the police, such relaxed time limits open new room for rights violations. And even if the CPL 2012 added that there should be 'necessary' time for rest and that meals should be provided during interrogations by summons, what should be considered 'necessity' in such a context was not explained. A judicial interpretation by the Supreme People's Court of 2012 did also not further shed light on it.[225] In the absence of meaningful institutional reforms, there is still barely any external supervision, so that 'necessity' remains at the discretion of the investigation authorities. Guo Zhiyuan's research about the enforcement of the exclusionary rules has shown that there exist divergent views among law enforcement personnel and defence lawyers on the notion of 'necessity', especially in less obvious and extreme cases.[226]

Overall, the reforms focused on tightening the conditions for custodial coercive measures and establishing mechanisms to challenge deprivations of liberty, which will be discussed in the next section. Article 79 CPL 2012 specified the social danger condition as a requirement to justify an arrest. As shown in the previous chapters, as part of the examination, prosecutors have been required to assess the necessity of arrest. One aspect of the necessity of arrest is the assessment of whether the criminal suspect or defendant poses a social danger. However, until 2012, the law had not explained under which conditions the accused poses a 'social danger', thus necessitating custody pending trial. The notion of 'social danger' (*shehui weixianxing*) has in practice been replaced by or equated with the term 'social harmfulness' (*shehui weihaixing*), as used in Chinese criminal law to distinguish between crimes and non-crimes.[227] The equation of these two terms has led to immediate arrest when a crime has been committed and prevents a case-by-case arrest examination.[228]

The CPL 2012 modified this requirement, and a social danger is assumed to be the case if they could obstruct criminal proceedings or endanger public security or social order. In addition, a suspect or defendant should be arrested if there is a possibility that they will be sentenced to fixed-term imprisonment of ten years or more, or if they have previously committed an intentional crime, or if that person violates or is in breach of the provisions on bail or residential surveillance. With regard to such vague conditions as the suspect or defendant 'might commit a new crime' or they 'endanger the national security, public security, or social order', provisions by the Supreme People's Procuratorate and the Ministry of

[225] CPL 2012, art 117; SPC's Interpretation on the Application of the CPL 2012, art 115.

[226] Guo (n 87) 56–57.

[227] This term is used in art 13 of the Criminal Law to distinguish between crimes and non-crimes. Accordingly, any act that violates the objects of protection (security of the state, social and economic order, etc), is not minor and causes great harm is considered a crime in accordance with the law.

[228] Yang Yi (n 164) 138.

Public Security have clarified that the former requirement can be assumed under the following circumstances: if a suspect plots, organises or prepares to commit a new crime after or before the criminal offence has been committed; if they are a repeated, serial or a fugitive offender; within one year intentionally established illegal activities of the same type and received administrative sanctions; if they used acquisitions obtained by committing crimes as major source of living. A suspect may 'endanger the national security, public security, or social order' and thus pose a social danger if they plot, organise or prepare to commit a new crime that endangers national security, public or social order; if they have already received criminal or administrative punishment in the past for endangering national security, etc, and have plotted, organised, ordered or actively participated in criminal offences endangering national security, crimes related to organised crime, terrorist activities or drug-related crimes.[229] However, for the authorities, it remains difficult to determine the social danger requirement in practice, as they often lack evidence to prove that a suspect is posing such a danger, let alone actually realising it. Therefore, they still simply state that 'arrest is necessary' or that the suspect 'poses a social danger' without providing any further explanation or evidence or facts to support the 'necessity' of the arrest.[230]

The anticipated sentence is part of the examination of the social danger requirement (fixed-term imprisonment of ten years or more). Yet, the requirement of a 'possible prison sentence of ten years or a heavier punishment' is an anticipated punishment by the case-handling authorities. Furthermore, the CPL 2012 did not specify the requirement of 'imprisonment or a heavier punishment', which remains relevant to almost all criminal offences provided under the criminal law; this thus prevents a case-by-case decision. Consequently, the procuratorial organs have continued to focus on whether the suspect's behaviour constitutes a criminal offence and what offence has been committed under the criminal law.[231] Therefore, the expected punishment seems to remain the main factor in the arrest examination, but the approval of an arrest solely based on the expected criminal punishment runs counter to the main purpose of pre-trial detention (ie, enforcing the appearance of a defendant in court) and the principle of proportionality. The expected criminal punishment may be *one* factor in assessing the conditions of obstruction of the proceedings by flight or suppression of evidence, etc.

Furthermore, the CPL 2012 barely addressed the lack of transparency of the arrest examination procedure. Although it added a provision, interrogation of the suspect during the arrest examination remains optional in most instances and is mandatory only if the prosecutor has doubts as to whether the conditions are met,

[229] Criminal Procedure Rules of the People's Procuratorate (2012) art 139; Notice of the Supreme People's Procuratorate and the Ministry of Public Security on Issuing the Provisions on Several Issues Concerning the Condition of Social Danger of Arrest (for Trial Implementation) (9 October 2015, No. 9 [2015] of the Supreme People's Procuratorate, arts 5 to 7.

[230] Xie Xiaojian, 'Jiya biyaoxing shencha zhidu shixiao yanjiu (Study on the Effect of Custody Necessity Examination)' [2016] *The Jurist* 136, 140–141.

[231] Yang Yi (n 164) 133–135.

the suspect requests to make a statement before the prosecutor, or if the prosecutor suspects unlawful behaviour on the part of the police during investigation.[232] After the CPL 2012 was put into effect, provisions by the Supreme People's Court have stipulated that the prosecutors dealing with the case shall interrogate the suspect and listen to the opinion of their defence lawyer; the scope of such mandatory interrogations remained limited to complex cases, cases involving major suspects or minors, in addition to the mandatory instances under the Criminal Procedure Law.[233] The provisions reasserted that, when examining an arrest, the prosecuting organ must only hear the opinion of the defence lawyer (if the suspect has appointed a defender) upon their request.[234]

The unchanged administrative nature of the arrest examination relates to a major shortcoming of the reform; the CPL 2012 did not address the lack of equality of arms between prosecution and defence. As discussed in the previous section, scholars criticised the insufficient checks and balances among the three agencies. In terms of personal liberty safeguards, the reforms clearly focused on internal reshuffling rather than external empowerment. For example, the power of arrest approval within the procuratorial organs was shifted to the Investigation Supervision Department, which had emerged as a result of the merger of the Prosecution Department and the Arrest Approval Department (*busu heyi*),[235] to ensure greater separation between prosecution and arrest approval authorities.[236] This shift has been met with criticism, as this merger of powers within the procuratorates could not increase neutrality.[237]

Considering that a defence lawyer still cannot access case files in the investigation phase,[238] it remains difficult for the defence to determine on what evidence or other criteria, such as necessity, threat to society, danger of absconding, etc, the arrest decision was based and whether it is lawful. If a suspect or defendant does not have a defence lawyer or access to legal counsel, it is unlikely that they can understand the reasons for arrest. Moreover, the CPL 2012 did not address the issue of being informed of the reasons for detention or arrest. The CPL 1996 indeed contained insufficient provisions on that matter. In fact, the measure of detention was not substantially reformed in terms of conditions, targets or time limits.[239] Conversely, the CPL 2012 incorporated de facto incommunicado

[232] CPL 2012, art 86 (added).

[233] Criminal Procedure Rules of the People's Procuratorate (2012) arts 304 and 305.

[234] ibid art 309.

[235] In 1999, the arrest powers were shifted to the Arrest Examination Departments, see Criminal Procedure Rules of the People's Procuratorate (1999) art 91.

[236] ibid art 303.

[237] Min Chunlei, 'Lun shencha daibu chengxu de susonghua (On the Legal Proceduralization of the Arrest Procedure)' [2016] *Law and Social Development* 62, 64; Zhang Zetao, 'Goujian zhongguoshi de tingzheng shencha daibu chengxu (Constructing the Hearing Procedure of Examination of Criminal Arrest with Chinese Characteristics)' (2018) 36 *Tribune of Political Science and Law* 18, 19–20.

[238] CPL 2012, art 38.

[239] CPL 2012, arts 80, 154 to 158 (renumbered).

detention by waiving the requirement of notification of family members in cases involving national security or terrorism.[240]

In comparison, Article 9(2) ICCPR requires that the accused be informed about the reasons for provisional arrest (in the ICCPR sense, meaning detention in the Chinese sense) and the charges, meaning reasons for the deprivation of liberty, reasons that concern 'not only the general legal basis [...] but also enough factual specification to indicate the substance of the complaint'.[241] Chen Guangzhong had tried to explain that the requirement of being informed about the charges was difficult to be realised in the Chinese system, as formal charges are brought against the accused only after completion of the investigation, when the case is transferred to the procuratorate for prosecution examination.[242] However, it should be borne in mind that the notion of a 'criminal charge', as used in the ICCPR, must be autonomously defined. And the requirement of being informed about the reasons serves only the purpose of determining whether the deprivation of personal liberty is appropriate; it does not require detailed information on the charges that will later be needed to prepare for trial.[243]

As regards arrest, the prosecuting organs are still only required to explain the reasons for disapproval.[244] A suspect will still receive an 'arrest approval decision notification' (*pizhun daibu juedingshu*) in a fixed form in which it is stated only that person X is suspected of having committed a criminal offence and meets the conditions for arrest in accordance with the law. Furthermore, the police power to request a reconsideration in the event of disapproval was retained, whereas a suspect still cannot immediately protest such a decision.[245]

Pursuant to official figures, from the early 2000s onwards, the percentage of suspects and defendants being held under the measure of arrest has steadily decreased, falling from around 91 per cent in 2002 to around 84 per cent in 2007 and 74.5 per cent in 2011. After passage of the CPL 2012, the percentage fell still further, reaching 68.7 per cent in 2012 and 58.5 per cent in 2016; it increased again to around 62.4 per cent in 2018, but fell to 59.8 per cent in 2019.[246] Therefore, in the post-CPL 2012 period, the percentage has stabilised at around 60 per cent (+/- 2 per cent). However, the reliability of these official figures should be treated with caution, and there is a lack of other data to verify these official figures. Irrespective of the reliability of these statistics, the decline in numbers cannot be

[240] CPL 2012, art 83.

[241] GC No. 35 para 25.

[242] Chen Guangzhong (n 3) 139.

[243] GC No. 35 paras 29 and 30.

[244] CPL 2012, art 88; Criminal Procedure Rules of the People's Procuratorate (2012) art 336; Criminal Procedure Rules of the People's Procuratorate (Amended by the Supreme People's Procuratorate on 30 December 2019, No. 4 [2019]) art 301.

[245] CPL 2012, art 90; Zhang Zetao (n 237) 20–21.

[246] The figures are based on the annually published Law Yearbook of China (*Zhongguo falü nianjian*) 1987 to 2018; the 2019 and 2020 figures are based on the Supreme People's Procuratorate Work Report (*Zuigao renmin jianchayuan gongzuo baogao*) of 2020 and 2021, see 'Supreme People's Procuratorate Work Report' www.spp.gov.cn/spp/gzbg/index.shtml accessed 9 September 2023.

attributed to the CPL 2012 alone, as the trend began in 2002, when the arrest conditions in the CPL 1996 were still vague. Moreover, the statistics are not exhaustive, as they do not include other compulsory measures, such as police detention, residential surveillance at a designated location, or various forms of administrative detention or illegal forms of deprivation of personal liberty.[247] Therefore, it is difficult to assess whether the number of arrests has actually decreased or whether other custodial measures are being applied instead.

Moreover, according to official data, only 23.7 per cent of those convicted of a criminal offence were given a heavier punishment of *more* than a three-year imprisonment in 2012, while the percentage of those given less amounted to 76.3 per cent, amongst which the percentage of those given less than three-year imprisonment amounted to 33.7.[248] In 2016, the number of people being convicted of a criminal offence and given a heavier punishment than three years' imprisonment even decreased to 15.7 per cent, while the percentage of those given less than three years' imprisonment amounted to 38.3 per cent.[249] Considering that an average of 60 per cent of suspects and defendants held in custody under the measure of arrest indicates that individuals accused of relatively minor offences are still arrested. In the view of scholars, clearer and different standards of social danger for major and minor crimes in the arrest examination are still missing.[250] The next section demonstrates why mechanisms remain ineffective to defend personal liberty in the criminal process.

## C. What are the Chances of Being Set Free?

The *habeas corpus* guarantee, as enshrined in Article 9(4) ICCPR, has been a point of controversy amongst scholars in China. As shown in chapter three, the CPL 1979 did not provide a legal basis for effectively challenging deprivations of personal liberty in the criminal justice process. A suspect could only demand their release if the time limit of police detention had been exceeded.[251] The CPL 1996 introduced the right to apply for bail and added that procuratorial organs and public security organs should cancel or modify the compulsory measure taken against a suspect if they discovered that the measure was inappropriate.[252] However, a positive guarantee to personal liberty, eg, a habeas corpus guarantee, was lacking.

[247] Furthermore, procuratorates could apply 'conditional arrest' (*fu tiaojian daibu*) to criminal suspects even though Criminal Procedure Law arrest conditions were not met, this practice was officially abolished by the Supreme People's Procuratorate in 2017, see Li Xunhu, 'Daibu zhidu gaige de fa shiyi xue jiedu (Doctrinal Legal Interpretation of the Reform of the Arrest System)' [2018] *Chinese Journal of Law* 155, 157.

[248] These figures refer to final judgments.

[249] *2017 Zhongguo falü nianjian (2017 China Law Yearbook)* (Beijing, Law Press China, 2017) 1165.

[250] Yang Yi (n 164) 139.

[251] CPL 1979, art 48(2).

[252] CPL 1996, arts 52 and 73.

Certain scholars have argued that the introduction of the constitutional human rights protection principle in 2004 would imply both the premise of and demand for the formulation of a habeas corpus law.[253] However, as early as the late 1990s, scholars were calling for habeas corpus 'with Chinese characteristics',[254] arguing that the procuratorates' authority over arrest approval should be maintained but that the law should provide a judicial remedy, meaning a review by a court to challenge such a decision.[255] Scholars producing draft proposals partly supported such an approach, but the CPL 2012 did not adopt such a provision.[256]

There are three different recourse measures available under the CPL 2012. First, the right to apply for bail in Article 52 CPL 1996 was revised and renumbered as Article 95 CPL 2012, granting a suspect or defendant – or their legal representative, close family member or defender – the right to apply for the modification of a compulsory measure (without formulating any exceptions) at any stage of the criminal proceedings. This provision is therefore applicable to *all* compulsory measures regulated under the Criminal Procedure Law. In this case, the agent of review can be a court, procuratorate, or public security organ. Yet, the revised law did not provide for detailed provisions on how exactly the relevant organ ought to conduct the review.

Second, Article 94 CPL 2012, which was introduced in CPL 1996 as Article 73 and only renumbered, empowered the relevant case-handling organ to review the necessity of custody in accordance with their procedural competences.[257] In other words, those organs were granted the final decision-making power based on their procedural competences.[258] However, the CPL 2012 did not clarify the specific processes of the two recourse measures if an application for the review and modification of a compulsory measure is not successful.

Third, newly added Article 93 CPL 2012 stipulates that *after* a suspect or defendant has been arrested a procuratorate must examine the necessity of their

[253] Deng Zhihui, 'renshen baohuling yu renquan baozhang – yi xingshi susong wei zhu shijiao (Habeas corpus and Human Rights Guarantees in the Context of Criminal Proceedings)' [2004] *China Legal Science* 158, 166.

[254] Chen Guangzhong and Zhang Jianwei, 'Lianheguo gongmin quanli he zhengzhi quanli guoji gongyue yu woguo xingshi susong (The ICCPR and Chinese Criminal Proceedings)' [1998] *China Legal Science* 98, 105–106.

[255] Chen Weidong, 'Jiya biyaoxing shencha shidian yanjiu baogao (Study on the Pilot Study of Custody Necessity Examination)' [2018] *Chinese Journal of Law* 175, 191; Chen Weidong and others, 'Jiya biyaoxing shencha de lilun renshi yu shishi yingyong (Theoretical Recognition and Practical Application of Custody Necessity Examination)' [2012] *Journal of National Prosecutors College* 3, 3; Chen Guangzhong and Zhang Jianwei (n 254) 106.

[256] Chen Guangzhong (n 9) 74 (art 129), 387–388; Xu Jingcun (n 33) 66 (Art 85). Chen and Xiong, who had advocated shifting the arrest powers to the courts, installed a review by the next higher court, see Chen Zexian and Xiong Qiuhong (n 79) 96–99.

[257] See also Criminal Procedure Rules of the People's Procuratorate (Amended by the Supreme People's Procuratorate in the 80th Meeting of the 11th Procuratorate Committee on 16 October 2012, No. 2012(2)) 2012, art 322; Criminal Procedure Rules of the People's Procuratorate (Amended by the Supreme People's Procuratorate on 2019, No. 4 [2019]) now art 298.

[258] Liu Qing, 'Jiya biyaoxing shencha zhidu yanjiu (Study on the System of Custody Necessity Examination)' [2013] *People's Procuratorial Semimonthly* 23, 24.

continued custody (*jiya biyaoxing shencha*). The idea seems simple: If custody is no longer deemed necessary, then the prosecuting organ should recommend that person's release or modification of the compulsory measure. The examination of necessity hence involves re-examination of the necessity of custody *after* the arrest has been approved.[259] Accordingly, the procuratorates are now legally obligated to review the necessity of custody after an arrest has been approved. For simplicity, I will refer to this as a review of custody. The objectives of this new review mechanism are to reduce the number of people being held in custody pending trial and to resolve the earlier mentioned phenomena of 'widespread custody' (*pubian jiya*) and 'being in custody throughout proceedings' (*yi ya dao di*). The prosecuting organs have the sole authority to carry out this review but have only 'recommendation power' (*jianyiquan*). As will be shown in this section, this review largely centres on the three conditions for arrest, namely, evidence, sentence and necessity.[260] This section discusses the 2012 mechanism of review of custody and explains why it can only have limited impact in practice. It should be observed that the two other measures (Articles 94 and 95) fall outside the scope of it.

Regarding the opening of a review, the CPL 2012 remains very vague, but provisions issued by the Supreme People's Procuratorate stipulate that a review of custody may be opened both ex officio and upon application.[261] Moreover, in 2016, it issued two important provisions that further regulate the review of custody upon application.[262] It may be worth mentioning that many of these provisions were later reproduced in The Rule of Criminal Procedure of the Supreme People's Procuratorate (2019 amendment), but the procedure and content of the review remained largely unchanged.[263]

Since the procuratorial organs are the agents of the review of custody due to legal supervision powers, this mechanism does not incorporate a judicial review by a court.[264] As regards the distribution of powers within a procuratorate, the Supreme People's Court initially stipulated the competences depending on the stage of the proceedings, ie, at the investigation stage, the investigation supervision department (*jiancha jiandu bumen*) of a procuratorate; at the trial stage, the

[259] Chen Weidong (n 255) 175.

[260] Xie Xiaojian (n 230) 136; Wang Shumao, '"Jiya biyaoxing shencha" de lijie yu shiyong (Understanding and Application of "Custody Necessity Examination")' [2013] *Law Review* 120, 121.

[261] Criminal Procedure Rules of the People's Procuratorate (Amended by the Supreme People's Procuratorate in the 80th Meeting of the 11th Procuratorate Committee on 16 October 2012, No. 2012(2)) 2012, art 616; Criminal Procedure Rules of the People's Procuratorate (Amended by the Supreme People's Procuratorate on 2019, No. 4 [2019]) now arts 573 and 574.

[262] Notice of the Supreme People's Procuratorate on Issuing the Provisions on the Handling of Custody Necessity Examination Cases by the People's Procuratorates (for Trial Implementation) (issued on 22 January 2016) (Provisions on the Handling of Custody Necessity Examination (2016)); Guiding Opinions of the Supreme People's Procuratorate on Implementing and Enforcing the Provisions on the Handling of Custody Necessity Examination Cases (For Trial Implementation) (issued on 11 July 2016) (Custody Necessity Examination Implementation Opinions 2016).

[263] See Criminal Procedure Rules of the People's Procuratorate (2019) ch 13, s 5.

[264] See ICCPR, art 9(4).

prosecution department (*gongsu bumen*) is responsible for the review of custody, and it may overturn decisions made by the investigation supervision department.[265] To increase neutrality,[266] the power of review of custody was centralised in 2015, and a decision was made to reorganise the functions of the procuratorial departments. Following this decision, the criminal execution procuratorial departments (*xingshi zhixing jiancha bumen*) possessed the exclusive competence to carry out the review of custody.[267]

However, if a given procuratorate had not yet established such a department, this power could be transferred to other personnel in charge of criminal execution procuratorial work.[268] In practice, both the investigation supervision and prosecution departments frequently conducted the review.[269] In 2019, the review powers were again reorganised and moved to the relevant arrest and prosecution department (*busu bumen*), responsible for the review in all stages of the criminal procedure.[270] In the view of some scholars, this redistribution could not overcome the problem of conflicting interests.[271] This internal reshuffling of powers demonstrates the efforts to ensure an efficient system without strengthening external supervision.

As far as a review of custody upon application is concerned, the thresholds for triggering such a review are very high. In triggering a review, the applicant bears the burden of proving a change in the case facts or evidence, as the procuratorate already examined the lawfulness of custody during the arrest approval stage.[272] Because the conditions of arrest remain unchanged for the arrestee, the grounds for arrest are the starting point in applying for a custody review. As shown in the previous sections, however, a person is not informed sufficiently about the reasons for arrest. Another (related) obstacle during the review application process is that the police stress the principle of confidentiality, ie, that during

[265] Criminal Procedure Rules of the People's Procuratorate (Amended by the Supreme People's Procuratorate in the 80th Meeting of the 11th Procuratorate Committee on 16 October 2012, No. 2012(2)) 2012, arts 616(1) and 617.

[266] Li Xiang, 'Zuigaojian xiangguan fuzeren xiangjie biyaoxing shencha xingui (Relevant Person of the SPP Explains the New Rules on Custody Necessity Examination)' *Legal Daily* (2 February 2016) www.legaldaily.com.cn/News_Center/content/2016-02/02/content_6474274.htm?node=54869 accessed 2 December 2018.

[267] Notice of the Supreme People's Procuratorate on Issuing the Decision of the Supreme People's Procuratorate on Comprehensively Strengthening and Regulating the Procuratorial Work in Criminal Execution (issued on 4 December 2015, No. 15 [2015]) art 5(4) and (5); Provisions on the Handling of Custody Necessity Examination Cases (2016) art 8.

[268] Custody Necessity Examination Implementation Opinions (2016) art 3.

[269] Xie Xiaojian (n 230) 140.

[270] Criminal Procedure Rules of the People's Procuratorate (2019) art 575.

[271] Liu Yonghong, Liu Jun and Li Kejuan, 'Xin xingsu guize xia jiya biyaoxing shencha de jinlu (Short Version of the Custody Necessity Examination Under the New Criminal Procedure Rules)' [2020] *Legal System and Society* 93, 93.

[272] Criminal Procedure Rules of the People's Procuratorate (2012) art 618; Zhang Lin, 'buhou jiya biyaoxing shengcha zhi zhengming guize yanjiu – yi yi shenqing qidong xia de jiya biyaoxing shencha wei shijiao (Study on the Rules of Proof for Custody Necessity Examination of Post-Arrest Detention: From the Perspective of Custody Necessity Examination upon Application)' [2017] *Criminal Science* 99; Provisions on the Handling of Custody Necessity Examination Cases (2016) art 7.

the examination procedure evidence collected at the pre-trial stage should not be revealed. The principle of confidentiality is not explicitly provided for in law; it is simply understood to be reflected in the Criminal Procedure Law, which entitles only a defence lawyer to learn the charges against a criminal suspect and obtain relevant case information from the criminal investigation authority.[273] As already discussed, lawyers still have no access to case files in the investigation phase, and, in most cases, a hearing during the arrest examination is still optional in most cases, which has led to inconsistent practices. For example, some procuratorates conduct a hearing only in those cases where arrest has been disapproved or only in certain cases such as rape. Scholars have therefore suggested that a hearing should be mandatory when the investigation authorities, the procuratorate, the criminal suspect, and/or their defender disagree as to the accusations, necessity of arrest or lawfulness of the obtained evidence.[274]

Based on the previous discussions, one likely explanation for the insistence on confidentiality is the 'thin evidence' produced by investigation authorities to constitute grounds for arrest. Another is the pressure to close criminal investigations. In the circumstances of the non-disclosure of evidence, from the defence perspective, an application for review of custody may be based only on the social danger requirement. However, as shown in the previous section, this requirement remains insufficiently specified and is thus difficult to grasp. The ineffectiveness of the review of custody largely stems from the shortcomings of the initial examination. Furthermore, in the light of the insistence on the principle of confidentiality, the initial burden of proving a change in evidence or case facts is unreasonably high.

Another major shortcoming of the mechanism is that it does not automatically and promptly trigger a review. The habeas corpus guarantee requires that a person who has been arrested or detained have the lawfulness of their deprivation of liberty reviewed by a court, and that court should decide on it 'without delay'.[275] As discussed, in the Chinese context, suspects who are initially detained by the police are not brought before a judge, and there is effectively no mechanism to review such a decision.[276] After a suspect (or defendant)[277] has been arrested, the prosecutor who has been dispatched to the detention centre must inform the arrestee of their right to apply for a review of custody within five working days.[278] If an arrestee applies for review of custody, the relevant procuratorial department must conduct an initial examination and, within three working days, decide whether to open the case for examination.[279]

[273] CPL 2012, art 36 (CPL 2018, art 38).
[274] Zhang Zetao (n 237) 23–26; Min Chunlei (n 237) 65–66.
[275] ICCPR, art 9(4); GC No. 35 para 42.
[276] CPL 2012, art 89 (CPL 2018, art 91).
[277] At this point, it will be mostly criminal suspects.
[278] Custody Necessity Examination Implementation Opinions (2016) art 8.
[279] Provisions on the Handling of Custody Necessity Examination Cases (2016) art 9; Custody Necessity Examination Implementation Opinions (2016) art 13.

Such an application shall be accepted if the conditions for a release or modification recommendation are met[280] or if there has been a major change in the evidence for the case, meaning that there is insufficient evidence to prove the link between the criminal facts or acts and the suspect or defendant. This would also be the case if a change in the criminal facts or case circumstances may lead to a 'lighter' punishment such as criminal detention (*juyi*), control (*guanzhi*) and independent supplementary punishment (*duli shiyong fujiaxing*); or they may be exempted from criminal punishment or even acquitted. Finally, a determination that the period of custody pending trial has exceeded the possible prison sentence or that the conditions for bail or residential surveillance have been met should trigger a review of custody and a release or modification recommendation.[281]

After an initial examination, a review application will generally not be accepted if the arrestee is accused of a serious crime or if their release may seriously obstruct the proceedings, including cases of homicide, national security, terrorism, organised crime, or corruption. Besides, it will not be accepted if the procuratorial decision to approve the arrest or extend the period of custody has not yet exceeded a period of one month.[282] This ground for exclusion means that a suspect is not entitled to a review within the first four weeks of the procuratorial organ having approved their arrest. In terms of time limits, the review of custody must be completed within ten working days (or within 15 working days for complicated cases) of the opening of a case, which is very generous in comparison to the requirement of 'without delay' under Article 9(4) ICCPR.[283] The initial case-opening threshold is hence the greatest obstacle to triggering a review, as the preconditions for opening a review are equivalent to the mandatory release or modification conditions.

Because the scope of custody review is not restricted a priori, such examination is intended to be applicable to all types of cases. Furthermore, neither the CPL 2012 nor any other legislation stipulates when and how many times a suspect or defendant may apply for a review of custody.[284] Yet, a unified standard remains lacking, and local regulations provide for different scopes of application.[285] According to official statistics, from January to November 2016, procuratorial

[280] Custody Necessity Examination Implementation Opinions (2016) arts 26 and 27.

[281] Notice of the Supreme People's Procuratorate on Issuing the Provisions on the Handling of Custody Necessity Examination Cases by the People's Procuratorates (for Trial Implementation) (issued on 22 January 2016) (Provisions on the Handling of Custody Necessity Examination (2016)) art 17 (see also Criminal Procedure Rules of the People's Procuratorate (Amended by the Supreme People's Procuratorate on 2019, No. 4 [2019]) art 579); Guiding Opinions of the Supreme People's Procuratorate on Implementing and Enforcing the Provisions on the Handling of Custody Necessity Examination Cases (For Trial Implementation) (issued on 11 July 2016) (Custody Necessity Examination Implementation Opinions 2016) art 26.

[282] Custody Necessity Examination Implementation Opinions (2016) art 15.

[283] Provisions on the Handling of Custody Necessity Examination Cases (2016) art 20.

[284] Chen Weidong (n 255) 190–191.

[285] Guo Bing, 'Jiya biyaoxing shencha zhidu shijian yunxing shenshi (Examination on the Practical Operation of the Custody Necessity Examination System)' [2016] *Criminal Science* 61, 70.

departments nationwide recommended the modification of the arrest measure for and release of 38,606 criminal suspects and defendants on the basis of review of custody.[286] From January to December 2016, 842,327 people were arrested.[287] Considering that approximately 772,133 people were arrested between January and November 2016 and that modification or release was recommended upon a review of custody, these figures mean that it was conducted for roughly five per cent of arrested persons in custody.[288] A judicial remedy would certainly trigger an examination procedure, whereas an application for review of custody does not necessarily trigger a review. After the adoption of this mechanism, scholars have suggested installing a relief mechanism, meaning the right to file an application with a higher-level procuratorate to have that decision reviewed in the case of an application's rejection.[289]

As already mentioned, legislation also regulates an ex-officio review of custody. Yet, it lacks a unified standard concerning the intervals at which it should take place, as the ex-officio procedure is mainly governed by local regulations. Scholars believe that the prosecution examination stage is the most relevant for an ex officio review, followed by the investigation and trial stages. This makes sense because the relevant evidential materials have been gathered at that stage. For most minor criminal offences, summary proceedings, which are completed in a relatively short period of time, are applied, and the trial stage is therefore less relevant for the review of custody.[290] As we will see in chapter six, the introduction of the 2018 plea leniency system is likely to further marginalise the review of custody at the trial stage.

Moreover, when a suspended prison sentence is anticipated, most defence lawyers will file an application with the courts for the modification of a compulsory measure.[291] What appears highly problematic is that ex officio review of custody is carried out primarily at the prosecution examination stage. At this point, a suspect may already have spent more than seven months in custody.[292] However, owing to the absence of clarity in terms of timing of ex officio review of custody, scholars have suggested that a review should be opened if, eg, any extensions of time limits for the handling of cases or for custody are requested in accordance with Criminal

[286] Xue Tao, 'Zhongguo zuigaojian: tuidong jiya biyaoxing shencha anjian shuliang zhiliang wen zhong you sheng (China's Supreme Procuratorate: Promote a Rise in Number and Quality of Custody Necessity Examination Cases)' *Xinhua Net* (14 February 2017) www.xinhuanet.com/legal/2017-02/14/c_129479212.htm accessed 6 November 2020.

[287] See *2016 Zhongguo falü nianjian (2016 China Law Yearbook)* (Beijing, Law Press China, 2016) 1163. Those numbers partly deviate from numbers provided in other official documents, such as the work reports of the Supreme People's Procuratorate.

[288] Information is lacking on whether a CNE was conducted upon application or carried out ex officio in these cases, as well as on how many applications were rejected.

[289] Wang Shumao (n 260) 123.

[290] CPL 2012, art 214 (now CPL 2018, art 220).

[291] Wang Shumao (n 260) 122; Zhang Yunpeng, 'Buhou jiya biyaoxing shancha zhidu de wanshan lujing (Ways to Improve the System of Custody Necessity after Arrest)' [2015] *Law Science* 151, 153–155.

[292] CPL 2018, arts 156 to 159.

Procedure Law provisions or a fixed time interval for review should be established, for example, every two months regardless of the stage of proceedings.[293] In the view of other scholars, ex officio reviews of custody would be dispensable in major and complex cases such as murder.[294] Admittedly, with more than 850,000 and perhaps as many as one million people being arrested every year,[295] carrying out reviews in every single case seems infeasible, if not impossible.[296] Therefore, neither a review ex officio nor upon application can ensure a review of custody, meaning arrest, in a prompt manner. More fundamentally, as a review of custody is not triggered in every case, its application is rather arbitrary.

The question that needs to be answered is whether the review of custody determines lawfulness and orders the release of an arrestee.[297] Regardless of whether the review was launched upon application or conducted ex officio, the examination content is the same. Many scholars agree that the review of custody deals only with the issue of the *reasonableness* of *continuing* custody.[298] As the review focuses on the necessity of custody, it should follow the principle of proportionality. Scholars have suggested that the principle of proportionality should centre on the issues of the purpose and objective of custody, as well as its necessity (consideration of alternative measures) and reasonableness (scope, limits and periods in relation to the sentence that could be imposed).[299] Therefore, as with the arrest examination, evidential materials and grounds are required to prove the necessity of custody.[300]

To determine the necessity of ongoing custody, the procuratorial organ should consider various factors, including the charges, nature and circumstances of the crime; the state and progress of case handling and the evidence in the case; the overall behaviour or attitude of the suspect or defendant; the overall physical condition and social factors, such as a fixed residence or stable job; the possible sentence; and whether the period of custody has exceeded the statutory limits, among others.[301] In addition, the procuratorial organ may, for example, examine the evidential materials, verify the health condition of the suspect or defendant, and hear the opinions of all parties involved.[302] However, use of the word 'may' in this provision indicates that it is rather optional.

In the course of examination, a suspect or defendant may collect 'bonus points' if they meet certain requirements, which largely correspond to those that are needed to trigger a review in the first case, such as a major change in evidence or

[293] Liu Qing (n 258) 27.
[294] Chen Weidong and others (n 255) 5.
[295] These figures are based on the annually published *Law Yearbook of China* (*Zhongguo falü nianjian*) (1986–2019).
[296] Chen Weidong (n 255) 180–181.
[297] ICCPR, art 9(4).
[298] Liu Qing (n 258) 27–28; Xie Xiaojian (n 230) 140.
[299] Liu Qing (n 258) 27.
[300] Wang Shumao (n 260) 124.
[301] Custody Necessity Examination Implementation Opinions (2016) art 20.
[302] Provisions on the Handling of Custody Necessity Examination Cases (2016) art 13; Custody Necessity Examination Implementation Opinions (2016) art 19.

case fact;[303] but such points may also be collected in cases of negligence, excessive self-defence, or minor crimes punishable by less than one year of imprisonment or other mitigating circumstances that may speak against continuing custody;[304] such points may moreover be collected if they are a minor, have a fixed residence or work, meet the conditions for residential surveillance, among others.[305] However, 'demerits' may also be collected, notably if they do not plead guilty or displays 'unstable' confessions or if the case-handling authorities protest it, among others.[306]

When changes in the evidence or case facts or other factors occur, the relevant department *must* make a recommendation to the case-handling organ to release the suspect or defendant or modify the compulsory measure. In other instances (notably negligent crimes, or self-defence or those concerning minor offenders or pregnant women), the procuratorial organ enjoys discretion on that matter.[307] The content of the examination thus correlates with the aforementioned mandatory case-opening preconditions.[308]

It may be worth noting that, in principle, as part of the review process, it is possible to conduct a 'public examination' (*gongkai shencha*) of the necessity of custody in the detention centre in which the suspect or defendant is being held, the location of the case-handling procuratorial organ, or a location fixed by the procuratorate.[309] Such a public examination is meant to enable a suspect or defendant, or their legal representative, close relative or defender, to explain the reasons for their application for release or modification of the compulsory measure.[310] However, to protect the principle of presumption of innocence, such an examination should be transparent (rather than 'public') and give an arrestee, as well as their lawyer, the opportunity to understand the evidence supporting the charges against him or her and the reasons for his or her arrest.

According to available data, the review mechanism has to date exerted only limited impact in practice. Because the review of custody is recognised by nature

[303] Custody Necessity Examination Implementation Opinions (2016) art 26; Criminal Procedure Rules of the People's Procuratorate (2012) art 619.

[304] Custody Necessity Examination Implementation Opinions (2016) art 27.

[305] ibid art 23.

[306] ibid art 24(1) to (6) and art 25.

[307] ibid arts 16, 26 and 27; see also Criminal Procedure Rules of the People's Procuratorate (2019) arts 579 and 580.

[308] Provisions on the Handling of Custody Necessity Examination Cases (2016) art 18(1) Nos. 1 to 12; Custody Necessity Examination Implementation Opinions (2016) art 27.

[309] Notice of the Supreme People's Procuratorate on Issuing the Provisions on the Handling of Custody Necessity Examination Cases by the People's Procuratorates (for Trial Implementation) (issued on 22 January 2016) (Provisions on the Handling of Custody Necessity Examination (2016)) art 14; Guiding Opinions of the Supreme People's Procuratorate on Implementing and Enforcing the Provisions on the Handling of Custody Necessity Examination Cases (For Trial Implementation) (issued on 11 July 2016) (Custody Necessity Examination Implementation Opinions 2016) arts 29 to 34; see also Criminal Procedure Rules of the People's Procuratorate (Amended by the Supreme People's Procuratorate on 2019, No. 4 [2019]) art 617; Chen Weidong, 'Jiya Biyaoxing Shencha Shidian Yanjiu Baogao (Study on the Pilot Study of Custody Necessity Examination)' [2018] *Chinese Journal of Law* 175, 193.

[310] Custody Necessity Examination Implementation Opinions (2016) art 32.

to belong to the legal supervision power of the procuratorates, these organs have only a recommendation power, as the innate character of legal supervision is 'recommend' (*jianyi*) not 'order'.[311] The relevant case-handling organs are therefore not obligated to follow the procuratorates' recommendations, and research on the ground has shown that they are indeed reluctant to do so, not even reaching 20 per cent in some localities.[312] Such research has moreover shown that the prosecuting organs display a very cautious attitude towards their legal supervision power due to a fear of a loss of reputation vis-à-vis the case-handling authorities. However, even if the procuratorate exercises its supervision powers, the law provides no sanctioning mechanism if the case-handling organ (usually the police) refuses to follow the correction opinion or recommendation. In fact, the 'recommendation power' of legal supervision has been identified as the main obstacle to the implementation of efficient custody review. In the view of Chen Weidong, the power to approve an arrest would by nature be a decision-making power. The power of custody review should thus also be recognised as a judicial power, granting immediate decision-making power.[313] Indeed, according to The Rule of Criminal Procedure of the Supreme People's Procuratorate (2019 amendment), the procuratorates seem now to have immediate decision-making powers in the stage of examination for prosecution, which appears most relevant for the review of custody, while it retains the recommendation powers at the investigation and trial stages.[314]

As with the procuratorial power to decide arrest, it remains open to question whether the procuratorates are the eligible agent for reviewing the necessity of custody. However, scholars are sceptical whether the transfer of this power to the courts would lead to a lower custody rate, as many courts prefer smooth proceedings and thus prefer a defendant to be in custody when cases are transferred to them.[315] In other words, they are likely to approve an arrest even if a procuratorate had previously rejected it.[316]

Overall, the review of the custody mechanism places a high burden on the arrestee to show that ongoing custody is not necessary, and there is no guarantee that an application will be accepted. A major weakness, moreover, is that it only reviews the reasonableness, or proportionality, of ongoing custody. It is essentially a form of internal procuratorial review, as it does not allow for the active participation of the suspect or defendant, let alone a defence lawyer, and hence does not constitute an effective limitation of compulsory state measures against individuals.

[311] Liu Qing (n 258) 24.
[312] Han Xu and Tao Tao, '(Problems Facing the Custody Necessity Review and Ways to Solve them)' (*Procuratorate Daily*, 16 April 2021) www.spp.gov.cn/spp/llyj/202104/t20210416_515857 accessed 20 November 2022.
[313] Chen Weidong (n 255) 191–193.
[314] Criminal Procedure Rules of the People's Procuratorate (2019) art 575.
[315] Chen Weidong and others (n 255) 4.
[316] Min Chunlei (n 237) 64.

# VI. Conclusions

Overall, the 2012 CPL was the result of a lengthy bargaining process that could barely satisfy the expectations of reform-minded scholars. Although a refinement of the law was already underway since 2003, disagreements and power struggles amongst the stakeholders brought the lawmaking to a halt. And even if the legislator did not formally assign scholars with the making of a refined law, scholars in China produced an extensive corpus of literature during the almost ten years and even compiled complete draft proposals. Well into the reform era, scholars had fully grasped the rationale of presumption of innocence, and conflicts were inevitable, and so it may not be surprising that the tensions between the official doctrine of national conditions and broader human rights claims steadily grew. In a way, the continued insistence on national conditions and thus the pressure to move within the cage of this rhetoric meant that scholars – perhaps out of conviction, perhaps because it was the only way to find a compromise among all stakeholders – dismantled the presumption of innocence into different elements, reflecting the expansion of a presumption of innocence 'with Chinese characteristics'. While this is possible because it is realised through a set of safeguards, without key safeguards like an effective right to silence and true equality of arms, the presumption of innocence is rendered meaningless. Especially individual safeguards like the right to silence or the habeas corpus guarantee that would have empowered accused persons in criminal proceedings could be suppressed by invoking the rhetoric of national conditions. Due to growing concerns of national security, such calls were supported by the Party Central. The 2012 CPL reform marked the beginning of a shift towards more illiberalism, or a further autocratisation of the autocratic system. While the period between the early 1990s and until around 2011 can be described as relatively liberal, from the late 2000s on, the human rights situation in China has significantly deteriorated. In February 2011, the party-state launched a crackdown on Chinese rights-defending (*weiquan*) lawyers and activists. After Xi Jinping took the helm in early 2013, the crackdown on human rights activists and civil society, more widely, continued and culminated in the '709 crackdown' on 9 July 2015.[317] These developments have also impacted academia more widely. In academic discourses, a decline of international human rights as a benchmark for criminal justice reforms was observable. Xi's human rights vision has become the most important point of reference for the legal framework. This also had implications for criminal justice.

[317] See, eg, Eva Pils, 'The Party's Turn to Public Repression: An Analysis of the "709" Crackdown on Human Rights Lawyers in China' (2018) 3 *China Law and Society Review* 1.

# 6

# Marginalisation of Presumption of Innocence in the New Era

As shown in chapter five, the CPL 2012 marked a crucial turning point. Criminal justice was at a crossroads, and it set the path of a more illiberal criminal justice system. On the discursive level, academic discourses peaked in the mid- to late 2000s. Indeed, after the CPL 2012 was put into effect, domestic research has not added much to the previous scholarship, and research on China's compliance with international human rights norms, especially the ICCPR, has decreased. There was no new round of presumption of innocence discourse, and in the law-making process, calls for the introduction of presumption of innocence standards were nearly absent. As for the reasons, it should be observed that the making of the CPL 2018 only took a few months. In contrast, the revision work of the CPL 2012 almost took ten years, during which a massive corpus of literature was published. Moreover, it is important to understand domestic developments that had taken place after 2012, especially the Party's elevated role as lawmaker and highest moral authority, as part of the agenda of law-based governance. Even if the official discourse frames the latest reform as progress due to further legalisation or standardisation of proceedings, the changes indicate a further return to crime control and illiberalism, which is further supported by the decline of academic discourses on liberal values such as presumption of innocence. Indeed, the CPL 2018 poses new challenges to any future acceptance of the presumption of innocence in China.

This concluding chapter focuses on two new mechanisms that serve as a case in point, ie, the anti-corruption mechanism and the plea leniency system. While the party-state pursues an efficient and cheap mechanism to dispose of minor cases through pleading leniency, it invests in the handling of types of cases perceived as a greater risk to stability and leadership. Both mechanisms, however, share the commonality of sacrificing due process for efficiency and crime control. I argue that the presumption of innocence has no future in the Chinese criminal justice system. Even if optimistically supporting the view that Chinese legislation, especially the CPL 2012, had shown some signs of a fragile presumption of innocence, the CPL 2018 seems to be the last nail in the coffin for it. To explain this, the first part of this chapter revisits the party-state's understanding of legal governance and explains how modified elements, such as reinforced Party leadership and individual discipline and obedience, have meant a further pushback for lobbying for values associated with liberalism is also more challenging.

# I. An Autocratic Value Claim and Implications for Criminal Justice

As the previous discussions have shown, in the reform era, legal scholars could negotiate, at least to some extent, for better rights protection, as the party-state had given the green light to elaborate on the notion of human rights in China and therefore tolerated more pluralistic views, while the official narrative has always framed socialism as the institutional guarantee of human rights and the Party as the vanguard through which they are realised. In other words, without socialism and the Party, there can be no human rights; the Party had stepped back, to some degree, in the reform era. However, as chapter five has already indicated, the room for advocacy of liberal values has considerably shrunk in the era of Xi Jinping. This is important because the domestic developments, especially the systemic closure and re-ideologisation, have impacted the underlying values of criminal justice. Under Xi, the Party has become the highest and sole moral authority, as crucially cemented in the issuance of the 'Socialist Core Values' (*shehuizhuyi hexin jiazhi guan*). These ideological modifications have closed a critical vacuum for advocacy of liberal values and facilitated a shift towards crime control, as envisaged by the Party to secure its leadership role. To explain this, it is necessary to look at the changing triangle relationship between the Party, the people and the law.

Evidently, the party-state's conception of a 'socialist rule of law with Chinese characteristics' is no liberal rule-of-law conception.[1] The party-state's limited commitment to international human rights has become more tangible in the era of Xi Jinping, though such tendencies were already evident earlier. In the late 1990s, observers criticised that legal reforms were never supposed to affect the Party's monopoly on power. On the contrary, the law was merely a tool for securing that monopoly.[2] Between the 16th CCP National Congress in 2002, at which Jiang emphasised that the integration of leadership of the Party and the people being the 'masters of their own affairs' with law-based governance was key to realising socialist democracy,[3] and the Fourth Plenum in 2014, the latter has not only been about accommodating the principle of Party leadership but also about a

[1] Eva Pils, 'Rule-of-Law Reform and the Rise of Rule by Fear in China' in Weitseng Chen and Hualing Fu (eds), *Authoritarian Legality in Asia: Formation, Development and Transition* (Cambridge, Cambridge University Press, 2020); Xiaodong Ding, 'Law According to the Chinese Communist Party: Constitutionalism and Socialist Rule of Law' (2017) 43 *Modern China* 322; Donald C Clarke, 'China's Legal System and the Fourth Plenum' [2015] *Asia Policy* 10.

[2] Pitman B Potter, 'The Chinese Legal System: Continuing Commitment to the Primacy of State Power' (1999) 159 *China Quarterly* 673.

[3] Ewan Smith, 'The Conception of Legality under Xi Jinping' in Rogier Creemers and Susan Trevaskes (eds), *Law and the Party in China: Ideology and Organisation* (Cambridge, Cambridge University Press, 2020) 104–105; Jiang Zemin, 'Quanmian jianshe xiaokang shehui, kaichuang zhongguo tese shehui zhuyi shiye xin jumian (Build a Well-off Society in an All-Round Way and Create a New Situation in Building Socialism with Chinese Characteristics), Report delivered to the 16th CCP National Congress on 8 November 2002' (2002) s 5 www.moe.gov.cn/jyb_sjzl/moe_364/moe_258/moe_44/tnull_5009.html accessed 20 March 2017.

shift towards regulating and disciplining individuals and thus less about how the power of the Party can be regulated and corrected through institutions, norms, and procedures.[4]

The Fourth Plenum of the 18th Central Committee of the CCP in October 2014 was first specifically devoted to the theme of 'law-based governance' and adopted the Decision on Several Major Issues Concerning the Comprehensive Promotion of Law Based Governance of 2014 ('2014 Fourth Plenum Decision'). The 2014 Fourth Plenum Decision unambiguously elevated the leadership role of the CCP, saying it was 'the most essential feature of socialism with Chinese characteristics',[5] as enshrined in the Constitution in 2018,[6] and it equates Party leadership with the socialist rule of law. The leadership of the Party is understood to guarantee the socialist rule of law. Following the official discourse, 'law-based governance' is a core element, and 'Party leadership' is a basic guarantee of the 'socialist rule of law'. This conceptualisation has been understood to create tensions between the two supremacies: supremacy of the Party versus supremacy of the law. However, as already mentioned, the Party had never fully endorsed the supremacy of the Constitution and the laws,[7] though it emphasised the increased reliance on law. In the view of the Party, there is no conflict between the two supremacies, and this raises the question, especially in the light of a reinforced disciplinary character of law, to what end the Party relies on law.

The party-state frames 'Party leadership', 'the people', and 'law-based governance' as a unity.[8] 'Law-based governance' is thus not an overarching principle but is equally ranked with Party leadership and the people. This crucially ties the Party to the state and the society. In other words, the Party basically becomes the agent through which the socialist rule of law is realised – as reiterated by Xi Jinping at the 20th Party Congress in 2022. Through this theoretical construct, the Party aims to create the reality that the socialist rule of law state cannot be realised without its leadership. A tautological claim indeed. However, at the same time, the supremacy of the law under the leadership of the Party is emphasised. In other words, the Party must follow the laws it created.[9] This creates an important bridge between the Party and the people and aims to legitimise the CCP.

[4] Smith (n 3) 98, 106–108.

[5] 'Decision of the Central Committee of the CCP on Several Major Issues Concerning the Comprehensive Promotion of Law Based Governance, Adopted at the Fourth Plenum of the 18th Central Committee on 23 October 2014' s 2 www.china.org.cn/chinese/2014-01/17/content_31226494_9.htm accessed 3 April 2020.

[6] See art 1(2) of the Constitution 1982 (2018 Amendment).

[7] Ding (n 1) 329.

[8] Li Yang, 'Fazhi: xiandai shehui zhili de jiben fangshi (Rule of Law: The Fundamental Means for the Contemporary Social Governance)' (*CCP News*, 6 May 2014) theory.people.com.cn/n/2014/0506/c384764-24981699.html accessed 10 October 2019.

[9] Xi Jinping, 'Gaoju zhongguo tese shehuizhuyi weida qizhi wei quanmian jianshe shehuizhuyi xiandaihua guojia er tuanjie fendou (Hold High the Great Banner of Socialism with Chinese Characteristics and Strive in Unity to Build a Modern Socialist Country in All Respects), Report to the 19th CCP National Congress on 16 October 2022)' (2022) ss 1 and 7 www.gov.cn/xinwen/2022-10/25/content_5721685.htm accessed 29 November 2023.

However, this raises the question of how this conception pairs with the reemphasis on individual discipline. In a sense, law-based governance suggests limits on the powers of individuals, including Party/state officials, but it does not limit the *power* of the party-state in terms of law-making. In the light of the reinforced emphasis on regulation and disciplining of individuals, Ding Xiaodong has elaborated on the CCP's understanding of law under the socialist rule of law, in contrast to liberal rule of law concepts. Ding believes that the Party does expect law to restrain the exercise of power and individuals to abide by law, as emphasised by the Fourth Plenum Decision 2014, but it would put more emphasis on the role of the people than on socialist rule of law. In the eyes of the Party, the socialist rule of law is an undertaking for the people, but it also relies on the people. This connects to the earlier mentioned equal ranking of law-based governance and the people mastering their own affairs. In the eyes of the Party, the sovereign people create, defend and guard the law. Because socialist law reflects the will of the people, it is a means through which the people exercise self-governance and self-discipline. In other words, the people exercise self-governance through socialist rule of law. The party, the vanguard and representative of the people, guides lawmaking, guarantees law enforcement, and so forth. Consequently, socialist law cannot exist as an independent system of positive norms detached from the people; it is the people's commitment to law that makes it meaningful and a reflection of the people's will. Since positive law does not exist independent from the people, it is not a standard to be observed independent from the individual's will. Law sets a behavioural standard that must be observed.[10] As also shown in chapter one, this disciplinary understanding of law, of course, has been a consistent attitude of the Party, as notably reflected in the Party's equation of state laws and party regulations, which both belong to the corpus of socialist law or discipline. A prominent example is the previous intra-party mechanism (*shuanggui*), which will be discussed in section II and which granted coercive powers to party organs to detain and investigate Party members outside the regular legal process. As already discussed, for the Party there is no conflict between leading and representing the people. To achieve self-governance, the CCP, in the role of leading the people, ought to decide and create a sense of collective will or consensus. Ding believes that the legitimacy of the Party depends on its ability to create consensus among the people. The party takes political action to lead the people through the socialist rule of law, amongst which the imposition of stricter laws on itself is one political activity; the socialist rule project is also the Party's efforts to self-discipline. Self-discipline thus becomes a political undertaking and is essential to creating the people's will.[11]

Taking the vanguard role, it may not be surprising that CCP members are expected to observe higher behavioural standards. What Ding calls the 'disciplinary' function of law is consistent with the socialist educational function of law. This explains why law is always political, and this illustrates why the Party

[10] Ding (n 1) 324.
[11] ibid.

construes it as being dependent on the leadership of the CCP. Here Ding touches upon some classical socialist attitudes towards law, as outlined in chapter one. If the people are the 'defenders and guardians' and exercise self-governance, they partake in the process of building a socialist rule of law state. This connects to the traditional emphasis on social mobilisation. Viewed from this perspective, the Party would engage the people in the process of building a socialist rule of law state but also holds them accountable in case of disobedience. An unresolved issue, of course, would be the precise determination of the 'will of the people', as 'the people' remains a rather fictitious conception, which appears particularly problematic in the absence of independent courts as a forum for contestation and consensus finding. The Party has reasserted classical socialist attitudes towards law, including the instrumentalist view and educational function of law. In contrast to the idealisation of individuals' observance of rules from inner conviction in Communist societies, the Party understands self-discipline to be achieved through laws, meaning externally through coercion rather than internally, even if Ding suggests that the Party understands self-regulation as a form of self-cultivation.[12] The question is how to deal with disobedient individuals such as alleged criminals, arguably the most extreme form of disobedience. In other words, the question is how the reinforced disciplinary or educational function of law in light of the Party's leadership role has affected the underlying values of criminal justice. To understand this, it is necessary to explain how the principle of Party leadership connects to the nature of law.

As the previous discussions have shown, in the reform era, the party-state remained imprecise as regards the meaning of human rights in the Chinese context, albeit the evident ideological constraints, and it had not monopolised the value discourse. In the early reform era, the leaders under Deng explicitly invited scholars to advance ideas as regards an especially 'Chinese' human rights view. This clearly opened room for more pluralistic discourses, and the party-state tolerated constructive criticism, to some degree. However, the Party seemed to have perceived such discourses increasingly as a threat, as it decided to close this vacuum by monopolising the discourse over morality. In this context, the combination of law-based governance and 'governing the country by moral virtue' (*yide zhiguo*, or virtue-based governance) and thus the combination of legal and moral norms has become a 'distinctive feature' of the socialist rule of law.[13]

Even if the relationship between law and morality has deep roots in Chinese legal culture and is not new, the current leadership brings it to a new level.[14] It has reached new heights under Xi, becoming an integral part of law-based

[12] ibid 335.

[13] 'Fazhi shehui jianshe shishi gangyao (2020–2025 nian) (Outline for the implementation of the Construction of a Rule of Law-based Society, 2020–2025), issued by Central Committee of the CCP on 7 December 2020' www.gov.cn/zhengce/2020-12/07/content_5567791.htm accessed 17 December 2021.

[14] Delia Lin and Susan Trevaskes, 'Creating a Virtuous Leviathan: The Party, Law, and Socialist Core Values' (2019) 6 *Asian Journal of Law and Society* 41, 42–43.

governance rather than running in parallel. Morality, therefore, becomes a centrally important means of governance.[15] As a concrete manifestation of virtue-based governance, the current leadership has pushed for a prescribed set of moral norms in the form of the Socialist Core Values since 2012.[16] These authoritative values make a claim of correctness and are understood – in the view of the Party – to be the only benchmark against which values may be measured. Considering the context, it may not come as a surprise that these values, instead of 'western values', are supposed to be a perfect fit and, hence, an apt alternative for the Chinese system.[17] The Central Committee's so-called 'Document No. 9' (2013) already explicitly emphasised the distinguishing characteristics and aims of 'capitalist states', thus making clear the rejection of central elements of a rule of law state such as judicial independence. Advocating such a model is seen as an attack on the Party's leadership and the socialist system.[18] Indeed, 'legal governance' (*fazhi*) itself is a designated Socialist Core Value at the societal level because, in official parlance, it is a value society strives for and it represents the particular type of governance through which such other values as freedom, equality, and justice are realised but can be exercised, of course, only within the constraints of the legal system.[19]

Such values have been understood to further 'enrich' the 'Chinese' human rights view.[20] In 2023, Xi Jinping emphasised that Socialist Core Values such as democracy, equality, justice and freedom are also at the core of human rights. Xi stresses the orthodox view of the societal notion of freedom, which presumes that genuine individual freedom can be realised only in the Communist society,

[15] Delia Lin and Susan Trevaskes, 'Law-Morality Ideology in the Xi Jinping Era', *Law and the Party in China: Ideology and Organisation* (Cambridge, Cambridge University Press, 2020) 132–133.

[16] The 12 Socialist Core Values are: prosperity (*fuqiang*), democracy (*minzhu*), civility (*wenming*), and harmony (*hexie*) at the national level; freedom (*ziyou*), equality (*pingdeng*), justice (*gongzheng*), 'rule of law' (*fazhi*) at the societal level; patriotism (*ai'guo*), dedication (*jingye*), integrity (*chengxin*), and friendship (*youshan*) at the individual level, see Hu Jintao, 'Jianding bugou yanzhe zhongguo tese shehuizhuyi daolu qianjin wei quanmian jiancheng xiaokangshehui er fendou (Firmly March on the Path of Socialism with Chinese characteristics and Strive to Complete the Building of a Moderately Prosperous Society in all Respects), Report to the 18th National Congress of the CCP on 8 November 2012' s 6, para 1 www.npc.gov.cn/zgrdw/npc/zggcddsbcqgdbdh/2012-11/09/content_1742519.htm accessed 8 May 2018.

[17] Xu Yao, 'Xuexi wenda 68: weishenme yao qizhi xianming fandui xifang suowei de "pushi jiazhi"? (Study Q&A 68. Why should we take a clear-cut stand on the so-called Western "universal values"?)' (*People's Daily*, 2 September 2021) www.12371.cn/2021/09/02/ARTI1630538734440951.shtml accessed 9 August 2022.

[18] 'Communiqué on the Current State of the Ideological Sphere, A Notice from the Central Committee of the Communist Party of China's General Office' www.chinafile.com/document9-chinafile-translation accessed 12 December 2023; Smith (n 3) 99.

[19] Yang Zhibo and Zhang Xiaodan, 'Xinshidai wenming shijian shehuizhuyi hexin jiazhi guan manhua tujie kan wan xiang wangji dou nan (Civilized Practice in the New Era|Comic illustration of Socialist Core Values, it is hard to forget after reading it!)' (*SOHU*, 17 September 2019) www.sohu.com/a/419248507_784627 accessed 1 January 2024.

[20] Liu Huawen, 'Zhongguo tese shehuizhuyi requan guan – jiehe Xi Jinping Zhi "2015" – Beijing Renquan Luntan" de Hexin (The Socialist Outlook on Human with Chinese Characteristics: Interpretation of Xi Jinping's Congratulatory Letter at the 2015 Beijing Human Rights Forum)' [2016] *Chinese Review of International Law* 3, 5.

and the collective notion of justice, which means treating everyone fairly, though emphasising that human rights are not individual rights but belong to the society as a whole ('the masses').[21] The Party's explicit rejection of liberal values and the Socialist Core Values indicate more strongly that fairness should not be measured against international human rights but *only* in accordance with 'Chinese' values and domestic legislation. This should be borne in mind for the discussions to follow.

Crucially, the CCP, as self-designated agent, creates the legal basis for such freedoms, etc, and thus defines the very nature of law. In the era of Xi, the claim that the Party leads over everything, including both the law-making process and the content of such laws, is thus more clearly articulated. And while 'in accordance with the law' (*yifa*) describes the *how* – the process by which leadership is exercised – the Socialist Core Values are an example of the *what*, they are a concrete manifestation of 'by virtuous' (*yide*). Their codification into legislation is thus the next logical step.[22] Therefore, the Party leaders rationalised the need to introduce the Socialist Core Values by creating the narrative of *yide* as an integral part of *yifa* from which a set of prescribed values follows. In a further step, it formulated the goal to institutionalise these values by integrating them into legislation, which is framed to reflect the will of the people. This is a departure from the orthodox Marxist view according to which morality cannot be legalised – or law cannot develop morality[23] – but the Socialist Core Values have become enforceable moral norms and serve as ideological gatekeepers. The declared anti-liberalism and the pivotal and elevated role of the Party in law-making should be borne in mind when looking at the criminal justice reforms after 2012 because the agenda of law-based governance has indeed become a platform to reframe criminal justice reforms.[24]

## II. The Legalisation of Efficiency and Discipline

Early in the tenure of Xi, strengthening Party discipline through anti-corruption became a major concern. From 2012 onwards, Xi has emphasised that the pressing issue of corruption within the Party needed to be resolved. In early 2013, an anti-corruption campaign that operates under the slogan of eliminating 'tigers and flies, and foxes' has been launched. This unprecedented campaign would soon bring down high-ranking Party officials, or 'tigers', like Bo Xilai or Zhou Yongkang, as

[21] Zhang Yonghe, 'Dangdai zhongguo renquan guan yu shehuizhuyi hexin jiazhi guan de neizai luoji (The Inner Logic of Human Rights and Socialist Core Values in Contemporary China)' *People's Daily* (26 March 2024) cpc.people.com.cn/BIG5/n1/2024/0326/c64387-40203176.html accessed 1 January 2025.

[22] 'Guanyu Peiyu He Shixing Shehuizhuyi Hexin Jiazhi Guan de Yijian (Opinions on Cultivating and Practicing the Socialist Core Values) (Adopted by the Central Committee of the CCP on 23 December 2013)' cpc.people.com.cn/n/2013/1223/c64387-23924110.html accessed 24 June 2018.

[23] George L Kline, '"Socialist Legality" and Communist Ethics' (1963) 8 *Natural Law Forum* 21, 27.

[24] Sarah Biddulph, Elisa Nesossi and Susan Trevaskes, 'Criminal Justice Reform in the Xi Jinping Era' (2017) 2 *China Law and Society Review* 63, 70–71.

well as many 'flies'. It should be observed that this campaign has a global reach and operations 'Foxhunt' (2014) and 'Skynet' (2015) aim to hunt down fugitives that are sought for economic crimes.[25] At the 19th National Party Congress in 2017, Xi reiterated the zero tolerance towards corruption, deeming it a threat to the leadership of the CCP.[26]

To implement this agenda, important documents of the Party Central guided the direction of criminal justice reforms. Besides the usual promises to rectify wrongful convictions, address the issue of coerced confessions, or improve human rights protections in the criminal process, more widely, the 2013 Third Plenum Decision and the 2014 Fourth Plenum Decision emphasised the need to combat corruption by legal means.[27] In addition, two other major themes soon dominated criminal justice discourses in the aftermath of the CPL 2012. The 2014 Fourth Plenum Decision formulated the goal of promoting trial centredness (*yi shenpan wei zhongxin*) and improving the plea leniency system (*renzui renfa congkuan zhidu*).[28]

While the delegates to the Criminal Procedure Association meeting in 2013 discussed the implementation of the CPL 2012 and largely expressed their satisfaction with the modifications, certain delegates raised concerns as to unresolved issues in terms of compulsory measures or exclusionary rules.[29] However, in the light of the set policy goals, the meetings of the Criminal Procedure Association between 2015 and 2018 centred on the major themes of anti-corruption legislation, trial-centredness, plea leniency, and trial *in absentia* against the broader backdrop of promoting law-based governance. In these contexts, even though

[25] 'Gongan'bu: "hu zhua" xingdong yi zhuahuo waitao jingji fan 680 ren, shuliang kongqian (Ministry of Public Security: Operation "Foxhunt" has already caught 680 Economic Fugitives that had fled abroad, an unprecedented Number)' (*The Paper*, 8 January 2015) m.thepaper.cn/kuaibao_detail.jsp?contid=1292442&from=kuaibao accessed 1 December 2021; '6 nian lai "tianwang" xingdong dafa buduan shengji zhenshe chixu qianghua zhuizang mubiao yujia jingzhun (In the past 6 years of Operation "Skynet" the Level of Deterrence has been raised and the Precision of the Goal of Hunting Fugitives and Returning Stolen Goods has continuingly been Strengthened)' (*CCDINSC web*, 1 March 2021) www.ccdi.gov.cn/yaowen/202103/t20210301_236665.html accessed 1 December 2021.

[26] Xi Jinping, 'Juesheng quanmian jiancheng xiaokangshehui duoqu xinshidai zhongguo tese shehuizhuyiweida shengli (Secure a Decisive Victory in Building a Moderately Prosperous Society in All Respects and Strive for the Great Success of Socialism with Chinese Characteristics for a New Era), Report to the 19th National Congress of the CCP on 18 October 2017' s 1 www.gov.cn/zhuanti/2017-10/27/content_5234876.htm accessed 13 July 2018.

[27] 'Decision of the Central Committee of the CCP on Some Major Issues Concerning Comprehensively Deepening the Reform, Adopted at the Third Plenary Session of the 18h Central Committee of the CCP on 12 November 2013' s 9, para 34 /www.gov.cn/jrzg/2013-11/15/content_2528179.htm accessed 25 March 2017; 'Decision of the Central Committee of the CCP on Several Major Issues Concerning the Comprehensive Promotion of Law Based Governance, Adopted at the Fourth Plenum of the 18th Central Committee on 23 October 2014' (n 5) s 36.

[28] 'Decision of the Central Committee of the CCP on Several Major Issues Concerning the Comprehensive Promotion of Law Based Governance, Adopted at the Fourth Plenum of the 18th Central Committee on 23 October 2014' (n 5) s 4, paras 2, 3.

[29] Tian Ye, 'Jujiao shiwu xin wenti, tuidong xingsufa guanche zhixing – zhongguo xingshi susong faxue yanjiuhui 2013 nian nianhui zongshu (Focusing on new Practical Issues and Promoting the Implementation of the Criminal Procedure Law – Summary of the 2013 Annual Meeting of the China Criminal Procedure Law Research Association)' [2013] *People's Procuratorial Semimonthly* 49.

being far from resolved, the question of presumption of innocence was occasionally but only superficially raised, and previously highly controversial issues such as the right to silence were no longer prominent on the agenda.[30]

In March 2018, a third overhaul of the Criminal Procedure Law was formally put on the legislative agenda,[31] and in October 2018, a refined version of the law was adopted (CPL 2018). Looking at the timeline, the lawmaking was finalised in a comparatively short period of time, presumably also because the reform was much smaller in scale than the previous reforms; only 18 provisions were amended and 18 articles were added.[32] The CPL 2018 mostly aimed at incorporating the political agenda, as outlined in this section, including the integration of the supervisory mechanism, the establishment of trials *in absentia*,[33] and the institutionalisation of the policy of combining leniency with severity through the set-up of a plea leniency system.[34] In contrast, changes with respect to pre-trial safeguards, including criminal defence or personal liberty, are almost not worthy of mention. This seems particularly startling when considering that these mechanisms have been codified in parallel to efforts of achieving greater trial-centredness, meaning a shift away from investigation-centralism.

In the light of the relatively short period of time, the scholarly discourse in the process of revising the CPL 2012 was far less extensive, and no Criminal Procedure Law draft proposals were produced. Chen Weidong has suggested that the CPL 2012 reform era marked a transition from the 'deepening' to the 'mature phase', as it had resolved fundamental issues in relation to objectives, values, competences or organisational structure. This would explain why the 2018 CPL reform was completed within a relatively short period, focusing on the connection of the system after the reform of the anti-corruption system, the inclusion of the system of pleading leniency, and the construction of the procedure of trial *in absentia*. Of these three elements, the most urgent issue was the harmonisation with the new anti-corruption mechanism.[35] Although the CPL 2018 left many controversial issues unresolved and showed few signs of improvements in terms

[30] Zhang Jixi, Xiang Yan and Ni Run, 'Zhongguo xingshi susong faxue yanjiuhui 2015 nian nianhui zongshu (Summary of the 2015 Annual Meeting of the China Criminal Procedure Law Society)' [2016] *Justice of China* 36.

[31] '2018 Legislative Work Plan of the Standing Committee of the NPC (Adopted 2 March 2018, No. 14 [2018])' www.gov.cn/gongbao/content/2018/content_5277687.htm accessed 17 October 2020.

[32] See Decision of the NPC Standing Committee to Amend the Criminal Procedure Law of the PRC (Adopted at the Sixth Meeting of the Standing Committee of the Thirteenth National People's Congress on 26 October 2018).

[33] CPL 2018, arts 170, 291 to 297; Fan Chongyi, 'Xingshi susong fa xiugai de zhongdian nandian wenti jiedu (Reading the Key and Difficult Issues in the Revision of the Criminal Procedure Law)' [2019] *Journal of Law Application* 81, 81.

[34] 'Explanations on the Criminal Procedure Law of the PRC (Draft Amendment) 26 October 2018' (26 October 2018) www.npc.gov.cn/zgrdw//npc//xinwen/2018-10/26/content_2064462.htm accessed 4 April 2021.

[35] Chen Weidong, 'Xingshi susong fazhi sishi nian: huigu yu zhanwang (40 Years' Development of Criminal Procedure Law: Retrospect and Prospect)' (2019) 37 *Tribune of Political Science and Law* 18, 23–24.

of fair trial, in a sense, it has continued a trend that had already become tangible in the making of the CPL 2012. The pendulum had swung towards crime control.

For example, the supervisory mechanism reflects pure crime control and does not even pretend to meet minimum fair trial standards. Interestingly, while many observers outside of China have criticised the new mechanism for basically codifying an unfair trial,[36] many scholars inside China have held that it means progress in terms of rights protection. The official discourse frames the new law as a further strengthening of law-based governance in China, which is partly echoed by scholars in China. Certain scholars have argued that the supervisory reforms mean progress in terms of 'legalisation', often mentioned together with 'standardisation' (*guifanhua*) and 'regularisation' (*zhengguihua*), against the backdrop of the agenda of law-based governance, suggesting that the wave of codification should be considered as progress in terms of rights protection; the new provisions would provide clarified competences, investigation procedure or evidence rules.[37] For example, Chen Guangzhong viewed the move from Party regulations to state law as very important. While arguing that some provision would need further clarification,[38] overall, Chen seems to consider the codification a positive step.

Moreover, the overall more repressive atmosphere suppressed the more nuanced and multifaceted discourses on human rights protection in the criminal justice process that had dominated the reforms in 1996 and 2012, and declining high-level support through the illiberal shift impacted the direction of criminal justice. The question of presumption of innocence was not of major concern, neither in academic nor in official discourses. The political agenda of the Party Central, the identification of corruption and national security as main areas of potential threat to social stability, was favourable to those relying on national conditions claims. Indeed, it can be observed that international law, which had become the most important benchmark for fair trial in the reform era, has been increasingly marginalised due to the emphasis on national conditions, ie, 'Chinese characteristics.' Especially after the adoption of the CPL 2018, a stronger emphasis on a 'Chinese theory of criminal justice' amongst legal scholars in China is

[36] Yu-Jie Chen, 'Human Rights in the Chinese Administration of Justice' (Taiwan Foundation for Democracy 2019) China Human Rights Report 2018, 94–96 www.tfd.org.tw/en/publication/human accessed 3 April 2020.

[37] Bian Jianlin, 'Jiaqian jijian jiancha jiguan zishen jianshe shi tigao jijian jiancha gongzuo guifanhua fazhihua zhengguhua shuiping de neizai yaoqiu (Strengthening the Self-Building of the Discipline Inspection and Supervisory Organs is an intrinsic Demand for improving the Standardisation, Legalisation and Regularisation of the Discipline Inspection and Supervision Work)' *China Discipline Inspection and Supervision Magazine* 2023; Zhang Yunxiao, 'Guojia jiancha tizhi gaige fazhihua jincheng chutan (A Preliminary Study on the Legalisation of the State Supervision System)' [2018] *Law Science Magazine* 29.

[38] 'Chen Guangzhong "jianchafa" shi danggui zhuanxiang guofa de zhongyao bianhua (Chen Guangzhong: The "Supervision Law" is an important shift from Party regulations towards state law)' *China News* (22 March 2018) www.chinanews.com/gn/2018/03-22/8473449.shtml accessed 1 August 2023.

observable, whereas international law as the most important benchmark and calls on the Chinese government to fulfil moral and legal obligations under international law are not advanced in the same manner and intensity as previously.[39]

While Supreme People's Court has portrayed the CPL 2018 as a success, completing a criminal justice system 'with Chinese characteristics.'[40] Shen Chunyao, chairperson of the SCNPC Legislative Affairs Commission, stressed that the CPL 2018 had successfully implemented the policies of the party-state, most notably the so-called 'Four-Pronged Comprehensive Strategy' (*sige quanmian zhanlüe buju*), which was first put forward by Xi Jinping in 2014 and includes building a moderately well-off society, pursuing an expanded in-depth reform agenda, implementing a comprehensive framework for promoting law-based governance and enforcing Party discipline.[41] In official parlance, the implementation of this policy will enhance the domestic protection of human rights.[42] This again illustrates the law-like treatment of policies, and since policies had shifted towards strengthening party and self-discipline, more widely, the focus had shifted towards crime control.

The sections to follow centre on the most prominent themes of the CPL 2018 reform, ie, plea leniency and the integration of the supervisory mechanism as part of an effort to strengthen legal governance. While the institutionalisation of plea leniency may be seen to suppress procedural fairness at the expense of efficiency, the Supervision Law manifests the party-state's understanding of fairness and demonstrates the denial of international standards of fairness. More resources are being allocated in – what is deemed – high-profile cases, whereas ordinary and minor cases should be handled efficiently, preferably through speedier procedures. Both these mechanisms heavily rely on confessions and have further institutionalised the policy of combining leniency with severity. While a detailed discussion on these mechanisms would go beyond the ambit of this book, the sections to follow aim to give a glimpse into the mechanisms in the light of a more illiberal and closed system, as discussed in the previous section, and demonstrate how problematic they are in the light of unresolved fair trial issues and especially in the absence of presumption of innocence.

[39] Liu Chuangao, 'Xin shidai xingshi susong zhidu de xin fazhan – Zhongguo xingshi susong faxue yanjiuhui 2018 nian nianhui guandian shuyao (New Development of the Criminal Procedure System in the New Era – Summary of Views from the 2018 Annual Meeting of the Criminal Procedure Association)' [2018] *People's Procuratorate Semimonthly* 35, 35; Zhang Lu and Luo Haimin, 'Zhongguo Xingshi Susong Faxue Yanjiuhui 2019 Nian Nianhui Zongshu (Summary of the Annual Meeting of the Criminal Procedure Association in 2019)' [2020] *Justice of China* 99.

[40] Notice of the Supreme People's Court on Earnestly Studying and Implementing the Decision of the Standing Committee of the National People's Congress to Amend the Criminal Procedure Law of the PRC (Adopted on 7 November 2018, No. 294 [2018] of Supreme People's Court) s 1.

[41] 'Explanations on the Criminal Procedure Law of the PRC (Draft Amendment) 26 October 2018' (n 33).

[42] '"Wei renmin mou xingfu: xin zhongguo renquan shiye fazhan 70 nian" baipishu (Seeking Happiness for People: 70 Years of Progress on Human Rights in China)' www.scio.gov.cn/zfbps/index.htm accessed 24 August 2020.

## A. Plea Leniency as a Symbol of Efficiency

As mentioned in the previous section, the 2014 Fourth Plenum Decision called for the promotion of a lenient punishment system in the criminal process. With the increasing abolition of administrative measures, such as re-education through labour, the judicial system had been burdened with the handling of minor offences, which make up the majority of all criminal cases. The question of efficient handling of such cases thus became an area of concern.[43] Speedier court procedures existed in China already before the enactment of the plea leniency system.[44] The simplified procedure, which was introduced in 1996, is applicable at the trial stage and means that a court can take a shortcut in certain cases, ie, those punishable by a maximum of three years' imprisonment.[45] In 2012, the CPL introduced admission of guilt as a prerequisite to entering the procedure and broadened the scope of application of the simplified procedure,[46] but the actual use of this procedure varied greatly across different localities.[47] In 2016, an initial pilot program for a plea deal mechanism was launched in 18 localities. The mechanism, a legalisation and institutionalisation of the policy of 'combining leniency with severity' (*kuan yan xiang ji*),[48] is promoted as fair, cheap and efficient.[49]

The plea leniency system was among the hot topics at the annual meeting of the Criminal Procedure Association in 2017. At the meeting, certain delegates emphasised that the plea leniency system was not comparable to plea bargaining. Rather, the key to leniency for those who plead guilty and accept punishment would lie in the simplified and expedited procedures. However, there were three areas of contestation, including the standard of proof required for conviction, the voluntariness of guilty pleas, and the involvement of lawyers. In the absence of a legally protected right to silence, the question of how to secure voluntariness of admissions of guilt was seen as problematic. And although the mechanism appears to lay great emphasis on the role of lawyers in securing voluntariness, delegates raised concerns that the CPL 2012 was still lacking fundamental

[43] Biddulph et al (n 23) 63, 70–71.

[44] Xin He, 'Plea Leniency and Prosecution Centredness in China's Criminal Process' (2023) 254 *The China Quarterly* 448, 451; Enshen Li, 'Haste Makes Waste: Why China's New Plea Leniency System Is Doomed to Fail' (2022) 17 *Asian Journal of Comparative Law* 76, 80.

[45] CPL 1996, arts 174 to 179 (CPL 2018, arts 214 to 221).

[46] CPL 2012, art 208(2).

[47] Zhang Jixi, Xiang Yan and Ni Run (n 29) 38.

[48] As pointed out by Chen Weidong at the annual meeting of the Criminal Procedure Association in 2017, see Chang Feng, 'Gaige beijing xia xingshi susong zhidu de fazhan – Zhongguo xingshi susong faxue yanjiuhui 2017 nian nianhui guandian zongshu (Development of the Criminal Procedure System against the Backdrop of Reforms – Summary of the Views at the 2017 Annual Meeting of the Criminal Procedure Association)' [2017] *People's Procuratorial Semimonthly* 36, 37.

[49] Decision of the NPC Standing Committee on Authorising the Supreme People's Court and the Supreme People's Procuratorate to Conduct the Pilot Program of the System for Imposing Lenient Punishments on Those Confessing to Their Crimes and Accepting Punishments in Criminal Cases in Certain Areas (Adopted at the Twenty-second Meeting of the Standing Committee of the Twelfth NPC on 3 September 2016).

guarantees such as a legal guarantee of mandatory presence of lawyers during first interrogation.[50]

The CPL 2018, then, enacted the plea leniency system by including the requirement of 'acknowledging guilt and accepting punishment' (*renzui renfa*) in the expedited procedure (*sucai chengxu*) for minor criminal cases, ie, those facing less than three years of imprisonment.[51] These two elements must both be met. It more explicitly reflects the confession value or the educational value of confessions in criminal trials, as an accused must make a '*truthful* admission' (*rushi gongshu*) of guilt.[52] The Guiding Opinions on the Application of the System of Accepting Guilt and Accepting Punishment of 2019 (Guiding Opinions 2019) stress an *upright* admission of guilt and a *genuine* regret and acceptance of punishment to fulfil the two elements of '*renzui*' and '*renfa*'. The acceptance of punishment is an important element of this mechanism, whereas only a confession of guilt or surrender will not be weighed as heavily in sentencing.[53] Otherwise it would indeed simply be someone who makes an admission of guilt in a standard court procedure. The evidentiary standard of clear facts and hard evidence is another precondition to enter the expedited procedure.[54]

Certain groups of defendants or types of cases are excluded from this proceeding, including disabled, minors, cases with significant social impact, cases of joint crimes in which not all defendants meet all requirements for a deal, or cases in which no compensation agreement with the victim's side has been reached yet.[55] Minor offences are considered to belong to 'contradictions among the people' (*minjian maodun*) – nothing the party-state is particularly concerned with and which may thus be handled efficiently through plea leniency; unlike other cases, such 'contradictions' do not belong to a group of cases perceived as posing a threat to its leadership.[56] Therefore, cases with great social harm are excluded from the expedited procedure.[57] Pleading for leniency by admitting reinforces the long-standing practice of rewarding cooperation, but the reforms have further legalised and standardised the proceedings of pleading for leniency.

However, it should be observed that the system of leniency for a guilty plea does not prescribe a specific mode of proceedings. Rather, it has been formulated as a general principle of the criminal process that is predominantly concerned with sentence reduction of the defendant. In other words, an admission of guilt may also lead to lenient punishment in the regular process. Once an accused makes an

[50] Chang Feng (n 47) 37–39.
[51] CPL 2018, arts 15 and 222 (added).
[52] CPL 2018, art 15.
[53] Guiding Opinions on the Application of the System of Accepting Guilt and Accepting Punishment (Adopted by the Supreme People's Court, the Supreme People's Procuratorate, the Ministry of Public Security, the Ministry of National Security and the Ministry of Justice on 24 October 2019) s 2, para 6; ss 3 and 9.
[54] CPL 2018, art 222; Guiding Opinions on the Application of the System of Accepting Guilt and Accepting Punishment 2019.
[55] CPL 2018, art 223.
[56] 2019 Opinions, art 1.
[57] CPL 2018, art 223(3).

admission of guilt, the case may be resolved by one of these speedier proceedings if it meets the requirements of the specific procedure.[58]

To ensure voluntariness of confessions, state agencies should sufficiently explain the nature and procedure of the plea leniency system, as well as the consequences of a confession, to an accused at every stage of the proceedings, with the court being the last checkpoint to make sure that they have understood the consequences of pleading for leniency.[59] Lawyers are understood to play a crucial role in securing the voluntariness of the accused's admission of guilt, and an effective right to defence is thus seen as a prerequisite. The CPL 2018 added a provision enabling access to duty lawyers where a suspect or defendant has not entrusted a defence lawyer to provide legal assistance as regards the choice of proceedings or assisting in applying for the modification of compulsory measures, among others.[60] While a suspect or defendant can refuse the assistance of a duty lawyer, a lawyer must be present when they sign the statement to plead guilty and accept punishment.[61] To meet this demand, a full coverage of (duty) lawyers in the plea deal system has been further promoted.[62]

Notwithstanding the role ascribed to lawyers in the plea leniency system, the CPL 2018 made only modest efforts to improve the overall criminal defence system, nor did it refine the interrogation procedure or address the question of silence in the phase of police investigation, despite decades-long debates about the relationship between the duty to cooperate, on the one hand, and that of silence. There are, moreover, various caveats with respect to duty lawyers.

After the CPL 2018 was put into effect, scholars like Chen Guangzhong voiced concerns, as duty lawyers are allowed to provide legal assistance to suspects and defendants who plead guilty and accept punishment, which means they enjoy fewer rights in terms of meetings with clients or access to case files. Because the application of plea leniency is not limited, except for cases tried using the summary proceedings, plea leniency cases are usually cases that carry a sentence of more than three years. In these cases, legal assistance by duty lawyers would not be sufficient and would lower the standard of defence.[63] The Guiding Opinions 2019 further elaborated on the rights of duty lawyers and stipulates that, for example, a duty lawyer may meet with a suspect or defendant in custody, even though in cases

[58] Yu Mou, *The Construction of Guilt in China, An Empirical Account of Routine Chinese Injustice* (Oxford, Hart Publishing, 2020) 140–142.

[59] CPL 2018, art 120(2); ibid s 10, para 39.

[60] CPL 2018, art 36.

[61] CPL 2018, art 174; Guiding Opinions on the Application of the System of Accepting Guilt and Accepting Punishment 2019, s 4, para 14.

[62] Measures on launching the pilot work of full coverage of legal defence in criminal cases (issued by the Supreme People's Court and the Ministry of Justice on 11 October 2017); Opinions of the Supreme People's Court, the Supreme People's Procuratorate and the Ministry of Justice on further deepening the pilot work of full coverage of legal defence in criminal cases (No. 49 [2022] of the Ministry of Justice); Provisions on the Legal Protection of Lawyers' Practicing Rights (Issued by the Supreme People's Court, the Supreme People's Procuratorate, the Ministry of Public Security, the Ministry of National Security and the Ministry of Justice on 16 September 2015).

[63] Chen Guangzhong, 'Dangqian Xingshi Susong Zhidu Gaige Mianlin de Jige Wenti (Several Issues Currently Facing the Reform of the Criminal Procedure System)' (2018) 26 *Evidence Science* 517, 518.

involving national security or terrorism, the meeting with a criminal suspect in custody during the investigation period requires the police's approval. Duty lawyers may moreover read case files from the day the procuratorial organ examines the case.[64] To some degree, these provisions harmonised or aligned the roles of duty lawyers with those of defence lawyers, as enshrined in the Criminal Procedure Law.[65] However, research on the ground has shown that the duty lawyer's right to meet with clients was limited in practice due to a lack of enthusiasm on the side of the police but also due to limited resources.[66]

However, as discussed in the previous chapters, Chinese legislation is understood to suggest that suspects do not have access to legal counsel *during* the first interrogation. The absence of a lawyer raises concerns as to the credibility of an admission of guilt made during the first questioning. Moreover, although CPL 2018 enables lawyers to submit defence opinions to the prosecution at the prosecution stage, they remain largely excluded from the prosecutorial interrogation, which seems particularly problematic with respect to suspects' decision on whether to plead guilty at this point.[67] The Opinions 2019 stipulate that the police should not make a concrete leniency promise; in the prosecution phase, leniency offers can be made. In other words, a suspect is left in the loop until the prosecution stage.[68]

To close the investigation in a case of plea leniency, the same evidentiary standard as for other cases is required, and all materials, including the recorded admission of guilt, must be transferred to the prosecution.[69] Recording is thus obligatory to ensure voluntariness, but the law does not say that the entire interrogation must be recorded.[70] The prosecutor must inform a suspect about their procedural rights and hear the opinions of all sides – including those of the defender or duty lawyer – as to the accusations and recommended punishment. As part of this process, the prosecutor should enable the duty lawyer access to the relevant case materials.[71] The procuratorial organ should review the voluntariness and lawfulness of the investigation when receiving a case for prosecution with the recommendation to apply a fast-track procedure. This includes, for example, reviewing whether a suspect was trapped or forced to plead guilty or whether a suspect understands the possible consequences of a guilty plea.[72]

[64] Guiding Opinions on the Application of the System of Accepting Guilt and Accepting Punishment 2019, s 4, para 12.
[65] See ch 5, IV.B.
[66] Sun Changyong and Guo Hang, 'Bei Zhuisu Ren Renzui Renfa Ziyuanxing Zai Shenshi (Review of the Voluntariness of the Accused's Admission of Guilt and Punishment)' (2024) 32 *Henan Social Sciences* 52, 56–60.
[67] Mou (n 57) 143.
[68] Guiding Opinions on the Application of the System of Accepting Guilt and Accepting Punishment 2019, s 7, para 23.
[69] CPL 2018, art 162(2).
[70] CPL 2018, art 172.
[71] CPL 2018, art 173; Guiding Opinions on the Application of the System of Accepting Guilt and Accepting Punishment 2019, s 8, para 27.
[72] ibid 8, para 28.

In the examination of punishment, an early and proactive as well as thorough and stable admission of guilt will be considered favourable for the degree of leniency.[73] Therefore, a late admission of guilt, for example, at trial will grant the defendant less leniency than one made in the pre-trial phases. However, the procuratorial organ may also decide not to prosecute in minor cases where punishment may be waived; where the facts are unclear and evidence is insufficient, it must not prosecute.[74]

The discussions in the previous chapters have shown that the Chinese criminal justice system heavily relies on admissions of guilt, and these are traditionally rewarded with leniency. The main novelty is that the agreed deal is written down and thus understood to be more trustworthy than any oral promises.[75] Therefore, the prosecution and defence basically agree on a punishment, and this serves as the basis for the court's hearing. Pleading for leniency is not plea bargaining but rather resembles an 'offer and consent' mechanism, which is supported by the wording of the law; there is no element of negotiation. As pointed out by Chen Weidong, leniency for an admission of guilt already existed before, but now the procedure of plea leniency has been legalised and standardised. The procedure follows trial-centralism in the sense that the court is understood to remain the last line of defence to check on pre-trial admissions of guilt and acceptance of punishment.[76]

However, scholars have raised concerns that the plea leniency system means a real pushback for trial-centredness. As emphasised in the White Paper on the Legal Protection of Human Rights of 2017, plea leniency proceedings should also be permeated by trial-centredness. The official stance considers trial-centralism as a means through which the innocent can be protected.[77] As mentioned in the preceding section, from 2014 onwards, the Party Central has pursued trial-centredness reforms.[78] There has been a debate as to the implications of these reforms, with many stakeholders agreeing that it aims at a shift away from investigation-centralism but not implying 'court' or 'judge centralism'; it would simply indicate that the activities should centre on the trial stage. Some nonetheless emphasised that such an envisaged shift would require some more adversarial

[73] Guiding Opinions on the Application of the System of Accepting Guilt and Accepting Punishment 2019, s 3, para 9.

[74] ibid 8, para 30.

[75] He (n 43) 452.

[76] CPL 2018, arts 190(2), 201 and 226; Chen Weidong, 'Renzui renfa congkuan zhidu de lilun wenti zai tantao (Re-examination of Theoretical Issues of the Plea Leniency System)' [2020] *Global Law Review* 23, 27–30.

[77] State Council Information Office, 'Zhongguo renquan fazhihua baozhang de xin jinzhan (New Progress in the Legal Protection of Human Rights in China) (White Paper on the Legal Protection of Human Rights in China)' (2017) www.scio.gov.cn/zfbps/index.htm accessed 12 January 2018.

[78] 'Decision of the Central Committee of the CCP on Several Major Issues Concerning the Comprehensive Promotion of Law Based Governance, Adopted at the Fourth Plenum of the 18th Central Committee on 23 October 2014' (n 5) para IV, s 3.

elements and respect for presumption of innocence.[79] Yet, trial-centralism neither implies an elevated role for the defence counsel. Rather, the trial ought to be the centre for the determination of facts to change the practices of confession reliance and pre-trial determination of facts.[80] Indeed, trial-centredness is understood to take place within the existing legal framework.[81]

To this end, as provisions issued by state agencies show, in the pre-trial phases, it especially entails a strengthening of the procuratorial supervision powers over investigation activities, as well as improvements to the investigation and interrogation proceedings. The standardisation of proceedings, such as the precise conditions under which supplementary investigations should be carried out, seems to be the overarching goal to eradicate pre-trial errors.[82] Indeed, looking at further instructions, many of the aspects of trial-centredness are not new but have been areas of concern before, including already established rules and principles of criminal justice, such as evidentiary-based judgments, the enforcement of exclusionary rules, the application of the principle of *in dubio pro reo* or overall procedural fairness, etc.[83] This raises the question of how trial-centredness expresses influence in the plea leniency system in light of the dominant role of the procuratorial organs in plea leniency.

At trial, a sole judge should assess whether the required standard of proof for conviction is met and whether the defendant indeed voluntarily confessed and agrees with the application of the fast-track sentencing procedure.[84] The judge should hear the opinion of the defendant as well as the defendant's statement.[85] However, the trial is more like window-dressing, an administrative procedure during which the judge announces the judgment. Observers have criticised that there is no meaningful involvement of courts in the plea leniency system,[86] while the procuratorial organs assume a central role due to their power to make sentencing recommendations. While such a sentencing recommendation is not binding on courts, they should generally follow the recommendations of the prosecutor unless the court finds inconsistencies with respect to the charges, involuntary admission of guilt, and acceptance of punishment or the defendant denies charges while reviewing the case.[87] According to official figures for the year 2023, courts

[79] Zhang Jixi, Xiang Yan and Ni Run (n 29) 36–37.
[80] Biddulph et al (n 23) 77–79.
[81] Zhang Lu and Luo Haimin (n 38) 101–102.
[82] Opinions of the Supreme People's Court, the Supreme People's Procuratorate, the Ministry of Public Security, the Ministry of State Security and the Ministry of Justice on Promoting the Reform of the Criminal Procedure System with Trials as the Centre (Adopted on 11 October 2016).
[83] Implementing Opinions on Comprehensively Promoting the Reform of the Criminal Procedure System with Trials as the Centre (Adopted on 17 February 2017, No. 5 [2017] of the Supreme People's Court) s 1.
[84] CPL 2018, art 190(2).
[85] CPL 2018, art 224.
[86] He (n 43) 451.
[87] CPL 2018, arts 176 and 201.

nevertheless followed the procuratorial's sentencing recommendation in 97.5 per cent of all cases.[88]

In 2020, the Supreme People's Procuratorate issued model cases that ought to guide the implementation of plea leniency. Some of these cases were closed within 48 hours, ie, from formal initiation of prosecution to judgment. Moreover, in Case No. 1, the suspect was taken into police detention and only had access to a duty lawyer when asked to sign the statement.[89] Such a quick closure of cases raises concerns as to the effectiveness of defence, as a lawyer should have adequate time to review such a statement and provide legal assistance to the accused.

Based on an analysis of criminal judgments of 2020 from courts in Shanghai processed through the simplified or expedited procedure, Li Enshen has shown that the defendant's arguments are rarely taken into consideration by the court when deciding on a sentence. Moreover, even if legal counsel plays a role in plea leniency, defence counsel was not present at trial in most of all cases that proceeded through these proceedings, which is partly due to the nature of the proceedings that require only mandatory counsel when reaching a plea deal, usually at the earlier stages. Those defence lawyers who attended the trial barely tried to challenge the criminal charges or the guilty pleas in terms of lawfulness or voluntariness. Rather, they focus on arguments for lenient punishment. This strategy may be partly due to their experience that troubling authorities may indeed be detrimental to reaching a more lenient sentence and therefore not in their client's best interest. However, it makes the trial a mere formality without adversarial elements.[90] Indeed, this further undermines procedural justice.

Notwithstanding efforts to standardise the plea leniency system, research by Enshen Li has shown that, owing to the absence of unified standards of application, the degree of leniency and the treatment of suspects and defendants may vary greatly across different localities.[91] From an official point of view, this mechanism does not conflict with the goal of a trial-centred system, because it upholds the principle of evidence-based judgments, which is at the core of trial centredness. The opinions thus make very clear that an admission of guilt does not lower the evidentiary standard. In other words, where evidence is insufficient – even in the event of a confession – a person should not be convicted.[92] However, scholars are sceptical if this is ever actually the case, as research has shown that the speedier

[88] '2023 nian quanguo jiancha jiguan zhuyao ban'an shuju (Main Data on Cases handled by the National Procuratorial Organs in 2023)' (10 March 2024) www.spp.gov.cn/xwfbh/wsfbt/202403/t20240310_648482.shtml#1 accessed 8 August 2024.

[89] 'Zuigao renmin jianchayuan fabu si qi renzui renfa anjian shiyong sucai chengxu dianxing anli (Supreme People's Procuratorate Publishes Four Model Cases where the Defendant Admits Guilt and Accepts Punishment and to which the Fast-Track Sentencing Procedure May Apply) (Issued by the SPP on 13 October 2020)' www.spp.gov.cn/spp/xwfbh/wsfbt/202010/t20201013_481664.shtml#2 accessed 25 September 2022.

[90] Li (n 43) 86–91.

[91] ibid 95–96.

[92] Guiding Opinions on the Application of the System of Accepting Guilt and Accepting Punishment 2019, s 1, para 3.

procedures do not require such strong evidence in practice but are rather convenient to deal with weak cases.[93] It would moreover require the courts to play an active role in plea deals. Yet, there is a clear asymmetry of powers between courts and the police and prosecution. Although the plea leniency system can be applied in all procedural phases, research has shown that most admissions of guilt take place in the pre-trial phases, and the procuratorial organs play the dominant role amongst the three agencies.[94]

As He Xin has argued, this plea deal system enhances the position of the procuratorates in the criminal process and facilitates 'prosecution centredness' – rather than 'trial centredness' – without providing proper safeguards for the accused. And because judges can be relieved of their heavy workload and close more cases conveniently, courts – though being further marginalised – have not protested this newly gained omnipotence of the prosecutors as investigator, prosecutor and judge – assuming all three powers at once. The prosecutor can withdraw a plea offer.[95]

The procuratorial organs undoubtedly assume a dominant role in the procedure and have tried to capture and establish 'prosecution-led' proceedings. While it may appear problematic that courts do not have to follow the sentencing recommendation and thus violate the leniency expectation of the defendant, they should ensure the lawfulness of proceedings and have the final adjudication power. Trying to further cement 'prosecution-led' proceedings, in 2021, the Supreme People's Court issued a judicial interpretation to Article 201 CPL 2018, compromising the court's power not to follow the procuratorial sentencing recommendation by stipulating the procuratorate's power to protest such judgments on the grounds that the court has violated the statutory procedures, basically replacing the court's discretionary power under this provision. This undermines trial centralism and erodes the exclusive adjudication power of courts.[96]

In this context, it may be worth noting that, in 2023, only six per cent of all defendants appealed the decision.[97] Therefore, only six per cent of all defendants challenge the conviction based on a plea deal. Here, the question is whether those who did only challenged the sentence or whether they withdrew their confessions. The problem is courts will not be able to properly assess whether a confession was indeed made voluntarily or whether a person was tricked or manipulated into making one. Indeed, wrongful convictions will decrease – at least on the surface.[98]

[93] Mou (n 57) 142.

[94] He (n 43) 460–461; Li (n 43) 86–87.

[95] He (n 43) 459.

[96] Ji Xiangde, 'Xi Jinping fazhi sixiang zhidao xia de renzui renfa congkuan zhidu (The Plea Leniency System under the Guidance of Xi Jinping's Rule-of-Law-Thought)' (2024) 42 *Tribune of Political Science and Law* 3, 5–7.

[97] 'Zuigao renmin fayuan zhang Yang Wanming: shiyong renzui renfa congkuan zhidu, tuijin qingzui shenli xiandaihua (Yang Wanming, Vice-President of the Supreme Court: applying the system of leniency in pleading guilty and accepting punishment, advancing the modernisation of trials for minor offences)' (*Supreme People's Court of the PRC*, 10 March 2024) www.court.gov.cn/zixun/xiangqing/427612.html accessed 12 June 2024.

[98] He (n 43) 454.

Even if the expedited procedure is applicable *only* to cases in which a prison sentence of under three years may be imposed, such minor cases make up the greatest proportion of all criminal cases in Chinese courts. According to the Supreme People's Court's numbers, between 2019 and 2024, the use of plea leniency in first instance cases has increased by 44.2 per cent. While the percentage was only 44 per cent of all criminal cases in 2019, it had risen to 86 per cent in 2022.[99] According to numbers issued by the Supreme People's Procuratorate for 2023, the plea leniency mechanism – there was no specification as to the procedure used – is now applied in over 90 per cent of all criminal cases.[100] This clearly illustrates the magnitude of this new mechanism. It basically means that the confession rate was also over 90 per cent. This raises the question of whether the mechanism provides incentives for an innocent person to make an admission of guilt.

## B. The Innocence Problem: Incentives for Pleading Guilty

The idea of bargaining about what is just and acceptable in the event of an admission of guilt – in other words, reaching a consensus or deal on that matter – is not new. And without doubt, an admission of guilt is usually met with leniency across different criminal justice systems. There is, however, the innocence problem – an innocent person pleading guilty. Against this backdrop, scholars have discussed the perils that may arise from such a mechanism. Indeed, false guilty pleas are not the exception.[101] The establishment of such a mechanism in a system that lacks presumption of innocence and minimum fair trial safeguards, in general, appears highly problematic. There is clear unfairness underlying the Chinese plea leniency system. Li Enshen is very critical of the claim that the plea leniency system can achieve the dual objective of efficient crime control and human rights protection, arguing that it has little regard for due process and fairness.[102]

Sun Chanyong has voiced concerns in terms of the voluntariness of admissions of guilt and acceptance of punishment. What precisely constitutes voluntariness would not clearly be defined by law. Whether an accused person has a choice, in the sense of choosing to make a confession without any external influence, would be debatable when considering the environment, ie, high detention, prosecution and conviction rates, as well as powerful state agencies. In the view of Sun, in the

[99] 'Zuigao renmin fayuan zhang Yang Wanming: shiyong renzui renfa congkuan zhidu, tuijin qingzui shenli xiandaihua (Yang Wanming, Vice-President of the Supreme Court: applying the system of leniency in pleading guilty and accepting punishment, advancing the modernisation of trials for minor offences)' (n 96).

[100] '2023 nian quanguo jiancha jiguan zhuyao ban'an shuju (Main Data on Cases handled by the National Procuratorial Organs in 2023)' (n 87).

[101] See, eg, Lucian E Dervan and Vanessa A Edkins, 'The Innocent Defendant's Dilemma: An Innovative Empirical Study of Plea Bargaining's Innocence Problem' (2013) 103 *Journal of Criminal Law and Criminology* 1.

[102] Li (n 43) 77. For a similar observation, see Mou (n 57) 152.

light of the duty to make truthful statements and owing to the absence of an effective privilege against self-incrimination and a right to silence, an accused could not choose between the two options of making a statement or choosing to be silent. Truthfulness and voluntariness were two different things. A truthful confession may be extorted, but that does not mean it was voluntary.[103] This is even worsened by the earlier discussed marginalised role of lawyers and the insufficient review by courts and ignorance towards the defence's view.

The plea leniency system may make detecting wrongful convictions nearly impossible. In the view of the vice-president of the Supreme People's Court, Yang Wanming, because the system was built on voluntariness, there was no incentive for authorities to present illegally obtained evidence and extort confessions, thereby effectively protecting the innocent.[104] However, wrongful convictions may still occur, as the pressure may become unsurmountable when punishment appears unescapable. The only problem is that errors will be even more difficult to detect than before. Considering the persistent shortcomings in the criminal justice system, the question is whether it is trust or fear that makes people plead for leniency. He Xin points out that because the chances of an acquittal are highly unlikely, once prosecution is inevitable, it seems the lesser of two evils to take a plea deal.[105] Indeed, considering the conviction rate of over 99 per cent, 'troublemakers' are likely to be convicted at trial anyway and, on top of that, may receive a harsher punishment for making a fuss.

As discussed in the previous section, the involvement of lawyers should function as a check on the lawfulness of proceedings, but they can hardly play this role in reality. The procuratorates are the designated organs for legal supervision and at the same time play a dominant role in plea deals. They have the most powerful position in the plea leniency system, and this begs the question as to whether they are expected to self-supervise their work. There is more cooperation than mutual restraint among the three agencies. The procuratorial organs' powerful position in plea leniency was further cemented through the merger of the arrest and prosecution work, meaning this procuratorial department combines the two powers of arrest approval and decision over prosecution. Being faced with the prospect of spending a prolonged time in custody awaiting trial in the event of showing resistance, making a confession may be an attractive alternative.[106]

[103] Sun Changyong and Guo Hang (n 65) 53.

[104] 'Zuigao renmin fayuan zhang Yang Wanming: shiyong renzui renfa congkuan zhidu, tuijin qingzui shenli xiandaihua (Yang Wanming, Vice-President of the Supreme Court: applying the system of leniency in pleading guilty and accepting punishment, advancing the modernisation of trials for minor offences)' (n 96).

[105] He (n 43) 459.

[106] Sun Changyong and Guo Hang (n 65) 58–60. The power over arrest approvals had been shifted, again, to the Arrest and Prosecution Department, see Criminal Procedure Rules of the People's Procuratorate (Amended by the Supreme People's Procuratorate on 30 December 2019, No. 4 [2019]) art 8.

The risk of being taken into custody pending trial may thus be another incentive for a suspect or defendant to consider a guilty plea. For those who are already in detention, a plea deal might be a chance to be set free.[107] As the previous discussions have shown, unlawful and arbitrary deprivations of liberty in criminal proceedings have long haunted Chinese authorities. Because the police are expected to crack cases and because unresolved cases will be detrimental to promotion, etc, pending cases meant that suspects and defendants often remained in custody for years – because such cases do not appear in any statistics. Another dilemma in such cases was that a court could not have given them a lesser sentence than the duration they had already spent in custody to avoid compensation claims; a relatively harsh punishment for a minor offence was thus not unusual. While the plea leniency mechanism may have a positive impact on the number of criminal suspects and defendants being unlawfully and arbitrarily deprived of personal liberty, it may increase indirect pressure to plead guilty.

However, the plea leniency system should influence the percentage of suspects and defendants being held in custody pending trial. To accommodate this new mechanism, the CPL 2018 indeed modified the social danger requirement and added a paragraph stating that the nature of the crime, the circumstances in which it was committed, and whether the suspect or defendant has confessed and accepts their punishment should be taken into account.[108] These circumstances could fall within the scope of non-social danger to allow for a clearer distinction between social danger and non-social danger cases when reviewing arrest requests.[109] The aim seems to be the improvement of evidence-based proof that an accused may pose a social danger,[110] in order to address the earlier mentioned practice of investigation authorities (the police) providing only evidential materials relating to conviction and sentencing to justify an arrest. Moreover, in the process of handling plea leniency cases, the procuratorates are now obliged to review the necessity of ongoing custody of suspects if they have pleaded leniency.[111]

From 2019 onwards, the nationwide percentage of non-arrest has reportedly increased from around 22 per cent in 2019, as shown in chapter five, to 41 per cent in 2023.[112] The gap between the number of persons being arrested and prosecuted in the same year has, again, widened. But the percentage remains high considering that most cases are disposed of through the plea leniency system. This suggests that people accused of relatively minor offences and guilty pleas are still being arrested.

[107] 2018 CPL, art 81(2); Guiding Opinions on the Application of the System of Accepting Guilt and Accepting Punishment 2019, s 6, paras 19-21.

[108] CPL 2018, art 81 (CPL 2012, art 79).

[109] The Supreme People's Procuratorate reorganised but only slightly clarified social danger instances of 'may commit a new crime', 'endangers national security, public security or social order', see arts 129 to 133 of the Criminal Procedure Rules of the People's Procuratorate (2019).

[110] ibid art 135.

[111] ibid art 270.

[112] '2023 nian quanguo jiancha jiguan zhuyao ban'an shuju (Main Data on Cases handled by the National Procuratorial Organs in 2023)' (n 87).

It should be observed that, in terms of protection of personal liberty, the CPL 2018 did not modify the review mechanisms, as outlined in chapter five.[113] It moreover failed to address the administrative nature of the arrest examination procedure, with a hearing still not being mandatory in most cases.[114] After the CPL 2012 was put into effect, scholars had continued to raise concerns as regards equality of arms between prosecution and defence, emphasising that the arrest examination should be transformed into a procedural hearing, regardless of whether the arrest powers are shifted to the courts.[115] The scope of arrest examination hearings remains very narrow and varies across regions due to a lack of financial and human resources.[116] Owing to the absence of effective oversight over pre-trial proceedings, Chinese scholars believe that hoping that authorities will respect the presumption of innocence when applying compulsory measures means 'asking a tiger for its skin'.[117]

Although the plea leniency system has arguably given the procuratorates more powers, there is no true empowerment of the defence to counterbalance state power. The legalisation of plea leniency in such a flawed system means a further pushback for the protection of human rights in the criminal process. This mechanism is a manifestation of efficient crime control.

## C. Presuming Guilt and Reinforcing Discipline Through Law

Even if the anti-corruption system targets only a certain group of suspects, it is nevertheless important to discuss it, as it indicates more clearly a departure from and rejection of international fair trial standards. This section is particularly concerned with the coercive powers in the investigation of corruption cases ascribed to the supervisory organs that emerged as part of the 2018 reform, as well as the emphasis on confession reliance and the integration of the policy of combining leniency with severity in the context of anti-corruption to further illustrate the more illiberal turn of criminal justice in China in the post-2012 era.

Before going into details, it may be helpful to briefly outline the previous anti-corruption system. It was described as a dual-track system, consisting of a party and a judicial track. The investigation of Party members was an extra-legal process, an intra-party mechanism (*shuanggui*), governed by Party regulations, and conducted by the

[113] CPL 2012, arts 93, 94, and 95 were renumbered (now CPL 2018, arts 95, 96, and 97).

[114] Article 88 of the CPL 2018 stipulates only three instances in which an interrogation is mandatory. Apart from adding cases of plea deals, 2019 SPP Criminal Procedure Rules retained the instances of mandatory interrogations as provided for by the 2012 SPP Criminal Procedure Rules, see art 280.

[115] Min Chunlei, 'Lun shencha daibu chengxu de susonghua (On the Legal Proceduralization of the Arrest Procedure)' [2016] *Law and Social Development* 62, 64.

[116] Zhang Zetao, 'Goujian zhongguoshi de tingzheng shencha daibu chengxu (Constructing the Hearing Procedure of Examination of Criminal Arrest with Chinese Characteristics)' (2018) 36 *Tribune of Political Science and Law* 18, 23–26; Min Chunlei (n 114) 65–66.

[117] Xi Danni, *Lun wuzui tuiding (On the Presumption of Innocence)* (Beijing, People's Court Press, 2015) 210–212.

Discipline and Inspection Commissions (DIC, *jiwei*), a party organ. After investigation, the case was handed over to the procuratorial organs and thus only then entered the formal legal process. In the other cases, meaning ordinary corruption cases not involving Party members, the investigation was in the hands of the procuratorial organs. However, this dual-track system, in which Party leaders were understood to play the dominant role, had faced a lot of criticism for being flawed and ineffective.[118]

A prominent case in point is Bo Xilai, a high-ranking Party official and member of the Politburo, who was targeted in 2012. He stood trial in August 2013. Even if Bo was not the only 'tiger' to be taken down, his case is interesting because it was touted as yet another crucial moment in China's 'rule of law' journey. As for the reasons, the alleged publicity and transparency and the relative length of the trial of four days were acclaimed as major improvements. Notwithstanding top leadership promises that his case would be handled in strict accordance with the law, Bo was initially extra-legally investigated by the Central Discipline and Inspection Commission and confessed under *shuanggui*. He was sentenced to lifelong imprisonment; his attempt to appeal the verdict was unsuccessful.[119] Bo could not choose his counsel freely, and because his confession was obtained during *shuanggui* – outside the regular process – there were concerns as to voluntariness not just by observers. Bo himself demanded the exclusion of his written materials, which were used as evidence in the case, saying they had been obtained under duress.[120] The complexities as to the evidence in his case cannot be outlined in detail at this point, but for many scholars it was precisely the use of such materials obtained during *shuanggui* in the legal process that was perceived as marginalisation of the legal process.

As already mentioned, in 2014, the Party Central called for a reform of the anti-corruption system. A trial run was initiated in November 2016 to cover three experimental locations, and a year later, a nationwide expansion of the reform of the national supervisory system and the establishment of supervisory commissions at all levels was put on the agenda.[121] To establish a normative framework for anti-corruption, a draft of a Supervision Law initially circulated in November 2017. However, constitutional scholars like Han Dayuan criticised that the law-making had not followed the principle of legal governance and questioned the constitutionality of the law because these new supervisory organs were not provided for by the Constitution.[122] In other words, a constitutional amendment was necessary first.

[118] Jinting Deng, 'The National Supervision Commission: A New Anti-Corruption Model in China' [2018] *International Journal of Law, Crime and Justice* 58, 58–59.

[119] Jerome A Cohen, 'Criminal Justice in China: From the Gang of Four to the Trial of Bo Xila' (Human Rights Watch 2013) www.hrw.org/news/2013/07/25/criminal-justice-china-gang-four-bo-xilai accessed 8 May 2021.

[120] Long Zongzhi, 'Bo Xilai'an shenpan zhong de ruogan zhengju fa wenti (Some Issues of Evidentiary Law in the Bo Xilai Trial)' [2013] *Law Science* 3, 3–5.

[121] Decision of the NPC Standing Committee on Pushing Forward the Pilot Reform of the State Supervisory System Across the Country (Adopted at the 13th Meeting of the Standing Committee of the Twelfth National People's Congress on 4 November 2017).

[122] Han Dayuan, '"Jiancha fa (cao'an)" quefa xianfa yiju (The Draft Supervision Law lacks a Constitutional Basis)' (*Weixin*, 12 November 2017) mp.weixin.qq.com/s?__biz=MzAxNDM2OTc0OQ==&mid=2650 …6bc1a&mpshare=1&scene=23&srcid=1112RNQsLpIKczMYnmdwZuli#rd accessed 1 August 2022.

In March 2018, a constitutional amendment established the National Supervisory Commission (*guojia jiancha weiyuanhui*), and the Supervision Law was adopted.[123]

The Supervision Law 2018 (SL 2018) enacted the supervision mechanism. However, the passage of this law raised questions as regards the relationship with the regular legal process and thus the Criminal Procedure Law.[124] While the supervisory system may indeed create legitimacy and increase standardisation of the anti-corruption work, the legal framework governing the procedure, which partly integrated Party practices, raises serious concerns with respect to fair trial.

The National Supervision Commission was established by integrating the anti-corruption force of the procuratorates with the disciplinary inspection system. In other words, they are now departments under the National Supervisory Commission's leadership.[125] This merger elevated the rank of the Party organisation into a national organisation, jointly working under two titles, even if sharing the same personnel.[126] Leaders of disciplinary inspection commissions often concurrently hold leadership positions in the supervisory commissions, often at the equivalent level; one team, two brands.[127] The National Supervisory Commission is the fourth branch of government, giving it the same constitutional status as the State Council, the Supreme People's Court and the Supreme People's Procuratorate. It is also responsible to the National People's Congress and its Standing Committee.[128] As a fourth and powerful player, the National Supervisory Commission has stirred up the other three agencies.[129] The new system is a single-track anti-corruption mechanism. It is the integration of the disciplinary inspection system, meaning the combination of party discipline and law, that suggests a greater Party influence on the newly established supervisory commissions. While observers outside of China have deemed this to further blur the lines between Party and state, or tighten Party control over the state,[130] the idea behind the centralisation and consolidation was to reduce local Party control over anti-corruption work.[131]

As already indicated, the most significant change is the transfer of the power to investigate duty-related crimes from the procuratorial to the supervisory organs. Indeed, the supervisory organs are not only in charge of investigating corruption

[123] Supervision Law of 20 March 2018.

[124] Fan Chongyi (n 32); Bian Jianlin, 'Peihe yu zhiyue: jiancha diaocha yu xingshi susong de jiejie (Cooperation and Constraints: the Nexus between Inspection Investigations and Criminal Proceedings)' [2019] *Studies in Law and Business* 15.

[125] Li Li and Peng Wang, 'From Institutional Interaction to Institutional Integration: The National Supervisory Commission and China's New Anti-Corruption Model' [2019] *The China Quarterly* 967.

[126] ibid 968.

[127] Li and Wang (n 124) 980.

[128] Constitution 1982 (2018 Amendment), arts 123, 125, and 126.

[129] Li and Wang (n 124) 982–983.

[130] Ling Li, 'The "Organisational Weapon" of the Chinese Communist Party: China's Disciplinary Regime from Mao to Xi Jinping' in Rogier Creemers and Susan Trevaskes (eds), *Law and the Party in China: Ideology and Organisation* (Cambridge, Cambridge University Press, 2021) 206–209.

[131] Deng (n 117) 60.

cases but also supervising all state officials, including their adherence to Party discipline. The supervisory organs thus hold two main powers, ie, supervision and investigation.[132] To further guide the work of the supervisory organs, the National Supervisory Commission issued more detailed provisions in 2021.[133] However, there is still considerable overlap between the investigation competences of procuratorial and supervisory organs because the former were not completely stripped of their power to investigate duty-related offences (as part of their legal supervision power), but the investigation of corruption cases is now in the hands of the latter.[134] And even if the people's procuratorates were deprived of their power to investigate corruption cases, they still monopolise the power of public prosecution, and they may request the relevant supervisory organ to conduct supplementary investigation or even decide to conduct further investigation themselves.[135]

There has been a debate, largely academic, about the nature of the power these new organs possess or about the question of where precisely the difference between the supervisory and procuratorial powers lies. The supervision power is understood to be distinct from the procuratorial legal supervision power. The supervisory commissions have law enforcement powers, as they are authorised to investigate corruption cases and impose sanctions. In the view of Zhong Tao, the most obvious distinction would lie in the supervisory commission's power to investigate individual persons, while the procuratorial legal supervision power covers the actions of state agencies, police and courts. It moreover oversees all state officials' observance of Party discipline and moral conduct, whereas the procuratorates would only check on the lawfulness of actions of state agencies. Therefore, these two powers were complementary not conflicting, and the new anti-corruption investigation would more clearly separate the investigation from the prosecution power.[136] This illustrates that the supervisory system is of a preventive nature, whereas the procuratorates conduct ex post supervision over state agencies' actions. However, even if it has not impacted the procuratorial legal supervision power as such, it has brought considerable challenges thereof.

In the phase of investigating duty-related violations or crimes, supervisory organs should work together with the other three agencies and may seek assistance also from the procuratorial organs.[137] However, the somewhat unclear relationship between these two in the phase of supervisory investigation has led to many questions. As Li Fenfei has pointed out, the procuratorial organs can and should

[132] SL 2018, art 3.

[133] Implementation Regulations for the PRC Supervision Law (Adopted by the National Supervisory Commission on 20 July 2021), art 10.

[134] SL 2018, art 11; Zhiyuan Guo, 'Anti-Corruption Mechanisms in China after the Supervision Law' [2023] *Journal of Economic Criminology* 1, 3.

[135] CPL 2018, art 170; SL 2018, art 47.

[136] Zhong Tao, 'Jiancha jiandu he jiancha jiandu de guanxi (Relationship between Procuratorial Supervision and Supervisory Supervision)' (*People's Procuratorate of Weibin*, 29 January 2019) www.sn.jcy.gov.cn/bjswbq/swdy/201901/t20190129_105037.html accessed 4 May 2020.

[137] SL 2018, art 4; Criminal Procedure Rules of the People's Procuratorate (2019), art 256(2).

lead the supervisory investigation, as he sees a risk of 'investigation-centralism', which evidently undermines the earlier mentioned efforts of trial-centralism. The Supervision Law has established a new model of 'investigation-prosecution' (*diaocha – gongsu*), but the concrete relationship remains unclear, especially the role of the procuratorates in the supervisory investigation. Although it effectively is the same as criminal investigation (*zhencha*), the supervisory commissions do not face the constraints of the Criminal Procedure Law. Therefore, it is also unclear how the procuratorial legal supervision power extends to supervisory investigation, even though it could improve the quality of case handling and the review of the lawfulness of procedures, which would be crucial to secure convictions.[138]

As part of the investigation (*diaocha*) power, supervisory organs collect evidential materials,[139] which may be used as evidence in criminal proceedings.[140] They may moreover freeze property,[141] conduct searches of the body or residences, among others.[142] Furthermore, supervisory organs may enforce a form of incommunicado confinement by taking the 'holding measure' (*liuzhi*), ie, confinement, without external (judicial) supervision. Although family members must generally be notified about the detention within 24 hours, the law allows for broad exceptions where there is a risk of destruction or falsification of evidence or other obstructions of the investigation.[143] Even more worrying, there is no external review of this measure.[144] A provision ensuring access to a lawyer is also missing from the new law. As a result, suspects held are de facto held in incommunicado confinement, which increases the risk of torture. The SL 2018 does not regulate the interrogation procedure but only states that 'time and length' should be 'reasonable'.[145] With the possibility of being placed in a form of incommunicado detention and without the right to legal counsel, the SL 2018 states that an accused may be 'required' to make statements about the allegations and to '*confess* truthfully to the accusations' (*rushi gongshu shexian fazui*).[146] In other words, these powers the supervisory organs hold are substantially comparable to those of the police in the regular process.

The procuratorates remain largely excluded from the supervisory investigation after a case has been filed, meaning when procedures are formally initiated, and only express influences in the phase of reviewing a case for prosecution, during which it conducts ex post review of the supervisory commission's actions.[147] Since the supervisory organs are neither a judicial nor an administrative organ, their

[138] Li Fenfei, 'Zhiwu fanzui diaocha zhong de jiancha yindao wenti yanjiu (A Study on the Question of how the Procuratorial Guides the Investigation of Duty-Related Offences)' [2019] *Journal of Comparative Law* 28, 28–29, 30–31.
[139] SL 2018, art 18.
[140] SL 2018, art 33.
[141] SL 2018, arts 23 and 25.
[142] SL 2018, art 24.
[143] SL 2018, art 44.
[144] SL 2018, art 60.
[145] SL 2018, art 44.
[146] See SL 2018, art 20.
[147] Li Fenfei (n 137) 37–38.

investigation power is neither criminal nor administrative but is of a hybrid nature, combining party discipline investigation, political discipline investigation and criminal investigation. The power of supervision and investigation would have a distinct 'political flavour', which would make it difficult to implement procuratorial-led investigations. Due to lacking supervision, Li Fenfei thus believes that there is a risk of secrecy and rights violations in the supervisory mechanism.[148]

Indeed, it is startling that the Supervision Law is characterised by a significant lack of minimum fair trial guarantees, and there is not even an attempt to hide it. The law has introduced a pre-trial presumption of guilt. As shown above, it places a burden on the accused to prove their own guilt. In cases of state officials, Chinese legislation very early had already codified a reversed onus, requiring such an accused to explain the sources of illicit enrichment.[149] But due to the missing link to the existing safeguards under the Criminal Procedure Law, it appears unlikely that the accused can invoke this law in the phase of investigation. Especially in corruption cases, authorities have always heavily relied on confessions as the 'king of evidence' to secure conviction,[150] but the educational function of a confession was made even clearer by the expressive denial of silence. The chances to challenge deprivations of personal liberty under the holding measure are also bleak, and protections are much weaker than those under the Criminal Procedure Law. In the investigation phase, a person can only apply for internal review within the supervisory system,[151] and if a case is transferred to the procuratorial organs and if the supervisory suspect was held (*liuzhi*), detention (*juliu*) must be applied, and the procurator may decide to arrest (*daibu*) the criminal suspect.[152] This almost automatic extension of confinement demonstrates that liberty ought to be the exception.

This educational function of the law is further illustrated by the ranking of punishments. The supervisory system combines severity with leniency by adopting a tiering system of case handling, ranging from education and criticism in minor cases of duty-related violations taking precedence over harsher sanctions and eventually criminal punishment.[153] Indeed, plea leniency is applicable in supervisory cases as well, but the threshold is different from the regular process. In addition to pleading guilty and accepting punishment, as outlined in the previous sections, the person under supervisory investigation must return ill-gotten gains or make a meritorious contribution, or the case involves national interests; especially the latter of course is very vague and lacks predictability.[154]

[148] ibid 35.
[149] See art 11 of the Supplementary Provisions on the Punishment of Corruption and Bribery Offenses, Adopted by the NPC Standing Committee on 21 January 1988, No. 63 [1988]); art 395 of the Criminal Law 1997 (CL 1997).
[150] Li Fenfei (n 137) 30.
[151] SL 2018, art 60.
[152] CPL 2018, art 170; SL 2018, art 47.
[153] SL 2018, art 45.
[154] SL 2018, art 31. A 'lenient punishment' may moreover be recommended if a person under investigation provides relevant clues conducive for the investigation of other cases, see art 32 of the SL 2018.

There are many caveats to plea leniency under the Supervision Law. It only refers to substantive leniency ('lenient punishment') in a very abstract and principled way, while the law makes no reference to procedural leniency ('lenient treatment')[155] in the sense of whether being eligible for speedier procedures or as a criterion when applying compulsory measures. This is the most obvious difference. The 'admission of guilt and acceptance of punishment' in the law is not treated as a separate mitigating circumstance. Rather, it is confused with lenient circumstances such as self-surrender or the returning of illegal gains. In other words, these are not additional circumstances that will be considered on top of admitting guilt and accepting punishment. However, these additional requirements are not new; the Supervision Law has absorbed the mitigating circumstances of the Criminal Law, and it has combined the Criminal Procedure Law and Criminal Law's requirements of plea leniency.[156]

However, the linkage to the regular process also remains partly unclear. Crucially, even if far from perfection, the safeguards to ensure voluntariness of guilty pleas in the pretrial phases of the regular process, eg, the recording or notification requirements, do not apply to supervisory investigations. Whether a person meets the conditions of plea leniency under the Supervision Law appears to reside in the hands of the supervisory commission, with the procuratorates and courts being largely unable to understand the reasons for this determination. For example, if a supervisory suspect admits guilt and accepts punishment during investigation but – in the view of the supervisory organ – cannot meet the requirements for leniency, this should be noted in the prosecution opinion.[157] Yet, it is unclear whether a procuratorate or a court can access all the relevant materials from the supervisory organ or send a case back for supplementary investigation. Regarding notification requirements, in contrast to the regular process, relevant provisions make no reference as to whether the supervisory organ should ensure that an investigated person understands the consequences of pleading guilty.[158] Interestingly, while the police cannot make a concrete leniency promise in the regular process, the supervisory organs appear to hold the power over sentencing recommendations, even though such decisions are not exclusively made by the handling supervisory organ but must be made collectively and approved by the next higher.[159]

In 2020, four agencies jointly issued provisions that aimed to clarify the interplay between supervisory and criminal proceedings. In terms of plea leniency,

[155] CPL 2018, art 15.

[156] Regulations on the Implementation of the PRC Supervision Law, Adopted on 20 July 2021 (No. 1 [2021] of the National Supervisory Commission) arts 83, 213, and 219; Zeng Zhijun and Fang Wen, 'Renzui renfa congkuan zhidu zai jiancha yu sifa zhong xianjie de xietiao yanjiu (A study on the Coordination of the Convergence of the System of Leniency for Pleading Guilty and Accepting Punishment with Supervision and Justice)' (*China Behaviour Law Association*, 25 September 2023) www.lawcd.net/xuehuidongtai/592.html accessed 8 January 2024.

[157] ibid art 219.

[158] ibid art 83.

[159] SL 2018, art 31; ibid art 213; Zeng and Fang (n 156).

they emphasise the distinctiveness of the plea leniency systems in both laws. Indeed, the supervisory commissions are called on to waive punishment only in exceptional cases, and the higher threshold to meet the conditions for lenient punishment under the Supervision Law is emphasised. Moreover, the supervisory commissions' predominant role in plea leniency is clearly highlighted. In making a decision, they must also consider Party discipline and policies. Thus, political factors play a role here.[160] Therefore, plea leniency in the supervisory mechanism is a political-legal exercise. In a way, all this makes sense, as corruption has been deemed a major threat to the leadership of the CCP and thus not minor or ordinary cases that fall within the scope of 'contradictions among the people'.

In terms of rights violations in the phase of supervisory investigations, the SL 2018, like the Criminal Procedure Law, prohibits the extortion of confessions by torture or other illegal means, as well as the unlawful deprivation of personal liberty, and stipulates that the supervisory personnel should be held accountable.[161] However, there has been a debate as to the qualification of the supervisory personnel as 'judicial personnel' (*sifa gongyuo renyuan*) in accordance with the Criminal Law to hold them legally liable for rights violations. While supervisory commissions are neither judicial nor administrative organs but rather political organs per definition, Li Xiang argues that they could and should be interpreted to fall within the scope of judicial personnel due to their investigation powers;[162] the previous chapters have shown that the exclusion of evidence is already difficult in the regular process. In the light of the secrecy of the supervisory investigation and the even weaker position of the accused, it is arguably even more difficult to challenge the legality of the evidence obtained by the supervision commissions in the investigation at a later stage of the proceedings.

After the Supervision Law was put into effect, the case of former INTERPOL president and high-ranking Party official Meng Hongwei was among the first to be handled under the new legal framework. He disappeared in September 2018 upon his arrival in Beijing, and it was later announced that he had been placed under investigation and held (*liuzhi*) at a secret place for months before re-emerging and publicly showing repentance. Meng was later sentenced to 13.5 years in prison for corruption; he did not appeal the verdict.[163] In his case, the lines between informal and formal means were clearly blurred, as Meng first disappeared only to reappear shortly before the opening of the trial so that any claims of strict adherence to the law are not sound. As part of the party-state's anti-corruption sweep, a revival

[160] Opinions on Strengthening and Improving the Mechanism for the Linkage between Supervisory Law Enforcement and Criminal Justice (for Trial Implementation) s 7, paras 1 and 2.

[161] SL 2018, arts 65(4), (7) and 66.

[162] Criminal Law, art 247; Li Xiang, '"Jiancha fa" shishi dui xingshi shiti fa de yingxiang ji wanshan (Impact of the implementation of the "Supervision Law" on Substantive Criminal Law and its Improvement)' [2019] *Journal of Southeast University (Philosophy and Social Science)* 97, 98–99.

[163] Chris Buckley, 'Ex-President of Interpol Is Sent to Prison for Bribery in China' *New York Times* (21 January 2020) www.nytimes.com/2020/01/21/world/asia/interpol-china-meng-hongwei.html accessed 2 February 2024.

of public denunciation of guilt in the form of TV confessions or publicly showing repentance with respect to (what is deemed) high-profile cases is observable, especially in the context of cases of alleged 'self-surrender' (*zishou*).[164]

Theoretically, the CPL 2018 enabled the conduct of a trial in absentia with respect to cases involving duty-related offences, national security or terrorism.[165] However, trial *in absentia* seems to have almost no practical significance, at least not so far. After the 2018 reforms, there has been only one known case where a fugitive was convicted *in absentia*. Cheng Sanchang was one of China's most wanted fugitives and an INTERPOL Red Notice subject. He reportedly had been on the run since 2001 and was put on China's '100 most wanted list' in 2015. After the supervisory reforms in 2018, his case was investigated. In 2022, the Zhengzhou Municipal Intermediate People's Court sentenced him to 12 years in prison for embezzlement *in absentia*. His case was coined another landmark case in China's 'rule of law' efforts, meaning combating corruption through legal means.[166]

A few years after the enactment of the SL 2018, an overhaul of the law was deemed necessary to make improvements and accommodate actual needs. Commenting on the draft Supervision Law of September 2024, Liu Jinguo, who heads the National Supervisory Commission, stressed that the law-making followed the 'correct political orientation', meaning the will of the Party was transformed into the state's will through legal procedures, and the supervisory system would have been a 'top level design', meaning full central control over law-making.[167]

In December 2024, the legislator adopted a refined version of the Supervision Law (SL 2024). A comparison between the 2018 and 2024 versions of the law reveals that the changes focused on the broadening of supervisory investigation powers with respect to compulsory measures.[168] Even if the SL 2024 integrated the constitutional human rights protection clause,[169] and even though the legislator has touted these changes as improvements in terms of legalisation of anti-corruption work,[170] the SL 2024 introduced new coercive measures that are functionally comparable to those that exist in the regular criminal process. For example, the revised law empowers supervisory organs to compel the appearance

[164] See, eg, Yunshu Li, 'Guojia jianwei yindu diyi ren yin jiji peihe, zhudong tui zang qing pan (First National Supervisory Commission extradited person received a Light Sentence for Actively Cooperating and Voluntarily returning Stolen Goods)' *Xinhua* (28 August 2020) www.xinhuanet.com/politics/2020-08/28/c_1126421972.htm accessed 5 June 2021.

[165] See ch 3 of the CPL 2018.

[166] 'Shi da anjian zhi Cheng Sanchang tanwu quexi shenpan an: jingwai bushi fawai, fawang jiushi tianwang (One of the Top Ten Cases: Cheng Sanchang's Corruption Trial in absentia: no Law outside the Country, the Law is the SkyNet)' *Beijing Daily* (1 February 2023) xinwen.bjd.com.cn/content/s63da2638e4b043bcce2c55bb.html accessed 13 January 2024.

[167] 'Explanations on the PRC Supervision Law (Draft Amendment) 10 September 2024' www.npc.gov.cn/npc/c2/c30834/202412/t20241225_442031.html accessed 16 January 2025.

[168] For a similar observation and a very helpful overview, see 'Supervision Law 2024 Revisions – Comparison of New vs. Old' (*China Law Translate*, 26 December 2024) www.chinalawtranslate.com/en/supervision-law-2025/ accessed 20 February 2025.

[169] SL 2024, art 5.

[170] 'Explanations on the PRC Supervision Law (Draft Amendment) 10 September 2024' (n 166).

(*qiangzhi dao'an*) of investigation subjects to enhance the 'authority of supervisory law enforcement'. Three new compulsory measures were added. The SL 2024 enables the supervisory organs to take a supervisory suspect into confinement for up to seven days – a measure comparable to police detention (*juliu*) in the regular legal process, but the supervisory organs do not need to produce a warrant, nor is there any notification requirement with respect to this measure in the SL 2024. Furthermore, the measure of 'order release pending investigation' (*zeling hou cha*) is comparable to bail in the regular criminal process, also in terms of conditions; and 'protective care' (*guan hu*), which is a measure that may be applied to investigated suspects for up to 24 hours before taking the holding measure (*liuzhi*), if there is a risk of obstruction of proceedings through suicide or flight. It moreover relaxed the time limits of holding (*liuzhi*) a supervisory suspect, which were reportedly too tight under the SL 2018, leading to problems in case handling. The possibility to apply for changes to compulsory measures appears to provide weak protection for an accused in view of the supervisory powers.[171] These new measures will likely lead to prolonged incommunicado detention in the phase of supervisory investigation.

Recalling the previous discussion about the Party's conception of legal governance, the supervision mechanism is fair – from an official point of view. Recalling the discussion about the relationship of law and morality in the context of legal governance, state officials assume a vanguard role in showing spotless discipline and obedience. They are expected to observe higher morals than 'ordinary' people; where those morals are violated, they are not considered to enjoy the same procedural safeguards as 'ordinary' citizens, which is justified by claiming to deliver fairness for the people. And, as discussed, the socialist rule of law sets no limits to rights restrictions. Moreover, fairness here is not procedural fairness, and international fair trial standards ought not to be the benchmark. This marked a clear departure from the reform era. The party-state has codified an idea of fairness that reflects its understanding of what ought to be fair, but it is not in line with international standards of fairness. The supervisory procedure presents a pure crime control model, a self-contained system that operates within a hybrid model of due process and crime control.

## III. Conclusions

Chapter five elaborated on how the illiberal shift that became tangible during the 2012 reform further expressed influence during the 2018 reform. This chapter has shown how, in the aftermath of the CPL 2012, the Party's elevated status as a distinctive feature of the 'socialist rule of law with Chinese characteristics' and the only agent through which it can be realised has expressed influence in the sphere

[171] ibid.

of criminal justice. As ideological gatekeepers, the Party has carved out specifically Chinese values that ought to be codified and thus guide lawmaking. This monopolisation over the meaning of values or legal governance closed the discursive vacuum that scholars could use in the reform era to lobby for presumption of innocence. Even if the official discourse frames the latest reform as progress due to further legalisation or standardisation of proceedings, the chapter has demonstrated that the changes indicate a further cementation of crime control and illiberalism. The CPL 2018 was largely devoted to implementing the new political agenda of the Party Central. Yet, the codification of an anti-corruption mechanism meant a legalisation of an unfair trial, and the plea leniency mechanism is a symbol of efficiency and an institutionalisation of the longstanding practice of confession reliance and the policy of combining leniency with severity. If anything, this reform has exacerbated existing problems. Indeed, the CPL 2018 poses new challenges to any future acceptance of the presumption of innocence in China.

# 7

# Concluding Remarks

This book has shed light on the fate of the presumption of innocence from the Mao era to today. I started this book by quoting a Chinese law professor, saying that 'There is no presumption of innocence in China.'[1] In the introduction, I outlined the argument that China has no presumption of innocence. So, it seems – as part of my concluding remarks – it is time to succinctly summarise the reasons. My book focused on the pre-trial phases of criminal proceedings, as observers have attributed most shortcomings to these early phases of proceedings due to powerful state agencies and the weak position of the accused, ie, the lack of equality of arms, while the trial itself is marginalised. Considering the high conviction rate, once a case is prosecuted, an acquittal is nearly impossible. Indeed, despite decades of criminal justice reforms, persistent shortcomings or problems have never been tackled at their roots and include the lack of effective defence, coerced confessions, and arbitrary and unlawful deprivations of personal liberty, to name a few. This book therefore paid particular attention to criminal pre-trial proceedings in China with respect to presumption of innocence. Looking at the processes of law-making and negotiations between scholars and party-state agencies from a discursive angle has deepened our understanding of the dynamics between the different actors that appear as stakeholders in lawmaking.

The main objective of chapter two was to illustrate the importance of the presumption of innocence. Considering the bottom-up conception of fairness, the presumption of innocence is not only a centrally important fair trial safeguard, but it is also rendered non-negotiable, as derogations from it are made almost impossible in practice due to the interplay of fair trial safeguards. Although the right to a fair trial with the presumption of innocence allows for flexible implementation, there are some key requirements that maintain the *essence* of fairness, which ultimately aim to protect the integrity and dignity of the accused. This includes the right to defence, protection against torture, the right to silence, and prohibition against self-incrimination. This book has supported a broad approach to presumption of innocence for a reason, encompassing the three dimensions of a rule, a right and a principle. While such a broad approach is not universally embraced, the presumption of innocence develops its full moral force only when recognising this broader moral legal principle. As a moral legal principle, it manifests the rule of law and thus suggests limits on state power.

[1] Conversation with a Chinese law professor#1 (Site A).

The Chinese criminal justice system is embedded in an autocratic system, and it is neither designed nor built on the premise of human rights protection. This book has shown that the debates on criminal justice in the late 1970s developed in parallel and independently from human rights discourses, even though the idea of national conditions was already a basic mantra of legal reforms, ie, the official stance of not blindly copying other systems but rather combining national conditions with foreign experience. The official conception of human rights 'with Chinese characteristics' follows the same premise. As demonstrated, both rest on the Marxist theory of historical and dialectical materialism, and the idea of a gradual development (historical materialism) is a claim of the official doctrine of national conditions, which has also shaped the understanding of rights protection in criminal process. Admittedly, a difficulty surely is that the party-state, as the sole determinator of what ought to constitute any national condition(s), has not explained – beyond the primary stage of socialism – what it or they ought to be. And even if official and academic discourses have divided national conditions vaguely into the historical, social, economic and cultural conditions, their interpretation depends on who invokes the claim of national conditions to argue either in one or the other direction. The book used the example of presumption of innocence to better understand how the doctrine of national conditions is applied in specific instances.

As shown in chapter three, discourses on human rights with 'Chinese characteristics' had not yet entered the sphere of criminal justice. In the Mao era, a tentative discourse on presumption of innocence was – understandably – short-lived and highly politicised due to waves of internal consolidation and re-organisation, as well as the many political campaigns. Mao himself was a declared anti-legalist, even if the party-state made some modest efforts to establish formal laws, procedures, and institutions in the mid-1950s. However, this more liberal atmosphere facilitated the first round of academic discourse on the presumption of innocence in China. Especially this short period gives a glimpse into different ideas of criminal justice and shows that there were more diverse than one may perhaps expect. In a way, the rejection of both the 'feudal' presumption of guilt and the 'bourgeois' presumption of innocence called for an alternative principle of fairness and truth-seeking. The CPL drafts from the 1950s and 1960s reveal that different proposals were made, which suggests that there was a debate and differing views about the construct and the values on which the administration of justice should rest. These drafts also reflect the fluidity of politics at the time. While the CPL draft (1957) showed more signs and indeed provided for an explicit presumption of innocence provision and overall showed more signs of due process, the drafts from the 1960s abandoned it and instead installed the principle of seeking truth from facts and stressed crime control. Those scholars, discussed in this book, who had advocated the presumption of innocence were later targeted by the Anti-Rightist Campaign (1957–58) that had brought the first round to a standstill. The turmoil of the Mao era did not allow for an expansion of these tentative debates.

The second phase of presumption of innocence discourses began in the late 1970s, after the Cultural Revolution (1966–76) that coincided with the end of the Mao era. The decision of the Third Plenum in 1978 under the leadership of Deng Xiaoping to foster the development of a socialist legal system had encouraged official and academic discourses on human rights and criminal justice, but these two initially developed in parallel strands. In the reform era, stability was emphasised to support economic development, and with the official end of the class struggle and the elevation of law over politics, the presumption of innocence gained new ground. The Party did step back, to some degree, and it allowed some more room for pluralistic discourses. At the time, recovering from the Cultural Revolution, Chinese scholars and Party leaders were not only more interested but also more dependent on international linkages and encouraged scholars to engage in research on the construction of a legal system.

In 1979, China's first Criminal Procedure law (CPL 1979) was enacted. The law was based on the more illiberal CPL drafts from the 1960s, meaning a choice was made not to use the CPL draft (1957). The CPL 1979 was greatly based on the idea of pursuing objective truth, as reflected in the principle of seeking truth from facts that was enshrined in the law – as an axiomatic national condition. Therefore, the official view was not to presume anything but instead to seek truth from facts, presenting these two as incompatible principles of criminal justice, even though they can exist alongside. Moreover, another common argument against the presumption of innocence was that it was simply obsolete, as especially the right to defence would provide sufficient protection. Some misconceptions of presumption of innocence had survived and were revived in the early reform era, most prominently the understanding of presumption of innocence as being a factually based presumption. This understanding led to the view of incompatibility of the two principles or the idea of a presumption of innocence but only in doubtful cases. At the time, scholars were critically examining the different expressions of the presumption of innocence in international discourses and human rights instruments. It should be borne in mind that academia was still recovering from the turmoil of the Mao era and began to seriously study the presumption of innocence.

Perhaps because the Party leaders did not like the use of 'presumptions', in the eyes of scholars, Beccaria's formulation seemed attractive and less tricky, as no recognition of a *presumption* of innocence was needed, whereas the UDHR formulation was deemed unreasonable. Consequently, scholars developed the idea of only adopting what were deemed the 'reasonable' elements, which very early reflected the idea of accommodating national conditions. While the label of 'presumption' was viewed with scepticism, the rule of presumption of innocence, ie, the evidential aspects, was generally accepted, or the idea that an accused should be found guilty in accordance with the prescribed procedure. Indeed, especially the evidence rules were used to argue that the CPL 1979 had manifested the expression of presumption of innocence. However, the law clearly fell short of international fair trial standards and showed no signs of presumption of innocence. Conversely, it retained socialist attitudes towards law, especially the educational function of law, and stressed crime control. However, the hope with which reform-minded scholars studied the law at the time may be understandable because it was seen only as the beginning, not the end, of a functioning criminal justice system.

Chapter four, then, has shown how human rights entered the sphere of criminal justice. In fact, many theorists and practitioners agreed that the CPL 1979 was flawed in the first place, and a first overhaul was thus soon discussed and supported by the Party Central. In the early 1990s, domestic scholarship on 'improving human rights' (*wanshan renquan*) in the criminal justice process was skyrocketing. There were different reasons for the growing reference to human rights in the context of criminal justice. From the late 1980s onwards, the Chinese government turned towards the international human rights regime and signed and/or ratified several international human rights treaties. This move has led to a greater convergence of legal systems and influenced academic discourses in China. Especially the issuance of the 1991 White Paper marked a crucial moment for scholars in China. While the idea of national conditions already existed in the context of criminal justice because it is the basic tenet of legal reforms, it crucially connected the spheres of human rights and criminal justice. The recognition that China had deficits in human rights protection was the green light for academia to push ahead with human rights research and examine the situation in the context of criminal justice. Moreover, assuming a more rights-based language in their writings, scholars in China reviewed the hostility with which the presumption of innocence was met largely on ideological and political grounds in the Mao era and early years of the reform era.

Even if not challenging the official position of national conditions, scholars artfully used the official parlance – meaning the interplay between base and superstructure – to argue in favour of better rights protections. The scholars who were entrusted with the production of a Criminal Procedure Law draft proposal supported the adoption of a provision on presumption of innocence, as well as associated key safeguards. Indeed, for many reform-oriented scholars, national conditions (be they economic, social, or cultural conditions) were not seen as an obstacle to the implementation of the label of presumption of innocence. In contrast, party-state agents have used national conditions as a codeword for political imperatives. They especially invoked the alleged limited capacities to argue against a broadening of procedural safeguards, notably key safeguards to realise presumption of innocence such as a right to silence, better personal liberty protections, or unlimited access to legal counsel, saying that they would overburden the system and lead to chaos. This echoed the Party's approved priorities to maintain stability and control and vested state agencies with a powerful rhetoric to suppress procedural safeguards by using the notion of national conditions.

The legislator did not follow the scholarly proposal and insisted that no presumption was needed, claiming the law had properly accommodated the socio-economic changes (ie, China's changing conditions). Of course, this is not to suggest that there was always agreement among scholars, and, in many areas, scholars disagreed on the precise extent to which procedural safeguards should be adopted in the light of alleged national conditions. However, it is fair to say that many scholars in the reform era were supportive of adopting fundamental fair trial guarantees, even if remaining pragmatic or moderate in many respects.

The official doctrine of national conditions had triumphed over presumption of innocence claims in the making of the CPL 1996, and even if it is difficult to maintain that the law had embraced the presumption of innocence, it is nonetheless fair to say that it showed signs of improvements in terms of procedural safeguards, including criminal defence or personal liberty protection, which further fuelled hopes that – eventually – the domestic system will comply with international fair trial standards. Interestingly, the view of a presumption of innocence 'with Chinese characteristics', one that echoes national conditions, received growing support from the 1990s onwards, crucially enabled by the adoption of Article 12 CPL 1996, stipulating the exclusive adjudication power of courts, and soon became the dominant view among scholars. Certain scholars believed that the CPL 1996 was the beginning of a presumption of innocence 'with Chinese characteristics', suggesting a partial acceptance of these safeguards, reflecting national conditions. Again, this must not necessarily indicate a rejection of international presumption of innocence standards; it may also have been motivated by optimism that a gradual transformation will be possible. Such optimism was not unfounded. In the late 1990s, not least due to the Chinese government's commitment to law-based governance and the signature to the ICCPR, many scholars believed that the ratification, and thus full compliance with the Covenant, was only a question of time.

Chapter five demonstrated the lengthy process of negotiations over the second overhaul of the Criminal Procedure Law. Although a refinement of the law was already underway since 2003, disagreements and power struggles amongst the stakeholders brought the lawmaking to a halt. Although the legislator did not formally assign scholars with the making of a refined law, scholars in China produced an extensive corpus of literature during the almost ten years and even compiled complete draft proposals. The chapter was especially devoted to highlighting these efforts. Even if the 1996 CPL reform was marked by a triumph of the official doctrine of national conditions over international presumption of innocence standards, scholars used the idea of a presumption of innocence 'with Chinese characteristics' to advocate either further or full acceptance. Well into the reform era, scholars had fully grasped the rationale of presumption of innocence, and certain scholars began to advocate the broader dimension of principle, as well as stressing the right to presumption of innocence. Conflicts were inevitable, and so it may not be surprising that the tensions between the official doctrine of national conditions and broader human rights claims steadily grew. In a way, the continued insistence on national conditions and thus the pressure to move within the cage of this rhetoric meant that scholars – perhaps out of conviction, perhaps because it was the only way to find a compromise among all stakeholders – dismantled the presumption of innocence into different elements. While this is possible because it is realised through a set of safeguards, without key safeguards like an effective right to silence and true equality of arms, the presumption of innocence is rendered meaningless.

However, it was precisely the principle of and the right to presumption of innocence with its underlying liberalism that would have challenged the Party's and the state's agencies' monopoly on power and could not mobilise sufficient support. In 2012, criminal justice was at a crossroads: the question was which direction criminal procedural law would take. It took a rather more illiberal direction. Especially individual safeguards like the right to silence or the habeas corpus guarantee that would have empowered accused persons in criminal proceedings could be suppressed by invoking the rhetoric of national conditions. Due to growing concerns of national security, such calls were supported by the Party Central, which demonstrates the political-legal nature of criminal justice in China. Although the CPL 2012 showed some signs of improvements, eg, it integrated a narrow privilege against self-incrimination, the three agencies opposed the adoption of a right to silence, and the duty to cooperate was maintained. Furthermore, while the CPL 2012 made some improvements in terms of personal liberty, exclusionary rules or the criminal defence system, their implementation remains weak due to many normative and institutional weaknesses, and the law installed potential counter-norms by enabling incommunicado confinement. Therefore, even the claim of a fragile presumption of innocence in the CPL 2012 is not very sound.

Chapter six elaborated on how this illiberal turn further expressed influence during the 2018 reform of the Criminal Procedure Law. Even if the party-state had stepped back a little in the reform era, it had never abandoned its autocratic and instrumentalist views on law and human rights, but pragmatism could suppress them for a while. Rather, they had facilitated the illiberal turn or autocratisation of the legal system. Moreover, the Party launched a crackdown on the civil society and installed ideological gatekeepers. These developments have made advocacy for international fair trial and presumption of innocence standards more difficult. On the discursive level, academic discourses peaked in the mid- to late 2000s and were in decline, especially after the 2012 reform. Indeed, after the CPL 2012 was put into effect, domestic research has not added much to the previous scholarship, and research on China's compliance with international human rights norms, especially the ICCPR, has decreased. Today, as can be seen by the more recent Chinese scholarship on criminal justice, 'Chinese' values – not international human rights law – ought to be the most important point of reference. In the so-called 'New Era', with the rise of especially 'Chinese' values, ie, the Socialist Core Values, on which laws and institutions should rest, meant a further pushback for the already limited freedoms. This marked a clear departure from the previously more open atmosphere. Especially the Party's elevated role as lawmaker and highest moral authority, as part of the agenda of law-based governance, expressed influence during the 2018 reform.

Even if the official discourse frames the latest reform as progress due to further legalisation or standardisation of proceedings, the CPL 2018 was largely devoted to implementing the new political agenda of the Party Central, and the changes indicate a further return to crime control and illiberalism. The codification of an anti-corruption mechanism meant a legalisation of an unfair trial, and the plea leniency mechanism is a symbol of efficiency and an institutionalisation of the longstanding practice of confession reliance and the policy of combining leniency with severity. If anything, this reform has exacerbated existing problems. It is observable that these developments have also impacted the underlying values of criminal justice, crucially supported by the Party Central.

While legal reforms are still underway, the focus seems to have shifted towards perfecting the criminal justice system 'with Chinese characteristics'. In September 2023, the Standing Committee of the 14th NPC put a fourth revision of the Criminal Procedure Law on the five-year legislative agenda.[2] At the time of writing the law-making is still underway, but tentative scholarly discussions in China support the suspicion that there will be no return of the question of presumption of innocence. An exception seems to be Chen Guangzhong,[3] who has been mentioned many times in this book and who has been lobbying for the presumption of innocence since the inception of the reform era in the late 1970s. Such voices have been marginalised, and it can be expected that it will be a refinement, focusing especially on improvements to the 2018 mechanisms, ie, the plea leniency system and the linkages between the supervisory and criminal proceedings. It is unlikely that this reform will bring any fundamental changes to the existing system, let alone a meaningful revival of liberal values such as presumption of innocence.

One may now wonder whether there is still hope for the presumption of innocence in China. While it is true that the Party leaders never felt comfortable with the label of presumption of innocence and its underlying liberalism, scholars in the reform era could not anticipate the pushback it would receive under Xi Jinping. However, the periodic approach of this book demonstrates that the genesis of criminal justice in China has not been linear, and there was a window during which a greater shift towards due process would have been possible. But it seems that this window of opportunity has closed and Chinese scholars' hope for a gradual transformation has not been fulfilled. I believe there is – unfortunately – enough reason to be sceptical.

[2] 'Legislative Plan of the Standing Committee of the Standing Committee of 14th NPC (130 Items)' npcobserver.com/wp-content/uploads/2023/10/14th-NPCSC-Legislative-Plan.pdf accessed 13 January 2024.

[3] See, eg, Chen Guangzhong, '"Xingshi susong fa" zao xiugai de ruogan zhongyao wenti tantao (Discussion on Some Important Issues of the Revision of Criminal Procedure Law)' (2024) 42 *Tribune of Political Science and Law* 35.

# BIBLIOGRAPHY


*1987 Zhongguo falü nianjian (1987 China Law Yearbook)* (Beijing, Law Press China, 1987).

*2016 Zhongguo falü nianjian (2016 China Law Yearbook)* (Beijing, Law Press China, 2016).

*2017 Zhongguo falü nianjian (2017 China Law Yearbook)* (Beijing, Law Press China, 2017).

Amnesty International, 'No End in Sight – Torture and Forced Confessions in China' (2015) www.amnesty.org/en/documents/asa17/2730/2015/en/.

Ashworth, A, 'Four Threats to the Presumption of Innocence' (2006) 10 *The International Journal of Evidence & Proof* 241.

Bai Dong, 'Rushi huida yu chenmoquan de gongneng zhuyi fenxi yu wenhua jieshi (Functional Analysis and Cultural Interpretation to Truthful Answer and Right to Silence)' [2012] *Law Science Magazine* 113.

——, 'Rushi huida yu chenmoquan feili zhizheng – jiyu quanqiu huayu zhong "women de" difangxing zhishi" zhi zai renshi (Conflicts between the Duty to Make Truthful Statements and the Right to Silence: Reconceptualising "Our" "Local Knowledge" in Global Discourse)' [2017] *Nankai Journal* (Philosophy, Literature and Social Science Edition) 62.

Ballestrem, KG, 'The Soviet Concept of Truth' (1964) 4 *Studies in Soviet Thought* 1.

Beccaria, C, On Crimes and Punishments and Other Writings, 4th edn (Cambridge, Cambridge University Press, 2003).

Beitz, C, *The Idea of Human Rights* (Oxford, Oxford University Press, 2009).

Belkin, I, 'China's Tortuous Path toward Ending Torture in Criminal Investigations', *Comparative Perspectives on Criminal Justice in China* (Cheltenham, Edward Elgar Publishing 2013).

Berman, HJ, 'What Makes "Socialist Law" Socialist?' (1971) 20 *Problems of Communism* 24.

Berman, HJ and Quigley, Jr. JB, 'Comment on the Presumption of Innocence under Soviet Law' (1968) 15 *UCLA Law Review* 1230.

Bian Jianlin, 'Peihe yu zhiyue: jiancha diaocha yu xingshi susong de jiejie (Cooperation and Constraints: The Nexus between Inspection Investigations and Criminal Proceedings)' [2019] *Studies in Law and Business* 15.

——, 'Jiaqian jijian jiancha jiguan zishen jianshe shi tigao jijian jiancha gongzuo guifanhua fazhihua zhengguhua shuiping de neizai yaoqiu (Strengthening the Self-Building of the Discipline Inspection and Supervisory Organs is an intrinsic Demand for improving the Standardisation, Legalisation and Regularisation of the Discipline Inspection and Supervision Work)' *China Discipline Inspection and Supervision Magazine* 2023.

Bian Jianlin and Guo Zhiyuan, 'Yingguo dui chenmoquan de xianzhi (Restrictions on the Right to Silence in England)' [1999] *Journal of Comparative Law* 283.

Biddulph, S, 'Democratic Centralism and Administration in China' in Hualing Fu and others (eds), *Socialist Law in Socialist East Asia* (Cambridge, Cambridge University Press, 2018).

Biddulph, S, Nesossi, E and Trevaskes, S, 'Criminal Justice Reform in the Xi Jinping Era' (2017) 2 *China Law and Society Review* 63.

Bo, Y and Duff, P, 'Criminal Procedure in Contemporary China: Socialist, Civilian, or Traditional?' (2010) 59 *International & Comparative Law Quarterly* 1099.

Bodde, D and Morris, C, *Law in Imperial China: Exemplified by 190 Ch'ing Dynasty Cases (Translated from the Hsing-an Hui-Lan), With Historical, Social, and Juridical Commentaries.* (Cambridge, MA, Harvard University Press, 1967).

Cao Peiqiang and Liu Junhan, *Mao Zedong sixiang he zhongguo tese shehui zhuyi lilun tixxi gainian (Mao Zedong Thought and the Theoretical System of Socialism with Chinese Characteristics)*, 2nd edn (Beijing, Beijing Institute of Technology Press, 2011).

Cascarelli, JC, 'Presumption of Innocence and Natural Law: Machiavelli and Aquinas' (1996) 41 *The American Journal of Jurisprudence*.

Central Political-Legal Cadre School, Department of Criminal Law and Criminal Procedure Law, *Zhonghua Renmin Gongheguo xingshi susong fa jiangyi (PRC Criminal Procedure Law Handout)* (Amherst, Mass Publishing House, 1981).

Chang Feng, 'Gaige beijing xia xingshi susong zhidu de fazhan – Zhongguo xingshi susong faxue yanjiuhui 2017 nian nianhui guandian zongshu (Development of the Criminal Procedure System against the Backdrop of Reforms – Summary of the Views at the 2017 Annual Meeting of the Criminal Procedure Association)' [2017] *People's Procuratorial Semimonthly* 36.

Chao, P, 'Socialism in Confucianism' (1971) 9 *Asian Studies: Journal of Critical Perspectives on Asia* 328.

Chen, A, *An Introduction to the Legal System of the People's Republic of China*, 4th edn (London, Lexis-Nexis, 2011).

Chen, D, 'Explaining China's Changing Discourse on Human Rights, 1978-2004' (2005) 29 *Asian Perspective* 155.

Chen Guangzhong, 'Yingdang pipan de jicheng wuzui tuiding yuanze (We Should Critically Inherit the Principle of Presumption of Innocence' [1980] *Chinese Journal of Law* 34.

——, 'Jiaqiang renquan baozhang shi gaige kaifang de xuyao (Strengthening the Protection of Human Rights is a Demand for Reform and Opening-up)' [1992] *China Legal Science* 18.

——, 'Lun xingshi susongfa xiugai de zhidao sixiang (On the Guiding Thought of the Revision of the Criminal Procedure Law' [1995] *Law and Social Development* 43.

——, '"Jianchi chengzhi fanzui yu baozhang renquan xiang jiehe lizu guoqing yu jiejian waiguo xiang jiehe" (Adhering to the Combination of Punishing Crimes and Safeguarding Human Rights, Being based on National Conditions and Drawing on Foreign Countries)' [1996] *Tribune of Political Science and Law* (Journal of CUPL) 25.

——, *'Gongmin quanli he zhengzhi quanli guoji gongyue yu woguo xingshi susong' (International Covenant on Civil and Political Rights and Criminal Process in China)* (Beijing, The Commercial Press, 2005).

——, *Zhonghua Renmin Gongheguo xingshi susongfa zai xiugai zhuanjia jianyigao yu lunzheng (Expert Draft for Re-Amendment to the PRC Criminal Procedure Law and Annotations)* (Beijing, China Legal Publishing House, 2006).

——, *Xingshi susong fa (Criminal Procedure Law)* (Peking, Peking University Press, 2013).

——, 'Dangqian Xingshi Susong Zhidu Gaige Mianlin de Jige Wenti (Several Issues Currently Facing the Reform of the Criminal Procedure System)' (2018) 26 *Evidence Science* 517.

——, '"Xingshi susong fa" zao xiugai de ruogan zhongyao wenti tantao (Discussion on Some Important Issues of the Revision of Criminal Procedure Law)' (2024) 42 *Tribune of Political Science and Law* 35.

Chen Guangzhong and Bian Jianlin, 'Xingshi susong faxue yanjiu xianzhuang yu fazhan qushi (The Present State and the Trend of Development of Criminal Procedure Law Research' [1996] *The Jurist* 34.

Chen Guangzhong, Chen Ruihua and Tang Weijian, 'Shichang jingji yu xingshi susong faxue de zhangwang (Perspectives on Market Economy and Criminal Procedure Studies)' [1993] *China Legal Science* 3.

Chen Guangzhong, Jiang Jiahua and Xiao Peiquan, 'Lun wuzui tuiding jiqi zai zhongguo de shiyong (On the Presumption of Innocence and its Application in China)' [2013] *Law Science Magazine* 1.

Chen Guangzhong and Yan Duan, *Zhonghua Renmin Gongheguo xingshi susongfa xiugai jianyigao yu lunzheng (Draft for Amendment to the PRC Criminal Procedure Law and Its Annotations)* (Zhengzhou, China Zhengzhou Publishing House, 1995).

Chen Guangzhong, Zeng Xinhua and Liu Linna, 'Xingshi susong fazhi jianshe de zhongda jinbu (Significant Progress in the Development of the Criminal Procedure Legal System)' (2012) 6 *Tsinghua Law Journal* 7.

Chen Guangzhong and Zhang Jianwei, 'Lianheguo gongmin quanli he zhengzhi quanli guoji gongyue yu woguo xingshi susong (The ICCPR and Chinese Criminal Proceedings)' [1998] *China Legal Science* 98.

Chen, H, 'Renquan wenti qian yi (A brief discussion on Human Rights)' [1985] *CASS Journal of Political Science* 12.

Chen, J, *Criminal and Criminal Procedure Law in the People's Republic of China* (Leiden, Brill Nijhoff, 2013).

Chen Qiwu, '"Shishi shi genju, falü shi zhunsheng" shi woguo xingshi susong de jiben zhidao yuanze ("Taking Facts as the Basis, and Law as the Yardstick" is the Basic Guiding Principle of Criminal Proceedings in China)' [1958] *Law Science* 37.

Chen Ruihua, *Xingshi zhengju faxue (Criminal Evidence Law)* (Peking, Peking University Press, 2014).

Chen Weidong, *Mofan xingshi susong fadian (Model Code of Criminal Procedure)* (Beijing, Renmin University Press, 2011).

——, 'Jiya biyaoxing shencha shidian yanjiu baogao (Study on the Pilot Study of Custody Necessity Examination)' [2018] *Chinese Journal of Law* 175.

——, 'Xingshi susong fazhi sishi nian: huigu yu zhanwang (40 Years' Development of Criminal Procedure Law: Retrospect and Prospect)' (2019) 37 *Tribune of Political Science and Law* 18.

——, 'Renzui renfa congkuan zhidu de lilun wenti zai tantao (Re-examination of Theoretical Issues of the Plea Leniency System)' [2020] *Global Law Review* 23.

——, 'Jiya biyaoxing shencha de lilun renshi yu shishi yingyong (Theoretical Recognition and Practical Application of Custody Necessity Examination)' [2012] *Journal of National Prosecutors College* 3.

Chen Weidong and Chen Fei, 'Lun chenmoquan yu tanbai congkuan (On the Right to Silence and Leniency for Those Who Confess)' [2005] *Journal of Henan Administrative Institute of Politics and Law* 50.

Chen Yaobin, 'Lun zhongguo tese de renquan guan (On the View of Human Rights with Chinese Characteristics)' [1995] *Hebei Tribune of Social Science* 33.

Chen Y-J, 'China's Challenge to the International Human Rights Regime' (2019) 51 *NYU Journal of International Law and Politics* 1179.

——, 'Human Rights in the Chinese Administration of Justice' (Taiwan Foundation for Democracy 2019) China Human Rights Report 2018 www.tfd.org.tw/en/publication/human.

Chen Youwu and Li Buyun, 'Zhongguo tese shehui zhuyi renquan lilun tixi lun gang (Outline of the Theoretical System of Socialist Human Rights with Chinese Characteristics)' [2012] *Political Science and Law* 54.

Chen Zexian and Xiong Qiuhong, *Xingshi susong fa xiugai jianyi gao yu lunzheng – yi bei kongzhi ren de quanli baohu wei hexin (Draft Proposal for Amendments to the Criminal Procedure Law and Argumentation – Centred on the Protection of the Rights of Accused Persons* (Beijing, China Social Sciences Press, 2009).

——, *Xingshi susong fa xiugai jianyi gao yu lunzheng – yi renquan baozhang wei shijiao (Draft Proposal for Amendments to the Criminal Procedure Law and Argumentation – from the Perspective of Human Rights Protection)* (Beijing, China Social Sciences Press, 2012).

Choo, ALT, *The Privilege Against Self-Incrimination and Criminal Justice* (Oxford, Hart Publishing, 2013).

Clarke, DC, 'China's Legal System and the Fourth Plenum' [2015] *Asia Policy* 10.

Clarke, DC and Feinerman, JV, 'Antagonistic Contradictions: Criminal Law and Human Rights in China' [1995] *The China Quarterly* 136.

Cohen, JA, *Criminal Process in the People's Republic of China, 1949-1963* (Cambridge, MA, Harvard University Press, 1966).

——, 'Criminal Justice in China: From the Gang of Four to the Trial of Bo Xila' (Human Rights Watch 2013) www.hrw.org/news/2013/07/25/criminal-justice-china-gang-four-bo-xilai.

Cook, AC, *The Cultural Revolution on Trial: Mao and the Gang of Four* (Cambridge, Cambridge University Press, 2016).

Cui Min, 'Guanyu xingshi susong fa xiugai yu wanshan de ruogan jianyi (Some Suggestions on the Revision and Improvement of the Criminal Procedure Law)' [1996] *The Jurist* 86.

Dai Peng, 'Shishi shang de wuzui yu falü shang de wuzui – Nie Shubin'an yu Wang Shujin'an luoji fenxi (Factual and Legal Innocence – Logical Analysis of the Nie Shubin and the Wang Shujin Cases)' *Tianjin Legal Science* 86.

Dai Y, 'An Important Thesis on Building Socialism' *Beijing Review* (9 November 1987).

Dai Yuzhong, 'Jianshe zhongguo tese shehui zhuyi xingshi susong zhidu (Building a Socialist Criminal Justice System with Chinese Characteristics)' *People's Procuratorate Monthly* (2007) 7.

Daly, Y and others, 'Human Rights Protections in Drawing Inferences from Criminal Suspects' Silence' (2021) 21 *Human Rights Law Review* 696.

Davis, MC, 'Chinese Perspectives on Human Rights', *Human Rights and Chinese Values* (Hong Kong, Oxford University Press, 1995).

de Schutter, O, *International Human Rights Law: Cases, Materials, Commentary*, 2nd edn (Cambridge, Cambridge University Press, 2014).

Deng, J, 'The National Supervision Commission: A New Anti-Corruption Model in China' [2018] *International Journal of Law, Crime and Justice* 58.

Deng, X, *Building Socialism with Chinese Characteristics* (Peking, Foreign Language Press, 1985).

——, 'Bourgeois Liberalization Means Taking the Capitalist Road, May and June 1985', *Deng Xiaoping wenxuan (Selected Works of Deng Xiaoping)*, vol III (Beijing, People's Publishing House, 1993).

Deng Zhihui, 'renshen baohuling yu renquan baozhang – yi xingshi susong wei zhu shijiao (Habeas corpus and Human Rights Guarantees in the Context of Criminal Proceedings)' [2004] *China Legal Science* 158.

Dervan, LE and Edkins, VA, 'The Innocent Defendant's Dilemma: An Innovative Empirical Study of Plea Bargaining's Innocence Problem' (2013) 103 *Journal of Criminal Law and Criminology* 1.

Ding, X, 'Law According to the Chinese Communist Party: Constitutionalism and Socialist Rule of Law' (2017) 43 *Modern China* 322.

Dong Yunhu, 'Zhongguo renquan fazhan lishi shang de yige zhongyao lichengbei – "zhongguo de renquan zhuangkuang" baipishu fabiao 10 zhounian huigu (An Important Milestone in the Development of Human Rights in China – a Review of the 10th Anniversary of the Publication of the White Paper "the Human Rights Situation in China")' [2002] *Human Rights* 24.

Donnelly, J, 'The Relative Universality of Human Rights' (2007) 29 *Human Rights Quarterly* 281.

——, *Universal Human Rights in Theory and Practice*, 3rd edn (Ithaca, Cornell University Press, 2013).

Dworkin, RM, 'The Model of Rules' (1967) 35 *The University of Chicago Law Review* 14.

Fan, C, 'The Process of Revising "The Criminal Procedure Law of the People's Republic of China" 1996' aw.unimelb.edu.au/__data/assets/pdf_file/0006/1546260/The_Process_of_Revising_The_Criminal_Procedure_Law_of_the_Peoples_Republic_of_China_19961.pdf.

Fan Chongyi, *Xingshi susongfa xiugai zhuanti yanjiu baogao (Thematic report on the revision of the Code of Criminal Procedure)* (China Police University Publishing House, 2004).

——, 'Xingshi susong fa xiugai de zhongdian nandian wenti jiedu (Reading the Key and Difficult Issues in the Revision of the Criminal Procedure Law)' [2019] *Journal of Law Application* 81.

Fan Fenglin, *Xingshi susong fa (Criminal Procedure Law)* (China Police University Publishing House, 1988).

Fang, Q, *The Communist Judicial System in China, 1927-1976* (Amsterdam University Press 2021).

Farrell, BR, *Habeas Corpus in International Law* (Cambridge University Press 2016).

Feng, C, 'China's Socialist Rule Of Law: A Critical Appraisal Of The Relationship Between The Communist Party And Comprehensive Law Reform' in John Garrick, and Yan Chang Bennett (eds), *China's Socialist Rule of Law Reforms Under Xi Jinping* (Abingdon, Routledge, 2016).

Feng Xin and Jiang Ke, 'Chenmoquan zai zhongguo de kunjing yu chulu – yi "xingshisusongfa" xiugai wei beijing (Dilemmas and Ways forward of the Right to Silence in China – against the Background of the Revision of the Criminal Procedure Law)' [2012] *Journal of Heilongjiang Administrative Cadre College of Politics and Law* 95.

Ferguson, PR, 'The Presumption of Innocence and Its Role in the Criminal Process' (2016) 27 *Criminal Law Forum* 131.

Fletcher, GP, 'The Presumption of Innocence in the Soviet Union' 15 *UCLA Law Review* 1203.

Freeman, M, *Human Rights: An Interdisciplinary Approach*, 2nd edn (Cambridge, Polity Press, 2011).

Fu, H, 'Criminal Defence in China: The Possible Impact of the 1996 Criminal Procedure Law Reform' [1998] *The China Quarterly* 31.

——, 'When Lawyers Are Prosecuted … The Struggle of a Profession in Transition' (2007) 2 *Journal of Comparative Law* 95.

Gao Jiapeng, 'Zhencha jiandu wenti de fajieshixue fenxi (Hermeneutic Analysis of Investigation Supervision Issues)' (2018) 36 *Tribune of Political Science and Law* 33.

Gelatt, T, 'The People's Republic of China and the Presumption of Innocence' (1982) 73 *The Journal of Criminal Law & Criminology* 259.

Gelatt, TA, 'Criminal Justice with Chinese Characteristics: China's Criminal Process and Violations of Human Rights' (New York, Lawyers Committee for Human Rights, 1993).

——, *Opening to Reform? An Analysis of China's Revised Criminal Procedure Law* (New York, Lawyers Committee for Human Rights, 1996).

Glöckner, A and Seelig, S, 'Falldarstellungen Und Ausführungen Zum Chinesischen Rechtssystem: Gespräch Mit Einem Richter Am Oberen Volksgericht in Shanghai' in Hans-Dieter Schwind and Konrad Wegmann (eds), *Studien zum chinesischen Recht* (Bochum, Studienverlag Dr N Brockmeyer, 1979).

Goldman, M, 'China's Anti-Confucian Campaign, 1973-74' [1975] *The China Quarterly* 435.

Guo Bing, 'Jiya biyaoxing shencha zhidu shijian yunxing shenshi (Examination on the Practical Operation of the Custody Necessity Examination System)' [2016] *Criminal Science* 61.

Guo Daohui, 'Renquan de benxing yu jiazhi wei jie (The Nature and Value Hierarchy of Human Rights)' (2004) 22 *Tribune of Political Science and Law (Journal of China University of Political Science and Law)* 3.

Guo, Z, 'Exclusion of Illegally Obtained Confessions in China: An Empirical Perspective' (2017) 21 *The International Journal of Evidence & Proof* 30.

——, 'The First Step of the Long March: Implementing the Exclusionary Rules in China' (2017) 25 *Asia Pacific Law Review* 48.

——, 'Torture and the Exclusion of Evidence in China' [2019] *China Perspectives* 45.

——, 'Anti-Corruption Mechanisms in China after the Supervision Law' [2023] *Journal of Economic Criminology* 1.

Gutmann, A, *Human Rights as Politics and Idolatry* (Princeton, Princeton University Press, 2001).

Habermas, J, 'The Concept of Human Dignity and the Realistic Utopia of Human Rights' (2010) 41 *Metaphilosophy* 464.

Hazard, JN, *Communists and Their Law* (Chicago, University of Chicago Press, 1969).

He, J, *Back from the Dead: Criminal Justice and Wrongful Convictions in China* (Honolulu, University of Hawaii Press, 2016).

He Jiahong, 'Zhongguoshi chenmoquan zhidu zhi wo Jian – yi "meiguoshi" wei canzhao (My views on the Chinese system of the right to silence – with reference to the American system)' (2013) 31 *Tribune of Political Science and Law* 107.

——, 'Miscarriage of Justice and Malpractice in Criminal Investigations in China' (2016) 16 *The China Review* 65.

——, 'Chenmoquan yhidu ji xingshi sifa de jiazhi quxiang (Right to Silence Regime and the Value Orientation of Criminal Justice)' 8 *Journal of National Prosecutors College* 32.

He, X, 'Plea Leniency and Prosecution Centredness in China's Criminal Process' (2023) 254 *The China Quarterly* 448.

Ho, HL, 'The Presumption of Innocence as a Human Right' in Paul Roberts and Jill Hunter (eds), *Criminal Evidence and Human Rights, Reimagining Common Law Procedural Traditions* (Oxford, Hart Publishing, 2012).

Hong Daode, 'Zhongguo faxuehui susongfaxue yanjiuhui 1991 nian nianhui (The 1991 Annual Meeting of the China Law Society Procedural Law Research Association' in Institute of Law at CASS (ed), *Zhongguo faxue yanjiu nianjian (China Law Research Yearbook)* (Beijing, China University of Political Science and Law Press, 1991).

Hsiung, JC, 'Introduction' in James C Hsiung (ed), *Symposium: The Trial of the "Gang of Four" and Its Implications in China* (1981) 40(3) Occasional papers/reprints series in contemporary Asian studies.

Huang Dao, 'Lüe lun xingshi susong zhong de wuzui tuiding yuanze (A Brief Discussion on Principle of the Presumption of Innocence in Criminal Procedure' [1957] *Law Science* 49.

——, 'Yinggai chedi pipan "wuzui tuiding" de miulun (The Fallacy of the "Presumption of Innocence" Should be Thoroughly Criticised)' [1958] *Law Science*.

Huang Dao and Tie Li, 'Wuzui tuiding zai xin zhongguo de mingyun – jianguo yilai faxuejie zhongda shijian yanjiu (er) (The Fate of the Presumption of Innocence in New China: A Study of Major Events in Jurisprudence since the Founding of the People's Republic of China (II))' [1997] *Law Science* 2.

Huang Haibo, 'Zhencha jiandu shiye zhong de xingshi juliu (Criminal Detention from the Perspective of Investigation Supervision)' [2007] *Chinese Criminal Science* 89.

Huang Yansheng, 'Wuzui tuiding yu shishi qiushi (The Presumption of Innocence and Seek Truth from Facts)' [1997] *People's Procuratorate* 13.

Human Rights Watch, 'World Report 2019 (China, Events of 2018)' (2019) www.hrw.org/world-report/2019/country-chapters/china-and-tibet.

Hunt, A, 'Marxist Theory of Law' in Dennis Patterson (ed), *A Companion to Philosophy of Law and Legal Theory*, 2nd edn (Chichester, Blackwell Publishing, 2010).

Jackson, JD and Summers, SJ, *The Internationalisation of Criminal Evidence* (Cambridge, Cambridge University Press, 2012).

Ji Xiangde, 'Xi Jinping fazhi sixiang zhidao xia de renzui renfa congkuan zhidu (The Plea Leniency System under the Guidance of Xi Jinping's Rule-of-Law-Thought)' (2024) 42 *Tribune of Political Science and Law* 3.

Jiang, N, 'The Presumption of Innocence and Illegally Obtained Evidence: Lessons from Wrongful Convictions in China' [2013] *Hong Kong Law Journal* 745.

——, 'Excluding Tortured Confessions in the People's Republic of China: A Long March towards the Eventual Abolition of Torture?' (2018) 54 *International Journal of Law, Crime and Justice* 1.

Jiang, T, 'The Development and Evaluation of "Presumption of Innocence in China' in Wei Zhang (ed), *Human Rights and Good Governance* (Leiden, Brill Nijhoff, 2016).

Kaiser, A, 'A New Model of Habeas Corpus in China? Procuratorial Necessity Examination of Pretrial Custody' in Björn Ahl (ed), *Post-2013 Reforms of Chinese Courts and Criminal Procedure* (Cambridge, Cambridge University Press, 2021).

——, 'The Shaping of Authoritarian Law under the "Socialist Rule of Law": Academics and Obedience in the Chinese Party-State' [2024] *Taiwan Human Rights Journal* 15.

Kälin, W and Künzli, J, *The Law of International Human Rights Protection*, 2nd edn (Oxford, Oxford University Press, 2019).

Kent, A, *Between Freedom and Subsistence, China and Human Rights* (Oxford, Oxford University Press, 1993).

Kinzelbach, K, 'Human Rights in Chinese Foreign Policy: A Battle for Global Public Opinion' in Sarah Biddulph and Joshua Rosenzweig (eds), *Handbook on Human Rights in China* (Cheltenham, Edward Elgar, 2019).

Kline, GL, '"Socialist Legality" and Communist Ethics' (1963) 8 *Natural Law Forum* 21.

Lan, R, 'A False Promise of Fair Trials: A Case Study of China's Malleable Criminal Procedure Law' (2010) 27 *Pacific Basin Law Journal* 153.

Law School of the East China University of Political Science and Law, 'Donghua zhengfa xueyuan juxing kexue taolunhui – pibo wuzui tuiding lun (Law School of the East China University of Political Science and Law holds an Academic Seminar – Rebuttal of the Presumption of Innocence)' [1958] *Law Science* 48.

Lee, K, 'China and the International Covenant on Civil and Political Rights: Prospects and Challenges' (2007) 6 *Chinese Journal of International Law* 445.

Lee, Y, 'Deontology, Political Morality, and the State: Political Theory and Criminal Punishment' (2011) 8 *Ohio State Journal of Criminal Law* 385.

Leng, S-C, *Justice in Communist China: A Survey of the Judicial System of the Chinese People's Republic* (New York, Oceana Publications, 1967).

Leng, S-C and Chiu, H, *Criminal Justice in Post-Mao China* (Albany, State University of New York Press, 1985).

Li Baomin, '"Wuzui tuiding" bu ying zuowei woguo xingshi susong de yuanze (The "Presumption of Innocence" should not be a Principle of Chinese Criminal Procedure)' [1958] *Law Science* 45.

Li, E, 'The Abuse of Guaranteed Pending Trial in the Chinese Criminal Process: A Violation of International Human Rights Law' (2011) 9 *Indonesian Journal of International Law* 79.

——, 'Haste Makes Waste: Why China's New Plea Leniency System Is Doomed to Fail' (2022) 17 *Asian Journal of Comparative Law* 76.

Li, Fenfei, 'Zhiwu fanzui diaocha zhong de jiancha yindao wenti yanjiu (A Study on the Question of how the Procuratorial Guides the Investigation of Duty-Related Offences)' [2019] *Journal of Comparative Law* 28.

Li, G, *A Glossary of Political Terms of the People's Republic of China* (Hong Kong, Chinese University Press, 1995).

Li Jingbing, 'Jiang wuzui tuiding yuanze zairu woguo xianfa (Write the Principle of the Presumption of innocence into the Chinese Constitution)' [1989] *Law Science* 4.

Li, L, 'The "Organisational Weapon" of the Chinese Communist Party: China's Disciplinary Regime from Mao to Xi Jinping' in Rogier Creemers and Susan Trevaskes (eds), *Law and the Party in China: Ideology and Organisation* (Cambridge, Cambridge University Press, 2021).

Li, L and Wang, P, 'From Institutional Interaction to Institutional Integration: The National Supervisory Commission and China's New Anti-Corruption Model' [2019] *The China Quarterly* 967.

Li Xiang, '"Jiancha fa" shishi dui xingshi shiti fa de yingxiang ji wanshan (Impact of the implementation of the "Supervision Law" on Substantive Criminal Law and its Improvement)' [2019] *Journal of Southeast University* (Philosophy and Social Science) 97.

Li Xunhu, 'Daibu zhidu gaige de fa shiyi xue jiedu (Doctrinal Legal Interpretation of the Reform of the Arrest System)' [2018] *Chinese Journal of Law* 155.

Li Zhongcheng, 'Zhongguo faxuehui susong faxue yanjiuhui 2003 nian nianhui zongshu (Summary of the 2003 Annual Meeting of the China Law Society Procedural Law Research Association)' [2004] *China Legal Science* 186.

Lin, D and Trevaskes, S, 'Creating a Virtuous Leviathan: The Party, Law, and Socialist Core Values' (2019) 6 *Asian Journal of Law and Society* 41.

——, 'Law-Morality Ideology in the Xi Jinping Era', *Law and the Party in China: Ideology and Organisation* (Cambridge, Cambridge University Press, 2020).

Lin, X and Watters, C, 'Understanding the Presumption of Innocence in China: Institution and Practice' in Yun Zhao and Michael Ng (eds), *Chinese Legal Reform and the Global Legal Order: Adoption and Adaptation* (Cambridge, Cambridge University Press, 2018).

Lin Xifen, 'Fenduan shencha yihuo guikou: jiya biyaoxing shencha de gaige luoji (Sectionalized or Centralized Examination: The Logic behind the Reform of Custody Necessity Examination)' [2015] *Chinese Journal of Law* 157.

Lin Xin, '"Wuzui tuiding" haishi "wuzui jiadong"? ("Presumption of Innocence" or "Assumption of Innocence"?' [1983] *Social Sciences in China* 173.

Lippke, RL, 'The Presumption of Innocence in the Trial Setting' (2015) 28 *Ratio Juris* 159.

——, *Taming the Presumption of Innocence* (Oxford, Oxford University Press, 2016).

——, 'Fundamental Values of Criminal Procedure' in Darryl K Brown, Jenia I Turner and Bettina Weisser (eds), *The Oxford Handbook of Criminal Process* (Oxford, Oxford University Press, 2019).

Liu Chuangao, 'Xin shidai xingshi susong zhidu de xin fazhan – Zhongguo xingshi susong faxue yanjiuhui 2018 nian nianhui guandian shuyao (New Development of the Criminal Procedure System in the New Era – Summary of Views from the 2018 Annual Meeting of the Criminal Procedure Association)' [2018] *People's Procuratorate Semimonthly* 35.

Liu Genju, 'Zai woguo queding chenmoquan yuanze jige wenti zhi yantao (Discussing Some Issues Regarding China's Establishment of the Principle of Right to Silence)' [2000] *China Legal Science* 43.

Liu Huawen, 'Zhongguo tese shehuizhuyi requan guan – jiehe Xi Jinping Zhi "2015" – Beijing Renquan Luntan" de Hexin (The Socialist Outlook on Human with Chinese Characteristics: Interpretation of Xi Jinping's Congratulatory Letter at the 2015 Beijing Human Rights Forum)' [2016] *Chinese Review of International Law* 3.

Liu Junning, 'Renquan de pubianxing ji qi fandiao (The Universality of Human Rights and their Antitheses)' [1998] *Open Times* 5.

Liu Qing, 'Jiya biyaoxing shencha zhidu yanjiu (Study on the System of Custody Necessity Examination)' [2013] *People's Procuratorial Semimonthly* 23.

Liu, S and Halliday, T, *Criminal Defense in China, The Politics of Lawyers at Work* (Cambridge, Cambridge University Press, 2016).

Liu Yonghong, Liu Jun and Li Kejuan, 'Xin xingsu guize xia jiya biyaoxing shencha de jinlu (Short Version of the Custody Necessity Examination Under the New Criminal Procedure Rules)' [2020] *Legal System and Society* 93.

Lo, CW, *China's Legal Awakening: Legal Theory and Criminal Justice in Deng's Era* (Hong Kong, Hong Kong University Press, 1995).

Lohmann, G, 'Zu Einer Relationalen Begründung Der Universalisierung Der Menschenrechte' in Günter Nooke, Georg Lohmann and Gerhard Wahlers (eds), *Gelten Menschenrechte universal?: Begründungen und Infragestellungen* (Freiburg im Breisgau, Herder Press, 2008).

——, 'Echo Des Naturrechts? Menschenwürde, Menschenrechte Und Demokratie' in Pirmin Stekeler-Weithofer and Benno Zabel (eds) (Tübingen, Mohr Siebeck GmbH and Co KG, 2018).

Long Zongzhi, 'Dui "wuzui tuiding" de xin siwei (New Thoughts on the 'Presumption of Innocence)' [1989] *Modern Law Science* 17.

——, 'Susong jizhi de chongtu yu xietiao – ping xingshi susongfa xiugai de xuezhe jianyigao (Conflict and Coordination of Procedural Mechanisms – Comment on the Scholars' Draft Proposal for the Revision of the Criminal Procedure Law)' [1995] *Modern Law Science* 54.

——, 'Bo Xilai'an shenpan zhong de ruogan zhengju fa wenti (Some Issues of Evidentiary Law in the Bo Xilai Trial)' [2013] *Law Science* 3.

Lu Jin, 'Qianxi gongmin ji zhengzhi quanli guoji gongyue zhong "arrest" yu woguo daibu zhidu de chayi – jian yi "arrest" de fanyi (Research on the Differences between "Arrest" under the ICCPR and the Chinese System of "Arrest")' [2012] *Law Science* 124.

Lü Zhongya, 'Xin xingshi susongfa jiangou qi shihe guoqing de "wuzui tuiding" yuanze (The New Criminal Procedure Law Established the Principle of Presumption of Innocence in Accordance with National Conditions)' [1996] *Law Science* 17.

Lubman, SB, *Bird in a Cage* (Redwood, Stanford University Press, 1999).

Luo Haocai, 'Zhongguo renquan shiye qianjing guangkuo (The Cause of Human Rights in China has a Bright Future)' (2014) 73 *Human Rights* 2.

Luo Rong, 'Shi lun xingshi susong zhong de beigaoren (On the Defendant in the Criminal Procedure' [1957] *Law Science* 56.

Luo Xinmin, 'Wuzui tuiding bu shi shehui zhuyi de susong yuanze (The Presumption of Innocence is not a Socialist Procedural Principle)' [1982] *Modern Law Science* 27.

Macfarlane, LJ, 'Marxist Theory and Human Rights' (1982) 17 *Government and Opposition* 414.

Mao, Z, 'Talks at the Yenan Forum on Literature and Art, May 1942', vol III. (Peking, Foreign Language Press, 1965).

Mao Zedong, 'On Practice, July 1937' in Foreign Language Press (ed), *Selected Works of Mao Tse-Tung*, vol I. (Beijing, Foreign Language Press, 1965).

Martin, FF and others, *International Human Rights and Humanitarian Law: Treaties, Cases, and Analysis* (Cambridge, Cambridge University Press, 2011).

Marx, K, *Critique of the Gotha Program* (Maryland, Wildside Press, 2008).

——, *Zur Kritik Der Politischen Ökonomie* (Karl-Maria Guth ed, Contumax, 2017).

McConville, M and (with Satnam Choongh, Pinky Choy, Dick Wan, Eric Chui, Wing Hong, Ian Dobinson and Carol Jones), *Criminal Justice in China: An Empirical Inquiry* (Cheltenham, Edward Elgar, 2011).

McCrudden, C, 'Human Dignity and Judicial Interpretation of Human Rights' (2008) 19 *The European Journal of International Law* 655.

Min Chunlei, 'Lun shencha daibu chengxu de susonghua (On the Legal Proceduralization of the Arrest Procedure)' [2016] *Law and Social Development* 62.

Morsink, J, *The Universal Declaration of Human Rights: Origins, Drafting, and Intent* (Philadelphia, University of Pennsylvania Press, 1999).
Mou, Y, 'Overseeing Criminal Justice: The Supervisory Role of the Public Prosecution Service in China' (2017) 44 *Journal of Law and Society* 620.
——, 'The Constructed Truth: The Making of Police Dossiers in China' (2017) 26 *Social & Legal Studies* 69.
——, *The Construction of Guilt in China, An Empirical Account of Routine Chinese Injustice* (Oxford, Hart Publishing, 2020).
Moulin, X and Miao, M, 'Miscarriage of Justice in Capital Cases in China' (2018) 41 *Hastings International & Comparative Law Review* 273.
Müllerson, R, 'Universal Human Rights in Multicultural World' in ER May and AE Laiou (eds), *The Dumbarton Oaks Conventions and the United Nations 1944–1994* (Dumbarton Oaks Research Library and Collection, 1998).
Nesossi, E, 'The Politics of Torture and Miscarriages of Justice in Contemporary China' (2017) 11 *Journal of Comparative Law* 166.
—— (eds), *Legal Reforms and Deprivation of Liberty in Contemporary China* (Abingdon, Routledge. 2016).
Nesossi, E and Trevaskes, S, *Procedural Justice and the Fair Trial in Contemporary Chinese Criminal Justice System* (Leiden, Brill Nijhoff, 2018).
Nickel, JW, *Making Sense of Human Rights* (Oakland, University of California Press, 1987).
Ning Hanlin, 'Lun wuzui tuiding (On the Presumption of Innocence)' [1982] *Social Sciences in China* 65.
Nowak, M, *U.N. Covenant on Civil and Political Rights, CCPR Commentary*, 2nd edn (Kehl, N P Engel, 2005).
Packer, HL, 'Two Models of the Criminal Process' (1964) 113 *University of Pennsylvania Law Review* 1.
Petev, V, *Kritik Der Marxistisch-Sozialistischen Rechts- Und Staatsphilosophie* (Berlin, Duncker & Humbolt 1989).
Pils, E, 'Disappearing China's Human Rights Lawyers' in Mike McConville and Eva Pils (eds), *Comparative Perspectives on Criminal Justice in China* (Cheltenham, Edward Elgar, 2013).
——, *China's Human Rights Lawyers: Advocacy and Resistance* (Abingdon, Routledge, 2014).
——, 'The Party's Turn to Public Repression: An Analysis of the "709" Crackdown on Human Rights Lawyers in China' (2018) 3 *China Law and Society Review* 1.
——, 'Rule-of-Law Reform and the Rise of Rule by Fear in China' in Weitseng Chen and Hualing Fu (eds), *Authoritarian Legality in Asia: Formation, Development and Transition* (Cambridge, Cambridge University Press, 2020).
Potter, PB, 'The Chinese Legal System: Continuing Commitment to the Primacy of State Power' (1999) 159 *China Quarterly* 673.
Przetacznik, F, 'The Socialist Concept of Human Rights: Its Philosophical Background and Political Justification' (1977) 13 *Revue Belge De Droit International* 238.
Qu Fu, 'Lüe tan xingshi susong zhong beigaoren de susong diwei (On the Procedural Position of the Defendant in the Criminal Process)' [1957] *Chinese Journal of Law* 22.
Rachels, J, *The Elements of Moral Philosophy*, 4th edn (New York, McGraw-Hill, 2003).
Rawls, J, *The Law of Peoples* (Massachusetts, Harvard University Press, 1999).
Robinson, JP, 'The Right to a Fair Trial in International Law, with Specific Reference to the Work of the ICTY' (2009) 3 *Berkeley Journal of International Law* 1.
Rosenzweig, J, 'Residential Surveillance: Evolution of a Janus-Faced Measure' in Elisa Nesossi and others (eds), *Legal Reforms and Deprivation of Liberty in Contemporary China* (Abingdon, Routledge, 2016).
Sapio, F, *Sovereign Power and the Law in China* (Leiden, Brill Nijhoff, 2010).
Schachter, O, 'Human Dignity as a Normative Concept' (1983) 77 *The American Journal of International Law* 848.
Schwikkard, PJ, 'The Presumption of Innocence: What Is It?' (1998) 11 *South African Journal of Criminal Justice* 396.

Seymour, JD and Wong, P, 'China and the International Human Rights Covenants' (2015) 47 *Critical Asian Studies* 514.

Shah, S, 'Detention and Trial' in Daniel Moeckli and others (eds), *International Human Rights Law*, 3rd edn (Oxford, Oxford University Press, 2017).

Shi Daxin, 'Lun renquan he renquan de guoji baohu (On Human Rights and the International Protection of Human Rights' [1982] *Journal of Anhui University* (Philosophy and Social Sciences Edition) 52.

Shytov, A and Duff, P, 'Truth and Procedural Fairness in Chinese Criminal Procedure Law' (2019) 23 *The International Journal of Evidence & Proof* 299.

Sikkink, K, *Evidence for Hope: Making Human Rights Work in the 21st Century* (Princeton, Princeton University Press, 2017).

Smith, E, 'The Conception of Legality under Xi Jinping' in Rogier Creemers and Susan Trevaskes (eds), *Law and the Party in China: Ideology and Organisation* (Cambridge, Cambridge University Press, 2020).

Smith, J and Gompers, M, 'Realizing Justice: The Development of Fair Trial in China' (2006) 2 *Chinese Law & Policy Review* 108.

Smith, RKM, *International Human Rights Law*, 8th edn (Oxford, Oxford University Press, 2018).

Song Yinghui, *Xingshi susong mudi lun (Objective Theory of Criminal Proceedings)* (China Police University Publishing House, 1995).

Stavros, S, 'The Right to a Fair Trial in Emergency Situations' (1992) 41 *Comparative Law Quarterly* 343.

Stuckenberg, C-F, *Untersuchungen Zur Unschuldsvermutung* (Berlin, De Gruyter, 1998).

——, 'Who Is Presumed Innocent of What by Whom?' (2014) 8 *Criminal Law and Philosophy* 301.

Stumer, A, *The Presumption of Innocence: Evidential and Human Rights Perspectives* (Oxford, Hart Publishing, 2010).

Sun Changyong, 'Chenmoquan yu zhongguo xingshi susong (The Right to Silence and the Chinese Criminal Process)' (2000) 22 *Modern Law Science* 18.

Sun Changyong and Guo Hang, 'Bei Zhuisu Ren Renzui Renfa Ziyuanxing Zai Shenshi (Review of the Voluntariness of the Accused's Admission of Guilt and Punishment)' (2024) 32 *Henan Social Sciences* 52.

Svensson, M, *Debating Human Rights in China: A Conceptual and Political History* (Lanham, Rowman & Littlefield, 2002).

Tang Congyao, *Xingshi beigaoren de susong quanli he yiwu (The Procedural Rights and Duties of the Criminal Defendant)* (Fuzhou, Fujian Renmin University Press, 1982).

Tang Guanda, 'Dui "wuzui tuiding" yao juti fenxi (A Detailed Analysis on the "Presumption of Innocence")' [1980] *Chinese Journal of Law* 64.

Tanner, MS, 'State Coercion and the Balance of Awe: The 1983-1986 "Stern Blows" Anti-Crime Campaign' [2000] *The China Journal* 93.

Tay, AE-S and Kamenka, E, 'Marxism and the Problem of Legal Continuity – Recent Trens in Communist Legal Theory' [1980] *Bulletin of the Australian Society of Legal Philosophy* 31.

Thieme, GV, 'The Debate on the Presumption of Innocence in the People's Republic of China' [1984] *Review of Socialist Law* 277.

Tian Ye, 'Jujiao shiwu xin wenti, tuidong xingsufa guanche zhixing – zhongguo xingshi susong faxue yanjiuhui 2013 nian nianhui zongshu (Focusing on new Practical Issues and Promoting the Implementation of the Criminal Procedure Law – Summary of the 2013 Annual Meeting of the China Criminal Procedure Law Research Association)' [2013] *People's Procuratorial Semimonthly* 49.

Trechsel, S, *Human Rights in Criminal Proceedings* (Oxford, Oxford University Press, 2005).

Ulväng, M, 'Presumption of Innocence Versus a Principle of Fairness, A Response to Duff' (2013) 42 *Netherlands Journal of Legal Philosophy* 205.

van Kempen, PH, *Pre-Trial Detention: Human Rights, Criminal Procedure Law and Penitentiary Law Comparative Law* (Cambridge, Intersentia, 2012).

Vogler, R and Foulavand, S, 'Standards for Making Factual Determination in Arrest and Pre-Trial Detention' in Jacqueline E Ross and Stephen C Thaman (eds), *Comparative Criminal Procedure* (Cheltenham, Edward Elgar, 2018).

von Senger, H, 'Die UNO-Konzeption Der Menschenrechte Und Die Offizielle Menschenrechts-Position Der Volksrepublik China' in Gregor Paul (ed), *Die Menschenrechtsfrage: Diskussion über China – Dialog mit China* (ein wissenschaftliches Symposium (Schriften der Deutschen China-Gesellschaft, 1998).

Waldron, J, 'How to Argue for a Universal Claim' (1999) 30 *Columbia Human Rights Law Review* 306.

——, 'How Law Protects Dignity' (2012) 71 *Cambridge Law Journal* 200.

Wan Qianhui, 'Zhongguo tese renquanguan de lishi fazhan yu neizai luoji (Historical Development and Internal Logic of the View of Human Rights with Chinese Characteristics)' [2017] *Human Rights* 33.

Wang Bingxin, 'Guanyu "wuzui tuiding" yuanze de tantao (On the Principle of "Presumption of Innocence"' [1979] *Modern Law Science* 10.

Wang, G, 'Power, Rights and Duties in Chinese History' [1980] *The Australian Journal of Chinese Affairs* 1.

Wang Guiwu, 'Ping "wuzui tuiding" de susong yuanze (A Comment on the Procedural Principle of the "Presumption of Innocence"' [1984] *Legal Forum* 1.

Wang Junmin, '"Wu cong panding" yu wuzui tuiding ("No Guilt without Punishment" and the "Presumption of Innocence")' [1996] *Law Science* 13.

Wang Liwan, 'Lifa guanliao: lijie zhongguo lifa guocheng de xin jiaodu (Legislative Bureaucracy: New Perspectives on Understanding Legislative Processes in China)' [2016] *China Law Review* 114.

Wang Minyuan, 'Woguo xingshi susongfa xiugai shu ping (Review of China's Criminal Procedure Law Revision)' [1996] *The Jurist* 41.

Wang Shumao, '"Jiya biyaoxing shencha" de lijie yu shiyong (Understanding and Application of "Custody Necessity Examination")' [2013] *Law Review* 120.

Wang Xiaohua and Ma Qingguo, '"Wuzui tuiding" bian (Defending the Presumption of Innocence)' [1980] *Chinese Journal of Law* 63.

Wang Xinqing, 'Woguo xingshi susongfa buyi caiyong "wuzui tuiding" yuanze (The Incompatibility of the Principle of the "Presumption of Innocence" in our Criminal Procedure Law)' [1987] *Legal Studies & Research* 58.

Wei Tong, 'Guanyu xiugai xingshi susong fa wenti de qingkuang fanying – zhongguo faxuehui susongfaxue yanjiuhui 1995 nian nianhui zongshu zhiyi (Some Reflections on the Issue of Revising the Criminal Procedure Law – A Summary of the 1995 Annual Meeting of the China Law Society Procedural Law Research Association)' [1996] *Journal of CUPL* 89.

Wei Yuening, 'Shenpan qian de jiya (Pre-trial Detention)' in Chen Guangzhong (ed), *Gongmin quanli he zhengzhi quanli guoji gongyue pizhun yu shishi wenti yanjiu (Study on the Ratification and Implementation of the International Covenant on Civil and Political Rights)* (Beijing, China Legal Publishing House, 2002).

Weigend, T, 'Should We Search for the Truth, and Who Should Do It?' (2011) 36 *North Carolina Journal of International Law and Commercial Regulation* 388.

——, 'There Is Only One Presumption of Innocence' (2013) 42 *Netherlands Journal of Legal Philosophy* 193.

——, 'Assuming the Defendant Is Not Guilty: The Presumption of Innocence in the German System of Criminal Justice' (2014) 8 *Criminal Law and Philosophy* 285.

——, 'The Suspect as a Source of Information' in Michael Lindemann and Andreas Ransiek (eds), *Interrogation, Confession, and Truth* (Baden-Baden, Nomos, 2020).

Wen Ziyang, 'Wuzui tuiding yuanze zai woguo xianzhuang ji fazhan (Status and Development of the Principle of Presumption of innocence in China)' [2018] *Legality Vision* 26.

Whitfort, A, 'The Right to a Fair Trial in China: The Criminal Procedure Law of 1996' (2006) 2 *Chinese Law & Policy Review* 141.

Wu Hongyao and Zhong Songzhi, *Zhongguo xingshi susong fadian bainian 1906 nian – 2012 nian (zhongce) (100 Years of the Chinese Criminal Procedure Law Codes (1906-2012) (middle volume))* (Beijing, China University of Political Science and Law Press, 2012).

Wu Lei, 'Guanyu woguo xingshi susong zhong bianhuren susong diwei de yanjiu (Research on the Procedural Status of the Defender in the Chinese Criminal Procedure)' [1957] *Chinese Journal of Law*.

——, 'Xingshi susong fa de jiben yuanze (Fundamental Principles of the Criminal Procedure Law)' in Central Political-Legal Cadres School (ed), *Xingshi susongfa jiangyi (Handouts on Criminal Procedure Law)* (Beijing, Renmin University, 1981).

Wu, W and Vander Beken, T, 'Police Torture in China and Its Causes: A Review of Literature' (2010) 43 *The Australian and New Zealand Journal of Criminology* 557.

Xi Danni, *Lun wuzui tuiding (On the Presumption of Innocence)* (Beijing, People's Court Press, 2015).

Xiao Hua, '"Wuzui tuiding" yuanze yu woguo xingshi susong shijian gegeburu (The Principle of "Presumption of Innocence" is incompatible with the Practice of Chinese Criminal Proceedings)' [1980] *Chinese Journal of Law* 62.

Xie Xiaojian, 'Jiya biyaoxing shencha zhidu shixiao yanjiu (Study on the Effect of Custody Necessity Examination)' [2016] *The Jurist* 136.

——, 'Lun woguo xingshi juliu de jinjixing yaojian (On the Requirement of Exigency of Criminal Detention in China' [2016] *Modern Law Science* 110.

Xie Yong and Tang Qiyou, 'Lun xingshi beigaoren xianfa quanli de baozhang – cong wuzui tuiding jiaodu suozuo de fenxi (On the Safeguarding of the Criminal Defendant's Constitutional Rights – An Analysis from the Perspective of Presumption of Innocence' [2012] *Law Science Magazine* 99.

Xie Youping, 'Wuzui tuiding yuanze pinglun (A Comment on the Principle of Presumption of Innocence)' [1993] *Law Science* 34.

——, '"hunhexing" xingshi susong moshi pinglun – «xingshi susongfa xiugai jueding» suixiang (Review of the "Hybrid" Model of Criminal Procedure – Reflections on the 'Decision on Amendments to the Criminal Procedure Law")' [1996] *Law Science* 10.

——, 'Lun gongmin renshen ziyouquan de xianfa baozhang yu sifa baohu – yi xingshi sifa wei zhongxin (On the Constitutional Guarantees and Judicial Protection of Citizens' Right to Personal Liberty – with a Focus on Criminal Justice)' (2013) 11 *Shanghai Jiaotong Journal* 10.

Xu Bing, 'Renquan lilun de chansheng he lishi fazhan (The Emergence and Historical Development of the Human Rights Theory)' [1989] *Chinese Journal of Law* 1.

Xu Jingcun, *Zhongguo xingshi susongfa (dier xiuzhengan) xuezhe nizhigao ji lifa liyou (China Criminal Procedure Law (Second Amendment) Scholarly Draft and Legislative Rationale)* (Beijing, Law Press China, 2005).

Xu, X, *Heaven Has Eyes: Law and Justice in Chinese History* (Oxford, Oxford University Press, 2020).

Xu Yichu, *Xingshi susong faxue yanjiu gaishu (An Account of the Research on Criminal Procedure Law)* (Tianjin, Tianjin Education Publishing House, 1989).

Yang Yi, 'Yi shehui weixianxing shencha wei hexin de daibu tiaojian chonggou – jiyu jingyan shishi de lilun fansi (Reconstruction of Arrest Conditions centred on the Examination of Social Danger – a Theoretical Reflection based on Empirical Facts)' [2018] *Journal of Comparative Law* 130.

Ye Qing and Xu Meijun, 'Zhongguo faxuehui xingshi susong faxue yanjiuhui 2008 nian nianhui zongshu (Summary of the 2008 Annual Meeting of the China Association of Criminal Procedure Law of the China Law Society)' [2008] *ECUPL Journal* 154.

Ye Xiaoxin, '1789 nian faguo "renquan xuanyan" de pipan – cong lao gen shang qingsuan youpai fenzi guanyu minzhu, ziyou, fazhi deng de huangyan (Critique of the 1789 French "Declaration of the Rights of Man" – Exposing the Lies of Rightists About Democracy, Freedom or Legal Systems from the Roots)' [1958] *Law Science* 35.

Yi Xiaozhong, '"Wuzui tuiding" yuanze he woguo "daibu juliu tiaoli" daxiangjingting (The Gap between the Principle of the "Presumption of Innocence" and China's "Detention and Arrest Regulation")' [1980] *Chinese Journal of Law* 63.

Yi, Y, 'Arrest as Punishment: The Abuse of Arrest in the People's Republic of China' (2008) 10 *Punishment and Society* 9.
——, 'China's Criminal Detention as a Compulsory Measure under Exigencies: A Comparative Analysis' (2014) 6 *Tsinghua China Law Review* 171.
Yi Yanyou, 'Lun fandui ziwo guizui de tequan (On the Privilege Against Committing Self-Incrimination)' [1999] *Journal of Comparative Law* 273.
——, 'Lun wuzui tuiding de hanyi yu xingshi susongfa de wanshan (On the Implications of the Presumption of Innocence and the Improvement of the Criminal Procedure Law)' [2012] *Tribune of Political Science and Law* 10.
Yue Hanwei, 'Fandui ziwo guizui quan de ying mei fa suyuan yu fali fenxi – jian lun woguo xingshisusongfa xiangguan guiding de wanshan (The Legal Sources in Anglo-American Law and the Jurisprudential Analysis of Privilege against Self-incrimination: And the Improvement of relevant Regulations about Criminal Procedure Law in China)' [2016] *Journal of Comparative Law* 96.
Yue Liling, *Gongmin quanli he zhengzhi quanli guoji gongyue yu zhongguo xingshi sifa (International Covenant on Civil and Political Rights and Criminal Justice in China)* (Beijing, Law Press China, 2007).
——, *Xingshi shenpan yu renquan baozhang (Criminal Trial and Human Rights Protection)* (Beijing, Law Press China, 2010).
Zhang Hui, Li Changchun and Zhang Zipei, 'Zhe bu shi woguo xingshi susong de jiben yuanze – ping Qu Fu "lüe tan xingshi susong zhong beigaoren de susong diwei (This is not a Fundamental Principle of China's Criminal Proceedings – Comment on Qu Fu's Discussion on the Procedural Position of the Defendant in Criminal Proceedings)' [1958] *Law Science* 76.
Zhang Jinjie, Zhang Tao and Wang Minyuan, 'Lun wuzui tuiding yuanze (On the Principle of the Presumption of Innocence)' (1991) 13 *Chinese Journal of Law* 34.
Zhang Jixi, Xiang Yan and Ni Run, 'Zhongguo xingshi susong faxue yanjiuhui 2015 nian nianhui zongshu (Summary of the 2015 Annual Meeting of the China Criminal Procedure Law Society)' [2016] *Justice of China* 36.
Zhang Lin, 'buhou jiya biyaoxing shengcha zhi zhengming guize yanjiu – yi yi shenqing qidong xia de jiya biyaoxing shencha wei shijiao (Study on the Rules of Proof for Custody Necessity Examination of Post-Arrest Detention: From the Perspective of Custody Necessity Examination upon Application)' [2017] *Criminal Science* 99.
Zhang Lu and Luo Haimin, 'Zhongguo Xingshi Susong Faxue Yanjiuhui 2019 Nian Nianhui Zongshu (Summary of the Annual Meeting of the Criminal Procedure Association in 2019)' [2020] *Justice of China* 99.
Zhang Q, *The Constitution of China: A Contextual Analysis* (Oxford, Hart Publishing, 2012).
Zhang Xiaohai, *Wuzui tuiding quanli lun (On the Right to Presumption of Innocence)* (Beijing, China Democracy Legislative Publishing House, 2015).
Zhang Yunpeng, 'Buhou jiya biyaoxing shancha zhidu de wanshan lujing (Ways to Improve the System of Custody Necessity after Arrest)' [2015] *Law Science* 151.
Zhang Yunxiao, 'Guojia jiancha tizhi gaige fazhihua jincheng chutan (A Preliminary Study on the Legalisation of the State Supervision System)' [2018] *Law Science* Magazine 29.
Zhang Zetao, 'Zui cong panding yu wuzui tuiding (No Guilt without Judgment and the Presumption of Innocence)' [1999] *Journal of Xinjiang Police College* 34.
——, 'Goujian zhongguoshi de tingzheng shencha daibu chengxu (Constructing the Hearing Procedure of Examination of Criminal Arrest with Chinese Characteristics)' (2018) 36 *Tribune of Political Science and Law* 18.
Zhang Zipei, 'Bo zichanjieji de "wuzui tuiding" yuanze (Reject the Bourgeois Principle of "Presumption of Innocence")' [1958] *Law Science* 37.
——, '"Wuzui tuiding" yuanze pouxi (An Analysis of the Principle of the "Presumption of Innocence")' [1980] *Chinese Journal of Law* 30.
——, 'Ping "wuzui tuiding" (Critique of the "Presumption of Innocence")' [1983] *Tribune of Political Science and Law* 14.

Zhao Guangyu, 'Guanyu "wuzui tuiding" yuanze de lijie he shiyong (On the Understanding and Application of the Principle of the Presumption of Innocence)' [1981] *Chinese Journal of Law* 23.

Zhao Shunrong, 'Chuyi wuzui tuiding yuanze (Some Suggestions on the Principle of the Presumption of Innocence)' [1999] *Hebei Law Science* 110.

Zheng Chengliang, 'Wuzui tuiding lun (On the Presumption of Innocence)' [1988] *Jilin University Social Sciences* 58.

Zhou Shimin, 'Shou xingshi kongzhizhe de chenmoquan (The Right to Silence of the Criminal Accused)' in Chen Guangzhong (ed), *Gongmin quanli he zhengzhi quanli guoji gongyue pizhun yu shishi wenti yanjiu (Study on the ratification and implementation of the International Covenant on Civil and Political Rights)* (Beijing, China Legal Publishing House, 2002).

Zhou Xiangyuan, 'Lun woguo xingshi susong zhong beigaoren de bianhuquan (On the Defedant's Right to Defence in the Chinese Criminal Proceedings)' [1956] *Chinese Journal of Law* 51.

Zhu, F, 'Human Rights and the Political Development of Contemporary China, 1979-1994' in Michael C Davis (ed), *Human Rights and Chinese Values* (Oxford, Oxford University Press, 1995).

Zhu Linyu and Lin Hongjiao, '"Shishi shi genju, falü shi zhunsheng" yuanze de xingcheng he fazhan (Formation and Development of the Principle of "Taking Facts as the Basis, and Law as the Yardstick")' [2013] *Journal of Law Application* 42.

Zhu Zongjie, 'Zai renquan baozhang shiye xia lun wuzui tuiding yuanze (On the Principle of the Presumption of Innocence from the Perspective of Human Rights Protection' [2011] *Human Rights* 23.

Zimmermann, A, 'The Right to a Fair Trial in Situations of Emergency and the Question of Emergency Courts' in David Weissbrodt and Rüdiger Wolfrum (eds), *The Right to a Fair Trial* (Princeton, Springer, 1998).

# INDEX

[*all references are to page number*]

www.ingramcontent.com/pod-product-compliance
Ingram Content Group UK Ltd.
Pitfield, Milton Keynes, MK11 3LW, UK
UKHW020246290926
15470UKWH00002B/772

9 781509 97310